D1245272

WITHDRAWN

SOCIAL WELFARE
FIGHTING POVERTY
AND HOMELESSNESS

ISSN 1937-3295

SOCIAL WELFARE

FIGHTING POVERTY
AND HOMELESSNESS

Melissa J. Doak

INFORMATION PLUS® REFERENCE SERIES
Formerly Published by Information Plus, Wylie, Texas

3 4085 00000 6552

MOLINE HIGH SCHOOL
MEDIA CENTER

Detroit • New York • San Francisco • New Haven, Conn. • Waterville, Maine • London

Social Welfare: Fighting Poverty and Homelessness

Melissa J. Doak

Paula Kepos, Series Editor

Project Editors
Kathleen J. Edgar, John McCoy

Permissions
Jacqueline Key, Jhanay Williams

Composition and Electronic Prepress
Evi Seoud

Manufacturing
Cynde Bishop

© 2008 The Gale Group.

Thomson and Star logos are trademarks and Gale is a registered trademark used herein under license.

For more information, contact
The Gale Group
27500 Drake Rd.
Farmington Hills, MI 48331-3535
Or you can visit our Internet site at http://www.gale.com

ALL RIGHTS RESERVED
No part of this work covered by the copyright hereon may be reproduced or used in any form or by any means—graphic, electronic, or mechanical, including photocopying, recording, taping, Web distribution, or information storage retrieval systems—without the written permission of the publisher.

For permission to use material from this product, submit your request via Web at http://www.gale-edit.com/permissions, or you may download our Permissions request form and submit your request by fax or mail to:

Permissions Department
The Gale Group
27500 Drake Rd.
Farmington Hills, MI 48331-3535
Permissions Hotline: 248-699-8006 or 800-877-4253, ext. 8006
Fax: 248-699-8074 or 800-762-4058

Cover photo reproduced by permission of Digital Stock.

While every effort has been made to ensure the reliability of the information presented in this publication, the Gale Group does not guarantee the accuracy of the data contained herein. The Gale Group accepts no payment for listing; and inclusion in the publication of any organization, agency, institution, publication, service, or individual does not imply endorsement of the editors or publisher. Errors brought to the attention of the publisher and verified to the satisfaction of the publisher will be corrected in future editions.

ISBN-13: 978-0-7876-5103-9 (set)
ISBN-10: 0-7876-5103-6 (set)
ISBN-13: 978-1-4144-0760-9
ISBN-10: 1-4144-0760-2
ISSN 1937-3295

This title is also available as an e-book.
ISBN-13: 978-1-4144-2948-9 (set), ISBN-10: 1-4144-2948-7 (set)
Contact your Gale Group sales representative for ordering information.

Printed in the United States of America
10 9 8 7 6 5 4 3 2 1

TABLE OF CONTENTS

PREFACE

Social Welfare: Fighting Poverty and Homelessness is part of the *Information Plus Reference Series*. The purpose of each volume of the series is to present the latest facts on a topic of pressing concern in modern American life. These topics include today's most controversial and most studied social issues: abortion, capital punishment, care of senior citizens, crime, the environment, health care, immigration, minorities, national security, social welfare, women, youth, and many more. Although written especially for the high school and undergraduate student, this series is an excellent resource for anyone in need of factual information on current affairs.

By presenting the facts, it is the Gale Group's intention to provide its readers with everything they need to reach an informed opinion on current issues. To that end, there is a particular emphasis in this series on the presentation of scientific studies, surveys, and statistics. These data are generally presented in the form of tables, charts, and other graphics placed within the text of each book. Every graphic is directly referred to and carefully explained in the text. The source of each graphic is presented within the graphic itself. The data used in these graphics are drawn from the most reputable and reliable sources, in particular from the various branches of the U.S. government and from major independent polling organizations. Every effort was made to secure the most recent information available. The reader should bear in mind that many major studies take years to conduct, and that additional years often pass before the data from these studies are made available to the public. Therefore, in many cases the most recent information available in 2007 dated from 2004 or 2005. Older statistics are sometimes presented as well, if they are of particular interest and no more-recent information exists.

Although statistics are a major focus of the *Information Plus Reference Series*, they are by no means its only content. Each book also presents the widely held positions and important ideas that shape how the book's subject is discussed in the United States. These positions are explained in detail and, where possible, in the words of their proponents. Some of the other material to be found in these books includes: historical background; descriptions of major events related to the subject; relevant laws and court cases; and examples of how these issues play out in American life. Some books also feature primary documents, or have pro and con debate sections giving the words and opinions of prominent Americans on both sides of a controversial topic. All material is presented in an even-handed and unbiased manner; the reader will never be encouraged to accept one view of an issue over another.

HOW TO USE THIS BOOK

Aid for the poor has long been a controversial topic in the United States. Most Americans agree that society should help those who have fallen on hard times, but there are many different opinions as to how this is best accomplished. The 1990s were a time of particularly heavy debate about this issue, resulting in major changes to the U.S. welfare system in 1996 with the introduction of the Personal Responsibility and Work Opportunity Reconciliation Act, requiring recipients to work in exchange for time-limited assistance. In this book both the old and the new welfare systems are examined, and their differences are highlighted. The volume also describes those who make use of the welfare system, why they use it, and what they get out of it.

Social Welfare: Fighting Poverty and Homelessness consists of seven chapters and three appendixes. Each chapter is devoted to a particular aspect of social welfare. For a summary of the information covered in each chapter, please see the synopses provided in the Table of Contents at the front of the book. Chapters generally begin with an overview of the basic facts and background information on the chapter's topic, then proceed to examine subtopics of particular interest. For example, Chapter 2, Who Are the Poor?, begins with an overview of the characteristics of those in poverty. It details the race, ethnicity, and age of the poor. Included is a look at how poverty impacts the youngest and oldest Americans. The chapter goes on to reveal the length of time that people generally spend in poverty and in assistance programs. It concludes with a discussion about why having a job does not guarantee freedom from poverty. Readers can find their way through a chapter by looking for the section and subsection headings, which are clearly set off from the text. Or, they can refer to the book's extensive Index if they already know what they are looking for.

Statistical Information

The tables and figures featured throughout *Social Welfare: Fighting Poverty and Homelessness* will be of particular use to the reader in learning about this topic. These tables and figures represent an extensive collection of the most recent and valuable statistics on social welfare, as well as related issues—for example, graphics in the book cover the amount of money spent each year for various government welfare programs; the demographics of poverty; the role of child support payments in preventing poverty; and the number of people without health insurance in the United States. The Gale Group believes that making this information available to the reader is the most important way in which we fulfill the goal of this book: to help readers understand the issues and controversies surrounding social welfare and reach their own conclusions.

Each table or figure has a unique identifier appearing above it for ease of identification and reference. Titles for the tables and figures explain their purpose. At the end of each table or figure, the original source of the data is provided.

In order to help readers understand these often complicated statistics, all tables and figures are explained in the text. References in the text direct the reader to the relevant statistics. Furthermore, the contents of all tables and figures are fully indexed. Please see the opening section of the Index at the back of this volume for a description of how to find tables and figures within it.

Appendixes

In addition to the main body text and images, *Social Welfare: Fighting Poverty and Homelessness* has three appendixes. The first is the Important Names and Addresses directory. Here the reader will find contact information for a number of government and private organizations that can provide further information on aspects of social welfare. The second appendix is the Resources section, which can also assist the reader in conducting his or her own research. In this section the author and editors of *Social Welfare: Fighting Poverty and Homelessness* describe some of the sources that were most useful during the compilation of this book. The final appendix is the Index.

ADVISORY BOARD CONTRIBUTIONS

The staff of Information Plus would like to extend its heartfelt appreciation to the Information Plus Advisory Board. This dedicated group of media professionals provides feedback on the series on an ongoing basis. Their comments allow the editorial staff who work on the project to continually make the series better and more user-friendly. Our top priorities are to produce the highest-quality and most useful books possible, and the Advisory Board's contributions to this process are invaluable.

The members of the Information Plus Advisory Board are:

- Kathleen R. Bonn, Librarian, Newbury Park High School, Newbury Park, California

- Madelyn Garner, Librarian, San Jacinto College—North Campus, Houston, Texas

- Anne Oxenrider, Media Specialist, Dundee High School, Dundee, Michigan

- Charles R. Rodgers, Director of Libraries, Pasco-Hernando Community College, Dade City, Florida

- James N. Zitzelsberger, Library Media Department Chairman, Oshkosh West High School, Oshkosh, Wisconsin

COMMENTS AND SUGGESTIONS

The editors of the *Information Plus Reference Series* welcome your feedback on *Social Welfare: Fighting Poverty and Homelessness*. Please direct all correspondence to:

Editors
Information Plus Reference Series
27500 Drake Rd.
Farmington Hills, MI 48331-3535

CHAPTER 1
POVERTY IN THE UNITED STATES

THE FEDERAL DEFINITION OF POVERTY

The federal government began measuring poverty in 1959. During the 1960s President Lyndon B. Johnson declared a national war on poverty. Researchers realized that few statistical tools were available to measure the number of Americans who continued to live in poverty in one of the most affluent nations in the world. To fight this "war," it had to be determined who was poor and why.

During the early 1960s Mollie Orshansky of the Social Security Administration suggested that the poverty income level be defined as the income sufficient to purchase a minimally adequate amount of goods and services. The necessary data for defining and pricing a full market basket of goods was not available then, nor is it available now. Orshansky noted, however, that in 1955 the U.S. Department of Agriculture (USDA) had published the Household Food Consumption Survey, which showed that the average family of three or more people spent approximately one-third of its after-tax income on food. She multiplied the USDA's 1961 economy food plan (a no-frills food basket meeting the then-recommended dietary allowances) by three.

Basically, this defined a poor family as any family or person whose after-tax income was not sufficient to purchase a minimally adequate diet if one-third of the income was spent on food. Differences were allowed for size of family, gender of the head of the household, and whether it was a farm or nonfarm family. The threshold (the level at which poverty begins) for a farm family was set at 70% of a nonfarm household. (The difference between farm and nonfarm households was eliminated in 1982.)

The poverty guidelines set by the U.S. Department of Health and Human Services (HHS) are based on the poverty thresholds as established by the U.S. Bureau of the Census. The poverty thresholds are updated each year to reflect inflation. People with incomes below the applicable threshold are classified as living below the poverty level.

The poverty guidelines vary by family size and composition. In 2007 a family of four earning $20,000 or less annually was considered impoverished. (See Table 1.1.) A person living alone who earned less than $9,800 was considered poor, as was a family of eight members making less than $33,600. The poverty level is considerably higher in Alaska and Hawaii, where the cost of living is higher than in the contiguous forty-eight states and the District of Columbia.

The poverty guidelines set by the HHS are important because various government agencies use them as the basis for eligibility to key assistance programs. The HHS uses the poverty guidelines to determine Community Services Block Grants, Low-Income Home Energy Assistance Block Grants, and Head Start allotments. The guidelines are also the basis for funding the USDA's Food Stamp Program, National School Lunch Program, and Special Supplemental Food Program for Women, Infants, and Children. The U.S. Department of Labor uses the guidelines to determine funding for the Job Corps and other employment and training programs under the Workforce Investment Act of 1998. Some state and local governments choose to use the federal poverty guidelines for some of their own programs, such as state health insurance programs and financial guidelines for child support enforcement.

THE HISTORICAL EFFORT TO REDUCE POVERTY

Since the late 1950s Americans have seen both successes and failures in the battle against poverty. For the total population in 1959, 22.4%, or 39.5 million people, lived below the poverty level. (See Table 1.2.) After an initial decline through the 1960s and 1970s, the poverty rate began to increase during the early 1980s, coinciding with a downturn in household and family incomes for all Americans. The poverty rate rose steadily until it reached

TABLE 1.1

Department of Health and Human Services (HHS) poverty guidelines, 2007

[For all states except Alaska and Hawaii and for the District of Columbia]

Size of family unit	100 percent of poverty	110 percent of poverty	125 percent of poverty	150 percent of poverty	175 percent of poverty	185 percent of poverty	200 percent of povety
1	$9,800	$10,780	$12,250	$14,700	$17,150	$18,130	$19,600
2	$13,200	$14,520	$16,500	$19,800	$23,100	$24,420	$26,400
3	$16,600	$18,260	$20,750	$24,900	$29,050	$30,710	$33,200
4	$20,000	$22,000	$25,000	$30,000	$35,000	$37,000	$40,000
5	$23,400	$25,740	$29,250	$35,100	$40,950	$43,290	$46,800
6	$26,800	$29,480	$33,500	$40,200	$46,900	$49,580	$53,600
7	$30,200	$33,220	$37,750	$45,300	$52,850	$55,870	$60,400
8	$33,600	$36,960	$42,000	$50,400	$58,800	$62,160	$67,200

Notes: For family units with more than 8 members, add $3,400 for each additional person at 100% of poverty, $3,740 at 110%, $4,250 at 125%, $5,100 at 150%, $5,950 at 175%, $6,290 at 185% and $6,800 at 200% of poverty. For optional use in federal fiscal year 2006 and mandatory use in federal fiscal year 2007.

SOURCE: "2007 HHS Poverty Guidelines," U.S. Department of Health and Human Services, Administration for Children and Families, National Center for Appropriate Technology, Low-Income Home Energy Assistance Program (LIHEAP) Clearinghouse, September 6, 2006, http://www.sustainable.doe.gov/profiles/povertytables/FY2007/popstate.htm (accessed January 23, 2007)

an eighteen-year high of 15.2% in 1983, a year during which the country was climbing out of a serious economic recession. The percentage of Americans living in poverty then began dropping, falling to 12.8% in 1989. After that, however, the percentage increased again, reaching 15.1% in 1993. It then dropped to 11.3% in 2000; however, because the nation's economy slowed, the poverty rate rose again to 12.7% in 2004, and then dropped slightly in 2005. Figure 1.1 provides a graphic representation of the number of poor people and the poverty rates between 1959 and 2005.

Analysts believe the overall decline in poverty is because of both the growth in the economy and the success of some of the antipoverty programs instituted in the late 1960s; yet not all demographic subcategories have experienced the same level of change. For example, the poverty rate of those aged sixty-five and older has dramatically improved from 35.2% in 1959 to 10.1% in 2005. For related children under eighteen years of age in African-American families, however, the improvement from 65.6% in 1959 to 33.2% in 2005 shows that antipoverty programs still have not reached many people in need. Table 1.3 shows the differences in the nation's historical poverty for people by categories of age, race, and ethnic background.

RATIO OF INCOME TO POVERTY LEVELS

For purposes of analysis, the Census Bureau uses income-to-poverty ratios that are calculated by dividing income by the respective poverty threshold for each family size. The resulting number is then tabulated on a scale that includes three categories: poor, near-poor, and nonpoor. Poor people have a poverty ratio below 1. People above the poverty level are divided into two groups: the near-poor and the nonpoor. The near-poor have a poverty ratio between 1 and 1.24 (100% to 124% of the poverty level),

and the nonpoor have an income-to-poverty ratio of 1.25 (125% of the poverty level) and above. In 2005, 12.6% of the total population had income-to-poverty ratios under 1; in other words, nearly thirty-seven million people in the United States had incomes below the poverty threshold, and 16.8% were classified as poor or near-poor.

HOW ACCURATE IS THE POVERTY LEVEL?

Almost every year since the Census Bureau first defined the poverty level observers have been concerned about its accuracy. Since the early 1960s, when Orshansky defined the estimated poverty level based on a family's food budget, living patterns have changed and food costs have become a smaller percentage of family spending. For example, the U.S. Bureau of Labor Statistics reports in the news release "Consumer Expenditures in 2005" (November 8, 2006, http://www.bls.gov/news.release/pdf/cesan.pdf) that the average family spent $5,931, or 12.8% of its total expenditures, on food per year. By contrast, housing accounted for $15,167, or 32.7% of family spending. The proportion of family income spent on food is not the only change in family budgets since the 1950s. In families headed by two parents, both parents are far more likely to be working than they were in the 1950s. There is also a much greater likelihood that a single parent, usually the mother, will be heading the family. Child care costs, which were of little concern during the 1950s, have become a major issue for working mothers and single parents in the twenty-first century.

Critics of the current poverty calculations tend to believe that the official poverty level has been set too low, because they are based on a fifty-year-old concept of American life that does not reflect today's economic and social realities. Even among those who feel the poverty level should be changed to more accurately reflect how many Americans have trouble paying for basic expenses

TABLE 1.2

Overall poverty status, 1959–2005

[Numbers in thousands. People as of March of the following year.]

| Year | All people | | | People in families | | |
| | Total | Below poverty level | | All families | Below poverty level | |
		Number	Percent	Total	Number	Percent
All races						
2005	293,135	36,950	12.6	242,389	26,068	10.8
2004	290,617	37,040	12.7	240,754	26,544	11.0
2003	287,699	35,861	12.5	238,903	25,684	10.8
2002	285,317	34,570	12.1	236,921	24,534	10.4
2001	281,475	32,907	11.7	233,911	23,215	9.9
2000	278,944	31,581	11.3	231,909	22,347	9.6
1999	276,208	32,791	11.9	230,789	23,830	10.3
1998	271,059	34,476	12.7	227,229	25,370	11.2
1997	268,480	35,574	13.3	225,369	26,217	11.6
1996	266,218	36,529	13.7	223,955	27,376	12.2
1995	263,733	36,425	13.8	222,792	27,501	12.3
1994	261,616	38,059	14.5	221,430	28,985	13.1
1993	259,278	39,265	15.1	219,489	29,927	13.6
1992	256,549	38,014	14.8	217,936	28,961	13.3
1991	251,192	35,708	14.2	212,723	27,143	12.8
1990	248,644	33,585	13.5	210,967	25,232	12.0
1989	245,992	31,528	12.8	209,515	24,066	11.5
1988	243,530	31,745	13.0	208,056	24,048	11.6
1987	240,982	32,221	13.4	206,877	24,725	12.0
1986	238,554	32,370	13.6	205,459	24,754	12.0
1985	236,594	33,064	14.0	203,963	25,729	12.6
1984	233,816	33,700	14.4	202,288	26,458	13.1
1983	231,700	35,303	15.2	201,338	27,933	13.9
1982	229,412	34,398	15.0	200,385	27,349	13.6
1981	227,157	31,822	14.0	198,541	24,850	12.5
1980	225,027	29,272	13.0	196,963	22,601	11.5
1979	222,903	26,072	11.7	195,860	19,964	10.2
1978	215,656	24,497	11.4	191,071	19,062	10.0
1977	213,867	24,720	11.6	190,757	19,505	10.2
1976	212,303	24,975	11.8	190,844	19,632	10.3
1975	210,864	25,877	12.3	190,630	20,789	10.9
1974	209,362	23,370	11.2	190,436	18,817	9.9
1973	207,621	22,973	11.1	189,361	18,299	9.7
1972	206,004	24,460	11.9	189,193	19,577	10.3
1971	204,554	25,559	12.5	188,242	20,405	10.8
1970	202,183	25,420	12.6	186,692	20,330	10.9
1969	199,517	24,147	12.1	184,891	19,175	10.4
1968	197,628	25,389	12.8	183,825	20,695	11.3
1967	195,672	27,769	14.2	182,558	22,771	12.5
1966	193,388	28,510	14.7	181,117	23,809	13.1
1965	191,413	33,185	17.3	179,281	28,358	15.8
1964	189,710	36,055	19.0	177,653	30,912	17.4
1963	187,258	36,436	19.5	176,076	31,498	17.9
1962	184,276	38,625	21.0	173,263	33,623	19.4
1961	181,277	39,628	21.9	170,131	34,509	20.3
1960	179,503	39,851	22.2	168,615	34,925	20.7
1959	176,557	39,490	22.4	165,858	34,562	20.8

SOURCE: Adapted from "Table 2. Poverty Status of People by Family Relationship, Race, and Hispanic Origin, 1959 to 2005," in *Current Population Survey, Annual Social and Economic Supplements*, U.S. Census Bureau, September 6, 2006, http://www.census.gov/hhes/www/poverty/histpov/hstpov2.html (accessed December 1, 2006)

there is disagreement about what would make a more accurate benchmark. Should the amount spent on food be multiplied by a factor of eight instead of three? Should the poverty level be based on housing or other factors? What about geographical differences in the cost of living?

Some are concerned because the poverty threshold is different for elderly and nonelderly Americans. When the poverty threshold was first established, it was thought that older people did not need as much food. Therefore, the value of their basic food needs was lower. Consequently, when this figure was multiplied by three to determine the poverty rate, it was naturally lower than the rate for non-elderly people. (The U.S. government, however, uses the poverty rate for nonelderly Americans when determining the eligibility for welfare services for all people, including the elderly.) Critics point out that while the elderly might eat less than younger people, they have greater needs in

FIGURE 1.1

Number in poverty and poverty rate, 1959–2005

[Numbers in millions, rates in percent]

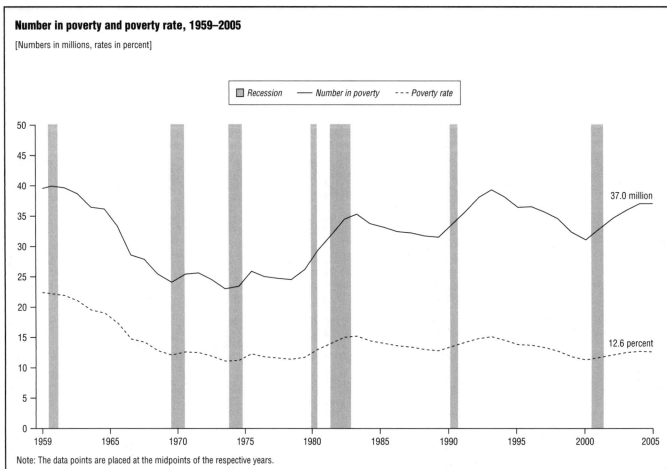

Note: The data points are placed at the midpoints of the respective years.

SOURCE: Carmen DeNavas-Walt, Bernadette D. Proctor, and Cheryl Hill Lee, "Figure 4. Number in Poverty and Poverty Rate: 1959 to 2005," in *Income, Poverty, and Health Insurance Coverage in the United States: 2005—Current Population Reports*, U.S. Census Bureau, August 2006, http://www.census .gov/prod/2006pubs/p60-231.pdf (accessed December 1, 2006)

other areas, which are not considered when their food needs are simply multiplied by three. Probably the most notable difference between the needs of the elderly and nonelderly is in the area of health care. The Bureau of Labor Statistics, in *Consumer Expenditures in 2004* (April 2006, http:// www.bls.gov/cex/csxann04.pdf), finds that while the total population interviewed spent $2,574, or 4.7% of their income, on health care, those over sixty-five years of age spent $3,899, or 11.1% of their income, on health care. These critics feel that the poverty level should be the same for everyone, no matter what their age.

In *Measuring Poverty: A New Approach* (1995), the National Research Council's Panel on Poverty and Family Assistance raises several important issues regarding poverty thresholds or measurement of need. It recommends that new thresholds be developed using consumer expenditure data to represent a budget for basic needs: food, clothing, shelter (including utilities), and a small allowance for miscellaneous needs. This budget would be adjusted to reflect the needs of different family types and geographic differences in costs.

In June 2004 the Committee on National Statistics met to research alternative methods for measuring poverty, as recommended in 1995. The panel recommended adopting a new poverty measure, taking into account the current dollar value of food, clothing, shelter, and utilities, as well as taxes, the value of food stamps and other near-cash benefits, and child support payments. In addition, the panel workshop recommended adjusting the new poverty measure based not only on inflation but also on data on yearly consumer expenditures. John Iceland, the rapporteur for the committee, notes in "The CNSTAT Workshop on Experimental Poverty Measures, June 2004" (*Focus*, Spring 2005), "The reasoning here is that CE [consumer expenditure]-based calculations will allow the thresholds to retain their social significance for longer periods of time than absolute thresholds."

INCOME AND POVERTY
How Should Income Be Defined?

Critics point out that the definition of income used to set the poverty figure is not accurate because it does not include the value of all welfare services as

TABLE 1.3

People's poverty status, by age, race, and Hispanic origin, 1959–2005

[Numbers in thousands. People as of March of the following year.]

	Under 18 years					
	All people			Related children in families		
		Below poverty level			Below poverty level	
Year and characteristic	Total	Number	Percent	Total	Number	Percent
All races						
2005	73,285	12,896	17.6	72,095	12,335	17.1
2004[m]	73,241	13,041	17.8	72,133	12,473	17.3
2003	72,999	12,866	17.6	71,907	12,340	17.2
2002	72,696	12,133	16.7	71,619	11,646	16.3
2001	72,021	11,733	16.3	70,950	11,175	15.8
2000[l]	71,741	11,587	16.2	70,538	11,005	15.6
1999[k]	71,685	12,280	17.1	70,424	11,678	16.6
1998	71,338	13,467	18.9	70,253	12,845	18.3
1997	71,069	14,113	19.9	69,844	13,422	19.2
1996	70,650	14,463	20.5	69,411	13,764	19.8
1995	70,566	14,665	20.8	69,425	13,999	20.2
1994	70,020	15,289	21.8	68,819	14,610	21.2
1993[j]	69,292	15,727	22.7	68,040	14,961	22.0
1992[i]	68,440	15,294	22.3	67,256	14,521	21.6
1991[h]	65,918	14,341	21.8	64,800	13,658	21.1
1990	65,049	13,431	20.6	63,908	12,715	19.9
1989	64,144	12,590	19.6	63,225	12,001	19.0
1988	63,747	12,455	19.5	62,906	11,935	19.0
1987[g]	63,294	12,843	20.3	62,423	12,275	19.7
1986	62,948	12,876	20.5	62,009	12,257	19.8
1985	62,876	13,010	20.7	62,019	12,483	20.1
1984	62,447	13,420	21.5	61,681	12,929	21.0
1983[f]	62,334	13,911	22.3	61,578	13,427	21.8
1982	62,345	13,647	21.9	61,565	13,139	21.3
1981[e]	62,449	12,505	20.0	61,756	12,068	19.5
1980	62,914	11,543	18.3	62,168	11,114	17.9
1979[d]	63,375	10,377	16.4	62,646	9,993	16.0
1978	62,311	9,931	15.9	61,987	9,722	15.7
1977	63,137	10,288	16.2	62,823	10,028	16.0
1976	64,028	10,273	16.0	63,729	10,081	15.8
1975	65,079	11,104	17.1	64,750	10,882	16.8
1974[c]	66,134	10,156	15.4	65,802	9,967	15.1
1973	66,959	9,642	14.4	66,626	9,453	14.2
1972	67,930	10,284	15.1	67,592	10,082	14.9
1971[b]	68,816	10,551	15.3	68,474	10,344	15.1
1970	69,159	10,440	15.1	68,815	10,235	14.9
1969	69,090	9,691	14.0	68,746	9,501	13.8
1968	70,385	10,954	15.6	70,035	10,739	15.3
1967[a]	70,408	11,656	16.6	70,058	11,427	16.3
1966	70,218	12,389	17.6	69,869	12,146	17.4
1965	69,986	14,676	21.0	69,638	14,388	20.7
1964	69,711	16,051	23.0	69,364	15,736	22.7
1963	69,181	16,005	23.1	68,837	15,691	22.8
1962	67,722	16,963	25.0	67,385	16,630	24.7
1961	66,121	16,909	25.6	65,792	16,577	25.2
1960	65,601	17,634	26.9	65,275	17,288	26.5
1959	64,315	17,552	27.3	63,995	17,208	26.9
White, not Hispanic						
2001	44,095	4,194	9.5	43,459	3,887	8.9
2000[l]	44,244	4,018	9.1	43,554	3,715	8.5
1999[k]	44,272	4,155	9.4	43,570	3,832	8.8
1998	45,355	4,822	10.6	44,670	4,458	10.0
1997	45,491	5,204	11.4	44,665	4,759	10.7
1996	45,605	5,072	11.1	44,844	4,656	10.4
1995	45,689	5,115	11.2	44,973	4,745	10.6
1994	46,668	5,823	12.5	45,874	5,404	11.8
1993[j]	46,096	6,255	13.6	45,322	5,819	12.8
1992[i]	45,590	6,017	13.2	44,833	5,558	12.4
1991[h]	45,236	5,918	13.1	44,506	5,497	12.4
1990	44,797	5,532	12.3	44,045	5,106	11.6
1989	44,492	5,110	11.5	43,938	4,779	10.9
1988	44,438	4,888	11.0	43,910	4,594	10.5
1987[g]	44,461	5,230	11.8	43,907	4,902	11.2
1986	44,664	5,789	13.0	44,041	5,388	12.2

TABLE 1.3

People's poverty status, by age, race, and Hispanic origin, 1959–2005 [CONTINUED]

[Numbers in thousands. People as of March of the following year.]

	Under 18 years					
	All people			Related children in families		
		Below poverty level			Below poverty level	
Year and characteristic	Total	Number	Percent	Total	Number	Percent
1985	44,752	5,745	12.8	44,199	5,421	12.3
1984	44,886	6,156	13.7	44,349	5,828	13.1
1983[f]	44,830	6,649	14.8	44,374	6,381	14.4
1982	45,531	6,566	14.4	45,001	6,229	13.8
1981[e]	45,950	5,946	12.9	45,440	5,639	12.4
1980	46,578	5,510	11.8	45,989	5,174	11.3
1979[d]	46,967	4,730	10.1	46,448	4,476	9.6
1978	46,819	4,506	9.6	46,606	4,383	9.4
1977	47,689	4,714	9.9	47,459	4,582	9.7
1976	48,824	4,799	9.8	48,601	4,664	9.6
1975	49,670	5,342	10.8	49,421	5,185	10.5
1974[c]	50,759	4,820	9.5	50,520	4,697	9.3
Black alone or in combination						
2005	12,159	4,074	33.5	11,975	3,972	33.2
2004[m]	12,190	4,059	33.3	12,012	3,962	33.0
2003	12,215	4,108	33.6	11,989	3,977	33.2
2002	12,114	3,817	31.5	11,931	3,733	31.3
Black alone						
2005	11,136	3,841	34.5	10,962	3,743	34.2
2004[m]	11,244	3,788	33.7	11,080	3,702	33.4
2003	11,367	3,877	34.1	11,162	3,750	33.6
2002	11,275	3,645	32.3	11,111	3,570	32.1
Black						
2001	11,556	3,492	30.2	11,419	3,423	30.0
2000[l]	11,480	3,581	31.2	11,296	3,495	30.9
1999[k]	11,488	3,813	33.2	11,260	3,698	32.8
1998	11,317	4,151	36.7	11,176	4,073	36.4
1997	11,367	4,225	37.2	11,193	4,116	36.8
1996	11,338	4,519	39.9	11,155	4,411	39.5
1995	11,369	4,761	41.9	11,198	4,644	41.5
1994	11,211	4,906	43.8	11,044	4,787	43.3
1993[j]	11,127	5,125	46.1	10,969	5,030	45.9
1992[i]	10,956	5,106	46.6	10,823	5,015	46.3
1991[h]	10,350	4,755	45.9	10,178	4,637	45.6
1990	10,162	4,550	44.8	9,980	4,412	44.2
1989	10,012	4,375	43.7	9,847	4,257	43.2
1988	9,865	4,296	43.5	9,681	4,148	42.8
1987[g]	9,730	4,385	45.1	9,546	4,234	44.4
1986	9,629	4,148	43.1	9,467	4,037	42.7
1985	9,545	4,157	43.6	9,405	4,057	43.1
1984	9,480	4,413	46.6	9,356	4,320	46.2
1983[f]	9,417	4,398	46.7	9,245	4,273	46.2
1982	9,400	4,472	47.6	9,269	4,388	47.3
1981[e]	9,374	4,237	45.2	9,291	4,170	44.9
1980	9,368	3,961	42.3	9,287	3,906	42.1
1979[d]	9,307	3,833	41.2	9,172	3,745	40.8
1978	9,229	3,830	41.5	9,168	3,781	41.2
1977	9,296	3,888	41.8	9,253	3,850	41.6
1976	9,322	3,787	40.6	9,291	3,758	40.4
1975	9,421	3,925	41.7	9,374	3,884	41.4
1974[c]	9,439	3,755	39.8	9,384	3,713	39.6
1973	(NA)	(NA)	(NA)	9,405	3,822	40.6
1972	(NA)	(NA)	(NA)	9,426	4,025	42.7
1971[b]	(NA)	(NA)	(NA)	9,414	3,836	40.4
1970	(NA)	(NA)	(NA)	9,448	3,922	41.5
1969	(NA)	(NA)	(NA)	9,290	3,677	39.6
1968	(NA)	(NA)	(NA)	(NA)	4,188	43.1
1967[a]	(NA)	(NA)	(NA)	(NA)	4,558	47.4
1966	(NA)	(NA)	(NA)	(NA)	4,774	50.6
1965	(NA)	(NA)	(NA)	(NA)	5,022	65.6

income. If the value of these services was counted as income, they believe the proportion of Americans considered to be living in poverty would be lower. In the 1990s the Census Bureau developed several experimental methods of estimating income for evaluating poverty levels, but the bureau has had considerable

TABLE 1.3

People's poverty status, by age, race, and Hispanic origin, 1959–2005 [CONTINUED]

[Numbers in thousands. People as of March of the following year.]

	Under 18 years					
	All people			Related children in families		
	Total	Below poverty level		Total	Below poverty level	
Year and characteristic	Total	Number	Percent	Total	Number	Percent
Asian alone or in combination						
2005	3,472	359	10.3	3,435	352	10.2
2004[m]	3,406	329	9.7	3,367	311	9.2
2003	3,316	420	12.7	3,279	406	12.4
2002	3,199	353	11.0	3,159	338	10.7
Asian alone						
2005	2,871	317	11.1	2,842	312	11.0
2004[m]	2,854	281	9.9	2,823	265	9.4
2003	2,759	344	12.5	2,726	331	12.1
2002	2,683	315	11.7	2,648	302	11.4
Asian and Pacific Islander						
2001	3,215	369	11.5	3,169	353	11.1
2000[l]	3,294	420	12.7	3,256	407	12.5
1999[k]	3,212	381	11.9	3,178	367	11.5
1998	3,137	564	18.0	3,099	542	17.5
1997	3,096	628	20.3	3,061	608	19.9
1996	2,924	571	19.5	2,899	553	19.1
1995	2,900	564	19.5	2,858	532	18.6
1994	1,739	318	18.3	1,719	308	17.9
1993[j]	2,061	375	18.2	2,029	358	17.6
1992[l]	2,218	363	16.4	2,199	352	16.0
1991[h]	2,056	360	17.5	2,036	348	17.1
1990	2,126	374	17.6	2,098	356	17.0
1989	1,983	392	19.8	1,945	368	18.9
1988	1,970	474	24.1	1,949	458	23.5
1987[g]	1,937	455	23.5	1,908	432	22.7
Hispanic (of any race)						
2005	14,654	4,143	28.3	14,361	3,977	27.7
2004[m]	14,173	4,098	28.9	13,929	3,985	28.6
2003	13,730	4,077	29.7	13,519	3,982	29.5
2002	13,210	3,782	28.6	12,971	3,653	28.2
2001	12,763	3,570	28.0	12,539	3,433	27.4
2000[l]	12,399	3,522	28.4	12,115	3,342	27.6
1999[k]	12,188	3,693	30.3	11,912	3,561	29.9
1998	11,152	3,837	34.4	10,921	3,670	33.6
1997	10,802	3,972	36.8	10,625	3,865	36.4
1996	10,511	4,237	40.3	10,255	4,090	39.9
1995	10,213	4,080	40.0	10,011	3,938	39.3
1994	9,822	4,075	41.5	9,621	3,956	41.1
1993[j]	9,462	3,873	40.9	9,188	3,666	39.9
1992[l]	9,081	3,637	40.0	8,829	3,440	39.0
1991[h]	7,648	3,094	40.4	7,473	2,977	39.8
1990	7,457	2,865	38.4	7,300	2,750	37.7
1989	7,186	2,603	36.2	7,040	2,496	35.5
1988	7,003	2,631	37.6	6,908	2,576	37.3
1987[g]	6,792	2,670	39.3	6,692	2,606	38.9
1986	6,646	2,507	37.7	6,511	2,413	37.1
1985	6,475	2,606	40.3	6,346	2,512	39.6
1984	6,068	2,376	39.2	5,982	2,317	38.7
1983[f]	6,066	2,312	38.1	5,977	2,251	37.7
1982	5,527	2,181	39.5	5,436	2,117	38.9
1981[e]	5,369	1,925	35.9	5,291	1,874	35.4
1980	5,276	1,749	33.2	5,211	1,718	33.0
1979[d]	5,483	1,535	28.0	5,426	1,505	27.7
1978	5,012	1,384	27.6	4,972	1,354	27.2
1977	5,028	1,422	28.3	5,000	1,402	28.0
1976	4,771	1,443	30.2	4,736	1,424	30.1
1975	(NA)	(NA)	(NA)	4,896	1,619	33.1
1974[c]	(NA)	(NA)	(NA)	4,939	1,414	28.6
1973	(NA)	(NA)	(NA)	4,910	1,364	27.8

difficulty determining the value of many of these subsidies. For example, it first tried to consider Medicare and Medicaid at full market value (this meant taking the total amount of money that the government spent on medical care for a particular group and then dividing it by the number of people in that group). The value was often

TABLE 1.3

People's poverty status, by age, race, and Hispanic origin, 1959–2005 [CONTINUED]

[Numbers in thousands. People as of March of the following year.]

	18 to 64 years			65 years and over		
	All people			Related children in families		
		Below poverty level			Below poverty level	
Year and characteristic	Total	Number	Percent	Total	Number	Percent
All races						
2005	184,345	20,450	11.1	35,505	3,603	10.1
2004[m]	182,166	20,545	11.3	35,209	3,453	9.8
2003	180,041	19,443	10.8	34,659	3,552	10.2
2002	178,388	18,861	10.6	34,234	3,576	10.4
2001	175,685	17,760	10.1	33,769	3,414	10.1
2000[l]	173,638	16,671	9.6	33,566	3,323	9.9
1999[k]	171,146	17,289	10.1	33,377	3,222	9.7
1998	167,327	17,623	10.5	32,394	3,386	10.5
1997	165,329	18,085	10.9	32,082	3,376	10.5
1996	163,691	18,638	11.4	31,877	3,428	10.8
1995	161,508	18,442	11.4	31,658	3,318	10.5
1994	160,329	19,107	11.9	31,267	3,663	11.7
1993[j]	159,208	19,781	12.4	30,779	3,755	12.2
1992[l]	157,680	18,793	11.9	30,430	3,928	12.9
1991[h]	154,684	17,586	11.4	30,590	3,781	12.4
1990	153,502	16,496	10.7	30,093	3,658	12.2
1989	152,282	15,575	10.2	29,566	3,363	11.4
1988	150,761	15,809	10.5	29,022	3,481	12.0
1987[g]	149,201	15,815	10.6	28,487	3,563	12.5
1986	147,631	16,017	10.8	27,975	3,477	12.4
1985	146,396	16,598	11.3	27,322	3,456	12.6
1984	144,551	16,952	11.7	26,818	3,330	12.4
1983[f]	143,052	17,767	12.4	26,313	3,625	13.8
1982	141,328	17,000	12.0	25,738	3,751	14.6
1981[e]	139,477	15,464	11.1	25,231	3,853	15.3
1980	137,428	13,858	10.1	24,686	3,871	15.7
1979[d]	135,333	12,014	8.9	24,194	3,682	15.2
1978	130,169	11,332	8.7	23,175	3,233	14.0
1977	128,262	11,316	8.8	22,468	3,177	14.1
1976	126,175	11,389	9.0	22,100	3,313	15.0
1975	124,122	11,456	9.2	21,662	3,317	15.3
1974[c]	122,101	10,132	8.3	21,127	3,085	14.6
1973	120,060	9,977	8.3	20,602	3,354	16.3
1972	117,957	10,438	8.8	20,117	3,738	18.6
1971[b]	115,911	10,735	9.3	19,827	4,273	21.6
1970	113,554	10,187	9.0	19,470	4,793	24.6
1969	111,528	9,669	8.7	18,899	4,787	25.3
1968	108,684	9,803	9.0	18,559	4,632	25.0
1967[a]	107,024	10,725	10.0	18,240	5,388	29.5
1966	105,241	11,007	10.5	17,929	5,114	28.5
1965	(NA)	(NA)	(NA)	(NA)	(NA)	(NA)
1964	(NA)	(NA)	(NA)	(NA)	(NA)	(NA)
1963	(NA)	(NA)	(NA)	(NA)	(NA)	(NA)
1962	(NA)	(NA)	(NA)	(NA)	(NA)	(NA)
1961	(NA)	(NA)	(NA)	(NA)	(NA)	(NA)
1960	(NA)	(NA)	(NA)	(NA)	(NA)	(NA)
1959	96,685	16,457	17.0	15,557	5,481	35.2
White not Hispanic						
2001	122,470	8,811	7.2	27,973	2,266	8.1
2000[l]	121,499	8,130	6.7	27,948	2,218	7.9
1999[k]	120,341	8,462	7.0	27,952	2,118	7.6
1998	120,282	8,760	7.3	27,118	2,217	8.2
1997	119,373	9,088	7.6	26,995	2,200	8.1
1996	118,822	9,074	7.6	27,033	2,316	8.6
1995	118,228	8,908	7.5	27,034	2,243	8.3
1994	119,192	9,732	8.2	26,684	2,556	9.6
1993[j]	118,475	9,964	8.4	26,272	2,663	10.1
1992[l]	117,386	9,461	8.1	26,025	2,724	10.5
1991[h]	117,672	9,244	7.9	26,208	2,580	9.8

greater than the actual earnings of the low-income family, which meant that, although the family's total earnings may not have been enough to cover food and housing, adding the market value of Medicare or Medicaid to its earnings put the family above the poverty threshold.

TABLE 1.3

People's poverty status, by age, race, and Hispanic origin, 1959–2005 [CONTINUED]

[Numbers in thousands. People as of March of the following year.]

Year and characteristic	18 to 64 years All people			65 years and over Related children in families		
	Total	Below poverty level Number	Below poverty level Percent	Total	Below poverty level Number	Below poverty level Percent
1990	117,477	8,619	7.3	25,854	2,471	9.6
1989	116,983	8,154	7.0	25,504	2,335	9.2
1988	116,479	8,293	7.1	25,044	2,384	9.5
1987[g]	115,721	8,327	7.2	24,754	2,472	10.0
1986	115,157	8,963	7.8	24,298	2,492	10.3
1985	114,969	9,608	8.4	23,734	2,486	10.5
1984	114,180	9,734	8.5	23,402	2,410	10.3
1983[f]	113,570	10,279	9.1	22,992	2,610	11.4
1982	113,717	10,082	8.9	22,655	2,714	12.0
1981[e]	112,722	9,207	8.2	22,237	2,834	12.7
1980	111,460	7,990	7.2	21,760	2,865	13.2
1979[d]	110,509	6,930	6.3	21,339	2,759	12.9
1978	107,481	6,837	6.4	20,431	2,412	11.8
1977	106,063	6,772	6.4	19,812	2,316	11.7
1976	104,846	6,720	6.4	19,565	2,506	12.8
1975	103,496	7,039	6.8	19,251	2,503	13.0
1974[c]	101,894	6,051	5.9	18,810	2,346	12.5
Black alone or in combination						
2005	23,338	4,735	20.3	3,053	708	23.2
2004[m]	22,842	4,638	20.3	3,005	714	23.8
2003	22,355	4,313	19.3	2,933	688	23.5
2002	22,170	4,376	19.7	2,922	691	23.6
Black alone						
2005	22,659	4,627	20.4	3,007	701	23.3
2004[m]	22,226	4,521	20.3	2,956	705	23.8
2003	21,746	4,224	19.4	2,876	680	23.7
2002	21,547	4,277	19.9	2,856	680	23.8
Black						
2001	21,462	4,018	18.7	2,853	626	21.9
2000[l]	21,160	3,794	17.9	2,785	607	21.8
1999[k]	21,518	4,000	18.6	2,750	628	22.8
1998	20,837	4,222	20.3	2,723	718	26.4
1997	20,400	4,191	20.5	2,691	700	26.0
1996	20,155	4,515	22.4	2,616	661	25.3
1995	19,892	4,483	22.5	2,478	629	25.4
1994	19,585	4,590	23.4	2,557	700	27.4
1993[j]	19,272	5,049	26.2	2,510	702	28.0
1992[i]	18,952	4,884	25.8	2,504	838	33.5
1991[h]	18,355	4,607	25.1	2,606	880	33.8
1990	18,097	4,427	24.5	2,547	860	33.8
1989	17,833	4,164	23.3	2,487	763	30.7
1988	17,548	4,275	24.4	2,436	785	32.2
1987[g]	17,245	4,361	25.3	2,387	774	32.4
1986	16,911	4,113	24.3	2,331	722	31.0
1985	16,667	4,052	24.3	2,273	717	31.5
1984	16,369	4,368	26.7	2,238	710	31.7
1983[f]	16,065	4,694	29.2	2,197	791	36.0
1982	15,692	4,415	28.1	2,124	811	38.2
1981[e]	15,358	4,117	26.8	2,102	820	39.0
1980	14,987	3,835	25.6	2,054	783	38.1
1979[d]	14,596	3,478	23.8	2,040	740	36.2
1978	13,774	3,133	22.7	1,954	662	33.9
1977	13,483	3,137	23.3	1,930	701	36.3
1976	13,224	3,163	23.9	1,852	644	34.8
1975	12,872	2,968	23.1	1,795	652	36.3
1974[c]	12,539	2,836	22.6	1,721	591	34.3
1973	(NA)	(NA)	(NA)	1,672	620	37.1
1972	(NA)	(NA)	(NA)	1,603	640	39.9
1971[b]	(NA)	(NA)	(NA)	1,584	623	39.3

This did not make much sense, so the Census Bureau began trying a fungible value (giving equivalent value to units) for Medicare and Medicaid. When the bureau measures a household's income, if the earners cannot cover the cost of housing and food, Medicare and Medicaid are given no value. However, if the family can cover the cost of food and shelter, the Census Bureau figures the difference between the household income and the amount needed to meet basic housing

TABLE 1.3

People's poverty status, by age, race, and Hispanic origin, 1959–2005 [CONTINUED]

[Numbers in thousands. People as of March of the following year.]

Year and characteristic	18 to 64 years All people			65 years and over Related children in families		
	Total	Below poverty level Number	Percent	Total	Below poverty level Number	Percent
1970	(NA)	(NA)	(NA)	1,422	683	48.0
1969	(NA)	(NA)	(NA)	1,373	689	50.2
1968	(NA)	(NA)	(NA)	1,374	655	47.7
1967[a]	(NA)	(NA)	(NA)	1,341	715	53.3
1966	(NA)	(NA)	(NA)	1,311	722	55.1
1965	(NA)	(NA)	(NA)	(NA)	711	62.5
Asian alone or in combination						
2005	9,115	999	11.0	1,144	144	12.6
2004[m]	8,780	819	9.3	1,104	147	13.3
2003	8,510	956	11.2	1,065	152	14.2
2002	8,292	804	9.7	995	86	8.7
Asian alone						
2005	8,591	941	11.0	1,118	143	12.8
2004[m]	8,294	774	9.3	1,083	146	13.5
2003	8,044	907	11.3	1,052	151	14.3
2002	7,881	764	9.7	977	82	8.4
Asian and Pacific Islander						
2001	8,352	814	9.7	899	92	10.2
2000[l]	8,500	756	8.9	878	82	9.3
1999[k]	7,879	807	10.2	864	96	11.1
1998	6,951	698	10.0	785	97	12.4
1997	6,680	753	11.3	705	87	12.3
1996	6,484	821	12.7	647	63	9.7
1995	6,123	757	12.4	622	89	14.3
1994	4,401	589	13.4	513	67	13.0
1993[j]	4,871	680	14.0	503	79	15.6
1992[l]	5,067	568	11.2	494	53	10.8
1991[h]	4,582	565	12.3	555	70	12.7
1990	4,375	422	9.6	514	62	12.1
1989	4,225	512	12.1	465	34	7.4
1988	4,035	583	14.4	442	60	13.5
1987[g]	4,010	510	12.7	375	56	15.0
Hispanic (of any race)						
2005	26,051	4,765	18.3	2,315	460	19.9
2004[m]	25,324	4,620	18.2	2,194	403	18.4
2003	24,490	4,568	18.7	2,080	406	19.5
2002	23,952	4,334	18.1	2,053	439	21.4
2001	22,653	4,014	17.7	1,896	413	21.8
2000[l]	21,734	3,844	17.7	1,822	381	20.9
1999[k]	20,782	3,843	18.5	1,661	340	20.5
1998	18,668	3,877	20.8	1,696	356	21.0
1997	18,217	3,951	21.7	1,617	384	23.8
1996	17,587	4,089	23.3	1,516	370	24.4
1995	16,673	4,153	24.9	1,458	342	23.5
1994	16,192	4,018	24.8	1,428	323	22.6
1993[j]	15,708	3,956	25.2	1,390	297	21.4
1992[l]	15,268	3,668	24.0	1,298	287	22.1
1991[h]	13,279	3,008	22.7	1,143	237	20.8
1990	12,857	2,896	22.5	1,091	245	22.5
1989	12,536	2,616	20.9	1,024	211	20.6
1988	12,056	2,501	20.7	1,005	225	22.4
1987[g]	11,718	2,509	21.4	885	243	27.5
1986	11,206	2,406	21.5	906	204	22.5
1985	10,685	2,411	22.6	915	219	23.9
1984	10,029	2,254	22.5	819	176	21.5
1983[f]	9,697	2,148	22.5	782	173	22.1
1982	8,262	1,963	23.8	596	159	26.6
1981[e]	8,084	1,642	20.3	568	146	25.7
1980	7,740	1,563	20.2	582	179	30.8

and food costs. It then values the health services at this difference (up to the amount of the market value of the medical benefits). Even though this is complicated, the formula is believed to give a fair value to these services. Similar problems have developed in trying to determine the value of housing subsidies, school lunches, and other benefits.

TABLE 1.3

People's poverty status, by age, race, and Hispanic origin, 1959–2005 [CONTINUED]

[Numbers in thousands. People as of March of the following year.]

	18 to 64 years			65 years and over		
	All people			Related children in families		
	Total	Below poverty level		Total	Below poverty level	
Year and characteristic		Number	Percent		Number	Percent
1979[d]	7,314	1,232	16.8	574	154	26.8
1978	6,527	1,098	16.8	539	125	23.2
1977	6,500	1,164	17.9	518	113	21.9
1976	6,034	1,212	20.1	464	128	27.7
1975	(NA)	(NA)	(NA)	(NA)	137	32.6
1974[c]	(NA)	(NA)	(NA)	(NA)	117	28.9
1973	(NA)	(NA)	(NA)	(NA)	95	24.9

NA=Not available.

[a]Implementation of a new March Current Population Survey (CPS) processing system.
[b]Implementation of 1970 census population controls.
[c]Implementation of a new March CPS processing system. Questionnaire expanded to ask eleven income questions.
[d]Implementation of 1980 census population controls. Questionnaire expanded to show 27 possible values from 51 possible sources of income.
[e]Implemented three technical changes to the poverty definition.
[f]Implementation of Hispanic population weighting controls.
[g]Implementation of a new March CPS processing system.
[h]CPS file for March 1992 (1991 data) was corrected after the release of the 1991 income and poverty reports. Weights for nine person records were omitted on the original file.
[i]Implementation of 1990 census population controls.
[j]Data collection method changed from paper and pencil to computer-assisted interviewing. In addition, the March 1994 income supplement was revised to allow for the coding of different income amounts on selected questionnaire items. Limits either increased or decreased in the following categories: earnings increased to $999,999; Social Security increased to $49,999; Supplemental Security Income and public assistance increased to $24,999; Veterans' benefits increased to $99,999; child support and alimony decreased to $49,999.
[k]Implementation of Census 2000 based population controls.
[l]Implementation of Census 2000 based population controls and sample expanded by 28,000 households.
[m]The 2004 data have been revised to reflect a correction to the weights in the 2005 Annual Social Economic Supplement (ASEC).

SOURCE: Adapted from "Table 3. Poverty Status of People, by Age, Race, and Hispanic Origin: 1959 to 2005," in *Current Population Survey, Annual Social and Economic Supplements*, U.S. Census Bureau, September 6, 2006, http://www.census.gov/hhes/www/poverty/histpov/hstpov3.html (accessed December 6, 2006)

Still other observers point out that most income definitions do not include assets and liabilities. Perhaps the poor household has some assets, such as a home or a car, that could be converted into income. One experimental definition of income includes capital gains on earnings, although it seems to make little difference—about 90% of all capital gains are earned by those in the upper fifth of the earnings scale. Michael Sherraden indicates in "Building Assets to Fight Poverty" (*Shelterforce Online*, March–April 2000) that including assets generally means little, because the overwhelming majority of poor families have few financial assets. For comparison purposes, the Census Bureau divides the population into five income groups (quintiles). According to Signe-Mary McKernan, in "Poor Finances: Assets and Low-Income Households" (June 7, 2006, http://www.acf.dhhs.gov/programs/opre/wrconference/presentations/Poor_Finances.ppt), the bureau reports that the bottom quintile of the population in income has a median asset holding of $17,000, whereas the second quintile has a median of $78,300 and the top quintile has $808,100. Clearly, poor and low-income families have relatively insignificant assets from which they could earn income.

Another major issue is the question of income before and after income taxes. Even though the Tax Reform Act of 1986 removed most poor households from the federal income tax rolls, many poor households still pay state and local taxes. Naturally, some critics claim, the taxes paid to local and state governments are funds that are no longer available for feeding and housing the family and, therefore, should not be counted as income.

Table 1.4 lists the various experimental definitions for income that the Census Bureau has considered. Table 1.5 illustrates that the use of these selected definitions typically lowers the poverty rate.

Growing Income Inequality

The Census Bureau has released a number of studies showing a change in the distribution of wealth and earnings in the United States. This change has resulted in an increase in the gap between the rich and the poor. Unlike many short-term economic changes that are often the product of normal economic cycles of growth and recession, these changes seem to indicate fundamental changes in American society.

The growing inequality in income in the United States began in the 1980s. In 2005 the income differences between income quintiles were close to record highs, with only the top fifth having increased its percentage of the nation's income since the 1980s. (See Table 1.6.) Census data show that in 2005 the quintile of households with the highest incomes received 50.4% of the national income, up from 50.1% the year before, about the same

TABLE 1.4

Median household income estimates based on alternative income definitions, 2002–03

[Income in 2003 dollars]

Alternative income definitions	Median income		Percent change in real income 2002 to 2003	Percent of money income
	2002 Estimate	2003 Estimate		
1. MI: Money income excluding capital gains or losses	43,381	43,318	−0.1	100.0
1b. MI−Tx: Definition 1 plus realized capital gains (losses), less taxes	38,049	38,306	0.7	88.4
2. Definition 1 less government cash transfers	39,998	39,896	−0.3	92.1
3. Definition 2 plus realized capital gains (losses)	40,450	40,263	−0.5	92.9
4. Definition 3 plus health insurance supplements to wage or salary income.	42,422	42,295	−0.3	97.6
5. Definition 4 less Social Security payroll taxes	39,664	39,695	0.1	91.6
6. Definition 5 less federal income taxes (excluding the Earned Income Credit [EIC])	36,868	37,274	1.1	86.0
7. Definition 6 plus the EIC*	37,061	37,490	1.2	86.5
8. Definition 7 less state income taxes	36,197	36,688	1.4	84.7
9. Definition 8 plus nonmeans-tested government cash transfers	40,024	40,605	1.5	93.7
10. Definition 9 plus the value of Medicare	42,222	42,679	1.1	98.5
11. Definition 10 plus the value of regular-price school lunches.	42,234	42,690	1.1	98.6
12. Definition 11 plus means-tested government cash transfers	42,432	42,876	1.5	99.0
13. Definition 12 plus the value of Medicaid	43,013	43,465	1.1*	100.3
14a. MI−Tx+NC−MM: Definition 13 plus the value of other means-tested government noncash transfers, less Medicare and Medicaid.	40,437	40,924	1.2	94.5
14. MI−Tx+NC: Definition 14a plus the value of Medicare and Medicaid	43,155	43,629	1.1	100.7
15. MI−Tx+NC+HE: Definition 14 plus imputed return on home equity.	44,884	45,154	0.6	104.2

*Twenty states (Arizona, Georgia, Hawaii, Illinois, Indiana, Iowa, Kansas, Kentucky, Maine, Maryland, Massachusetts, Minnesota, New Jersey, New Mexico, New York, Oklahoma, Oregon, Rhode Island, Virginia, and Wisconsin) and the District of Columbia have Earned Income Credit (EIC) or Low Income Credit (LIC) programs modeled in the state tax programs. The remaining states do not have such programs.
Note: Definition numbering reflects historical series identification.

SOURCE: Robert W. Cleveland, "Table 1. Median Household Income Estimates Based on Alternative Income Definitions: 2002 and 2003," in *Alternative Income Estimates in the United States: 2003—Current Population Reports*, U.S. Census Bureau, June 2005, http://www2.census.gov/prod2/popscan/p60-228.pdf (accessed December 13, 2006)

as that received by the other 80% of the population combined. The lowest quintile received only 3.4% of the national income in 2005. (Table 1.7.)

Why Is the Income Gap Growing?

Many reasons exist to explain the growing inequality, although observers disagree about which are more important. One reason is that the proportion of the elderly population, who are likely to earn less, is growing. According to the Census Bureau, 23.5 million of 114.4 million households in 2005 were headed by a householder sixty-five years of age or older. (See Table 1.8.) (A household may consist of a single individual or a group of related or unrelated people living together, whereas a family consists of related individuals.) In addition, more people than in previous years were living in nonfamily situations (either alone or with nonrelatives). In 2005, 37 million of 114.4 million households were nonfamily households. These nonfamily households earned a median income of $27,326 in 2005, compared with the $57,278 median income of family households.

The increase in the number of households headed by females, as well as the increased labor force participation of women, has also contributed to growing income inequality in the United States. In 2005, 14.1 million of 77.4 million family households, or 18.2%, were headed by women; 20.2 million of 37 million nonfamily households, or 54.7%, were headed by women. (See Table 1.8.) Female-headed households typically earn significantly less than other types of households. According to Carmen DeNavas-Walt, Bernadette D. Proctor, and Cheryl Hill Lee, in *Income, Poverty, and Health Insurance Coverage in the United States: 2005—Current Population Reports* (August 2006, http://www.census.gov/prod/2006pubs/p60-231.pdf), on average, women earned 77% of what men earned in 2005.

In *The Changing Shape of the Nation's Income Distribution* (June 2000, http://www.census.gov/prod/2000pubs/p60-204.pdf), Arthur F. Jones Jr. and Daniel H. Weinberg note that other factors contribute to the growing income gap, including the decline in the influence of unions and the changing occupational structure, in general, from better-paying manufacturing positions to lower-paying service jobs. In addition, DeNavas-Walt, Proctor, and Hill Lee indicate that the proportion of low-wage workers who receive employer-based health insurance and pension benefits dropped significantly between 1987 and 2005.

HOMELESSNESS

Homelessness is a complex social problem. According to the National Coalition for the Homeless fact sheet "How Many People Experience Homelessness?" (June 2006, http://www.nationalhomeless.org/publications/facts/How _Many.pdf), approximately 3.5 million Americans, 1.3 million of them children, lack a place to sleep at some time during the year. Social researchers—educators, sociologists, economists, and political scientists—have studied homelessness in the past and present and have determined that homelessness is caused by a combination of poverty, misfortune, illness, and behavior.

TABLE 1.5

Poverty estimates based on alternative measures of income, 2002–03

[Numbers of people in thousands, poverty rates in percentage points]

Selected alternative income definitions	2002		2003		Change (2003 less 2002)*	
	Number below poverty	Poverty rate	Number below poverty	Poverty rate	Number below poverty	Poverty rate
Thresholds adjusted for inflation using CPI-U						
MI (money income; used in official measure of poverty)	34,570	12.1	35,861	12.5	1,291	0.3
MI−Tx (money income plus realized capital gains (losses), less income and payroll taxes)	33,035	11.6	34,409	12.0	1,374	0.4
MI−Tx+NC−MM (money income plus realized capital gains (losses), less income and payroll taxes, plus value of employer-provided health benefits and all noncash transfers except Medicare and Medicaid)	28,074	9.8	29,243	10.2	1,169	0.4
MI−Tx+NC (money income plus capital gains (losses), less income and payroll taxes, plus value of all noncash transfers)	26,662	9.3	27,792	9.7	1,130	0.4
MI−Tx+NC+HE (money income plus capital gains (losses), less income and payroll taxes, plus value of all noncash transfers, plus imputed return to home equity)	24,581	8.6	25,956	9.0	1,375	0.4
Thresholds adjusted for inflation using CPI-U-RS						
MI (money income; used in official measure of poverty)	28,909	10.1	30,304	10.5	1,395	0.4
MI−Tx (money income plus realized capital gains (losses), less income and payroll taxes)	27,038	9.5	28,205	9.8	1,167	0.3
MI−Tx+NC−MM (money income plus realized capital gains (losses), less income and payroll taxes, plus value of employer-provided health benefits and all noncash transfers except Medicare and Medicaid)	22,393	7.8	23,224	8.1	831	0.3
MI−Tx+NC (money income plus capital gains (losses), less income and payroll taxes, plus value of all noncash transfers)	21,872	7.7	22,704	7.9	832	0.2
MI−Tx+NC+HE (money income plus capital gains (losses), less income and payroll taxes, plus value of all noncash transfers, plus imputed return to home equity)	20,188	7.1	21,228	7.4	1,040	0.3

*Details may not sum to totals because of rounding.

SOURCE: Joe Dalaker, "Table 1. Poverty Estimates Based on Alternative Measures of Income: 2002 and 2003," *Alternative Poverty Estimates in the United States: 2003—Current Population Reports*, U.S. Census Bureau, June 2005, http://www.census.gov/prod/2005pubs/p60-227.pdf (accessed December 13, 2006)

What Does It Mean to Be Homeless?

During a period of growing concern about homelessness in the mid-1980s, the first major piece of federal legislation aimed specifically at helping the homeless was adopted: the Stewart B. McKinney Homeless Assistance Act of 1987, today known as the McKinney-Vento Homeless Assistance Act. Part of the act officially defined a homeless person as:

1. An individual who lacks a fixed, regular, and adequate nighttime residence; and

2. An individual who has a primary nighttime residence that is:

A. A supervised publicly or privately operated shelter designed to provide temporary living accommodations (including welfare hotels, congregate shelters, and transitional housing for the mentally ill);

B. An institution that provides a temporary residence for individuals intended to be institutionalized; or

C. A public or private place not designed for, or ordinarily used as, a regular sleeping accommodation for human beings.

The government's definition of a homeless person focuses on whether a person is housed. Broader definitions of homelessness take into account whether a person has a home. For example, Martha R. Burt et al. report in *Helping America's Homeless: Emergency Shelter or Affordable Housing?* (2001) that as late as 1980 the Census Bureau identified people who lived alone and did not have a "usual home elsewhere"—in other words, a larger family—as homeless. In this sense the term *home* describes living within a family, rather than having a roof over one's head.

Burt et al. also state that homeless people themselves, when interviewed in the 1980s and 1990s, drew a distinction between having a house and having a home. Even when homeless people had spent significant periods of time in a traditional shelter, such as an apartment or

TABLE 1.6

Household income dispersion, 1967–2005

[Income in 2005 Consumer Price Index adjusted dollars]

Measures of income dispersion	2005	2004[a]	2003	2002	2001	2000[b]	1999[c]	1998	1997	1996	1995[d]	1994[e]	1993[f]	1992[g]	1991	1990	1989	1988	1987[h]	1986
Household income at selected percentiles																				
10th percentile upper limit	11,288	11,271	11,181	11,528	11,784	11,995	12,119	11,602	11,177	11,038	11,036	10,460	10,225	10,227	10,374	10,602	10,946	10,408	10,250	10,165
20th percentile upper limit	19,178	19,104	19,085	19,448	19,817	20,314	20,073	19,275	18,678	18,294	18,317	17,493	17,251	17,181	17,599	18,104	18,390	18,047	17,748	17,413
50th (median)	46,326	45,817	45,970	46,036	46,569	47,599	47,671	46,508	44,883	43,967	43,346	42,038	41,562	41,774	42,108	43,366	43,946	43,168	42,827	42,309
80th percentile upper limit	91,705	90,945	92,185	91,202	92,083	92,688	92,813	89,703	86,721	84,256	82,840	81,878	80,221	79,095	79,334	79,953	81,656	80,221	79,477	78,139
90th percentile lower limit	126,090	124,908	125,436	123,872	125,308	126,960	126,252	121,159	118,453	114,030	111,556	110,597	108,746	105,743	106,065	107,319	109,393	106,236	104,852	102,555
95th percentile lower limit	166,000	162,408	163,555	162,831	165,969	164,617	166,340	158,116	153,490	148,084	143,740	143,089	139,209	135,019	134,742	137,223	139,489	135,792	132,993	131,030
Household income ratios of selected percentiles																				
90th/10th	11.17	11.08	11.22	10.75	10.63	10.58	10.42	10.44	10.60	10.33	10.11	10.57	10.64	10.34	10.22	10.12	9.99	10.21	10.23	10.09
95th/20th	8.66	8.50	8.57	8.37	8.38	8.10	8.29	8.20	8.22	8.09	7.85	8.18	8.07	7.86	7.66	7.58	7.59	7.52	7.49	7.52
95th/50th	3.61	3.57	3.57	3.54	3.57	3.46	3.52	3.41	3.43	3.40	3.32	3.41	3.37	3.27	3.21	3.17	3.17	3.16	3.11	3.10
80th/50th	1.99	2.00	2.01	1.99	1.98	1.95	1.96	1.93	1.94	1.93	1.92	1.95	1.94	1.91	1.89	1.85	1.86	1.86	1.86	1.85
80th/20th	4.78	4.76	4.83	4.69	4.65	4.56	4.62	4.65	4.64	4.61	4.52	4.68	4.65	4.60	4.51	4.42	4.44	4.45	4.48	4.49
20th/50th	0.42	0.42	0.42	0.42	0.43	0.43	0.42	0.42	0.42	0.42	0.42	0.42	0.42	0.42	0.42	0.42	0.42	0.42	0.42	0.41
Mean household income of quintiles																				
Lowest quintile	10,655	10,587	10,608	10,845	11,178	11,514	11,614	11,031	10,721	10,648	10,616	10,050	9,790	9,894	10,101	10,378	10,633	10,250	10,077	9,813
Second quintile	27,357	27,089	27,250	27,572	28,086	28,748	28,518	27,854	26,802	26,135	25,946	25,047	24,819	24,791	25,369	26,112	26,455	25,873	25,611	25,240
Third quintile	46,301	45,896	46,256	46,462	47,011	47,874	47,735	46,607	45,091	43,959	43,384	42,196	41,603	41,766	42,139	43,131	43,976	43,273	42,818	42,236
Fourth quintile	72,825	72,368	73,218	73,085	73,709	74,423	74,293	72,081	69,840	68,036	66,691	65,661	64,654	64,115	64,236	65,030	66,518	65,413	64,721	63,629
Highest quintile	159,583	156,502	156,082	156,038	160,975	161,272	158,432	152,531	148,898	143,096	139,175	138,039	134,704	124,233	123,179	126,199	130,031	124,881	123,082	120,434
Shares of household income of quintiles																				
Lowest quintile	3.4	3.4	3.4	3.5	3.5	3.6	3.6	3.6	3.6	3.6	3.7	3.6	3.6	3.8	3.8	3.8	3.8	3.8	3.8	3.8
Second quintile	8.6	8.7	8.7	8.8	8.7	8.9	8.9	9.0	8.9	9.0	9.1	8.9	9.0	9.4	9.6	9.6	9.5	9.6	9.6	9.7
Third quintile	14.6	14.7	14.8	14.8	14.6	14.8	14.9	15.0	15.0	15.1	15.2	15.0	15.1	15.8	15.9	15.9	15.8	16.0	16.1	16.2
Fourth quintile	23.0	23.2	23.4	23.3	23.0	23.0	23.2	23.2	23.2	23.3	23.3	23.4	23.5	24.2	24.2	24.0	24.0	24.2	24.3	24.3
Highest quintile	50.4	50.1	49.8	49.7	50.1	49.8	49.4	49.2	49.4	49.0	48.7	49.1	48.9	46.9	46.5	46.6	46.8	46.3	46.2	46.1
Summary measures																				
Gini index of income inequality	0.469	0.466	0.464	0.462	0.466	0.462	0.458	0.456	0.459	0.455	0.450	0.456	0.454	0.433	0.428	0.428	0.431	0.426	0.426	0.425
Mean logarithmic deviation of income	0.545	0.543	0.530	0.514	0.515	0.490	0.476	0.488	0.484	0.464	0.452	0.471	0.467	0.416	0.411	0.402	0.406	0.401	0.414	0.416
Theil	0.411	0.406	0.397	0.398	0.413	0.404	0.386	0.389	0.396	0.389	0.378	0.387	0.385	0.323	0.313	0.317	0.324	0.314	0.311	0.310
Atkinson: e=0.25	0.098	0.097	0.095	0.095	0.098	0.096	0.092	0.093	0.094	0.093	0.090	0.092	0.092	0.080	0.078	0.078	0.080	0.078	0.077	0.077
e=0.50	0.192	0.190	0.187	0.186	0.189	0.185	0.180	0.181	0.183	0.179	0.175	0.180	0.178	0.160	0.156	0.156	0.158	0.155	0.155	0.155
e=0.75	0.289	0.286	0.283	0.279	0.282	0.275	0.268	0.271	0.272	0.266	0.261	0.268	0.266	0.242	0.237	0.236	0.239	0.236	0.238	0.237

TABLE 1.6

Household income dispersion, 1967–2005 [CONTINUED]

[Income in 2005 Consumer Price Index adjusted dollars]

Measures of income dispersion	1967[o]	1968	1969	1970	1971[n]	1972[m]	1973	1974[l]	1975	1976	1977	1978	1979[k]	1980	1981	1982	1983[j]	1984	1985[i]
Household income at selected percentiles																			
10th percentile upper limit	8,073	8,781	9,017	8,821	8,954	9,540	9,990	10,067	9,786	9,842	9,956	10,410	10,228	10,097	9,969	9,801	9,775	10,187	10,204
20th percentile upper limit	14,859	15,825	16,314	16,057	15,841	16,379	16,734	16,829	15,990	16,347	16,302	17,222	17,442	16,780	16,459	16,268	16,640	16,986	17,202
50th (median)	35,379	36,873	38,282	38,026	37,634	39,216	40,008	38,774	37,736	38,368	38,585	41,061	41,015	39,739	39,125	39,064	39,081	40,079	40,868
80th percentile upper limit	58,643	60,422	63,431	63,830	63,363	66,728	68,552	66,947	65,111	66,750	68,232	71,656	72,259	70,637	70,357	70,494	71,765	73,990	75,406
90th percentile lower limit	74,493	76,194	80,485	81,306	81,288	85,735	88,487	86,325	83,467	85,592	87,024	92,677	93,535	91,782	91,905	92,965	93,927	97,324	98,905
95th percentile lower limit	94,106	94,529	99,482	100,898	100,622	107,391	110,181	105,963	102,748	105,856	108,034	114,633	116,760	113,677	113,228	116,365	118,071	122,481	124,594
Household income ratios of selected percentiles																			
90th/10th	9.23	8.68	8.93	9.22	9.08	8.99	8.86	8.58	8.53	8.70	8.74	8.90	9.14	9.09	9.22	9.48	9.61	9.55	9.69
95th/20th	6.33	5.97	6.10	6.28	6.35	6.56	6.58	6.30	6.43	6.48	6.63	6.66	6.69	6.77	6.88	7.15	7.10	7.21	7.24
95th/50th	2.70	2.58	2.62	2.67	2.68	2.75	2.78	2.76	2.74	2.76	2.80	2.80	2.87	2.86	2.91	3.00	3.04	3.06	3.05
80th/50th	1.68	1.65	1.67	1.69	1.69	1.71	1.73	1.74	1.73	1.74	1.77	1.75	1.77	1.78	1.81	1.82	1.85	1.85	1.85
80th/20th	3.95	3.82	3.89	3.98	4.00	4.07	4.10	3.98	4.07	4.08	4.19	4.16	4.14	4.21	4.27	4.33	4.31	4.36	4.38
20th/50th	0.43	0.43	0.43	0.42	0.42	0.42	0.42	0.44	0.43	0.43	0.42	0.42	0.43	0.42	0.42	0.42	0.43	0.42	0.42
Mean household income of quintiles																			
Lowest quintile	7,923	8,599	8,816	8,672	8,721	9,233	9,663	9,636	9,304	9,535	9,481	10,045	9,982	9,671	9,440	9,276	9,395	9,720	9,714
Second quintile	21,955	23,060	23,803	23,492	23,050	23,849	24,297	23,951	22,852	23,341	23,337	24,669	24,828	24,071	23,515	23,475	23,602	24,210	24,618
Third quintile	35,054	36,572	38,036	37,830	37,370	38,921	39,853	38,602	37,494	38,384	38,606	40,732	40,934	39,720	38,955	38,857	39,021	40,120	40,863
Fourth quintile	49,045	51,018	53,276	53,324	53,129	55,876	57,330	55,748	54,479	55,742	56,565	59,666	60,069	58,517	58,068	57,790	58,555	60,408	61,466
Highest quintile	88,263	88,651	93,642	94,403	94,139	100,314	102,579	98,772	96,188	98,654	100,868	106,526	107,803	104,333	103,726	105,991	107,509	111,075	114,816
Shares of household income of quintiles																			
Lowest quintile	4.0	4.2	4.1	4.1	4.1	4.1	4.2	4.3	4.3	4.3	4.2	4.2	4.1	4.2	4.1	4.0	4.0	4.0	3.9
Second quintile	10.8	11.1	10.9	10.8	10.6	10.4	10.4	10.6	10.4	10.3	10.2	10.2	10.2	10.2	10.1	10.0	9.9	9.9	9.8
Third quintile	17.3	17.6	17.5	17.4	17.3	17.0	17.0	17.0	17.0	17.0	16.9	16.8	16.8	16.8	16.7	16.5	16.4	16.3	16.2
Fourth quintile	24.2	24.5	24.5	24.5	24.5	24.5	24.5	24.6	24.7	24.7	24.7	24.7	24.6	24.7	24.8	24.5	24.6	24.6	24.4
Highest quintile	43.6	42.6	43.0	43.3	43.5	43.9	43.9	43.5	43.6	43.7	44.0	44.1	44.2	44.1	44.3	45.0	45.1	45.2	45.6
Summary measures																			
Gini index of income inequality	0.397	0.386	0.391	0.394	0.396	0.401	0.400	0.395	0.397	0.398	0.402	0.402	0.404	0.403	0.406	0.412	0.414	0.415	0.419
Mean logarithmic deviation of income	0.380	0.356	0.357	0.370	0.370	0.370	0.355	0.352	0.361	0.361	0.364	0.363	0.369	0.375	0.387	0.401	0.397	0.391	0.403
Theil	0.287	0.273	0.268	0.271	0.273	0.279	0.270	0.267	0.270	0.271	0.276	0.275	0.279	0.274	0.277	0.287	0.288	0.290	0.300
Atkinson:																			
e=0.25	0.071	0.067	0.067	0.068	0.068	0.070	0.068	0.067	0.067	0.068	0.069	0.069	0.070	0.069	0.070	0.072	0.072	0.073	0.075
e=0.50	0.143	0.135	0.135	0.138	0.138	0.140	0.136	0.134	0.136	0.137	0.139	0.139	0.141	0.140	0.141	0.146	0.147	0.147	0.151
e=0.75	0.220	0.208	0.209	0.214	0.214	0.216	0.210	0.207	0.210	0.211	0.213	0.213	0.216	0.216	0.220	0.226	0.226	0.225	0.231

TABLE 1.6

Household income dispersion, 1967–2005 [CONTINUED]

[a]Data have been revised to reflect a correction to the weights in the 2005 Annual Social Economic Supplement (AESC).
[b]Implementation of a 28,000 household sample expansion.
[c]Implementation of Census 2000-based population controls.
[d]Full implementation of 1990 census-based sample design and metropolitan definitions, 7,000 household sample reduction, and revised editing of responses on race.
[e]Introduction of 1990 census sample design.
[f]Data collection method changed from paper and pencil to computer-assisted interviewing. In addition, the 1994 ASEC was revised to allow for the coding of different income amounts on selected questionnaire items. Limits either increased or decreased in the following categories: earnings limits increased to $999,999; social security limits increased to $49,999; supplemental security income and public assistance limits increased to $24,999; veterans' benefits limits increased to $99,999; child support and alimony limits decreased to $49,999.
[g]Implementation of 1990 census population controls.
[h]Implementation of a new Current Population Survey (CPS) AESC processing system.
[i]Recording of amounts for earnings from longest job increased to $299,999. Full implementation of 1980 census-based sample design.
[j]Implementation of Hispanic population weighting controls and introduction of 1980 census-based sample design.
[k]Implementation of 1980 census population controls. Questionnaire expanded to allow the recording of up to 27 possible values from a list of 51 possible sources of income.
[l]Implementation of a new CPS ASEC processing system. Questionnaire expanded to ask 11 income questions.
[m]Full implementation of 1970 census-based sample design.
[n]Introduction of 1970 census sample design and population controls.
[o]Implementation of a new CPS ASEC processing system.

SOURCE: Carmen DeNavas-Walt, Bernadette D. Proctor, and Cheryl Hill Lee, "Table A3. Selected Measures of Household Income Dispersion: 1967 to 2005," in *Income, Poverty, and Health Insurance Coverage in the United States: 2005—Current Population Reports*, U.S. Census Bureau, August 2006, http://www.census.gov/prod/2006pubs/p60-231.pdf (accessed December 1, 2006)

TABLE 1.7

Shares of household income, by quintile, 2004–05

[Income in 2005 dollars. Households and people as of March of the following year.]

Characteristic	2004[a] Number (thousands)	2004[a] Median income (dollars) Estimate	2005 Number (thousands)	2005 Median income (dollars) Estimate	Percentage change in real median income (2005 less 2004) Estimate
Households					
All households	113,343	45,817	114,384	46,326	1.1
Type of household					
Family households	76,858	57,179	77,402	57,278	0.2
Married-couple	57,975	65,946	58,179	66,067	0.2
Female householder, no husband present	13,981	30,823	14,093	30,650	−0.6
Male householder, no wife present	4,901	46,526	5,130	46,756	0.5
Nonfamily households	36,485	27,129	36,982	27,326	0.7
Female householder	19,942	22,594	20,230	22,688	0.4
Male householder	16,543	33,083	16,753	34,048	2.9
Race[b] and Hispanic origin of householder					
White	92,880	48,218	93,588	48,554	0.7
White, not Hispanic	81,628	50,546	82,003	50,784	0.5
Black	13,809	31,101	14,002	30,858	−0.8
Asian	4,123	59,427	4,273	61,094	2.8
Hispanic origin (any race)	12,178	35,417	12,519	35,967	1.6
Age of householder					
Under 65 years	90,192	52,562	90,926	52,287	−0.5
15 to 24 years	6,733	28,497	6,795	28,770	1.0
25 to 34 years	19,314	46,985	19,120	47,379	0.8
35 to 44 years	23,248	58,578	23,016	58,084	−0.8
45 to 54 years	23,393	63,068	23,731	62,424	−1.0
55 to 64 years	17,503	52,077	18,264	52,260	0.4
65 years and older	23,151	25,336	23,459	26,036	2.8
Nativity of householder					
Native	98,842	46,786	99,579	46,897	0.2
Foreign born	14,502	40,692	14,806	42,040	3.3
Naturalized citizen	6,741	47,642	6,990	50,030	5.0
Not a citizen	7,761	35,749	7,815	36,740	2.8
Region					
Northeast	21,187	49,462	21,054	50,882	2.9
Midwest	25,939	46,134	26,351	45,950	−0.4
South	41,224	42,108	41,805	42,138	0.1
West	24,993	49,245	25,174	50,002	1.5
Residence					
Inside metropolitan statistical areas	(NA)	(NA)	95,107	48,474	(X)
Inside principal cities.	(NA)	(NA)	38,008	41,166	(X)
Outside principal cities	(NA)	(NA)	57,098	53,544	(X)
Outside metropolitan statistical areas[c]	(NA)	(NA)	19,278	37,564	(X)
Shares of household income quintiles					
Lowest quintile	22,669	3.4	22,877	3.4	−0.7
Second quintile	22,669	8.7	22,877	8.6	−0.4
Third quintile	22,669	14.7	22,877	14.6	−0.5
Fourth quintile	22,669	23.2	22,877	23.0	−0.7
Highest quintile	22,669	50.1	22,877	50.4	0.6

rented room, if they felt those houses were transitional or insecure, they identified themselves as having been homeless while living there. According to Burt et al., these answers "reflect how long they have been without significant attachments to people."

Burt et al. and other homeless advocates disagree with the narrow government definition of a homeless person, which focuses on a person's sleeping arrangements. They assert that the definition should be broadened to include groups of people who, while they may have somewhere to live, do not really have a home in the conventional sense. Considerable debate has resulted over expanding the classification to include people in situations such as the following:

- People engaging in prostitution who spend each night in a different hotel room, paid for by clients

- Children in foster or relative care

- People living in stable but inadequate housing (for example, having no plumbing or heating)

TABLE 1.7

Shares of household income, by quintile, 2004–05 [CONTINUED]

[Income in 2005 dollars. Households and people as of March of the following year.]

Characteristic	2004[a] Median income (dollars)		2005 Median income (dollars)		Percentage change in real median income (2005 less 2004)
	Number (thousands)	Estimate	Number (thousands)	Estimate	Estimate
Earnings of full-time, year-round workers					
Men with earnings	60,088	42,160	61,500	41,386	−1.8
Women with earnings	42,380	32,285	43,351	31,858	−1.3
Per capita income[d]					
Total[b]	**291,166**	**24,655**	**293,834**	**25,036**	**1.5**
White	234,116	26,067	235,903	26,496	1.6
White, not Hispanic	195,347	28,357	195,893	28,946	2.1
Black	36,548	16,561	36,965	16,874	1.9
Asian	12,241	27,040	12,599	27,331	1.1
Hispanic origin (any race)	41,840	14,577	43,168	14,483	−0.6

(NA) Not available.
(X) Not applicable.
[a]The 2004 data have been revised to reflect a correction to the weights in the 2005 Annual Social and Economic Supplement.
[b]Federal surveys now give respondents the option of reporting more than one race. Therefore, two basic ways of defining a race group are possible. A group such as Asian may be defined as those who reported Asian and no other race (the race-alone or single-race concept) or as those who reported Asian regardless of whether they also reported another race (the race-alone-or-in-combination concept). This table shows data using the first approach (race alone). The use of the single-race population does not imply that it is the preferred method of presenting or analyzing data. The Census Bureau uses a variety of approaches. Information on people who reported more than one race, such as white and American Indian and Alaska Native or Asian and black or African American, is available from Census 2000 through American FactFinder. About 2.6 percent of people reported more than one race in Census 2000.
[c]The "outside metropolitan statistical areas" category includes both micropolitan statistical areas and territory outside of metropolitan and micropolitan statistical areas.
[d]The data shown in this section are per capita incomes and their respective confidence intervals. Per capita income is the mean income computed for every man, woman, and child in a particular group. It is derived by dividing the total income of a particular group by the total population in that group (excluding patients or inmates in institutional quarters).

SOURCE: Carmen DeNavas-Walt, Bernadette D. Proctor, and Cheryl Hill Lee, "Table 1. Income and Earnings Summary Measures by Selected Characteristics: 2004 and 2005," in *Income, Poverty, and Health Insurance Coverage in the United States: 2005—Current Population Reports*, U.S. Census Bureau, P60-231, August 2006, http://www.census.gov/prod/2006pubs/p60-231.pdf (accessed December 1, 2006).

- People doubled up in conventional dwellings for the short term

- People in hotels paid for by vouchers to the needy

- Elderly people living with family members because they cannot afford to live elsewhere

Official definitions are important because total counts of the homeless influence levels of funding authorized by Congress for homeless programs. With the availability of federal funds since the passage of the McKinney-Vento Homeless Assistance Act, institutional constituencies have formed that advocate for additional funding, an effort in which more expansive definitions are helpful.

Causes of Homelessness

In 2006 the U.S. Conference of Mayors, a nonpartisan organization of cities with populations higher than thirty thousand, surveyed the mayors of major cities on the extent and causes of urban homelessness, and most of the mayors named mental illness and lack of needed services, and lack of affordable housing as major causes of homelessness (eighteen and seventeen out of twenty-three mayors surveyed, respectively). (See Table 1.9.) The next three causes were, in rank order, substance abuse and the lack of needed services (identified by sixteen mayors), low-paying jobs (identified by thirteen mayors), and domestic violence and prisoner reentry (both identified

by seven mayors). The lowest ranking causes, cited by five mayors each, were unemployment and poverty. These results indicate that in the Conference of Mayors opinion, homelessness is a complex social problem arising from three fundamental and interacting causes: lack of means, medical conditions, and behavioral problems.

COUNTING THE HOMELESS

Methodology

An accurate count of the U.S. homeless population has proved to be a problem for statisticians. The most formidable obstacle is the nature of homelessness itself. Typically, researchers contact people in their homes using in-person or telephone surveys to obtain information regarding income, education levels, household size, ethnicity, and other demographic data. Because homeless people cannot be counted at home, researchers have been forced to develop new methods for collecting data on these transient groups. Martha R. Burt explored this issue for the U.S. Department of Housing and Urban Development (HUD) and the HHS and published in August 1999 a table of the most common methods of data collection for homeless people. (See Table 1.10.)

Counting each and every person without a home would be the most accurate way to establish the number of homeless people. However, such a count is almost

TABLE 1.8

Selected characteristics of households, by income in dollars, 2005

[Numbers in thousands. Households as of March of the following year.]

	Total	Under $2,500	$2,500 to $4,999	$5,000 to $7,499	$7,500 to $9,999	$10,000 to $12,499	$12,500 to $14,999	$15,000 to $17,499	$17,500 to $19,999	$20,000 to $22,499	$22,500 to $24,999	$25,000 to $27,499
All races												
All households	114,384	2,622	1,109	2,513	3,157	3,786	3,546	3,691	3,424	3,934	3,090	3,820
Type of household												
Family households	77,402	1,202	565	897	954	1,268	1,479	1,694	1,883	2,125	1,787	2,237
Married-couple families	58,179	493	162	233	295	618	723	875	1,062	1,252	1,140	1,461
Male householder, nsp*	5,130	105	50	72	77	116	104	134	177	160	119	190
Female householder, nsp*	14,093	603	353	593	582	534	652	686	644	713	528	586
Nonfamily households	36,982	1,421	545	1,616	2,202	2,518	2,067	1,997	1,541	1,809	1,302	1,584
Male householder	16,753	546	212	501	688	900	671	739	592	806	576	695
Living alone	13,061	480	194	471	618	852	613	660	508	709	495	576
Female householder	20,230	875	332	1,115	1,514	1,618	1,396	1,258	949	1,003	726	889
Living alone	17,392	803	316	1,078	1,470	1,560	1,343	1,192	873	912	667	773
Age of householder												
Under 65 years	90,926	2,211	893	1,742	1,735	2,047	1,901	2,263	2,149	2,783	1,901	2,652
15 to 24 years	6,795	381	180	265	255	317	299	325	312	383	206	358
25 to 34 years	19,120	455	237	317	325	463	393	524	482	689	480	658
35 to 44 years	23,016	467	133	360	328	373	382	498	441	585	475	589
45 to 54 years	23,731	484	167	398	410	415	399	447	485	532	362	511
55 to 64 years	18,264	425	177	403	416	480	428	469	430	595	379	536
65 years and over	23,459	411	216	771	1,422	1,738	1,645	1,428	1,275	1,152	1,189	1,168
65 to 74 years	11,687	176	77	328	554	660	612	571	524	498	568	538
75 years and over	11,772	235	139	443	868	1,079	1,033	857	751	654	621	630
Mean age of householder	49.2	45.7	46.3	52.2	57.3	57.2	57.6	54.5	53.8	50.8	54.1	51.0
Size of household												
One person	30,453	1,283	510	1,549	2,088	2,412	1,955	1,852	1,381	1,621	1,162	1,349
Two people	37,775	729	285	463	546	741	895	970	1,175	1,256	1,143	1,411
Three people	18,924	304	164	275	259	283	312	386	420	510	336	474
Four people	15,998	174	93	122	142	199	221	280	231	298	253	328
Five people	7,306	82	38	59	82	93	112	115	140	167	137	167
Six people	2,562	34	10	30	28	38	29	49	44	46	37	57
Seven people or more	1,366	18	8	13	11	20	20	40	33	37	23	34
Mean size of household	2.57	1.97	2.04	1.76	1.66	1.71	1.84	1.99	2.10	2.11	2.14	2.21
Number of earners												
No earners	24,224	2,089	592	1,672	2,246	2,258	2,018	1,633	1,381	1,219	1,208	1,111
One earner	42,066	482	461	732	812	1,367	1,330	1,726	1,662	2,238	1,397	2,026
Two earners or more	48,095	51	55	109	98	161	198	332	381	478	484	684
2 earners	38,327	48	53	104	90	148	191	311	361	443	452	629
3 earners	7,337	3	3	4	6	11	6	20	17	32	31	49
4 earners or more	2,430	0	0	0	3	3	0	2	2	3	1	6
Mean number of earners	1.36	0.23	0.52	0.39	0.33	0.46	0.50	0.67	0.73	0.84	0.79	0.93

TABLE 1.8

Selected characteristics of households, by income in dollars, 2005 [CONTINUED]

[Numbers in thousands. Households as of March of the following year.]

Educational attainment of householder	Total	Under $2,500	$2,500 to $4,999	$5,000 to $7,499	$7,500 to $9,999	$10,000 to $12,499	$12,500 to $14,999	$15,000 to $17,499	$17,500 to $19,999	$20,000 to $22,499	$22,500 to $24,999	$25,000 to $27,499
Total, 25 yrs & over	107,589	2,241	930	2,248	2,902	3,469	3,247	3,367	3,112	3,552	2,884	3,462
Less than 9th grade	6,088	186	108	437	590	558	389	407	340	323	244	277
9th to 12th grade, no diploma	9,130	359	162	454	600	612	554	528	450	514	380	421
High school graduate (includes equivalency)	32,345	785	312	754	983	1,256	1,274	1,314	1,223	1,466	1,111	1,316
Some college, no degree	19,311	356	184	301	358	486	507	536	518	629	478	673
Associate degree	9,563	157	54	111	129	203	204	237	213	212	231	257
Bachelor's degree or more	31,153	398	108	191	241	354	318	346	367	407	440	518
Bachelor's degree	19,843	268	79	148	179	264	247	237	268	287	346	363
Master's degree	7,943	91	18	32	53	63	50	90	77	97	110	110
Professional degree	1,789	20	3	6	6	11	8	7	19	10	16	23
Doctorate degree	1,578	18	8	4	4	15	13	12	3	12	8	21

	$27,500 to $29,999	$30,000 to $32,499	$32,500 to $34,999	$35,000 to $37,499	$37,500 to $39,999	$40,000 to $42,499	$42,500 to $44,999	$45,000 to $47,499	$47,500 to $49,999	$50,000 to $52,499	$52,500 to $54,999	$55,000 to $57,499
All races												
All households	2,798	3,882	2,530	3,506	2,470	3,464	2,306	2,913	2,345	3,142	1,975	2,490
Type of household												
Family households	1,742	2,477	1,686	2,116	1,677	2,284	1,658	2,037	1,667	2,137	1,453	1,840
Married-couple families	1,181	1,667	1,153	1,361	1,194	1,653	1,213	1,519	1,234	1,645	1,102	1,454
Male householder, nsp*	145	206	140	221	150	184	109	152	129	185	111	107
Female householder, nsp*	416	604	393	534	333	447	335	366	304	307	241	279
Nonfamily households	1,056	1,405	844	1,389	793	1,180	648	875	679	1,005	523	649
Male householder	444	758	403	738	399	627	315	445	362	566	272	315
Living alone	349	650	325	626	297	480	243	339	253	430	193	233
Female householder	612	648	441	651	394	553	334	430	317	439	251	334
Living alone	535	567	350	569	328	497	262	347	259	340	179	261
Age of householder												
Under 65 years	1,918	3,081	1,876	2,832	1,876	2,910	1,804	2,409	1,971	2,740	1,601	2,184
15 to 24 years	233	283	199	264	149	218	157	174	141	210	114	110
25 to 34 years	459	811	449	742	438	737	368	559	481	652	374	578
35 to 44 years	442	731	454	699	428	725	445	637	491	768	394	574
45 to 54 years	401	687	424	641	445	682	461	581	467	646	379	520
55 to 64 years	382	571	349	486	415	548	373	458	391	465	340	401
65 years and over	879	800	654	674	594	554	502	504	374	402	374	306
65 to 74 years	454	427	355	337	315	292	272	271	203	247	233	187
75 years and over	426	374	299	337	279	262	231	232	171	155	141	119
Mean age of householder	51.6	47.8	49.6	47.1	50.1	46.9	49.5	47.5	47.1	45.4	48.1	45.7
Size of household												
One person	884	1,217	676	1,196	624	977	506	685	511	770	371	494
Two people	1,112	1,355	999	1,106	948	1,228	877	1,026	866	1,065	709	867
Three people	334	553	384	537	389	526	419	514	425	579	413	454
Four people	246	413	295	369	287	426	284	398	293	429	278	396

TABLE 1.8

Selected characteristics of households, by income in dollars, 2005 [CONTINUED]

[Numbers in thousands. Households as of March of the following year.]

	$27,500 to $29,999	$30,000 to $32,499	$32,500 to $34,999	$35,000 to $37,499	$37,500 to $39,999	$40,000 to $42,499	$42,500 to $44,999	$45,000 to $47,499	$47,500 to $49,999	$50,000 to $52,499	$52,500 to $54,999	$55,000 to $57,499
Five people	133	220	108	187	143	186	124	169	156	181	124	160
Six people	52	77	43	77	51	80	54	69	77	84	51	66
Seven people or more	37	48	25	35	26	41	44	52	18	34	29	53
Mean size of household	2.30	2.38	2.39	2.36	2.49	2.46	2.60	2.60	2.62	2.60	2.72	2.75
Number of earners												
No earners	800	676	533	521	449	416	385	342	280	252	184	169
One earner	1,334	2,280	1,198	1,967	1,151	1,827	920	1,386	926	1,500	752	967
Two earners or more	663	926	798	1,018	870	1,220	1,001	1,185	1,139	1,390	1,039	1,354
2 earners	604	831	723	877	786	1,088	843	1,006	979	1,220	870	1,146
3 earners	48	82	67	129	78	119	142	159	125	151	144	179
4 earners or more	11	14	8	11	7	13	17	19	36	20	24	29
Mean number of earners	1.01	1.12	1.17	1.22	1.25	1.31	1.38	1.39	1.49	1.46	1.58	1.61
Educational attainment of householder												
Total, 25 yrs & over	2,564	3,599	2,331	3,242	2,321	3,246	2,149	2,739	2,204	2,932	1,861	2,380
Less than 9th grade	201	258	156	183	104	145	115	101	80	112	58	72
9th to 12th grade, no diploma	298	418	241	267	248	274	178	205	140	180	135	161
High school graduate (includes equivalency)	904	1,176	897	1,169	843	1,047	676	941	740	956	599	756
Some college, no degree	494	733	456	664	451	654	483	543	477	639	394	472
Associate degree	248	345	178	317	207	355	243	232	213	277	178	274
Bachelor's degree or more	420	670	403	641	467	772	454	716	553	768	497	644
Bachelor's degree	300	504	267	479	324	501	291	472	391	494	329	404
Master's degree	98	116	104	138	105	219	115	184	131	219	120	202
Professional degree	13	30	19	12	22	21	20	34	19	27	18	19
Doctorate degree	9	21	13	12	17	30	27	25	12	28	30	19

	$57,500 to $59,999	$60,000 to $62,499	$62,500 to $64,999	$65,000 to $67,499	$67,500 to $69,999	$70,000 to $72,499	$72,500 to $74,999	$75,000 to $77,499	$77,500 to $79,999	$80,000 to $82,499	$82,500 to $84,999	$85,000 to $87,499
All races												
All households	1,745	2,702	1,703	2,073	1,660	2,094	1,447	1,893	1,271	1,704	1,233	1,320
Type of householder												
Family households	1,388	2,045	1,389	1,633	1,343	1,653	1,190	1,502	1,047	1,372	1,052	1,114
Married-couple families	1,079	1,633	1,125	1,317	1,092	1,401	1,015	1,260	900	1,181	885	974
Male householder, nsp*	110	162	80	106	92	108	55	105	51	96	52	49
Female householder, nsp*	199	249	184	210	159	145	120	137	96	95	115	91
Nonfamily households	357	657	313	440	317	441	257	391	223	332	181	206
Male householder	174	342	174	236	144	231	149	233	127	207	97	110
Living alone	108	246	120	153	93	140	90	152	73	106	54	59
Female householder	183	315	139	204	173	210	108	157	96	125	84	96
Living alone	117	212	94	137	103	138	79	110	48	84	44	59
Age of householder												
Under 65 years	1,498	2,432	1,450	1,861	1,425	1,882	1,248	1,715	1,138	1,575	1,090	1,204
15 to 24 years	85	127	64	58	97	71	55	102	35	59	44	34
25 to 34 years	382	628	306	423	262	453	249	391	229	314	204	235

TABLE 1.8

Selected characteristics of households, by income in dollars, 2005 [CONTINUED]

[Numbers in thousands. Households as of March of the following year.]

	$57,500 to $59,999	$60,000 to $62,499	$62,500 to $64,999	$65,000 to $67,499	$67,500 to $69,999	$70,000 to $72,499	$72,500 to $74,999	$75,000 to $77,499	$77,500 to $79,999	$80,000 to $82,499	$82,500 to $84,999	$85,000 to $87,499
35 to 44 years	376	643	428	501	364	492	327	431	315	481	280	387
45 to 54 years	359	583	357	566	359	528	379	507	314	449	347	354
55 to 64 years	296	451	295	313	343	339	239	285	245	271	216	193
65 years and over	246	270	253	212	235	213	199	178	133	130	143	116
65 to 74 years	159	179	163	129	152	140	125	112	78	93	92	77
75 years and over	88	90	89	83	83	73	74	65	55	37	51	39
Mean age of householder	46.5	45.2	47.5	46.0	48.0	45.8	47.7	45.2	46.9	45.3	47.4	45.6
Size of household												
One person	224	458	213	289	195	278	169	261	121	189	98	118
Two people	657	973	665	715	701	796	528	660	467	590	439	500
Three people	376	506	328	450	356	379	290	368	257	345	268	281
Four people	290	414	289	362	225	390	259	350	244	378	256	249
Five people	117	232	126	163	119	180	126	169	140	140	110	119
Six people	56	76	57	68	41	50	47	54	25	47	41	26
Seven people or more	23	41	24	25	22	22	28	31	16	16	21	26
Mean size of household	2.87	2.82	2.89	2.93	2.80	2.88	3.00	2.95	3.04	3.01	3.10	3.00
Number of earners												
No earners	128	138	111	84	148	110	93	85	73	54	58	51
One earner	561	1,108	492	668	466	655	393	597	267	485	277	293
Two earners or more	1,056	1,456	1,100	1,321	1,046	1,329	962	1,211	930	1,165	898	975
2 earners	886	1,240	878	1,089	850	1,101	764	953	706	908	671	791
3 earners	142	175	182	171	157	173	153	205	162	205	180	132
4 earners or more	28	42	40	62	38	55	44	53	62	52	48	53
Mean number of earners	1.70	1.63	1.79	1.81	1.74	1.77	1.82	1.82	1.98	1.89	1.97	1.94
Educational attainment of householder												
Total, 25 yrs & over	1,660	2,575	1,639	2,015	1,562	2,023	1,393	1,791	1,236	1,645	1,189	1,285
Less than 9th grade	33	68	57	56	41	39	20	37	24	16	20	21
9th to 12th grade, no diploma	96	149	90	96	62	72	45	47	44	60	40	45
High school graduate (includes equivalency)	509	794	477	589	462	576	393	488	344	432	282	306
Some college, no degree	340	466	295	392	263	394	271	333	259	296	236	270
Associate degree	181	258	201	206	179	239	159	215	133	184	128	142
Bachelor's degree or more	500	840	518	676	556	703	505	672	431	657	483	500
Bachelor's degree	311	533	353	454	367	475	331	440	262	425	313	350
Master's degree	145	250	124	166	141	164	116	163	129	170	118	115
Professional degree	18	28	24	33	28	30	22	35	17	23	22	23
Doctorate degree	26	28	17	22	20	33	36	34	24	39	30	12

TABLE 1.8

Selected characteristics of households, by income in dollars, 2005 [CONTINUED]

[Numbers in thousands. Households as of March of the following year.]

	$87,500 to $89,999	$90,000 to $92,499	$92,500 to $94,999	$95,000 to $97,499	$97,500 to $99,999	$100,000 and over	Median income Value (Dol.)	Mean income Value (Dol.)
All races								
All households	**1,084**	**1,456**	**881**	**1,038**	**854**	**19,716**	**46,326**	**63,344**
Type of household								
Family households	926	1,213	787	911	755	17,219	57,278	74,390
Married-couple families	798	1,068	677	803	658	15,622	66,067	83,757
Male householder, nsp*	35	56	41	36	38	715	46,756	59,533
Female householder, nsp*	92	88	68	71	58	883	30,650	41,131
Nonfamily households	158	243	95	128	99	2,496	27,326	40,225
Male householder	102	152	68	83	57	1,497	34,048	47,355
Living alone	46	91	36	49	30	824	30,020	41,279
Female householder	56	92	27	44	42	999	22,688	34,321
Living alone	30	62	9	31	19	537	20,166	29,233
Age of householder								
Under 65 years	977	1,328	826	942	781	18,074	52,287	69,195
15 to 24 years	18	19	18	23	26	330	28,770	37,265
25 to 34 years	164	307	152	188	119	2,445	47,379	57,746
35 to 44 years	266	389	242	293	243	5,139	58,084	74,259
45 to 54 years	318	404	266	287	232	6,181	62,424	81,141
55 to 64 years	210	209	150	152	161	3,980	52,260	71,155
65 years and over	107	128	55	97	72	1,641	26,036	40,668
65 to 74 years	77	82	41	74	46	1,170	31,670	49,477
75 years and over	31	46	15	22	26	471	21,842	31,923
Mean age of householder	47.7	45.7	46.0	45.9	46.7	47.8	(X)	(X)
Size of household								
One person	76	153	44	80	50	1,361	23,736	34,400
Two people	405	473	309	296	239	6,589	49,294	65,336
Three people	261	330	204	234	214	4,230	58,917	74,879
Four people	225	304	191	253	221	4,641	69,605	86,517
Five people	78	158	84	120	86	1,956	66,487	84,641
Six people	25	27	28	37	27	645	61,342	80,886
Seven people or more	13	11	20	18	17	293	56,796	75,543
Mean size of household	3.03	3.03	3.25	3.29	3.33	3.20	(X)	(X)
Number of earners								
No earners	46	39	21	22	28	501	16,893	24,032
One earner	244	364	137	220	145	4,253	37,541	52,562
Two earners or more	794	1,053	724	796	681	14,961	75,293	92,575
2 earners	589	813	519	594	488	10,688	70,952	88,205
3 earners	164	194	161	154	148	2,874	87,905	104,940
4 earners or more	42	46	43	49	45	1,399	100,000	124,164
Mean number of earners	1.98	1.95	2.17	2.06	2.12	2.10	(X)	(X)
Educational attainment of householder								
Total, 25 yrs & over	1,066	1,437	864	1,015	827	19,386	47,716	64,991
Less than 9th grade	19	15	19	17	10	131	20,224	27,986
9th to 12th grade, no diploma	42	59	16	43	29	312	24,675	33,214

TABLE 1.8

Selected characteristics of households, by income in dollars, 2005 [CONTINUED]

[Numbers in thousands. Households as of March of the following year.]

	$87,500 to $89,999	$90,000 to $92,499	$92,500 to $94,999	$95,000 to $97,499	$97,500 to $99,999	$100,000 and over	Median income Value (Dol.)	Mean income Value (Dol.)
High school graduate (includes equivalency)	286	310	200	244	146	3,011	38,191	49,131
Some college, no degree	204	267	186	199	184	2,965	48,284	60,963
Associate degree	127	162	98	98	98	1,679	54,709	65,733
Bachelor's degree or more	388	624	345	414	360	11,288	77,179	100,272
Bachelor's degree	258	409	233	275	234	6,377	72,424	91,421
Master's degree	96	146	84	123	88	3,101	81,023	104,274
Professional degree	9	41	13	6	20	1,011	100,000	154,278
Doctorate degree	25	28	15	10	18	799	100,000	130,187

Note: (X) Not applicable.
*No spouse present

SOURCE: Adapted from "HINC-01. Selected Characteristics of Households, by Total Money Income in 2005," in *Current Population Survey, 2006 Annual Social and Economic Supplement*, U.S. Census Bureau, August 29, 2006, http://pubdb3.census.gov/macro/032006/hhinc/new01_001.htm (accessed December 13, 2006)

TABLE 1.9

Main causes of homelessness, as reported by city officials, November 2005–October 2006

Number of positive survey responses	Causes of homelessness	Cities replying in the affirmative that the listed cause of homelessness was one of the main or primary causes in their city
18	Mental illness and the lack of needed services	Boston, Charleston, Chicago, Cleveland, Denver, Los Angeles, Louisville Metro, Miami, Philadelphia, Phoenix, Portland, Salt Lake City, San Francisco, Santa Monica, Seattle, St. Paul, and Trenton
17	Lack of affordable housing	Boston, Charleston, Cleveland, Denver, Des Moines, Los Angeles, Louisville Metro, Miami, Philadelphia, Phoenix, Portland, Salt Lake City, San Francisco, Santa Monica, Seattle, St. Paul, and Trenton
16	Substance abuse and the lack of needed services	Chicago, Cleveland, Los Angeles, Louisville Metro, Miami, Nashville, Norfolk, Philadelphia, Phoenix, Portland, Salt Lake City, San Francisco, Santa Monica, Seattle, St. Paul, and Trenton
13	Low-paying jobs	Boston, Chicago, Cleveland, Denver, Louisville Metro, Norfolk, Philadelphia, Phoenix, Portland, Salt Lake City, San Francisco, St. Paul, and Trenton
7	Domestic violence	Charleston, Chicago, Kansas City, Los Angeles, Salt Lake City, San Francisco, and Seattle
7	Prisoner re-entry	Boston, Cleveland, Denver, Los Angeles, Louisville Metro, Phoenix, and San Francisco
5	Unemployment	Charleston, Chicago, Denver, Des Moines, and Los Angeles
5	Poverty	Cleveland, Phoenix, Seattle, St. Paul, and Trenton

SOURCE: Adapted from "Main Causes of Homelessness," in *Hunger and Homelessness Survey: A Status Report on Hunger and Homelessness in America's Cities—A 23-City Survey*, U.S. Conference of Mayors and Sodexho, December 2006, http://usmayors.org/uscm/hungersurvey/2006/ report06.pdf (accessed January 21, 2007)

TABLE 1.10

Common methods for collecting planning information

Method	Usual places to find people for study	Usual period of data collection and of estimate	Probable complexity of data collected
Full counts and other non-probability methods			
Analysis of agency records	Specific agency	Varies; usually not done to develop a population estimate	Whatever the agency routinely records in its case documents
Simple count, involving significant amounts of data by observation or from minimal agency records	Shelters, streets	1 night; point-in-time estimate	Enumeration+very simple population characteristics (gender, adult/child, race)
Simple count with brief interview	Shelters, meal programs, streets	1 night; point-in-time estimate	Enumeration+basic information as reported by respondent
Screener, counts and brief interviews for anyone screened in, plus unduplication using unique identifiers	Service agencies of all types	Several weeks or months; point-in-time and period prevalence estimate	Enumeration+basic information as reported by respondent
Complete enumeration through multiple agency search and referral followed by extensive interview (also unduplication)	Service agencies and key informants	Several weeks or months; point-in-time and period prevalence estimate	Usually extensive
Probability-based methods			
Block probability with substantial interview	Streets	Several weeks or months; point-in-time estimate	Usually extensive
Other probability approaches	Abandoned buildings, conventional housing in poor neighborhoods	Several days or weeks; point-in-time estimate	Enumeration+basic information as reported by respondent
Service-based random sampling	Usually homeless assistance programs	Several weeks, months, or years; point-in-time estimate	Usually extensive
Shelter and other service tracking systems that allow unduplication across all services in a jurisdiction over time	Service agencies	On going; point-in-time or period prevalence for periods of any length	Whatever the system collects, but usually simple data for administrative purposes
Other interesting methods			
Surveys of the housed population	At home	Multi-year; produces period prevalence for periods asked about	Basic information as reported by respondent
Longitudinal studies	Shelters, soup kitchens, streets	Multi-year; does not produce a population estimate	Extensive information, collected from the same person at several points in time

SOURCE: Martha R. Burt, "Table 3. Common Methods for Collecting Planning Information," in "Demographics and Geography: Estimating Needs," *Practical Lessons: The 1998 Symposium on Homelessness Research*, edited by Linda B. Fosburg and Deborah L. Dennis, U.S. Department of Housing and Urban Development and the U.S. Department of Health and Human Services, August 1999, http://aspe.os.dhhs.gov/progsys/homeless/symposium/1-demograp.htm (accessed January 2, 2007)

impossible. Anita Drever, in *Homeless Count Methodologies: An Annotated Bibliography* (February 1999, http://weingart.org/institute/research/projects/pdf/HomelessCountMethodologies.pdf), discusses other methods. One way to estimate the number of homeless people is to search records at homeless service provider locations. Alternatively, a sampling of those records combined with projections, called probability-based methods, can be used to count the number of homeless. Another way to count the homeless is to count the number of homeless at one particular time in one particular place. This snapshot method estimates the number of homeless at any one time. Longitudinal studies are a way to estimate the proportion of people in a population who may become homeless at some point in their lives. These studies follow individuals over a period to determine if they become homeless.

As Table 1.10 reveals, methods vary in scope and design. Different designs will produce different results even if the intention is the same—namely to accurately enumerate the homeless population. For example, Table 1.11 shows results of surveys conducted in 2004 and 2005 by the Association of Gospel Rescue Missions (AGRM). The data presented are based on the snapshot method—counts of a population at a point in time. The AGRM counted all people receiving homeless services during one specific night in each year.

Table 1.12 shows results of an Urban Institute study conducted in 1996. Data in Table 1.12 are based on a sample of seventy-six geographical areas selected by the Urban Institute as being representative of all service providers in the United States. The Urban Institute then compared its results by demographic characteristics with the total population as enumerated by the U.S. census. The male-female ratios in the AGRM study are quite different from the Urban Institute's study, with the AGRM finding that males were more than three-quarters of the homeless (76% in 2005), whereas the Urban Institute's study showed that males were just over two-thirds of the homeless population (68% in 1996). Both studies showed that males outnumbered females among the homeless, but the proportions were different.

Counting the Homeless for the U.S. Census

The official U.S. census, which takes place at ten-year intervals, is intended to count everyone in the United States. The results of the census are critical in determining how much federal money goes into different programs and to various regions of the country. Representation of the population in Congress is also based on the census. Because the Census Bureau counts people in their homes, counting the homeless presents special challenges.

TABLE 1.11

Demographic overview of the homeless population, 2004–05

	2005	2004
Gender		
Male	76%	77%
Female	24%	23%
Age groups		
Under 18	10%	9%
18–25	10%	10%
26–35	20%	18%
36–45	29%	30%
46–65	27%	29%
65+	4%	4%
Race/ethnic groups		
Caucasian	45%	44%
African-American	38%	40%
Hispanic	10%	10%
Asian	1%	1%
Native American	5%	5%
Women/children/families		
Couples	14%	16%
Women with children	61%	60%
Men with children	6%	7%
Intact families	19%	17%
Other information		
Veterans—male	22%	23%
Veterans—female	3%	3%
Served in Korea	4%	5%
Served in Vietnam	38%	41%
Served in Persian Gulf	12%	12%
Homeless less than 1 year	59%	62%
Never before homeless	34%	35%
Homeless once before	26%	26%
Homeless twice before	18%	18%
Homeless 3+ times before	22%	21%
More than 6 month resident	73%	72%
Harder to find work today than 6 mos. ago	55%	58%
Lost government benefits in last 12 mos.	19%	20%
Prefer spiritual emphasis in services	81%	80%
Comes to the mission daily for assistance	77%	78%
In long-term rehab—male	33%	35%
In long-term rehab—female	32%	25%

SOURCE: "Snapshot Survey of the Homeless Statistical Comparison," in *Statistics and Studies: 2005 Snapshot Survey of the Homeless*, Association of Gospel Rescue Missions, 2005, http://www.agrm.org/statistics/05-snap.html (accessed October 31, 2006)

In "The 1990 Census Shelter and Street Night Enumeration" (March 1992, http://www.amstat.org/sections/srms/proceedings/papers/1992_029.pdf), Diane F. Barrett, Irwin Anolik, and Florence H. Abramson indicate that census officials, on what was known as Shelter and Street Night, or S-Night, counted homeless people found in shelters, emergency shelters, shelters for abused women, shelters for runaway and neglected youth, low-cost motels, Young Men's Christian Associations and Young Women's Christian Associations, and subsidized units at motels. Additionally, they counted people found in the early morning hours sleeping in abandoned buildings, bus and train stations, all-night restaurants, parks, and vacant lots. The results of this count were released the following year in the Census Bureau publication "Count of Persons in Selected Locations Where Homeless Persons Are Found."

TABLE 1.12

Basic demographic characteristics of homeless and formerly homeless individuals, 1996

Characteristics	Currently homeless clients (2,938)[a]	Formerly homeless clients (677)[b]	U.S. adult population
Sex			
Male	68(%)	54(%)	48(%)
Female	32	46	52
Race/ethnicity			
White non-Hispanic	41	46	76
Black non-Hispanic	40	41	11
Hispanic	11	9	9
Native American	8	2	1
Other	1	2	3
Age			
17	1	0	NA
18–21	6	2	7
22–24	5	2	5
25–34	25	17	21
35–44	38	36	22
45–54	17	26	17
55–64	6	11	11
65 and older	2	6	17
Education/highest level of completed schooling			
Less than high school	38	42	18
High school graduate/G.E.D.	34	34	34
More than high school	28	24	48
Marital status			
Never married	48	45	23
Married	9	9	60
Separated	15	14	[c]
Divorced	24	25	10
Widowed	3	6	7
Living situation			
Client ages 17 to 24			
Clients in families			
Men	*	*	NA
Women	3	1	NA
Single clients			
Men	5	2	NA
Women	4	1	NA
Client ages 25 and older			
Clients in families			
Men	2	3	NA
Women	9	13	NA
Single clients			
Men	62	50	NA
Women	16	30	NA
Veteran status	**23**	**22**	**13**

Note: Numbers do not sum to 100 percent due to rounding.
NA=Not available.
*Denotes values that are less than 0.5 but greater than 0 percent.
[a]Population=2,938.
[b]Population=677.
[c]Included in "married."

SOURCE: Martha R. Burt and others, "Table 3.1. Basic Demographic Characteristics, by Homeless Status," in *Homelessness: Programs and the People They Serve: Findings of the National Survey of Homeless Assistance Providers and Clients*, Urban Institute, December 1999, http://www.huduser.org/publications/homeless/homelessness/ch_3b.html#fig3.1 (accessed January 2, 2007)

Homeless advocates criticized S-Night as inadequate, and sued the government alleging that the methodology of S-Night was unconstitutional. They charged the Census Bureau with excluding segments of the homeless population in the 1990 population count by not counting those in hidden areas and by not allocating adequate funds for S-Night. In *National Law Center on Homelessness and Poverty et al. v. Ronald H. Brown et al.* (1994), the law center cited an internal Census Bureau memorandum that stated, in part, "We know we will miss people by counting the 'open' rather than 'concealed' (two studies showed that about two-thirds of the street population sleep concealed)." Advocates were greatly concerned that this underrepresentation would negatively affect the funding of homeless initiatives.

In 1994 the district court dismissed the case. The ruling, which was upheld on appeal, found that a failure to count all the homeless was not a failure to perform a constitutional duty, because the Constitution does not give individuals a right to be counted or a right to a perfectly accurate census. The court stated that the "methods used by the Bureau on S-Night were reasonably designed to count as nearly as practicable all those people residing in the United States and, therefore, easily pass constitutional muster."

The controversy surrounding the 1990 census had several consequences. The Census Bureau undertook a special operation, called Service-Based Enumeration (SBE), for the 2000 census. The SBE lasted longer than the old S-Night program and attempted to count homeless people at a wider variety of locations. The SBE methods were considered an improvement over the methods used in the 1990 census survey. Homeless citizens and advocates alike expected to see an increase in the number of homeless people reported by the Census Bureau in the 2000 census as compared with the 1990 census. Expectations that the higher population counts would translate into higher funding levels for services to the homeless were also raised.

These hopes were disappointed, because the Census Bureau chose not to release a specific count of the homeless due to the liability issues raised after the S-Night count in 1990. The homeless would be included among those living in "emergency and transitional shelters." or "other noninstitutional group quarters population." These categories included people not generally considered to be homeless, such as college students living in dormitories, and the homeless portion of the category could not be extracted.

People involved in the receipt or delivery of services to the homeless were worried that their programs would suffer from the lack of SBE night information. A detailed homeless count was thought to be essential for city officials and advocacy groups to plan budgets for shelters and other homeless outreach programs. Results from the 2006 Conference of Mayors study illustrate the negative impact that inadequate information and funding can have on the delivery of human

TABLE 1.13

City data on homelessness, November 2005–October 2006

City	Percent increase in requests for emergency shelter	Percent increase in requests by families for emergency shelter	Shelter beds	Transitional housing units	Family breakup for shelter?	Family leave during day	Percentage need unmet	Turn away families?	Turn others away?
Boston	12	28	Increased	Increase	Yes	Yes	15	Yes	Yes
Charleston	7	NA	Stay the same	Stay the same	No	No	16%	Yes	Yes
Charlotte	NA	NA	NA	NA	NA	NA		NA	NA
Chicago	3.3	1.2	Increased	Increase	Yes	No	0%	No	No
Cleveland	−1	NA	Increased	Decrease	No	No		No	No
Denver	18	10	Increased	Increase	Yes	Yes	12	Yes	Yes
Des Moines	14	14	Stay the same	Decrease	No	Yes	13%	Yes	Yes
Detroit	0	0	Stay the same	Increase	No	Yes		Yes	Yes
Kansas City	−13	−19	Stay the same	Stay the same	No	Yes	29%	Yes	Yes
Los Angeles	30	20	Stay the same	Stay the same	Yes	Yes		Yes	Yes
Louisville Metro	43	−36	Decreased	Increase	Yes	No	NA	Yes	Yes
Miami	0	0	Stay the same	Decrease	Yes	Yes		Yes	Yes
Nashville	9	20	Stay the same	Stay the same	Yes	No	15	Yes	Yes
Norfolk	10	10	Stay the same	Stay the same	No	Yes		Yes	Yes
Philadelphia	−2.4	−2.8	Increased	Decrease	Yes	No	NA	No	No
Phoenix	7.35	−20.32	Increased	Increase	Yes	No	54%	Yes	Yes
Portland	NA	NA	Decreased	Increase	Yes	Yes	27%	Yes	Yes
Salt Lake City	8	12	Stay the same	Increase	No	No	43	Yes	Yes
San Francisco	−5.31	10	Decreased	Stay the same	No	No	0	Yes	No
Santa Monica	20	25	Increased	Decrease	Yes	Yes		Yes	Yes
Seattle	NA	NA	Stay the same	Decrease	No	Yes	NA	Yes	Yes
St. Paul	7.7	10.8	Stay the same	Stay the same	No	Yes	10%	Yes	Yes
Trenton	28	15	Increased	Increase	Yes	No	NA	Yes	No

NA=Not available.

SOURCE: "City Data on Homelessness," in *Hunger and Homelessness Survey: A Status Report on Hunger and Homelessness in America's Cities—A 23-City Survey*, U.S. Conference of Mayors and Sodexho, December 2006, http://usmayors.org/uscm/hungersurvey/2006/report06.pdf (accessed January 21, 2007).

services. (See Table 1.13.) For example, the needs of 54% of homeless people for shelter could not be met in Phoenix because of lack of resources. Homeless program funding for most cities was already strained. Almost two-thirds of cities surveyed (60.9%) in 2006 showed increased requests for emergency shelter services.

Only Estimates Are Available

The actual number of homeless people is unknown. Most organizations consider the Urban Institute study *America's Homeless II: Populations and Services* (February 1, 2000, http://www.urban.org/Presentations/AmericasHomelessII/toc.htm) the most authoritative estimate. That study estimated that 3.5 million people were homeless at some point of time during 1996.

The 2000 census counted 170,706 individuals in emergency and transitional shelters, down from 178,638 individuals in 1990. (See Table 1.14.) However, the Census Bureau expressly stated that this number was not a total count of the homeless. In the news release "Bush Administration Announces Record $1.4 Billion to Help Hundreds of Thousands of Homeless Individuals and Families" (January 25, 2005, http://www.hud.gov/news/release.cfm?content=pr05-007.cfm), HUD estimates that 150,000 people in 2005 were chronically homeless—

homeless for a year or more—and states that this population was only about 10% of all homeless individuals. This would put the overall homeless population at approximately 1.5 million people.

PUBLIC INTEREST IN HOMELESSNESS

Interest in and attitudes toward homelessness in the United States have changed over time. The mid- to late 1980s was a period of relatively high concern about homelessness. In 1986 the American public demonstrated concern over the plight of the homeless by initiating the Hands across America fund-raising effort. Some six million people locked hands across 4,152 miles to form a human chain across the country, bringing an outpouring of national attention and concern to the issue. In 1986 the comedians Robin Williams, Whoopi Goldberg, and Billy Crystal hosted the HBO comedy special *Comic Relief* to help raise money for the homeless. The show was a success and became an annual event. Magazines, art shows, books, and songs turned the nation's attention toward homelessness. Well-funded research studies came out by the dozens. The country was awash in statistical information regarding the homeless. All these activities pointed to the widely held belief that people became homeless because of circumstances outside their control.

TABLE 1.14

Population in emergency and transitional shelters by state, 1990 and 2000

Area	1990		2000	
	Number	Percent	Number	Percent
State/territory				
Alabama	1,530	0.9	1,177	0.7
Alaska	447	0.3	558	0.3
Arizona	2,735	1.5	2,312	1.4
Arkansas	489	0.3	754	0.4
California	30,806	17.2	27,701	16.2
Colorado	2,554	1.4	2,281	1.3
Connecticut	4,194	2.3	2,291	1.3
Delaware	313	0.2	847	0.5
District of Columbia	4,682	2.6	1,762	1.0
Florida	7,110	4.0	6,766	4.0
Georgia	3,930	2.2	4,774	2.8
Hawaii	854	0.5	747	0.4
Idaho	461	0.3	703	0.4
Illinois	7,481	4.2	6,378	3.7
Indiana	2,251	1.3	2,384	1.4
Iowa	989	0.6	1,013	0.6
Kansas	940	0.5	587	0.3
Kentucky	1,284	0.7	1,626	1.0
Louisiana	1,559	0.9	1,986	1.2
Maine	419	0.2	458	0.3
Maryland	2,507	1.4	2,545	1.5
Massachusetts	6,207	3.5	5,405	3.2
Michigan	3,784	2.1	4,745	2.8
Minnesota	2,253	1.3	2,738	1.6
Mississippi	383	0.2	572	0.3
Missouri	2,276	1.3	2,164	1.3
Montana	445	0.2	477	0.3
Nebraska	764	0.4	913	0.5
Nevada	1,013	0.6	1,553	0.9
New Hampshire	377	0.2	523	0.3
New Jersey	7,470	4.2	5,500	3.2
New Mexico	667	0.4	934	0.5
New York	32,472	18.2	31,856	18.7
North Carolina	2,637	1.5	3,579	2.1
North Dakota	279	0.2	178	0.1
Ohio	4,277	2.4	5,224	3.1
Oklahoma	2,222	1.2	1,478	0.9
Oregon	3,254	1.8	3,011	1.8
Pennsylvania	8,237	4.6	5,463	3.2
Rhode Island	469	0.3	634	0.4
South Carolina	973	0.5	1,528	0.9
South Dakota	396	0.2	414	0.2
Tennessee	1,864	1.0	2,252	1.3
Texas	7,816	4.4	7,608	4.5
Utah	925	0.5	1,494	0.9
Vermont	232	0.1	239	0.1
Virginia	2,657	1.5	2,692	1.6
Washington	4,565	2.6	5,387	3.2
West Virginia	451	0.3	525	0.3
Wisconsin	1,555	0.9	1,700	1.0
Wyoming	183	0.1	270	0.2
United States totals	178,638	100.00	170,706	100.00
Puerto Rico	445	*	586	*

*Not applicable.

SOURCE: Adapted from Annetta C. Smith and Denise I. Smith, "Table 1. Population in Emergency and Transitional Shelters for the United States, Regions, States, and Puerto Rico: 1990 and 2000," in *Emergency and Transitional Shelter Population: 2000*, Census 2000 Special Reports, CENSR/01-2, U.S. Census Bureau, October 2001, http://www.census.gov/prod/2001pubs/censr01-2.pdf (accessed January 2, 2007).

By 2007, however, national concern about homelessness had faded. One could only see *Comic Relief* in reruns. The annual fund-raiser ran out of steam in 1996 except for a revival show two years later. After that, there was no resurgence of public interest in the homeless problem, even though the problem remained and the Conference of Mayors reported in 2006 that the demand for services continued to increase. In "The Real Face of Homelessness" (*Time*, January 13, 2003), Joel Stein explores a change in the national mood about homelessness. A campaign was launched in Philadelphia to discourage giving money to panhandlers. In San Francisco, Proposition N ("Care Not Cash") reduced county housing support payments from $395 to $59 a month. In Orlando, Florida, people could be jailed for sleeping on the sidewalk.

Treating the Homeless as Criminals

Orlando's jailing of people who sleep on the sidewalks is an example of what some call the criminalization of homelessness. Across the United States there have been efforts to force the homeless out by passing laws that make activities engaged in by homeless people, such as panhandling, illegal. This is because many consider the homeless to be a nuisance or an eyesore.

According to "Georgia County Outlaws Panhandling and 'Urban Camping'" (*American City and County*, November 22, 2006), Gwinnett County, Georgia, passed a law in November 2006 making panhandling and "urban camping" illegal. In "OK, Sister, Drop That Sandwich!" (*Newsweek*, November 6, 2006), Matthew Philips notes that in Orlando, Florida, city lawmakers have passed ordinances making it illegal to feed large groups of people in public parks—making not only homelessness, but also helping the homeless, illegal.

There have been victories for those who oppose criminal penalties for homelessness. Betsy Streisand reports in "Homeless Sprawl" (*U.S. News and World Report*, December 10, 2006) that Los Angeles, the homeless capital of the nation, attempted to enforce a law that would prevent people from sleeping on the streets and sidewalks. The city was stopped when the American Civil Liberties Union sued. The U.S. Ninth Circuit Court of Appeals ruled that in a city without enough space in its homeless shelters for everyone, the law amounted to cruel and unusual punishment. Forrest Norman, in "Proposed Ordinance Targeting Shantytown Pulled" (*Miami Daily Business Review*, January 9, 2007), discusses how an ordinance in Miami that would make it illegal for homeless people to sleep on vacant city-owned lots missed emergency passage in December 2006 by only one vote and was pulled from the agenda the following month because city commissioners "needed more time to consider the ordinance" because of community support of the targeted shantytown.

Addressing Homelessness Is a Low Priority

When asked, Americans in the twenty-first century stated that they continued to be troubled by the existence of homelessness. According to "Americans Say Homelessness in U.S. Is a Serious Problem" (February 26, 2005, http://www.ipsos-na.com/news/pressrelease.cfm?id=2580), a survey of 1,001 adults by the Associated Press/Ipsos-Public Affairs, nine out of ten adults considered homelessness a serious or somewhat serious problem. However, only half of adults surveyed believed that chronic homelessness was caused by external circumstances (56%), and more than a third (38%) believed that homeless people were responsible for their homelessness. In a February 2007 Gallup Poll (http://www.galluppoll.com/content/?ci=1675&pg=1), when asked about the most important problem facing the nation, just 3% of Americans stated that the combination of poverty, hunger, and homelessness was the most important problem facing the nation today.

Research studies, once so plentiful, were outdated by 2007, but some well-funded research centers and organizations continued to study the homeless population. Their studies are used throughout this book.

HOMELESS SERVICES

A substantial number of organizations provide services to homeless people across the country. Faith-based organizations have been providing assistance to the needy throughout history, including programs for the homeless. Many secular nonprofits (organizations with no religious affiliation) also provide such assistance. Since 1987, with the passage of the McKinney-Vento Homeless Assistance Act, federal funding targeted to help homeless people has been available. In August 2006 HUD announced in the *Annual Performance Plan, Fiscal Year 2007* (http://www.hud.gov/offices/cfo/reports/pdfs/app2007.pdf) that President George W. Bush's proposed fiscal year 2007 budget contained a record level of funding for homeless programs, $1.54 billion, an increase of $209 million over 2006.

The most recent comprehensive study of assistance programs dates to 1996. In that year, according to the Urban Institute, about half of all assistance programs (19,388) were located in central cities, about one-fifth (7,694) in suburban fringe communities, and the rest in rural areas. (See Table 1.15.) All told, 39,664 programs operated nationwide, with the largest number in the South and Midwest and the lowest in the Northeast. (See Table 1.16.) Some of these programs were aimed directly at homeless people, such as homeless shelters. Others were programs open to a wider group of needy people but also intended to serve the homeless (for example, free health clinics for the poor).

Martha R. Burt et al. also study the utilization rates of homeless services. A section of their landmark study *Homelessness: Programs and the People They Serve, Findings of the National Survey of Homeless Assistance Providers and Clients* (December 1999, http://www.urban.org/UploadedPDF/homelessness.pdf) illustrates the scope of

TABLE 1.15

Homeless assistance programs by sponsorship, type, and urban or rural status, 1996

Areas and program types	Total number of programs	Percentage by sponsor type			
		Faith-based non-profit	Secular non-profit	Government	For-profit
All program types	39,664	31.8	47.3	13.4	0.6
Central cities					
All	19,388	36.8	45.9	9.9	0.7
Housing	7,894	28.7	53.8	9.6	0.8
Food	6,018	63.4	28.3	2.6	0.2
Health	1,379	7.5	56.8	29.1	0.7
Other	4,097	23.5	53.0	14.6	1.2
Suburbs					
All	7,694	35.1	48.0	7.4	1.1
Housing	3,230	24.2	53.6	8.7	1.8
Food	3,020	53.0	40.0	2.6	0.4
Health	251	2.9	51.0	32.0	2.6
Other	1,192	26.2	52.9	11.0	0.4
Rural areas					
All	12,583	21.9	48.9	22.6	0.2
Housing	4,754	15.5	56.6	18.6	NA
Food	3,965	37.6	49.1	10.3	0.7
Health	1,110	1.8	11.1	68.4	NA
Other	2,754	18.3	50.7	28.6	NA

NA=Not available.
Note: Rows may not add to 100 percent because programs that did not identify their source of sponsorship in the survey are not listed.

SOURCE: Laudan Y. Aron and Patrick T. Sharkey, "Table 1a. NSHAPC Programs by Urban/Rural Status," in *The 1996 National Survey of Homeless Assistance Providers and Clients: A Comparison of Faith-Based and Secular Non-Profit Programs*, The Urban Institute and the U.S. Department of Health and Human Services, March 2002, http://aspe.hhs.gov/hsp/homelessness/NSHAPC02/report.htm (accessed January 2, 2007)

food programs: 26% of the surveyed providers expected between 101 and 299 requests daily, and 11% expected more than three hundred contacts per day. For walk-in services and health programs, about half this percentage expected the same volume of clients; 5% of walk-in programs and 4% of health programs expected more than three hundred people per day. Housing programs served the lowest number of people per day: On average only 2% of the programs expected three hundred contacts per day. Food, health, and walk-in services (such as job counseling) are geared toward multiple returns and have high traffic. By contrast, housing programs provide single-client service delivery over a longer period. Housing programs are also geared specifically toward helping the homeless, whereas many food, health, and walk-in programs are open to a wider group of people.

Secular nonprofit organizations provided nearly half (47.3%) of all homeless services in 1996. (See Figure 1.2.) Secular organizations also ran most of the housing programs (54.6%) and "other" services (52.2%), including outreach, drop-in centers, and financial/housing assistance. Faith-based organizations were most active in providing

TABLE 1.16

Homeless assistance programs by sponsorship, type, and region, 1996

Regions and program types	Number of programs	Percentage by sponsor type			
		Faith-based non-profit	Secular non-profit	Government	For-profit
All programs	39,664	31.8	47.3	13.4	0.6
Northeast					
All programs	7,097	28.6	53.6	10.1	0.6
Housing	2,870	16.4	61.3	12.9	0.6
Food	2,401	53.1	37.2	3.6	0.5
Health	306	6.6	69.1	14.1	0.7
Other	1,521	17.4	62.1	14.5	0.7
South					
All programs	11,101	39.0	40.7	13.6	0.5
Housing	4,309	30.0	50.3	10.3	1.1
Food	4,113	58.1	32.2	6.1	NA
Health	863	4.7	26.9	57.0	0.1
Other	1,817	33.5	43.5	17.9	0.1
Midwest					
All programs	11,853	31.6	43.7	16.2	0.5
Housing	4,678	24.5	47.6	16.9	0.4
Food	3,945	54.6	34.3	6.7	0.8
Health	736	2.8	39.7	35.5	NA
Other	2,494	16.8	52.6	24.0	0.4
West					
All programs	9,333	25.8	54.6	12.4	1.0
Housing	3,892	21.2	62.9	8.0	1.0
Food	2,478	42.4	51.0	1.7	0.2
Health	816	6.0	34.7	53.8	1.7
Other	2,147	22.3	51.3	17.2	1.6

NA=Not available

Note: Rows may not add to 100 percent because programs that did not identify their source of sponsorship in the survey are not listed.

SOURCE: Laudan Y. Aron and Patrick T. Sharkey, "Table 1b. NSHAPC Programs by Region of the Country," in *The 1996 National Survey of Homeless Assistance Providers and Clients: A Comparison of Faith-Based and Secular Non-Profit Programs*, The Urban Institute and the U.S. Department of Health and Human Services, March 2002, http://aspe.hhs.gov/hsp/homelessness/NSHAPC02/report.htm (accessed January 2, 2007)

food services (53.1% of all such programs), including food pantries, soup kitchens, and mobile food distribution. Government agencies led in the provision of health services (45.3% of all such services).

Special Populations

Many homeless assistance programs are open to anyone who wants to use them, but other programs are designed to serve only specific groups of people. The population served may be defined in several different ways: for example, men by themselves, women by themselves, households with children, youth by themselves, battered women, or veterans. The Urban Institute reveals in *The 1996 National Survey of Homeless Assistance Providers and Clients: A Comparison of Faith-Based and Secular Non-Profit Programs* (March 2002, http://aspe.hhs.gov/search/hsp/homelessness/NSHAPC02/report.htm) that 42.1% of all homeless service programs named a specific population group as a focus. After meeting the basic needs of food, shelter, and health care, these homeless programs provided for other special needs. When an emergency shelter had a specific focus, it was most likely to offer shelter to victims of domestic violence (30.3% of emergency shelters), followed by a focus on chemical dependency (8.6%), youth (8.3%), or families (5.6%). (See Table 1.17.) The transitional shelters that report specialized assistance programs divided their focus between domestic violence (14%) and chemical dependence (14.4%). Permanent housing programs that target specific population groups focused heavily on those in need of mental health services (15.7% of programs).

FIGURE 1.2

Homeless programs by type and operating entity, 1996

[Percent of programs]

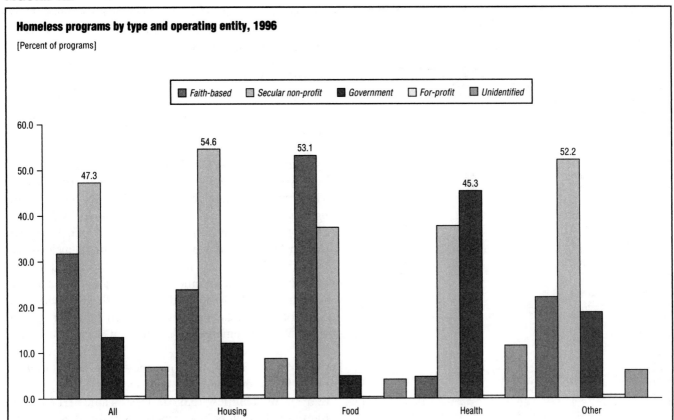

Note: The "other" category includes outreach, drop-in centers, financial/housing assistance, and miscellaneous aid programs.

SOURCE: Adapted from Laudan Y. Aron and Patrick T. Sharkey, "Table 1. NSHAPC Programs by Type of Agency Operating Programs," in *The 1996 National Survey of Homeless Assistance Providers and Clients: A Comparison of Faith-Based and Secular Non-Profit Programs*, The Urban Institute and the U.S. Department of Health and Human Services, March 2002, http://aspe.hhs.gov/search/hsp/homelessness/NSHAPC02/report.htm (accessed January 2, 2007)

TABLE 1.17

Homeless assistance programs by type, sponsorship, and focus, 1996

Program type and focus	Programs by all sponsors		Faith-based non-profit		Secular non-profit		Government	
	Number	Percent	Number	Percent	Number	Percent	Number	Percent
Emergency shelter with	5,320	100%	1,520	100%	3,480	100%	320	100%
No specialization		40.6		63.2		30.4		44.6
Mental health (MH) focus		3.7		2.5		4.1		5.2
Chemical dependency (CD) focus		8.6		15.5		5.3		12.6
MH/CD focus		1.4		2.7		0.9		1.0
HIV/AIDS focus		1.4		1.8		1.3		0.3
Domestic violence focus		30.3		5.2		42.1		20.1
Youth focus		8.3		1.7		11.3		6.8
Family focus		5.6		7.4		4.5		9.3
Transitional shelter with	4,149	100%	1,181	100%	2,535	100%	433	100%
No specialization		43.4		54.8		35.6		57.6
Mental health focus		8.3		3.5		9.6		14.2
Chemical dependency focus		14.4		16.6		15.2		4.2
MH/CD focus		5.2		2.9		6.3		5.2
HIV/AIDS focus		3.1		1.2		4.2		1.7
Domestic violence focus		14.0		7.7		18.2		6.6
Youth focus		4.4		5.6		4.6		0.2
Family focus		7.1		7.6		6.3		10.2
Permanent housing with	1,719	100%	205	100%	980	100%	534	100%
No specialization		63.6		61.6		52.8		84.2
Mental health focus		15.7		8.8		22.1		6.6
Chemical dependency focus		5.2		11.0		5.2		2.9
MH/CD focus		5.8		5.6		7.8		2.2
HIV/AIDS focus		9.8		13.0		12.1		4.2
Soup kitchen with	3,284	100%	2,131	100%	1,057	100%		NA
No specialization		83.2		84.9		79.4		NA
Mental health focus		6.1		4.4		9.8		NA
Chemical dependency focus		6.7		7.6		5.2		NA
Family focus		2.4		2.9		1.6		NA
HIV/AIDS focus		1.5		0.2		4.0		NA

NA=Not available

SOURCE: Adapted from Laudan Y. Aron and Patrick T. Sharkey, "Table 6. What Special Focus Do NSHAPC Programs Have?" in *The 1996 National Survey of Homeless Assistance Providers and Clients: A Comparison of Faith-Based and Secular Non-Profit Programs*, The Urban Institute and the U.S. Department of Health and Human Services, March 2002, http://aspe.hhs.gov/search/hsp/homelessness/NSHAPC02/report.htm (accessed January 2, 2007)

CHAPTER 2
WHO ARE THE POOR?

CHARACTERISTICS OF THE POOR

In 2005 almost thirty-seven million people in the United States, or 12.6% of the population, were poor. (See Table 2.1.) Another 4.2% had income-to-poverty ratios between 1 and 1.25, meaning that 16.8% of the U.S. population was poor or near-poor.

Race and Ethnicity

Historically, poverty rates have been consistently lower for whites than for minorities in the United States. According to the Census Bureau in *Poverty in the United States: 2000* (September 2001, http://www.census.gov/prod/2001pubs/p60-214.pdf), in 1959, 18.1% of all whites, or 28.5 million people, lived below the poverty level; in the same year, 55.1% of African-Americans, or 9.9 million people, lived in poverty. By 1970 the rate of poverty of white Americans had declined to 9.9%, about where it remained for the next ten years. The poverty rate for African-Americans was still almost triple that of whites in 1970, at 33.5%. By 2000, a year in which the U.S. economy was strong, only 9.4% of whites lived in poverty, whereas over one-fifth (22.1%) of all African-Americans did.

In 2005 African-Americans and Hispanics continued to be disproportionately affected by poverty. In 2005, 8.3% of non-Hispanic whites were poor, compared with 24.9% of African-Americans and 21.8% of Hispanics. (See Table 2.1.) Even more African-American and His-panic children suffered from poverty. Over one-third (33.5%) of African-Americans under the age of eighteen and 28.3% of Hispanics under the age of eighteen were poor, compared with only 14.4% of white children in the same age group. (See Table 1.3 in Chapter 1.)

According to the Census Bureau, the overall Asian-American poverty rate in 2005 was 11.1% (or 1.4 million people). (See Table 2.1.) The rate was slightly lower than it was in 1987, the first year that the Census Bureau kept

statistics on Asians and Pacific Islanders, when 12.7% lived below the poverty level. See Table 1.3 for the breakdown of poverty rates by different age groups among Asians and Pacific Islanders.

Age

CHILD POVERTY. Young adults and children under eighteen years of age were the age groups most likely to be poor (18.2% and 17.6%, respectively). Among these groups, it was the youngest children that suffered the most from poverty and deprivation. In 2005 one in five (20%) children under age six were poor, and more than one in four (25.4%) children under age six were poor or near-poor. Almost one in ten children this age (8.9%) were desperately poor, living in families with income-to-poverty ratios of under 0.5. (See Table 2.1.) In *Poor Kids in a Rich Country: America's Children in Comparative Perspective* (2003), Lee Rainwater and Timothy M. Smeeding indicate that the United States has the highest rate of child poverty among the fifteen richest nations in the world.

In 2005 children living with a female householder were particularly likely to live in poverty. Over a quarter of these children (28.7%) lived in poverty, compared with 13% of children living with a single dad and 5.1% of children living with married parents. (See Table 2.2.) Data from 2004 provide a more detailed look at children in female-householder families. In that year 53% of children under age six living in female-household families were poor, compared with 37% of children aged six to seventeen. (See Table 2.3.) Almost half (49%) of African-American children and over half (52%) of Hispanic children living in female-householder families were poor, compared with about a third (32%) of white, non-Hispanic children living in female-householder families.

Children are not only more likely than adults to be poor but they also arguably suffer more from the deprivations

TABLE 2.1

People with income below specified ratios of their poverty thresholds, by age, race, and family status, 2005

[Numbers in thousands. People as of March of the following year.]

| | | Income-to-poverty ratio | | | | | |
| | | Under 0.50 | | Under 1.00 | | Under 1.25 | |
Characteristic	Total	Number	Percent	Number	Percent	Number	Percent
All people	293,135	15,928	5.4	36,950	12.6	49,327	16.8
Age							
Under 18 years	73,285	5,648	7.7	12,896	17.6	16,679	22.8
18 to 24 years	27,965	2,625	9.4	5,094	18.2	6,379	22.8
25 to 34 years	39,480	2,248	5.7	4,965	12.6	6,574	16.7
35 to 44 years	43,121	1,842	4.3	4,186	9.7	5,599	13.0
45 to 54 years	42,797	1,494	3.5	3,504	8.2	4,573	10.7
55 to 59 years	17,827	663	3.7	1,441	8.1	1,923	10.8
60 to 64 years	13,153	498	3.8	1,260	9.6	1,684	12.8
65 years and older	35,505	909	2.6	3,603	10.1	5,917	167
Race* and Hispanic origin							
White	235,430	10,288	4.4	24,872	10.6	33,864	14.4
White, not Hispanic	195,553	6,916	3.5	16,227	8.3	22,262	11.4
Black	36,802	4,302	11.7	9,168	24.9	11,484	31.2
Asian	12,580	647	5.1	1,402	11.1	1,909	15.2
Hispanic (any race)	43,020	3,701	8.6	9,368	21.8	12,582	29.2
Family status							
In families	242,389	10,573	4.4	26,068	10.8	35,362	14.6
Householder	77,418	3,230	4.2	7,657	9.9	10,442	13.5
Related children under 18	72,095	5,209	7.2	12,335	17.1	16,028	22.2
Related children under 6	23,914	2,127	8.9	4,784	20.0	6,070	25.4
Unrelated subfamilies	1,220	308	25.2	456	37.4	568	46.5
Unrelated individual	49,526	5,048	10.2	10,425	21.1	13,397	27.1
Male	24,158	2,239	9.3	4,315	17.9	5,564	23.0
Female	25,367	2,809	11.1	6,111	24.1	7,833	30.9

*Federal surveys now give respondents the option of reporting more than one race. Therefore, two basic ways of defining a race group are possible. A group such as Asian may be defined as those who reported Asian and no other race (the race-alone or single-race concept) or as those who reported Asian regardless of whether they also reported another race (the race-alone-or-in-combination concept). This table shows data using the first approach (race alone). The use of the single-race population does not imply that it is the preferred method of presenting or analyzing data. The Census Bureau uses a variety of approaches. About 2.6 percent of people reported more than one race in Census 2000.
Note: Details may not sum to totals because of rounding.

SOURCE: Carmen DeNavas-Walt, Bernadette D. Proctor, and Cheryl Hill Lee, "Table 6. People with Income Below Specified Ratios of Their Poverty Thresholds by Selected Characteristics: 2005," in *Income, Poverty, and Health Insurance Coverage in the United States: 2005—Current Population Reports*, U.S. Census Bureau, August 2006, http://www.census.gov/prod/2006pubs/p60-231.pdf (accessed December 1, 2006)

of poverty than do adults. Childhood poverty is a matter of great concern because strong evidence suggests that food insecurity and lack of good medical care caused by poverty can limit a child's physical and cognitive development. In addition, poverty is the largest predictor of child abuse and neglect. In fact, the Children's Defense Fund (2006, http://www.childrensdefense.org/site/PageNavigator/c2pp_poverty) argues that "poverty is the largest driving force behind the 'Cradle to Prison Pipeline,'" a life trajectory that the organization believes leads children to marginalized lives and premature deaths. In addition, the National Center for Children in Poverty states in "Children's Mental Health: Facts for Policymakers" (November 2006, http://www.nccp.org/media/ ucr06b_text.pdf) that children in poverty are more likely to suffer from mental health problems than are other children.

POVERTY AMONG THE ELDERLY. In contrast with children, senior citizens are underrepresented among the poor. Barely one in ten (10.1%) adults aged sixty-five

and older were poor, up by 0.3% from the year before. (See Table 2.2.) From 1959 to 2002 the number of people sixty-five years and older living in poverty dropped significantly, from about 35% to 10.4%. (See Figure 2.1.) Most observers credit Social Security for the sharp decline in poverty among the elderly.

Urban Areas

People living in inner cities are most likely to suffer from poverty. In 2005, 17% of people living in inner cities lived below the poverty line. (See Table 2.2.) Only 9.3% of people who lived in suburban areas—inside metropolitan statistical areas but outside principal cities—lived below the poverty line. In rural areas the poverty rate was also high—14.5%.

Family Status

In 2005 people living in families (10.8%) were less likely to suffer from poverty than people living in unrelated

TABLE 2.2

People and families living in poverty, by demographic characteristics, 2004–05

[Numbers in thousands. People as of March of the following year.]

Characteristic	Below poverty in 2004[a]		Below poverty in 2005		Change in poverty (2005 less 2004)[b]	
	Number	Percentage	Number	Number	Number	Percentage
People						
Total	37,040	12.7	36,950	12.6	−90	−0.1
Family status						
In families	26,544	11.0	26,068	10.8	−476	−0.3
Householder	7,835	10.2	7,657	9.9	−177	−0.3
Related children under 18	12,473	17.3	12,335	17.1	−138	−0.2
Related children under 6	4,747	20.0	4,784	20.0	37	—
In unrelated subfamilies	570	45.4	456	37.4	−114	−8.1
Reference person	234	45.4	181	35.9	−53	−9.5
Children under 18	315	46.6	270	39.7	−45	−6.9
Unrelated individual	9,926	20.4	10,425	21.1	499	0.6
Male	4,316	18.2	4,315	17.9	−1	−0.4
Female	5,611	22.5	6,111	24.1	500	1.6
Race[c] and Hispanic origin						
White	25,327	10.8	24,872	10.6	−456	−0.3
White, not Hispanic	16,908	8.7	16,227	8.3	−682	−0.4
Black	9,014	24.7	9,168	24.9	154	0.2
Asian	1,201	9.8	1,402	11.1	201	1.3
Hispanic origin (any race)	9,122	21.9	9,368	21.8	246	−0.1
Age						
Under 18 years	13,041	17.8	12,896	17.6	−145	−0.2
18 to 64 years	20,545	11.3	20,450	11.1	−95	−0.2
65 years and older	3,453	9.8	3,603	10.1	150	0.3
Nativity						
Native	31,023	12.1	31,080	12.1	57	−0.1
Foreign born	6,017	17.1	5,870	16.5	−147	−0.6
Naturalized citizen	1,326	9.8	1,441	10.4	115	0.6
Not a citizen	4,691	21.6	4,429	20.4	−262	−1.3
Region						
Northeast	6,260	11.6	6,103	11.3	−156	−0.3
Midwest	7,545	11.7	7,419	11.4	−126	−0.2
South	14,817	14.1	14,854	14.0	38	−0.1
West	8,419	12.5	8,573	12.6	154	—
Residence						
Inside metropolitan statistical areas	(NA)	(NA)	30,098	12.2	(X)	(X)
Inside principal cities	(NA)	(NA)	15,966	17.0	(X)	(X)
Outside principal cities	(NA)	(NA)	14,132	9.3	(X)	(X)
Outside metropolitan statistical areas[d]	(NA)	(NA)	6,852	14.5	(X)	(X)
Work experience						
All workers (16 years and older)	9,384	6.1	9,340	6.0	−45	−0.1
Worked full-time, year-round	2,891	2.8	2,894	2.8	3	−0.1
Not full-time, year-round	6,493	12.8	6,446	12.8	−47	—
Did not work at least one week	15,871	21.7	16,041	21.8	170	—
Families						
Total	7,835	10.2	7,657	9.9	−177	−0.3

subfamilies (37.4%) or in households with unrelated individuals (21.1%). (See Table 2.1.) However, there was a great difference in the poverty rate between different family structures. Even though about one in every ten families in the United States was living in poverty in 2005, families headed by married couples had the lowest poverty rate (5.1%). More than a quarter (28.7%) of all families with a female householder (no husband present) were living in poverty, a 0.4% increase over the previous year. Male householders were also more likely than married-couple families to be in poverty (13%), but they were much less likely than female householders to be poor. (See Table 2.2.)

SINGLE-PARENT FAMILIES. An increasing number of children are being raised by one parent, usually the mother. The proportion of single-parent families grew rapidly between 1970 and the mid-1990s, whereas the proportion of families headed by married couples dropped. Since then the structure of U.S. households and families has remained relatively stable. In 2003, 23.3% of all households were married couples with children, down from 40.3% in 1970. (See Figure 2.2.) Another 28.2% of all households were married couples without children, down slightly from 30.3% in 1970. The percentage of other family households, including single-parent households headed by single

TABLE 2.2

People and families living in poverty, by demographic characteristics, 2004–05 [CONTINUED]

[Numbers in thousands. People as of March of the following year.]

Characteristic	Below poverty in 2004[a]		Below poverty in 2005		Change in poverty (2005 less 2004)[b]	
	Number	Percentage	Number	Number	Number	Percentage
Type of family						
Married-couple	3,216	5.5	2,944	5.1	−271	−0.5
Female householder, no husband present	3,962	28.3	4,044	28.7	82	0.4
Male householder, no wife present	657	13.4	669	13.0	12	−0.4

— Represents zero or rounds to zero.
(NA) Not available.
(X) Not applicable.
[a]The 2004 data have been revised to reflect a correction to the weights in the 2005 Annual Social and Economic Supplement (ASEC).
[b]Details may not sum to totals because of rounding.
[c]Federal surveys now give respondents the option of reporting more than one race. Therefore, two basic ways of defining a race group are possible. A group such as Asian may be defined as those who reported Asian and no other race (the race-alone or single-race concept) or as those who reported Asian regardless of whether they also reported another race (the race-alone-or-in-combination concept). This table shows data using the first approach (race alone). The use of the single-race population does not imply that it is the preferred method of presenting or analyzing data. The Census Bureau uses a variety of approaches. Information on people who reported more than one race, such as white and American Indian and Alaska Native or Asian and black or African American, is available from Census 2000 through American FactFinder. About 2.6 percent of people reported more than one race in Census 2000.
[d]The "Outside metropolitan statistical areas" category includes both micropolitan statistical areas and territory outside of metropolitan and micropolitan statistical areas.

SOURCE: Carmen DeNavas-Walt, Bernadette D. Proctor, and Cheryl Hill Lee, "Table 4. People and Families in Poverty by Selected Characteristics: 2004 and 2005," in *Income, Poverty, and Health Insurance Coverage in the United States: 2005—Current Population Reports*, U.S. Census Bureau, August 2006, http://www.census.gov/prod/2006pubs/p60-231.pdf (accessed December 1, 2006)

women and single men, had risen to 16.4% of all households in 2003 from 10.6% in 1970. Most of these other family households were headed by female householders. Table 2.4 shows that in 2003 there were almost three times as many single female-headed families as there were single male-headed families (13.6 million female householders versus 4.6 million male householders).

One factor in the rise of single-parent families is the rise in the divorce rate. In 1970 only 3.5% of men and 5.7% of women were separated or divorced. (See Figure 2.3.) By 2003, 10.1% of men and 13.3% of women were divorced. The percentage of divorced women is consistently higher than the percentage of divorced men because divorced men are more likely to remarry. After divorce, women most often raise the children. As Table 2.5 shows, almost two-thirds (64.2%) of custodial parents in 2003 were women.

Another reason for the increase in single-parent families is the rise in people who never marry yet still have children. Jason Fields reports in *America's Families and Living Arrangements: 2003* (November 2004, http://www.census.gov/prod/2004pubs/p20-553.pdf) that the percentage of people aged fifteen or older who had never married rose from 24.9% in 1970 to 28.6% in 2003. The proportion of those who have never married has increased as young adults delay the age at which they marry. Between 1970 and 2003 the median age at first marriage had risen from 20.8 years to 25.3 years for women, and from 23.2 years to 27.1 years for men. In addition, the proportion of all households that were unmarried-partner heterosexual households steadily rose

between 1996 and 2003, from 2.9% to 4.2% of all households. (See Figure 2.4.)

Single-parent women are more likely than single-parent men to have never been married. In 2003, 4.4 million of 10.1 million single mothers (43.6%), compared with 601,000 of 1.7 million single fathers (35.3%), had never been married. (See Table 2.6.) In 2003 African-American single mothers were most likely to have never been married (1.9 million of 3.1 million, or 61.3%), followed by Hispanic women (850,000 of 1.8 million, or 47.2%), and non-Hispanic white women (1.5 million of 4.9 million, or 30.6%).

In 2002 African-American children were far more likely to live with a single parent than were white or Hispanic children. In that year 48% of African-American children lived with their mothers and 5% with their fathers. Twenty-five percent of Hispanic children lived with their mothers and 5% with their fathers. Sixteen percent of white children lived with their mothers and 4% with their fathers. (See Figure 2.5.)

Jason Fields reports in *Children's Living Arrangements and Characteristics: March 2002* (June 2003, http://www.census.gov/prod/2003pubs/p20-547.pdf) that in 2002 a higher percentage of African-American children (9%) than Hispanics (6%) or whites (4%) lived with neither parent. In part, this is because African-American children are more likely to live with grandparents without the presence of either parent.

CHILD SUPPORT. Child support is an important source of income for single parents, especially mothers. In 2003, 64.2% of custodial mothers and 39.8% of custodial

TABLE 2.3

Percentage of all children and related children living below selected poverty levels, by demographic characteristics, 1980–2004

Characteristic	1980	1981	1982	1983	1984	1985	1986	1987	1988	1989	1990	1991	1992	1993	1994	1995	1996	1997	1998	1999	2000	2001	2002	2003	2004
Below 100% poverty																									
All children[b]	18	20	22	22	22	21	21	20	20	20	21	22	22	23	22	21	21	20	19	17	16	16	17	18	18
Gender																									
Male	—	—	—	—	—	—	—	20	20	20	21	21	22	23	21	20	20	20	18	17	16	16	17	18	18
Female	—	—	—	—	—	—	—	20	19	20	21	22	23	23	22	21	21	20	19	17	16	16	17	18	18
Age																									
Ages 0–5	—	—	—	—	—	—	—	23	22	23	24	25	26	26	25	24	23	22	21	19	18	18	19	20	20
Ages 6–17	—	—	—	—	—	—	—	19	18	18	19	20	20	21	20	19	19	19	18	16	15	15	16	16	17
Race and Hispanic origin[c]																									
White, non-Hispanic	12	13	14	15	14	13	13	12	11	12	12	13	13	14	13	11	11	11	11	9	9	10	9	10	11
Black	42	45	48	47	47	44	43	45	44	44	45	46	47	46	44	42	40	37	37	33	31	30	32	34	34
Hispanic[d]	33	36	40	38	39	40	38	39	38	36	38	40	40	41	42	40	40	37	34	30	28	28	29	30	29
Region																									
Northeast	—	—	—	—	—	—	—	17	16	16	18	20	20	21	20	19	19	20	19	16	15	15	15	15	16
Midwest	—	—	—	—	—	—	—	19	16	19	19	20	20	20	19	17	16	15	15	14	13	13	13	15	17
South	—	—	—	—	—	—	—	24	24	23	24	24	26	25	24	24	23	22	20	19	18	19	19	20	20
West	—	—	—	—	—	—	—	19	20	20	20	22	22	23	23	22	23	22	21	18	17	16	17	18	18
Related children[a]																									
Children in all families, total	18	20	21	22	21	20	20	20	19	19	20	21	22	22	21	20	20	19	18	17	16	16	16	17	17
Related children ages 0–5	20	22	23	25	23	23	22	22	22	22	23	24	26	26	25	24	23	22	21	18	18	18	19	20	20
Related children ages 6–17	17	18	20	20	20	19	19	18	17	17	18	20	19	20	20	18	18	18	17	16	15	15	15	16	16
White, non-Hispanic	11	12	14	14	13	12	12	11	11	11	12	12	12	13	12	11	10	11	10	9	9	9	9	9	10
Black	42	45	47	46	46	43	43	44	43	43	44	46	46	46	43	42	40	37	36	33	31	30	32	34	33
Hispanic[d]	33	35	39	38	39	40	37	39	37	36	38	40	39	40	41	39	40	36	34	30	28	27	28	29	29
Children in married-couple families, total	—	—	—	—	—	—	—	10	10	10	10	11	11	12	11	10	10	10	9	9	8	8	9	9	9
Related children ages 0–5	—	—	—	—	—	—	—	12	11	12	12	12	13	13	12	11	12	11	10	9	9	9	10	10	10
Related children ages 6–17	—	—	—	—	—	—	—	10	9	9	10	10	10	11	10	9	9	9	9	8	8	7	8	8	8
White, non-Hispanic	—	—	—	—	—	—	—	7	6	7	7	7	7	8	7	6	5	5	5	5	5	5	5	5	5
Black	—	—	—	—	—	—	—	18	17	18	18	15	18	18	15	13	14	13	12	11	9	10	12	11	13
Hispanic[d]	—	—	—	—	—	—	—	27	25	25	27	29	29	30	30	28	29	26	23	22	21	20	21	21	21
Children in female-householder families, no husband present, total	51	52	56	55	54	54	54	54	53	51	53	56	55	54	53	50	49	49	46	42	40	39	40	42	42
Related children ages 0–5	65	66	67	68	65	66	65	66	64	62	66	66	66	64	64	62	59	59	55	51	50	49	49	53	53
Related children ages 6–17	46	47	51	50	49	48	50	48	48	46	47	50	49	49	47	45	45	45	42	39	36	35	36	37	37
White, non-Hispanic	—	—	—	—	—	—	—	38	37	36	40	41	40	39	38	34	35	37	33	29	28	29	29	31	32
Black	65	52	56	55	54	67	67	67	65	63	65	68	67	66	63	62	58	55	55	52	49	47	48	50	49
Hispanic[d]	65	52	56	55	54	72	67	70	70	64	68	69	66	66	68	66	67	63	60	52	50	49	48	51	52

TABLE 2.3

Percentage of all children and related children living below selected poverty levels, by demographic characteristics, 1980–2004 [CONTINUED]

Characteristic	1980	1981	1982	1983	1984	1985	1986	1987	1988	1989	1990	1991	1992	1993	1994	1995	1996	1997	1998	1999	2000	2001	2002	2003	2004
Below 50% poverty																									
All children[b]	—	—	—	—	—	—	—	9	9	8	9	10	10	10	10	9	9	9	8	7	7	7	7	8	8
Gender																									
Male	—	—	—	—	—	—	—	9	9	8	9	10	10	10	10	8	8	9	8	7	7	7	7	8	8
Female	—	—	—	—	—	—	—	9	9	9	9	10	11	10	10	9	10	9	8	7	7	7	7	8	8
Age																									
Ages 0–5	—	—	—	—	—	—	—	10	11	10	11	12	13	12	12	11	11	10	10	8	8	8	8	10	9
Ages 6–17	—	—	—	—	—	—	—	9	8	7	8	9	9	9	9	7	8	8	7	7	6	7	6	7	7
Race and Hispanic origin[c]																									
White, non-Hispanic	—	—	—	—	—	—	—	5	5	4	5	5	6	6	5	4	5	5	4	4	4	4	4	4	5
Black	—	—	—	—	—	—	—	23	25	23	23	26	27	26	24	21	21	20	18	15	15	16	15	18	17
Hispanic[d]	—	—	—	—	—	—	—	15	16	13	14	15	16	15	17	16	15	16	14	11	10	11	11	11	10
Region																									
Northeast	—	—	—	—	—	—	—	7	7	6	8	9	9	10	9	9	10	10	8	8	6	7	6	7	8
Midwest	—	—	—	—	—	—	—	9	8	9	9	9	10	9	9	7	7	6	6	6	6	6	6	7	7
South	—	—	—	—	—	—	—	12	12	11	11	12	13	12	12	10	11	10	9	7	8	8	8	9	9
West	—	—	—	—	—	—	—	6	8	6	6	8	8	8	9	8	8	9	8	6	6	6	6	8	7
Related children[a]																									
Children in all families, total	—	7	—	9	9	8	8	9	9	8	8	9	10	10	9	8	8	8	8	6	6	7	7	7	7
Related children ages 0–5	—	—	—	—	—	—	—	10	10	10	10	11	12	12	12	10	11	10	9	8	8	8	8	9	9
Related children ages 6–17	—	—	—	—	—	—	8	8	8	7	7	8	9	8	8	7	7	8	7	6	6	6	6	6	6
White, non-Hispanic	—	—	—	—	—	—	—	5	4	4	4	5	5	5	4	3	4	4	4	3	3	3	3	4	4
Black	17	21	23	23	23	22	23	23	24	22	22	25	27	26	23	20	20	20	17	15	15	16	15	17	17
Hispanic[d]	—	—	—	—	—	—	—	15	16	12	14	14	15	14	17	16	14	16	13	11	9	10	11	11	10
Children in married-couple families, total	—	—	—	—	—	—	—	3	3	3	3	3	3	3	3	3	3	3	3	2	2	2	2	2	2
Related children ages 0–5	—	—	—	—	—	—	—	3	3	3	3	4	4	4	4	3	3	3	3	2	2	3	3	3	3
Related children ages 6–17	—	—	—	—	—	—	—	3	3	2	2	3	3	3	3	3	3	3	2	2	2	2	2	2	2
White, non-Hispanic	—	—	—	—	—	—	—	2	2	2	2	2	2	2	2	1	2	1	2	1	2	2	2	1	2
Black	—	—	—	—	—	—	—	6	7	4	4	6	7	7	6	3	3	5	3	3	3	3	3	4	4
Hispanic[d]	—	—	—	—	—	—	—	8	7	6	7	8	9	7	9	9	7	7	5	5	4	5	5	5	4
Children in female-householder families, no husband present, total	—	—	—	—	—	—	—	28	29	26	28	29	30	29	28	24	26	26	23	20	19	20	20	22	22
Related children ages 0–5	—	—	—	—	—	—	—	36	38	34	37	37	39	36	37	34	35	34	31	27	28	28	28	31	31
Related children ages 6–17	—	—	—	—	—	—	—	25	25	22	23	25	26	25	24	19	22	22	19	17	15	17	16	17	18
White, non-Hispanic	—	—	—	—	—	—	—	19	18	16	19	19	20	19	18	13	18	17	15	13	12	13	12	15	15
Black	—	—	—	—	—	—	—	38	38	36	37	40	41	40	36	32	33	31	29	25	24	27	25	27	27
Hispanic[d]	—	—	—	—	—	—	—	32	39	30	32	31	31	30	36	33	34	36	32	27	25	26	26	25	28

TABLE 2.3

Percentage of all children and related children living below selected poverty levels, by demographic characteristics, 1980–2004 [CONTINUED]

Characteristic	1980	1981	1982	1983	1984	1985	1986	1987	1988	1989	1990	1991	1992	1993	1994	1995	1996	1997	1998	1999	2000	2001	2002	2003	2004
Below 150% poverty																									
All children[b]	—	—	—	—	—	—	—	31	30	31	31	33	33	34	33	32	32	31	30	28	27	28	28	29	28
Gender																									
Male	—	—	—	—	—	—	—	31	30	31	31	32	33	34	33	32	31	30	29	28	27	27	28	29	28
Female	—	—	—	—	—	—	—	31	30	31	32	33	34	34	33	33	33	31	30	29	27	28	28	29	28
Age																									
Ages 0–5	—	—	—	—	—	—	—	33	34	34	35	36	38	38	37	36	35	34	32	31	29	30	31	32	32
Ages 6–17	—	—	—	—	—	—	—	29	28	28	30	31	31	32	31	31	30	29	28	28	25	26	27	27	27
Race and Hispanic origin[c]																									
White, non-Hispanic	—	—	—	—	—	—	—	21	20	20	21	22	22	22	22	20	20	20	18	18	16	17	17	18	17
Black	—	—	—	—	—	—	—	58	57	58	58	60	60	61	58	57	56	52	52	48	46	46	48	49	48
Hispanic[d]	—	—	—	—	—	—	—	56	54	55	56	59	58	60	59	59	58	56	53	50	47	47	47	48	47
Region																									
Northeast	—	—	—	—	—	—	—	25	25	25	27	28	29	29	29	29	29	28	28	26	23	25	25	25	23
Midwest	—	—	—	—	—	—	—	29	27	28	29	30	30	30	30	27	26	24	25	23	22	23	23	25	26
South	—	—	—	—	—	—	—	35	35	36	36	37	38	39	36	36	35	34	32	31	30	31	31	32	31
West	—	—	—	—	—	—	—	31	31	32	31	34	34	35	36	35	35	34	33	31	29	28	30	30	30
Related children[a]																									
Children in all families, total	29	32	34	34	32	32	30	30	30	30	31	32	33	33	32	32	31	30	29	28	26	27	27	28	28
Related children ages 0–5	—	—	—	—	—	—	—	33	34	34	34	36	37	38	37	35	35	33	32	30	29	30	31	31	31
Related children ages 6–17	—	—	—	—	—	—	—	29	28	28	29	30	30	31	30	30	29	28	27	27	25	25	26	27	26
White, non-Hispanic	—	—	—	—	—	—	—	20	20	20	21	21	21	22	21	19	19	19	18	17	16	17	17	17	17
Black	57	62	63	62	61	59	57	57	56	57	57	60	60	61	58	56	56	51	52	48	45	46	48	48	48
Hispanic[d]	—	—	—	—	—	—	—	56	54	54	55	58	58	60	58	59	57	56	52	49	47	46	47	48	47
Children in married-couple families, total	—	—	—	—	—	—	—	20	19	20	20	21	21	22	21	20	20	19	18	17	16	17	18	18	17
Related children ages 0–5	—	—	—	—	—	—	—	22	23	23	22	24	24	25	23	21	22	21	20	19	18	19	20	20	20
Related children ages 6–17	—	—	—	—	—	—	—	19	17	18	19	19	20	20	19	19	19	17	17	17	15	16	16	17	16
White, non-Hispanic	—	—	—	—	—	—	—	15	14	14	15	15	15	15	15	13	13	12	11	11	10	11	11	11	10
Black	—	—	—	—	—	—	—	32	30	33	32	32	33	35	28	26	28	24	26	21	21	21	25	22	23
Hispanic[d]	—	—	—	—	—	—	—	46	45	45	47	50	49	51	49	50	48	47	43	41	39	39	40	41	40
Children in female-householder families, husband present, total	—	—	—	—	—	—	—	67	67	66	67	69	68	68	67	65	65	64	62	60	57	57	57	58	58
Related children ages 0–5	—	—	—	—	—	—	—	77	77	75	77	78	79	77	78	75	74	74	71	68	67	66	65	68	68
Related children ages 6–17	—	—	—	—	—	—	—	63	63	62	62	64	63	63	62	60	60	60	58	56	53	54	53	54	53
White, non-Hispanic	—	—	—	—	—	—	—	53	53	53	54	55	54	53	53	49	50	52	48	45	44	46	45	46	46
Black	—	—	—	—	—	—	—	79	79	77	77	81	79	80	78	76	75	72	72	71	66	66	65	67	66
Hispanic[d]	—	—	—	—	—	—	—	81	81	79	80	81	80	81	81	82	81	78	76	71	70	66	66	68	68

TABLE 2.3

Percentage of all children and related children living below selected poverty levels, by demographic characteristics, 1980–2004 [CONTINUED]

Characteristic	1980	1981	1982	1983	1984	1985	1986	1987	1988	1989	1990	1991	1992	1993	1994	1995	1996	1997	1998	1999	2000	2001	2002	2003	2004
Below 200% poverty																									
All children[b]	—	—	—	—	—	—	—	41	41	41	42	44	44	45	44	43	43	41	40	39	38	38	38	39	39
Gender																									
Male	—	—	—	—	—	—	—	41	41	41	43	44	44	45	44	43	43	41	40	39	38	38	38	39	39
Female	—	—	—	—	—	—	—	41	41	42	42	44	45	45	44	44	44	42	41	38	38	38	38	40	40
Age																									
Ages 0–5	—	—	—	—	—	—	—	44	45	45	46	48	48	50	48	47	47	45	43	42	41	42	42	42	43
Ages 6–17	—	—	—	—	—	—	—	40	39	39	41	42	42	43	42	42	42	40	39	38	36	37	37	38	38
Race and Hispanic origin[c]																									
White, non-Hispanic	—	—	—	—	—	—	—	31	31	30	32	33	33	33	32	31	31	30	28	27	26	27	26	26	27
Black	—	—	—	—	—	—	—	68	67	68	68	70	71	72	68	68	68	64	64	61	59	57	60	61	61
Hispanic[d]	—	—	—	—	—	—	—	68	66	67	70	72	71	73	72	73	72	69	67	64	63	62	62	63	62
Region																									
Northeast	—	—	—	—	—	—	—	34	34	35	36	38	39	39	38	38	39	38	37	35	33	34	34	34	32
Midwest	—	—	—	—	—	—	—	39	38	38	40	41	42	41	41	37	37	36	34	33	31	33	33	34	36
South	—	—	—	—	—	—	—	46	46	47	48	49	49	50	48	48	48	46	43	42	42	42	42	44	43
West	—	—	—	—	—	—	—	42	43	42	43	45	45	46	47	46	47	44	44	42	41	40	40	41	42
Related children[a]																									
Children in all families, total	—	—	—	—	—	—	—	40	41	41	42	43	44	44	43	43	43	41	40	38	37	38	38	39	39
Related children ages 0–5	—	—	—	—	—	—	—	44	45	45	45	47	48	49	48	46	46	45	43	41	41	41	41	42	42
Related children ages 6–17	—	—	—	—	—	—	—	39	38	39	40	41	41	42	41	41	41	39	38	37	35	36	36	37	37
White, non-Hispanic	—	—	—	—	—	—	—	30	30	30	31	33	32	32	32	30	30	29	27	26	25	26	25	26	26
Black	—	—	—	—	—	—	—	68	67	68	68	70	71	72	68	68	68	64	64	60	59	57	60	61	60
Hispanic[d]	—	—	—	—	—	—	—	68	66	67	69	72	70	72	72	73	72	69	66	64	62	61	61	62	62
Children in married-couple families, total	—	—	—	—	—	—	—	30	30	30	31	33	32	33	32	31	31	29	28	27	26	27	27	27	27
Related children ages 0–5	—	—	—	—	—	—	—	34	35	34	34	36	35	36	35	33	34	33	31	29	29	30	30	30	31
Related children ages 6–17	—	—	—	—	—	—	—	29	28	28	30	31	31	31	30	30	30	27	27	26	25	25	25	26	26
White, non-Hispanic	—	—	—	—	—	—	—	24	25	24	25	26	25	25	25	23	23	21	20	19	18	19	19	19	18
Black	—	—	—	—	—	—	—	46	44	46	45	46	47	50	42	39	43	38	39	35	36	33	36	36	36
Hispanic[d]	—	—	—	—	—	—	—	60	58	60	62	65	64	65	64	66	65	63	59	58	55	54	56	56	56
Children in female-householder, no husband present, total	—	—	—	—	—	—	—	77	76	77	77	78	79	78	78	76	76	75	73	72	69	70	69	70	71
Related children ages 0–5	—	—	—	—	—	—	—	85	85	84	85	86	87	86	87	84	84	83	80	80	78	79	76	78	79
Related children ages 6–17	—	—	—	—	—	—	—	73	73	73	73	74	74	74	73	72	73	72	70	68	66	66	66	67	67
White, non-Hispanic	—	—	—	—	—	—	—	65	65	66	67	66	67	66	66	61	64	64	61	59	56	59	58	59	60
Black	—	—	—	—	—	—	—	86	86	85	86	88	88	88	85	87	85	83	82	82	79	77	76	78	79
Hispanic[d]	—	—	—	—	—	—	—	89	87	87	89	87	88	89	90	88	89	86	84	82	82	80	79	80	80

TABLE 2.3

Percentage of all children and related children living below selected poverty levels, by demographic characteristics, 1980–2004 [CONTINUED]

— = Not available.

[a]A related child is a person ages 0–17 who is related to the householder by birth, marriage, or adoption, but is not the householder or the householder's spouse.

[b]Includes children not related to the householder.

[c]For race and Hispanic origin data in this table: From 1980 to 2002, following the 1977 Office of Management and Budget (OMB) standards for collecting and presenting data on race, the Current Population Survey (CPS) asked respondents to choose one race from the following: white, black, American Indian or Alaskan Native, or Asian or Pacific Islander. Beginning in 2003, following the 1997 OMB standards for collecting and presenting data on race, the CPS asked respondents to choose one or more races from the following: white, black, Asian, American Indian or Alaska Native, and Native Hawaiian or other Pacific Islander. All race groups discussed in this table from 2002 onward refer to people who indicated only one racial identity within the racial categories presented. People who responded to the question on race by indicating only one race are referred to as the race-alone population. The use of the race-alone population in this table does not imply that it is the preferred method of presenting or analyzing data. Data from 2002 onward are not directly comparable with data from earlier years. Data on race and Hispanic origin are collected separately; Hispanics may be any race.

[d]Persons of Hispanic origin may be of any race.

Note: Data for 1999, 2000, and 2001 use Census 2000 population controls. Data for 2000 onward are from the expanded Current Population Survey sample. The poverty level is based on money income and does not include noncash benefits, such as food stamps. Poverty thresholds reflect family size and composition and are adjusted each year using the annual average Consumer Price Index level. The average poverty threshold for a family of four was $19,307 in 2004. The levels shown here are derived from the ratio of the family's income to the family's poverty threshold.

SOURCE: "Table ECON1.A. Child Poverty: Percentage of All Children and Related Children Ages 0–17 Living Below Selected Poverty Levels by Selected Characteristics, Selected Years 1980–2004," in *America's Children in Brief: Key National Indicators of Well-Being, 2006*, Federal Interagency Forum on Child and Family Statistics, 2006, http://www.childstats.gov/americaschildren/tables/econ1a.asp (accessed January 2, 2007)

FIGURE 2.1

Poverty rates, by age, 1959–2005

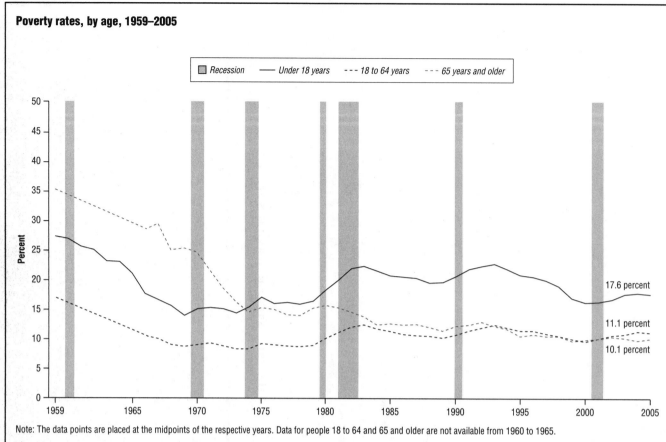

Note: The data points are placed at the midpoints of the respective years. Data for people 18 to 64 and 65 and older are not available from 1960 to 1965.

SOURCE: Carmen DeNavas-Walt, Bernadette D. Proctor, and Cheryl Hill Lee, "Figure 5. Poverty Rates by Age: 1959 to 2005," in *Income, Poverty, and Health Insurance Coverage in the United States: 2005—Current Population Reports*, U.S. Census Bureau, P60-231, August 2006, http://www.census.gov/prod/2006pubs/p60-231.pdf (accessed December 1, 2006)

fathers were awarded child support. (See Table 2.5.) However, less than half of all custodial parents received all child support payments owed to them (46.2% of custodial fathers and 45.2% of custodial mothers). Almost a quarter of all custodial mothers (23%) and 28.4% of all custodial fathers due child support payments did not receive any.

Child support is often not enough to keep custodial mothers and their children out of poverty. According to the Census Bureau, between 1993 and 2001 the percent of custodial parents and their children living below the poverty level declined from 33.3% to 23.4%, and then remained statistically unchanged in 2002 and 2003. (See Figure 2.6.) However, the poverty rate among custodial mothers (26.1%) remained significantly higher than the poverty rate among custodial fathers (13.4%).

The Census Bureau further breaks down whether custodial parents received their child support payments by whether their families were below the poverty level in 2001. A lower proportion of custodial parents with incomes below the poverty level received child support payments in 2001 (65.6%) than did all custodial parents (73.9%). (See

Table 2.7.) In addition, a lower proportion of the poor custodial parents (30.8%) than all custodial parents (44.8%) received the full amount of child support due them.

The average amount of child support due to custodial mothers in 2003 was $5,176; they actually received an average of $3,579. (See Table 2.5.) The average amount of child support due to custodial fathers in 2003 was $4,471; they actually received an average of $2,797. According to the Census Bureau, the mean total income of custodial mothers who actually received child support in 2001 was $28,258, substantially less than the mean total income of custodial fathers who received child support ($36,255). (See Table 2.7.)

By Race

The Census Bureau calculates the three-year average poverty rate of different racial and ethnic groups in the United States. It finds that non-Hispanic whites had the lowest rate, at 8.4%, followed by Asians, at 10.9%, and Native Hawaiians or other Pacific Islanders, at 12.2%. (See Table 2.8.) In contrast, more than one in five Americans of Hispanic origin (22%) and one in four African-Americans

FIGURE 2.2

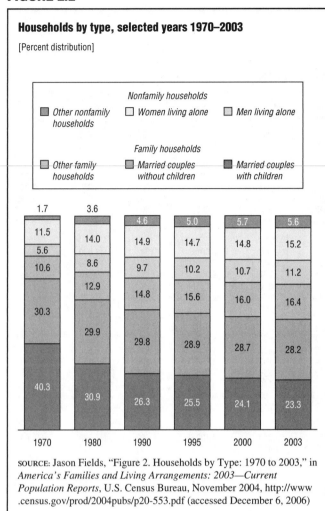

Households by type, selected years 1970–2003

[Percent distribution]

Nonfamily households
- ■ Other nonfamily households
- ☐ Women living alone
- ▨ Men living alone

Family households
- ☐ Other family households
- ▨ Married couples without children
- ■ Married couples with children

	1970	1980	1990	1995	2000	2003
Other nonfamily households	1.7	3.6	4.6	5.0	5.7	5.6
Women living alone	11.5	14.0	14.9	14.7	14.8	15.2
Men living alone	5.6	8.6	9.7	10.2	10.7	11.2
Other family households	10.6	12.9	14.8	15.6	16.0	16.4
Married couples without children	30.3	29.9	29.8	28.9	28.7	28.2
Married couples with children	40.3	30.9	26.3	25.5	24.1	23.3

SOURCE: Jason Fields, "Figure 2. Households by Type: 1970 to 2003," in *America's Families and Living Arrangements: 2003—Current Population Reports*, U.S. Census Bureau, November 2004, http://www.census.gov/prod/2004pubs/p20-553.pdf (accessed December 6, 2006)

(24.7%) and Native Americans and Alaskan Natives (25.3%) lived in poverty.

Work Experience

The probability of a family living in poverty is influenced by three primary factors: the size of the family, the number of workers, and the characteristics of the wage earners. As the number of wage earners in a family increases, the probability of poverty declines. The likelihood of a second wage earner is greatest in families headed by married couples.

In 2004 most Americans aged sixteen and older, at or above the poverty level, worked at some point during the year (144.4 million of 200 million, or 72.2%). About 6.7% of all Americans who worked lived in poverty, compared with 21% of those who did not work that year. The rate of poverty was higher for those who worked only twenty-six weeks or less (18.4%) than for those who worked twenty-seven weeks or more (5.6%). (See Table 2.9.)

Most poor children live in families where one or more adults work. However, millions of working parents

are not able to earn enough to lift their families out of poverty—even those who work full time all year.

Education

Not surprisingly, poverty rates drop sharply as years of schooling rise. In 2005 the median income for men aged twenty-five and older who had not completed high school was $22,138; for women it was only $13,076. (See Table 2.10.) Male high school graduates earned a median of $31,683, whereas females earned $20,179. Men with a four-year college degree earned a median of $53,693, whereas women earned $36,250. Heather Koball, Michelle Chau, and Ayana Douglas-Hall report in the fact sheet "Parents' Low Education Leads to Low Income, Despite Full-Time Employment" (October 2006, http://www.nccp.org/pub_pei06b.html) that most children who live in low-income or poor families have parents without any college education and that full-time employment does not protect families from low earnings.

GOVERNMENT ASSISTANCE

With few exceptions, the demand for welfare assistance increased sharply in the 1990s. However, because of decreased funding and welfare reform measures that gave states more flexibility in dispersing benefits, a smaller proportion of eligible families actually received benefits. In the fact sheet "Decade of Welfare Reform: Facts and Figures—Assessing the New Federalism" (June 2006, http://www.urban.org/UploadedPDF/900980_welfarereform.pdf), the Urban Institute reports that even though 80% of eligible families were enrolled in welfare programs in 1996, by 2002 only 48% were enrolled. Some were ineligible because they had assets such as a car or a savings account that brought them above permitted limits. Others did not know they were eligible for benefits, whereas some knew they were eligible but chose not to accept benefits or thought the effort was not worth the amount of benefits they would receive.

Who Receives Benefits?

The Census Bureau reports that in 2004 about 76.7 million people, or 26.4% of the total U.S. population, lived in households that received some form of means-tested assistance—assistance based on earning below a certain amount. (See Table 2.11.) Approximately thirty-seven million people were living below the poverty level in 2004. (See Table 2.12.) Of those living in poverty, twenty-five million, or 67.6%, were receiving some form of means-tested aid.

Certain types of households were more likely than others to receive means-tested assistance. Almost nine out of ten (86.9%) poor families with children under eighteen years of age received government assistance. (See Table 2.12.) Poor families headed by a single mother were most likely to receive government assistance; 91.6% of these families received some form of government assistance.

TABLE 2.4

Households, by type and selected characteristics, 2003

[In thousands, except average size]

Characteristic	All households Number	Family households Total	Married couple	Other families Male householder	Other families Female householder	Nonfamily households Total	Nonfamily households Male householder	Nonfamily households Female householder
All households	111,278	75,596	57,320	4,656	13,620	35,682	16,020	9,662
Age of householder								
15 to 24 years	6,611	3,551	1,379	789	1,383	3,060	1,507	1,552
25 to 34 years	19,056	13,438	9,536	1,011	2,892	5,617	3,343	2,274
35 to 44 years	24,069	18,741	14,001	1087	3,652	5,328	3,278	2,051
45 to 54 years	22,623	16,863	13,297	922	2,644	5,760	2,971	2,789
55 to 64 years	16,260	11,261	9,543	413	1,305	4,999	2,023	2,976
65 years and over	22,659	11,741	9,565	434	1,743	10,918	2,898	8,020
Race and ethnicity of householder								
White only	91,645	62,297	49,915	3,500	8,881	29,349	13,070	16,278
Non-Hispanic	81,166	53,845	44,101	2,674	7,070	27,321	11,968	15,353
Black only	13,465	8,928	4,165	762	4,000	4,538	2,043	2,495
Asian only	3,917	2,845	2,286	223	337	1,073	526	547
Hispanic (of any race)	11,339	9,090	6,189	872	2,029	2,249	1,228	1,021
Size of households								
1 person	29,431	(X)	(X)	(X)	(X)	29,431	12,511	16,919
2 people	37,078	32,047	24,310	1,992	5,745	5,031	2,660	2,371
3 people	17,889	17,076	11,526	1,403	4,147	813	556	257
4 people	15,967	15,672	12,754	733	2,185	295	212	83
5 people	7,029	6,969	5,719	296	955	60	42	17
6 people	2,521	2,489	2,004	142	344	31	19	12
7 or more people	1,364	1,343	1,007	90	246	22	19	2
Average size	2.57	3.19	3.22	3.11	3.12	1.24	1.32	1.17
Number of related children under 18								
No related children	72,367	36,685	30,261	2,240	4,183	35,682	16,020	19,662
With related children	38,911	38,911	27,059	2,416	9,437	(X)	(X)	(X)
1 child	16,511	16,511	10,378	1,429	4,704	(X)	(X)	(X)
2 children	14,333	14,333	10,800	683	2,850	(X)	(X)	(X)
3 children	5,771	5,771	4,235	220	1,317	(X)	(X)	(X)
4 or more children	2,296	2,296	1,646	84	566	(X)	(X)	(X)
Presence of own children under 18								
No own children	75,310	39,628	31,406	2,741	5,481	35,682	16,020	19,662
With own children	35,968	35,968	25,914	1,915	8,139	(X)	(X)	(X)
With own children under 12	26,251	26,251	19,168	1,295	5,788	(X)	(X)	(X)
With own children under 6	15,584	15,584	11,743	729	3,111	(X)	(X)	(X)
With own children under 3	9,081	9,081	7,014	451	1,615	(X)	(X)	(X)
With own children under 1	2,917	2,917	2,255	181	481	(X)	(X)	(X)
Tenure								
Owner	75,909	57,092	47,676	2,721	6,695	18,817	7,742	11,075
Renter	33,799	17,604	9,007	1,873	6,724	16,195	7,951	8,244
Occupies without payment	1,570	900	637	62	201	670	327	343

X Not applicable.
Note: Data are not shown separately for the other race groups because of the small sample sizes in the Current Population Survey in the 2003 Annual Social and Economic Supplement.

SOURCE: Jason Fields, "Table 1. Households by Type and Selected Characteristics: 2003," in *America's Families and Living Arrangements: 2003—Current Population Reports*, U.S. Census Bureau, November 2004, http://www.census.gov/prod/2004pubs/p20-553.pdf (accessed December 6, 2006)

In fact, more than two out of three of all families with children headed by a single mother (69.6%) received some form of means-tested assistance in 2004. (See Table 2.11.) In comparison, about half (49.7%) of families headed by a single father received means-tested assistance in that year.

In 2004 a slightly higher proportion of females (27.6%) than males (25.2%) lived in a household that received means-tested assistance, or welfare benefits of any kind. (See Table 2.11.) About 40.8 million females received program assistance during 2004, compared with nearly 35.9 million males. Among those living below the poverty level, 14.2 million women, or 68.8% of females living below the poverty line, received benefits during some part of the year, compared with 10.8 million males, or 66.1% of males living below the poverty line. (See Table 2.12.)

One reason for the larger percentage of females receiving assistance is that women are more likely to live in a family without a spouse present. Another reason is

FIGURE 2.3

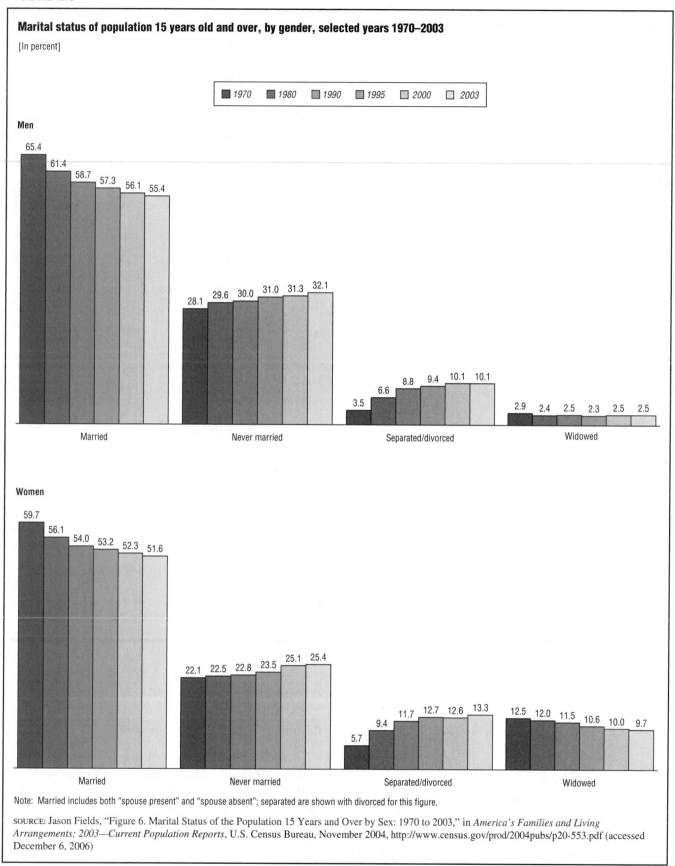

Marital status of population 15 years old and over, by gender, selected years 1970–2003

[In percent]

Legend: 1970 | 1980 | 1990 | 1995 | 2000 | 2003

Men

Married: 65.4, 61.4, 58.7, 57.3, 56.1, 55.4
Never married: 28.1, 29.6, 30.0, 31.0, 31.3, 32.1
Separated/divorced: 3.5, 6.6, 8.8, 9.4, 10.1, 10.1
Widowed: 2.9, 2.4, 2.5, 2.3, 2.5, 2.5

Women

Married: 59.7, 56.1, 54.0, 53.2, 52.3, 51.6
Never married: 22.1, 22.5, 22.8, 23.5, 25.1, 25.4
Separated/divorced: 5.7, 9.4, 11.7, 12.7, 12.6, 13.3
Widowed: 12.5, 12.0, 11.5, 10.6, 10.0, 9.7

Note: Married includes both "spouse present" and "spouse absent"; separated are shown with divorced for this figure.

SOURCE: Jason Fields, "Figure 6. Marital Status of the Population 15 Years and Over by Sex: 1970 to 2003," in *America's Families and Living Arrangements: 2003—Current Population Reports*, U.S. Census Bureau, November 2004, http://www.census.gov/prod/2004pubs/p20-553.pdf (accessed December 6, 2006)

TABLE 2.5

Award status given and support payments made to custodial parents, by demographic characteristics, 2003

[Numbers in thousands, as of spring 2004. Parents living with own children under 21 years of age whose other parent is not living in the home.]

				With child support agreements or awards						
				Due child support payments in 2003						
Characteristic	Total	Total	Percent	Total	Average due (dollars)	Average received (dollars)	Received all payments		Did not receive payments	
							Total	Percent	Total	Percent
All custodial parents										
Total	13,951	8,376	60.0	7,256	5,104	3,499	3,290	45.3	1,708	23.5
Sex										
Male	2,364	940	39.8	740	4,471	2,797	342	46.2	210	28.4
Female	11,587	7,436	64.2	6,516	5,176	3,579	2,948	45.2	1,498	23.0
Age										
Under 30 years	3,296	1,888	57.3	1,653	3,872	1,964	503	30.4	423	25.6
30 to 39 years	5,118	3,260	63.7	2,894	5,024	3,815	1,347	46.5	766	26.5
40 years and over	5,538	3,228	58.3	2,710	5,941	4,097	1,439	53.1	519	19.2
Race and ethnicity										
White alone	9,601	6,048	63.0	5,313	5,243	3,840	2,595	48.8	1,048	19.7
White alone, non-Hispanic	7,837	5,184	66.1	4,576	5,396	3,943	2,266	49.5	830	18.1
Black alone	3,554	1,852	52.1	1,547	4,607	2,104	522	33.7	532	34.4
Hispanic (any race)	1,977	975	49.3	832	4,320	3,782	371	44.6	246	29.6
Current marital status										
Married	3,075	2,035	66.2	1,875	4,876	3,301	880	46.9	377	20.1
Divorced	5,023	3,309	65.9	2,865	5,768	4,196	1,486	51.9	610	21.3
Separated	1,632	880	53.9	682	5,093	3,035	282	41.3	183	26.8
Never married	4,005	2,037	50.9	1,736	4,245	2,801	609	35.1	505	29.1
Educational attainment										
Less than high school diploma	2,200	1,208	54.9	988	3,826	3,682	404	40.9	326	33.0
High school graduate	5,123	3,078	60.1	2,685	4,740	2,781	1,101	41.0	714	26.6
Less than 4 years of college	4,589	2,849	62.1	2,541	5,275	3,608	1,199	47.2	493	19.4
Bachelor's degree or more	2,039	1,241	60.9	1,042	6,836	4,910	586	56.2	176	16.9
Selected characteristics										
Family income below 2003 poverty level	3,343	1,964	58.7	1,689	4,248	2,548	594	35.2	530	31.4
Worked full-time, year-round	7,523	4,480	59.6	3,904	5,364	3,667	1,965	50.3	856	21.9
Public assistance program participation*	4,229	2,520	59.6	2,157	4,224	2,742	776	36.0	595	27.6
With 1 child	7,958	4,409	55.4	3,787	4,610	3,074	1,689	44.6	863	22.8
With 2 or more children	5,994	3,967	66.2	3,469	5,643	3,964	1,601	46.2	846	24.4
Child had contact with other parent in 2003	9,269	5,931	64.0	5,200	5,255	3,914	2,686	51.7	906	17.4

*Public assistance program participation includes receiving at least one of the following: Medicaid, food stamps, public housing or rent subsidy, Temporary Assistance for Needy Families (TANF), or general assistance.

SOURCE: Timothy S. Grall, "Table 2. Demographic Characteristics of Custodial Parents by Award Status and Payments Received: 2003," in *Custodial Mothers and Fathers and Their Child Support: 2003—Current Population Reports*, U.S. Census Bureau, July 2006, http://www.census.gov/prod/2006pubs/p60-230.pdf (accessed December 6, 2006)

that, as reported by many government and private studies, women, on average, earned approximately 76.7% of what men earn in 2005. (See Table 2.10.) Another reason is that fewer single mothers participate in the workforce permanently and full time than do single fathers. In *Custodial Mothers and Fathers and Their Child Support: 2003* (July 2006, http://www.census.gov/prod/2006pubs/p60-230.pdf), Timothy S. Grall reports that although 80.1% of custodial mothers worked in 2003, only 50.5% of them worked full time, year round, whereas 70.6% of custodial fathers held full-time, full-year jobs. Grall notes one reason that might be part of the cause of this disparity: Custodial mothers were more likely than

custodial fathers to have two or more children living with them (44.4% and 35.9%, respectively).

African-Americans and Hispanics were more likely than non-Hispanic whites and Asians to received some form of means-tested assistance in 2004. The Census Bureau notes in *Current Population Survey, 2005 Annual Social and Economic Supplement* (2005, http://pubdb3.census.gov/macro/032005/pov/new26_000.htm) that 17.6% of non-Hispanic whites, 23.3% of Asians, 46.8% of African-Americans, and 49.6% of Hispanics lived in households receiving some form of means-tested assistance in 2004. Among those with incomes below the poverty line, 55.1% of non-Hispanic whites,

FIGURE 2.4

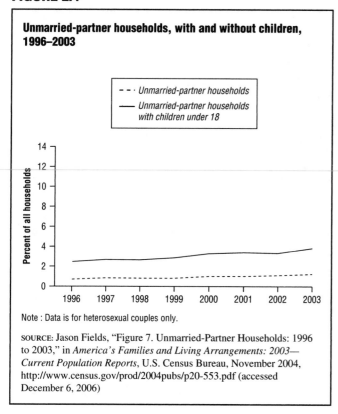

Unmarried-partner households, with and without children, 1996–2003

- - - Unmarried-partner households
—— Unmarried-partner households with children under 18

Note : Data is for heterosexual couples only.

SOURCE: Jason Fields, "Figure 7. Unmarried-Partner Households: 1996 to 2003," in *America's Families and Living Arrangements: 2003—Current Population Reports*, U.S. Census Bureau, November 2004, http://www.census.gov/prod/2004pubs/p20-553.pdf (accessed December 6, 2006)

54.7% of Asians, 80.4% of African-Americans, and 79.8% of Hispanics received benefits.

More than one-third (39.6%) of children under eighteen years old lived in households that received means-tested assistance at some time during 2004. Approximately one out of six people aged sixty-five or older (17.6%) received assistance. (See Table 2.11.)

Only 20.4% of those living in families headed by married couples received assistance in 2004. (See Table 2.11.) However, well over half (57.7%) of individuals in female-headed families with no spouse present received benefits. In contrast, about a third (36.2%) of those living in families headed by single men received means-tested benefits. The highest rate of assistance was provided to families headed by women with children under the age of six (75.1%).

LENGTH OF TIME IN POVERTY AND IN ASSISTANCE PROGRAMS

Entering and Exiting Poverty

For most poor Americans poverty is not a static condition. Some people near the poverty level improve their economic status within two years or less, whereas others at near-poverty levels become poor through economic catastrophes, such as an illness or job loss. Most data collected by the Census Bureau reflect a single point in time—in other words, showing how many people are in poverty or participating in a means-tested government program in a certain month. These surveys, however, do not reflect the dynamic nature of poverty for individual people and families.

The Census Bureau collects longitudinal information (measurements over time for specific individuals or families) about poverty and government program participation rates in its Survey of Income and Program Participation (SIPP). This makes it possible to measure the movement of individuals and families into and out of poverty (entry and exit rates) and the duration of poverty spells (the number of months in poverty for those who were not poor during the first interview month, but who became poor at some point in the study) as well as the length of time individuals and families use government programs.

In *Dynamics of Economic Well-Being, Poverty 1996–1999* (July 2003, http://www.census.gov/prod/2003pubs/p70-91.pdf), John Iceland uses data from the 1996 SIPP panel to examine poverty in the period from January 1996 through December 1999. He focuses on monthly measures of poverty and distinguishes between short- and long-term poverty. Some highlights of the survey include:

- More than one in three people (34.2%) were poor for at least two months in the four years between 1996 and 1999.

- About 2% of the population were chronically poor. That is, they were poor during all forty-eight months from January 1996 through December 1999. (See Figure 2.7.)

- Nonelderly adults were more likely to exit poverty than children and the elderly.

- Children had the highest entry rates into poverty and, along with retirement-age adults, had a low exit rate.

- More than half of all poverty spells lasted two to four months, whereas 11.9% lasted more than twenty-one months. (See Figure 2.8.)

RACE AND AGE. Of the poor in 1996, non-Hispanic whites (57.1%) were more likely to have left poverty by 1999 than either African-Americans (42.4%) or Hispanics (41.6%). (See Figure 2.9.) Figure 2.10 shows the newly poor as a percent of the population that was not poor in 1996. Non-Hispanic whites were less likely to have entered poverty by 1999 than African-Americans or Hispanics.

The elderly (often on fixed incomes) and children were less likely to exit poverty than were people of other ages. About 32.4% of the elderly and 47.9% of children under eighteen years of age who were poor in 1996 were able to escape poverty by 1999. (See Figure 2.9.) Adults eighteen to sixty-four years of age were the most likely to escape—53.9% moved out of poverty. Only 3.3% of the elderly entered poverty by 1999, compared with 4.5% of children under eighteen years of age. (See Figure 2.10.)

MOLINE HIGH SCHOOL MEDIA CENTER

TABLE 2.6

Single parents, by sex and demographic characteristics, 2003

[In thousands]

	Single fathers					Single mothers				
		Race and ethnicity						Race and ethnicity			
			White only			Hispanic			White only			Hispanic
Characteristic	Total	Total	Non-Hispanic	Black only	(of any race)	Total	Total	Non-Hispanic	Black only	(of any race)
All single parents	2,260	1,758	1,330	353	450	10,142	6,471	4,870	3,124	1,807
Type of family group										
Family household	1,915	1,506	1,176	285	346	8,139	5,155	3,960	2,591	1,357
Related subfamily	260	175	97	62	84	1,596	1,003	645	475	390
Unrelated subfamily	84	78	58	6	20	407	313	265	58	61
Number of own children under 18										
1 child	1422	1101	863	228	254	5,529	3,670	2,866	1,563	904
2 children	609	485	353	84	137	2,935	1,876	1,396	915	530
3 children	170	133	90	28	43	1,223	697	484	443	246
4 or more children	58	39	24	13	15	455	228	125	203	127
Presence of own children under 18										
With own children under 18	2,260	1,758	1,330	353	450	10,142	6,471	4,870	3,124	1,807
With own children under 12	1,547	1,187	846	254	360	7,417	4,624	3,385	2391	1,405
With own children under 6	878	668	430	139	253	4,234	2,575	1,811	1,395	872
With own children under 3	530	404	261	84	152	2,287	1,364	956	789	453
With own children under 1	203	162	112	27	55	734	446	309	241	155
Education										
Less than high school	450	356	170	64	195	1,966	1,267	600	585	736
High school graduate	953	742	590	146	156	3,577	2,235	1,726	1,169	586
Some college	580	426	269	113	62	3,298	2,065	1,722	1,055	396
Bachelor's degree or higher	277	234	302	29	35	1,301	904	822	315	90
Marital status										
Never married	852	601	359	183	257	4,413	2,255	1,507	1,924	850
Married spouse absent*	344	264	203	53	63	1,810	1,193	773	479	480
Divorced	956	817	707	95	115	3,504	2,725	2,363	632	394
Widowed	107	76	62	22	15	416	298	228	89	83
Poverty status in 2002										
Below poverty level	357	239	142	93	100	3,268	1,849	1,214	1,237	730
At or above poverty level	1,903	1,520	1,188	260	349	6,875	4,622	3,656	1,887	1,077

*Married spouse absent includes separated.

SOURCE: Jason Fields, "Table 4. Single Parents by Sex and Selected Characteristics: 2003," in *America's Families and Living Arrangements: 2003—Current Population Reports*, U.S. Census Bureau, November 2004, http://www.census.gov/prod/2004pubs/p20-553.pdf (accessed December 6, 2006)

FAMILY STATUS. Poor families headed by married couples were much more likely than other poor family types to have left poverty by 1999, underscoring how having two potential wage earners in a family helps protect a family from poverty. Of the poor families headed by married couples in 1996, 59.7% were able to escape poverty by 1999. Only 39.4% of the poor families of other types recovered from poverty by 1999. (See Figure 2.9.) Nonpoor families headed by married couples were also significantly less likely to have entered poverty by 1999. (See Figure 2.10.) With at least two adults in the household, these families are more likely to have at least one person working than a family headed by a single person.

Having a Job Does Not Guarantee Escape from Poverty

The working poor are those people who participated in the labor force for at least twenty-seven weeks (either working or looking for work) and who lived in families with incomes below the official poverty level. Over 7.8 million workers in 2004 (5.6% of individuals aged sixteen and over in the labor force) found that their jobs did not provide enough income to keep them out of poverty. (See Table 2.13.)

Working women had a higher poverty rate (4 million workers, or 6.2%) than working men (3.8 million workers, or 5%). (See Table 2.13.) Although nearly three-quarters of the working poor were white (5.6 million workers, or 71.6%), African-American and Hispanic workers continued to experience poverty while employed at more than twice the rates of whites. African-Americans (10.6%) and Hispanics (10.5%) with at least twenty-seven weeks in the labor force had a far higher poverty rate than whites (4.9%) or Asians (4.4%). Younger workers were more likely to be in poverty than older workers. Much of the reason for this is that many younger workers are still in

FIGURE 2.5

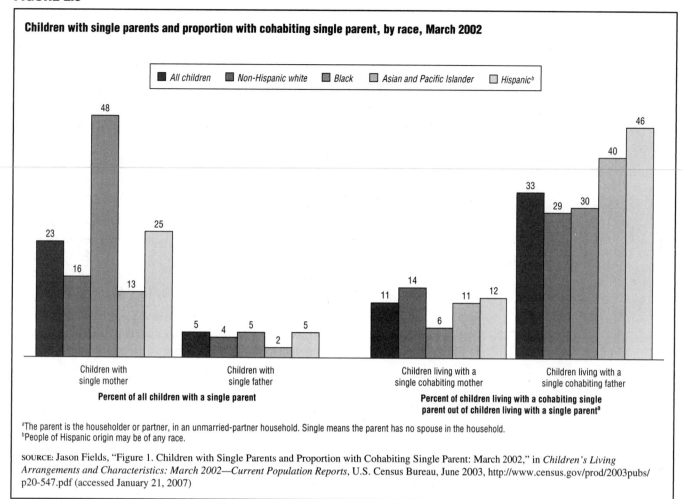

FIGURE 2.5

Children with single parents and proportion with cohabiting single parent, by race, March 2002

Legend: ■ All children ■ Non-Hispanic white ■ Black ■ Asian and Pacific Islander □ Hispanic[b]

[a]The parent is the householder or partner, in an unmarried-partner household. Single means the parent has no spouse in the household.
[b]People of Hispanic origin may be of any race.

SOURCE: Jason Fields, "Figure 1. Children with Single Parents and Proportion with Cohabiting Single Parent: March 2002," in *Children's Living Arrangements and Characteristics: March 2002—Current Population Reports*, U.S. Census Bureau, June 2003, http://www.census.gov/prod/2003pubs/p20-547.pdf (accessed January 21, 2007)

school and work at part-time or entry-level jobs that often do not pay well.

In general, the lower the educational level, the higher the risk of poverty. Among workers in the labor force for at least twenty-seven weeks in 2004, those with less than a high school diploma had a much higher poverty rate (15.2%) than high school graduates (6.5%). (See Table 2.14.) Far lower poverty rates were reported for workers with an associate's degree (3.1%) or a four-year college degree (1.7%). African-American and Hispanic workers, regardless of education levels, had higher poverty rates than white workers. The highest poverty rate (31.5%) was for African-American women workers without a high school diploma.

In 2004 working families headed by married couples without children were less likely than other family types to be poor (1.8%). (See Table 2.15.) The presence of children under age eighteen increased the married-couple poverty rate to 5.9%, reflecting the added monetary burdens of raising children and the decreased likelihood that a family will have two adults working full time. Single women with families were most likely to be living in

poverty (23.3%). Single men with children were also relatively likely to be poor (12.4%).

In a family headed by a married couple, there is a greater likelihood that two members of the family are working than in a single-parent family. Two-income families are rarely poor. Only 1.5% of families headed by married couples with two or more wage earners were poor in 2004. (See Table 2.15.) Of the 4.2 million working-poor families, 1.9 million families (45.2%) were families maintained by women. Working women who were the sole supporters of their families had the highest poverty rate: 24.2%.

Several factors affect the poverty status of working families: the size of the family, the number of workers in the family, the characteristics of the workers, and various labor market problems. The addition of a child puts a financial strain on the family and increases the chances that a parent might have to stay home to care for the child. Even though a child in a single-parent family may work, children are usually employed for low pay and at part-time jobs. In addition, the more education a person has, the more his or her job is likely to pay. Single

FIGURE 2.6

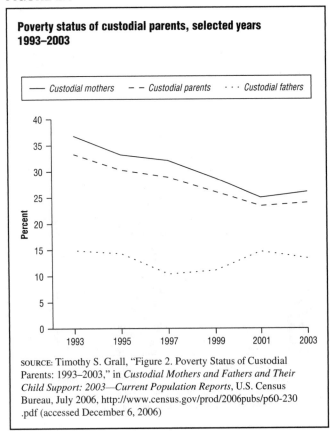

Poverty status of custodial parents, selected years 1993–2003

— Custodial mothers   – – Custodial parents   · · · Custodial fathers

SOURCE: Timothy S. Grall, "Figure 2. Poverty Status of Custodial Parents: 1993–2003," in *Custodial Mothers and Fathers and Their Child Support: 2003—Current Population Reports*, U.S. Census Bureau, July 2006, http://www.census.gov/prod/2006pubs/p60-230.pdf (accessed December 6, 2006)

mothers are more likely to have less education than married women with children.

Finally, the labor market plays a major role in whether a working family lives in poverty. Three major labor market problems contributed to poverty among workers in 2004: unemployment, low earnings, and involuntary part-time employment. Only 0.8% of workers who did not suffer from any of these problems were poor in 2004, whereas 22.4% of low-paid workers were in poverty. (See Table 2.16.) Unemployment accounted for the poverty of 7.6% of workers, and involuntary part-time work for 2.4%. However, it was the combination of two or more factors that had the most devastating effect on families. Unemployment coupled with low earnings and involuntary part-time employment accounted for 38.8% of workers in poverty.

Duration of Program Spells

The most recent Census Bureau report using SIPP data focused on the use of government assistance programs by families and individuals. In *Dynamics of Economic Well-Being: Participation in Government Programs, 2001 through 2003—Who Gets Assistance* (October 2006, http://www.census.gov/prod/2006pubs/p70-108.pdf), Tracy A. Loveless and Jan Tin examine the use of government programs over the survey period. Some highlights of the survey include:

- In 2003 one in five people (20%) took part in one or more major aid programs (Housing Assistance, Supplemental Security Income [SSI], Temporary Assistance for Needy Families [TANF]/general assistance, Food Stamps, or Medicaid) for at least one month. (See Figure 2.11.)

- More individuals participated in Medicaid (16% for at least one month in 2003) than in any other single aid program. (See Figure 2.11.)

- In an average month in 2003, 50.8% of people in poverty received benefits, compared with only 9.7% of people who were not poor. (See Figure 2.12.)

- In 2003, 48% of all households headed by a single female participated in a major means-tested program for at least one month, compared with 25.7% of households headed by a single male and 13.7% of married-couple households. (See Figure 2.13.)

- Adults who had not graduated from high school were more likely than high school graduates to participate in means-tested programs in an average month in 2003 (25.6% and 11.7%, respectively). (See Figure 2.14.)

The length of time people received assistance, referred to as a spell, differed by program. As Figure 2.15 shows, the average number of months for receiving any means-tested assistance between 2001 and 2003 was 7.2 months. The spell length for TANF/general assistance (4.9 months) was shorter than that for food stamps (7.7 months) and Medicaid (7.6 months). The spell length for SSI was longest (fifteen months).

Table 2.17 gives more detail about the characteristics of people by the length of time they participated in major means-tested programs between 2001 and 2003. Among racial and ethnic groups, non-Hispanic whites (7 months), Hispanics (7.2 months), and African-Americans (7.5 months) had similar median durations of participation in means-tested programs, whereas Asians and Pacific Islanders had a significantly lower median duration of program participation (3.9 months). Adults who had not graduated from high school had a longer median duration of participation (7.4 months) than did high school graduates (5.6 months) or those with at least some college (3.9 months), reflecting the increased economic opportunities of those with higher educational attainments.

Families had a longer median duration of participation in major means-tested programs than did households of unrelated individuals (7.2 months and 5.2 months, respectively). (See Table 2.17.) Among families, those headed by a single female spent the longest time in these programs (7.7 months), compared with single male-headed households (7.3 months) and married-couple families (6.9 months).

TABLE 2.7

Custodial parents awarded child support and actually receiving it, by poverty level, 2001

[In thousands except as noted (13,383 represents 13,383,000). Custodial parents 15 years and older with own children under 21 years of age present from absent parents as of spring 2002. Covers civilian noninstitutional population. Based on Current Population Survey.]

Award and recipiency status	All custodial parents				Custodial parents below the poverty level			
	Total				Total			
	Number	Percent distribution	Mothers	Fathers	Number	Percent distribution	Mothers	Fathers
Total	**13,383**	**(X)**	**11,291**	**2,092**	**3,131**	**(X)**	**2,823**	**308**
With child support agreement or award	7,916	(X)	7,110	807	1,706	(X)	1,571	135
Supposed to receive payments in 2001	6,924	100.0	6,212	712	1,469	100.0	1,339	130
Actually received payments in 2001	5,119	73.9	4,639	480	963	65.6	885	77
Received full amount	3,099	44.8	2,821	278	453	30.8	423	30
Received partial payments	2,020	29.2	1,818	202	510	34.7	463	47
Did not receive payments in 2001	1,804	26.1	1,573	232	507	34.5	454	53
Child support not awarded	5,466	(X)	4,181	1,285	1,425	(X)	1,253	172
Mean income and child support								
Received child support payments in 2001:								
Mean total money income ($)	29,008	(X)	28,258	36,255	7,571	(X)	7,604	7,189
Mean child support received ($)	4,274	(X)	4,274	4,273	3,041	(X)	3,078	2,622
Received the full amount due:								
Mean total money income ($)	32,338	(X)	31,734	38,479	7,963	(X)	7,958	8,032
Mean child support received ($)	5,665	(X)	5,655	5,768	4,576	(X)	4,701	2,831
Received partial payments:								
Mean total money income ($)	23,899	(X)	22,865	33,199	7,223	(X)	7,281	6,647
Mean child support received ($)	2,141	(X)	2,132	2,219	1,677	(X)	1,595	2,487
Received no payments in 2001:								
Mean total money income ($)	23,571	(X)	21,835	35,348	6,832	(X)	6,755	7,492
Without child support agreement or award:								
Mean total money income ($)	24,055	(X)	19,339	39,396	6,113	(X)	6,089	6,287

X Not applicable.

SOURCE: "Table 558. Child Support—Award and Recipiency Status of Custodial Parent: 2001," in *Statistical Abstract of the United States: 2006—Social Insurance and Human Services*, U.S. Census Bureau, http://www.census.gov/compendia/statab/social_insurance_human_services/socinsur.pdf (accessed January 2, 2007)

Not surprisingly, people who were not employed full time and families with incomes under the poverty line had the longest median durations of participation in means-tested programs. Those who were employed full time spent a median of 3.8 months in these programs, compared with 6.6 months for those employed part time and 7.2 months for those who were either unemployed or not in the labor force. (See Table 2.17.) Families under the poverty line spent a median of ten months participating in means-tested programs, whereas families with incomes above the poverty line spent a median of only six months in these programs.

TABLE 2.8

Three-year average of poverty statistics, by race and Hispanic origin, 2003–05

[Numbers in thousands. People as of March of the following year]

	3-year average 2003–2005[b]	
Race[a] and Hispanic origin	Number estimate	Percentage estimate
All races	**36,617**	**12.6**
White	24,824	10.6
White, not Hispanic	16,346	8.4
Black	8,988	24.7
American Indian and Alaska Native	573	25.3
Asian	1,335	10.9
Native Hawaiian and other Pacific Islander	79	12.2
Hispanic origin (any race)	9,180	22.0

[a]Federal surveys now give respondents the option of reporting more than one race. Therefore, two basic ways of defining a race group are possible. A group such as Asian may be defined as those who reported Asian and no other race (the race-alone or single-race concept) or as those who reported Asian regardless of whether they also reported another race (the race-alone-or-in-combination concept). This table shows data using the first approach (race alone). The use of the single-race population does not imply that it is the preferred method of presenting or analyzing data. The Census Bureau uses a variety of approaches. Information on people who reported more than one race, such as white and American Indian and Alaska Native or Asian and black or African American, is available from Census 2000 through American FactFinder. About 2.6 percent of people reported more than one race in Census 2000.
[b]The 2004 data have been revised to reflect a correction to the weights in the 2005 Annual Social and Economic Supplement (ASEC).

SOURCE: Carmen DeNavas-Walt, Bernadette D. Proctor, and Cheryl Hill Lee, "Table 5. Number in Poverty and Poverty Rates by Race and Hispanic Origin Using 3-Year Average: 2003 to 2005," in *Income, Poverty, and Health Insurance Coverage in the United States: 2005—Current Population Reports*, U.S. Census Bureau, August 2006, http://www.census.gov/prod/2006pubs/p60-231.pdf (accessed December 1, 2006).

TABLE 2.9

Poverty status and work experience of people in families and unrelated individuals, 2004

[Numbers in thousands. The unrelated individuals category includes people who live by themselves or with others not related to them.]

Poverty status and work experience	Total persons	In married-couple families				In families maintained by women			In families maintained by men			Unrelated individuals
		Husbands	Wives	Related children under 18	Other relatives	House-holder	Related children under 18	Other relatives	House-holder	Related children under 18	Other relatives	
Total												
All people[a]	225,236	57,326	57,911	5,712	17,641	13,968	2,089	10,977	4,869	513	5,093	49,137
With labor force activity	154,796	45,408	37,142	2,166	11,869	10,137	651	6,916	3,872	157	3,451	33,029
1 to 26 weeks	13,888	1,464	3,435	1,363	2,495	814	415	942	183	90	353	2,334
27 weeks or more	140,908	43,944	33,707	803	9,375	9,323	236	5,973	3,689	67	3,099	30,694
With no labor force activity	70,440	11,918	20,770	3,546	5,771	3,831	1,438	4,061	998	356	1,642	16,109
At or above poverty level												
All people[a]	200,049	54,156	54,702	5,324	16,856	10,009	1,484	9,259	4,217	463	4,576	39,003
With labor force activity	144,411	43,582	36,235	2,101	11,624	7,911	518	6,333	3,498	147	3,256	29,205
1 to 26 weeks	11,338	1,304	3,164	1,317	2,423	306	322	754	127	82	288	1,253
27 weeks or more	133,073	42,279	33,071	784	9,201	7,605	196	5,579	3,372	65	2,968	27,952
With no labor force activity	55,638	10,574	18,466	3,223	5,232	2,098	966	2,926	719	316	1,320	9,798
Below poverty level												
All people[a]	25,187	3,170	3,210	388	784	3,959	605	1,717	652	50	518	10,134
With labor force activity	10,385	1,826	906	64	245	2,226	133	582	373	10	196	3,823
1 to 26 weeks	2,549	161	270	46	72	508	94	188	56	8	65	1,081
27 weeks or more	7,836	1,665	636	19	173	1,718	39	394	317	2	130	2,742
With no labor force activity	14,802	1,344	2,304	323	539	1,733	472	1,135	279	40	322	6,310
Rate[b]												
All people[a]	11.2	5.5	5.5	6.8	4.4	28.3	29.0	15.6	13.4	9.7	10.2	20.6
With labor force activity	6.7	4.0	2.4	3.0	2.1	22.0	20.4	8.4	9.6	6.3	5.7	11.6
1 to 26 weeks	18.4	11.0	7.9	3.4	2.9	62.5	22.5	20.0	30.7	8.7	18.5	46.3
27 weeks or more	5.6	3.8	1.9	2.3	1.8	18.4	16.8	6.6	8.6	(C)	4.2	8.9
With no labor force activity	21.0	11.3	11.1	9.1	9.3	45.2	32.8	27.9	28.0	11.3	19.6	39.2

[a]Data on families include people in primary families and unrelated subfamilies.
[b]Number below the poverty level as a percent of the total.
[c]Data not shown where base is less than 80,000.
Note: Data in this table may vary slightly from that previously published due to corrections to the sample weights.

SOURCE: "Table 6. People in Families and Unrelated Individuals: Poverty Status and Work Experience, 2004," *A Profile of the Working Poor, 2004*, U.S. Department of Labor, Bureau of Labor Statistics, May 2006, http://www.bls.gov/cps/cpswp2004.pdf (accessed April 30, 2007)

TABLE 2.10

Past-year median earnings of workers, by gender, race and Hispanic origin, and educational level, 2005

[In 2005 inflation-adjusted dollars. Data are limited to the household population and exclude the population living in institutions, college dormitories, and other group quarters.]

Selected characteristic	Men Median earnings (dollars) estimate	Women Median earnings (dollars) estimate	Percent of men's earnings estimate
Race and Hispanic origin			
Full-time, year-round workers 16 years and older with earnings	41,965	32,168	76.7
White alone	44,850	33,237	74.1
White alone, not Hispanic	46,807	34,190	73.0
Black alone	34,433	29,588	85.9
American Indian and Alaska Native alone	33,520	27,977	83.5
Asian alone	48,693	37,792	77.6
Native Hawaiian and other Pacific Islander alone	35,426	30,041	84.8
Some other race alone	27,041	23,678	87.6
Two or more races	38,621	31,249	80.9
Hispanic (any race)	27,380	24,451	89.3
Educational attainment			
Population 25 years and older with earnings	38,514	25,736	66.8
Less than high school graduate	22,138	13,076	59.1
High school graduate (includes equivalency)	31,683	20,179	63.7
Some college or associate's degree	39,601	25,736	65.0
Bachelor's degree	53,693	36,250	67.5
Graduate or professional degree	71,918	47,319	65.8

Note: Data are based on a sample and are subject to sampling variability.

SOURCE: Adapted from Bruce H. Webster, Jr., and Alemayehu Bishaw, "Table 5. Median Earnings in the Past 12 Months of Workers by Sex and Women's Earnings as a Percentage of Men's Earnings by Selected Characteristics for the United States: 2005," in *Income, Earnings, and Poverty Data from the 2005 American Community Survey*, U.S. Census Bureau, August 2006, http://www.census.gov/prod/2006pubs/acs-02.pdf (accessed January 2, 2007)

TABLE 2.11

Program participation status of household—all income levels, 2004

[Numbers in thousands. People who lived with someone (a nonrelative or a relative) who received aid. Not every person tallied here received the aid themselves.]

	Total	In household that received means-tested assistance		In household that received means-tested assistance excluding school lunch		In household that received means-tested cash assistance		In household that received food stamps		In household in which one or more persons were covered by Medicaid		Lived in public or authorized housing	
		Number	Percent	Number	Percent	Number	Percent	Number	Percent	Number	Percent	Number	Percent
All races													
Both sexes													
Total[a]	**290,605**	**76,745**	**26.4**	**66,659**	**22.9**	**18,484**	**6.4**	**21,905**	**7.5**	**59,107**	**20.3**	**10,618**	**3.7**
Under 18 years	73,271	28,986	39.6	23,974	32.7	5,553	7.6	9,573	13.1	22,250	30.4	3,995	5.5
18 to 24 years	27,972	8,025	28.7	7,300	26.1	1,986	7.1	2,289	8.2	6,434	23.0	1,238	4.4
25 to 34 years	39,307	10,968	27.9	9,479	24.1	2,147	5.5	3,248	8.3	8,522	21.7	1,331	3.4
35 to 44 years	43,350	10,337	23.8	8,633	19.9	2,280	5.3	2,589	6.0	7,748	17.9	1,073	2.5
45 to 54 years	41,960	7,591	18.1	6,757	16.1	2,489	5.9	1,824	4.3	5,831	13.9	918	2.2
55 to 59 years	16,763	2,690	16.0	2,565	15.3	1,096	6.5	623	3.7	2,104	12.5	347	2.1
60 to 64 years	12,769	1,958	15.3	1,893	14.8	826	6.5	472	3.7	1,551	12.1	318	2.5
65 years and over	35,213	6,189	17.6	6,058	17.2	2,107	6.0	1,286	3.7	4,669	13.3	1,399	4.0
65 to 74 years	18,388	3,178	17.3	3,074	16.7	1,114	6.1	722	3.9	2,469	13.4	665	3.6
75 years and over	16,825	3,011	17.9	2,984	17.7	993	5.9	564	3.4	2,200	13.1	733	4.4
Male													
Total	**142,426**	**35,906**	**25.2**	**31,109**	**21.8**	**8,555**	**6.0**	**9,549**	**6.7**	**27,759**	**19.5**	**4,285**	**3.0**
Under 18 years	37,481	14,960	39.9	12,417	33.1	2,908	7.8	4,910	13.1	11,537	30.8	2,041	5.4
18 to 24 years	14,048	3,549	25.3	3,171	22.6	900	6.4	857	6.1	2,761	19.7	433	3.1
25 to 34 years	19,675	4,816	24.5	4,208	21.4	918	4.7	1,169	5.9	3,761	19.1	438	2.2
35 to 44 years	21,468	4,692	21.9	3,987	18.6	1,065	5.0	1,037	4.8	3,614	16.8	379	1.8
45 to 54 years	20,555	3,579	17.4	3,154	15.3	1,115	5.4	783	3.8	2,714	13.2	353	1.7
55 to 59 years	8,003	1,189	14.9	1,133	14.2	524	6.6	217	2.7	945	11.8	121	1.5
60 to 64 years	6,044	834	13.8	807	13.3	357	5.9	173	2.9	653	10.8	97	1.6
65 years and over	15,151	2,287	15.1	2,233	14.7	767	5.1	404	2.7	1,774	11.7	424	2.8
65 to 74 years	8,466	1,305	15.4	1,261	14.9	449	5.3	248	2.9	1,043	12.3	221	2.6
75 years and over	6,685	981	14.7	972	14.5	318	4.8	156	2.3	731	10.9	202	3.0
Female													
Total	**148,179**	**40,840**	**27.6**	**35,551**	**24.0**	**9,929**	**6.7**	**12,355**	**8.3**	**31,348**	**21.2**	**6,333**	**4.3**
Under 18 years	35,790	14,026	39.2	11,557	32.3	2,645	7.4	4,663	13.0	10,713	29.9	1,953	5.5
18 to 24 years	13,924	4,477	32.2	4,129	29.7	1,086	7.8	1,432	10.3	3,673	26.4	805	5.8
25 to 34 years	19,632	6,152	31.3	5,271	26.8	1,228	6.3	2,079	10.6	4,761	24.3	893	4.6
35 to 44 years	21,882	5,645	25.8	4,646	21.2	1,215	5.6	1,552	7.1	4,133	18.9	695	3.2
45 to 54 years	21,405	4,013	18.7	3,604	16.8	1,374	6.4	1,042	4.9	3,117	14.6	565	2.6
55 to 59 years	8,760	1,501	17.1	1,433	16.4	572	6.5	406	4.6	1,158	13.2	225	2.6
60 to 64 years	6,724	1,125	16.7	1,087	16.2	469	7.0	299	4.4	897	13.3	221	3.3
65 years and over	20,063	3,902	19.5	3,825	19.1	1,340	6.7	883	4.4	2,895	14.4	975	4.9
65 to 74 years	9,922	1,873	18.9	1,813	18.3	665	6.7	475	4.8	1,426	14.4	444	4.5
75 years and over	10,140	2,029	20.0	2,012	19.8	675	6.7	408	4.0	1,469	14.5	531	5.2

TABLE 2.11

Program participation status of household—all income levels, 2004 [CONTINUED]

[Numbers in thousands. People who lived with someone (a nonrelative or a relative) who received aid. Not every person tallied here received the aid themselves.]

Household relationship	Total	In household that received means-tested assistance		In household that received means-tested assistance excluding school lunch		In household that received means-tested cash assistance		In household that received food stamps		In household in which one or more persons were covered by Medicaid		Lived in public or authorized housing	
		Number	Percent	Number	Percent	Number	Percent	Number	Percent	Number	Percent	Number	Percent
Total[a]	**290,605**	**76,745**	**26.4**	**66,659**	**22.9**	**18,484**	**6.4**	**21,905**	**7.5**	**59,107**	**20.3**	**10,618**	**3.7**
65 years and over	35,213	6,189	17.6	6,058	17.2	2,107	6.0	1,286	3.7	4,669	13.3	1,399	4.0
In families[b]	241,153	67,084	27.8	57,277	23.8	15,413	6.4	18,801	7.8	52,030	21.6	8,005	3.3
Householder	77,019	18,554	24.1	16,074	20.9	4,480	5.8	5,278	6.9	14,359	18.6	2,505	3.3
Under 65 years	64,877	16,618	25.6	14,207	21.9	3,736	5.8	4,870	7.5	12,794	19.7	2,295	3.5
65 years and over	12,142	1,935	15.9	1,868	15.4	744	6.1	409	3.4	1,565	12.9	210	1.7
Related children under 18 years[c]	72,164	28,392	39.3	23,450	32.5	5,450	7.6	9,386	13.0	21,757	30.1	3,962	5.5
Under 6 years	23,750	9,839	41.4	8,880	37.4	1,961	8.3	3,638	15.3	8,362	35.2	1,588	6.7
6 to 17 years	48,414	18,553	38.3	14,571	30.1	3,490	7.2	5,748	11.9	13,395	27.7	2,374	4.9
Own children 18 year and over[d]	22,262	6,272	28.2	5,706	25.6	2,194	9.9	1,474	6.6	5,073	22.8	620	2.8
In married-couple families[f]	185,226	37,809	20.4	31,503	17.0	6,878	3.7	6,779	3.7	28,790	15.5	2,035	1.1
Husbands[f]	58,118	9,396	16.2	7,998	13.8	1,884	3.2	1,639	2.8	7,139	12.3	599	1.0
Under 65 years	47,516	8,189	17.2	6,825	14.4	1,469	3.1	1,451	3.1	6,155	13.0	465	1.0
65 years and over	10,601	1,207	11.4	1,173	11.1	415	3.9	188	1.8	984	9.3	134	1.3
Wives[f]	58,118	9,396	16.2	7,998	13.8	1,884	3.2	1,639	2.8	7,139	12.3	599	1.0
Under 65 years	49,892	8,548	17.1	7,166	14.4	1,596	3.2	1,509	3.0	6,465	13.0	499	1.0
65 years and over	8,225	848	10.3	832	10.1	288	3.5	130	1.6	674	8.2	100	1.2
Related children under 18 years[c]	51,220	14,604	28.5	11,536	22.5	1,757	3.4	2,934	5.7	10,826	21.1	719	1.4
Under 6 years	17,397	5,269	30.3	4,600	26.4	582	3.3	1,231	7.1	4,338	24.9	344	2.0
6 to 17 years	33,823	9,335	27.6	6,936	20.5	1,175	3.5	1,703	5.0	6,488	19.2	375	1.1
Own children 18 years and over[d]	14,197	3,020	21.3	2,720	19.2	958	6.7	406	2.9	2,489	17.5	98	0.7
In families with male householder, no spouse present	13,886	5,028	36.2	4,252	30.6	1,100	7.9	1,180	8.5	3,867	27.8	431	3.1
Householder	4,893	1,667	34.1	1,436	29.3	387	7.9	405	8.3	1,296	26.5	142	2.9
Under 65 years	4,425	1,538	34.8	1,311	29.6	340	7.7	376	8.5	1,195	27.0	131	3.0
65 years and over	468	129	27.6	124	26.6	47	10.1	29	6.2	101	21.6	11	2.4
Related children under 18 years[c]	3,915	1,944	49.7	1,556	39.7	295	7.5	495	12.6	1,471	37.6	165	4.2
Under 6 years	1,262	747	59.2	668	52.9	116	9.2	229	18.2	645	51.1	69	5.5
6 to 17 years	2,653	1,197	45.1	888	33.5	179	6.7	266	10.0	826	31.1	96	3.6
Own children 18 years and over[d]	1,450	379	26.2	346	23.8	115	8.0	80	5.5	282	19.5	36	2.5
In families with female house-holder, no spouse present	42,040	24,247	57.7	21,522	51.2	7,435	17.7	10,842	25.8	19,373	46.1	5,539	13.2

TABLE 2.11

Program participation status of household—all income levels, 2004 [CONTINUED]

[Numbers in thousands. People who lived with someone (a nonrelative or a relative) who received aid. Not every person tallied here received the aid themselves.]

	Total	In household that received means-tested assistance		In household that received means-tested assistance excluding school lunch		In household that received means-tested cash assistance		In household that received food stamps		In household in which one or more persons were covered by Medicaid		Lived in public or authorized housing	
		Number	Percent	Number	Percent	Number	Percent	Number	Percent	Number	Percent	Number	Percent
Householder	14,009	7,491	53.5	6,641	47.4	2,208	15.8	3,234	23.1	5,924	42.3	1,764	12.6
Under 65 years	12,207	6,767	55.4	5,951	48.7	1,884	15.4	3,022	24.8	5,328	43.6	1,687	13.8
65 years and over	1,801	724	40.2	690	38.3	324	18.0	212	11.8	596	33.1	77	4.3
Related children													
under 18 years[e]	17,029	11,845	69.6	10,358	60.8	3,398	20.0	5,957	35.0	9,459	55.5	3,079	18.1
Under 6 years	5,091	3,823	75.1	3,611	70.9	1,262	24.8	2,178	42.8	3,379	66.4	1,176	23.1
6 to 17 years	11,938	8,022	67.2	6,747	56.5	2,136	17.9	3,779	31.7	6,080	50.9	1,903	15.9
Own children 18 years and over[g]	6,614	2,872	43.4	2,640	39.9	1,121	16.9	987	14.9	2,302	34.8	486	7.3
In unrelated subfamilies[c]	1,255	664	52.9	584	46.5	102	8.2	212	16.9	564	44.9	35	2.8
Under 18 years	675	369	54.7	325	48.1	61	9.0	125	18.5	314	46.5	18	2.6
Under 6 years	202	109	53.8	103	50.8	22	10.6	48	23.9	97	48.0	8	3.7
6 to 17 years	473	261	55.1	222	46.9	39	8.3	77	16.2	217	45.9	10	2.2
18 years and over	580	295	50.8	259	44.7	42	7.2	87	15.0	250	43.1	17	2.9
Unrelated individuals[d]	48,198	8,997	18.7	8,798	18.3	2,969	6.2	2,891	6.0	6,513	13.5	2,579	5.4
Male	23,442	4,276	18.2	4,149	17.7	1,448	6.2	1,334	5.7	3,218	13.7	1,027	4.4
Under 65 years	20,121	3,585	17.8	3,459	17.2	1,250	6.2	1,203	6.0	2,757	13.7	757	3.8
Living alone	9,807	1,113	11.3	1,113	11.3	488	5.0	422	4.3	780	8.0	429	4.4
65 years and over	3,321	691	20.8	690	20.8	198	6.0	131	3.9	461	13.9	269	8.1
Living alone	2,908	585	20.1	585	20.1	148	5.1	102	3.5	370	12.7	260	8.9
Female	24,756	4,721	19.1	4,649	18.8	1,521	6.1	1,557	6.3	3,295	13.3	1,552	6.3
Under 65 years	16,628	3,028	18.2	2,956	17.8	1,047	6.3	1,127	6.8	2,243	13.5	797	4.8
Living alone	9,543	1,430	15.0	1,430	15.0	576	6.0	655	6.9	946	9.9	640	6.7
65 years and over	8,128	1,693	20.8	1,693	20.8	474	5.8	430	5.3	1,052	12.9	755	9.3
Living alone	7,708	1,559	20.2	1,559	20.2	416	5.4	391	5.1	938	12.2	748	9.7

[a]Universe: All people except unrelated individuals under age 15 (such as foster children). Since the Current Population Survey (CPS) asks income questions not only to people age 15 and over, if a child under 15 is not part of a family by birth, marriage, or adoption, we do not know their income and cannot determine whether or not they are poor. Those people are excluded from the totals so as not to affect the percentages.

[b]People in families: People who are related to the householder by birth, marriage, or adoption. People who are related to each other but not to the householder are counted elsewhere (usually as unrelated subfamilies).

[c]People in unrelated subfamilies: People who are not related to the householder, but who are related to each other, either as a married couple or as a parent-child relationship with an unmarried child under 18.

[d]Unrelated individuals: People who are not in primary families (the householder's family) or unrelated subfamilies.

[e]People in families with related children. People living in a family where at least one member is a related child—a person under 18 who is related to the householder but is not the householder or spouse.

[f]In married-couple families the householder may be either the husband or wife.

[g]Own children: Sons and daughters, including stepchildren and adopted children, of the householder.

SOURCE: "Pov26: Program Participation Status of Household—Poverty Status of People: 2004, All Races—All Income Levels," in *Current Population Survey, 2005 Annual Social and Economic Supplement*, U.S. Census Bureau, 2005, http://pubdb3.census.gov/macro/032005/pov/new26_001_01.htm (accessed January 2, 2007)

TABLE 2.12

Program participation status of household—persons below poverty level, 2004

[Numbers in thousands. People who lived with someone (a nonrelative or a relative) who received aid. Not every person tallied here received the aid themselves].

	Total	In household that received means-tested assistance		In household that received means-tested assistance excluding school lunch		In household that received means-tested cash assistance		In household that received food stamps		In household in which one or more persons were covered by Medicaid		Lived in public or authorized housing	
		Number	Percent	Number	Percent	Number	Percent	Number	Percent	Number	Percent	Number	Percent
All races													
Below poverty level													
Both sexes													
Total[a]	**36,997**	**25,022**	**67.6**	**22,681**	**61.3**	**7,552**	**20.4**	**13,390**	**36.2**	**20,009**	**54.1**	**5,959**	**16.1**
Under 18 years	13,027	11,230	86.2	9,973	76.6	3,096	23.8	6,552	50.3	9,165	70.4	2,716	20.9
18 to 24 years	5,068	2,742	54.1	2,583	51.0	818	16.1	1,382	27.3	2,260	44.6	685	13.5
25 to 34 years	4,924	3,368	68.4	3,036	61.7	857	17.4	1,856	37.7	2,719	55.2	711	14.4
35 to 44 years	4,272	2,946	69.0	2,570	60.2	841	19.7	1,443	33.8	2,247	52.6	555	13.0
45 to 54 years	3,507	2,040	58.2	1,888	53.8	801	22.8	994	28.3	1,549	44.2	453	12.9
55 to 59 years	1,416	674	47.6	648	45.7	284	20.0	317	22.4	510	36.0	173	12.2
60 to 64 years	1,326	530	40.0	522	39.4	257	19.4	260	19.6	423	31.9	159	12.0
65 years and over	3,457	1,492	43.2	1,461	42.3	598	17.3	586	17.0	1,136	32.9	508	14.7
65 to 74 years	1,721	792	46.0	769	44.7	340	19.7	347	20.2	615	35.8	272	15.8
75 years and over	1,736	700	40.3	691	39.8	259	14.9	239	13.8	520	30.0	235	13.5
Male													
Total	**16,381**	**10,828**	**66.1**	**9,753**	**59.5**	**3,129**	**19.1**	**5,569**	**34.0**	**8,606**	**52.5**	**2,312**	**14.1**
Under 18 years	6,667	5,782	86.7	5,147	77.2	1,577	23.6	3,335	50.0	4,714	70.7	1,383	20.8
18 to 24 years	2,157	1,023	47.4	952	44.1	288	13.4	455	21.1	794	36.8	208	9.7
25 to 34 years	1,907	1,112	58.3	986	51.7	250	13.1	539	28.3	858	45.0	161	8.5
35 to 44 years	1,788	1,138	63.7	1,004	56.1	300	16.8	511	28.6	875	48.9	179	10.0
45 to 54 years	1,631	904	55.4	823	50.5	327	20.0	390	23.9	673	41.3	148	9.1
55 to 59 years	594	232	39.1	223	37.6	115	19.4	90	15.1	183	30.9	53	9.0
60 to 64 years	579	201	34.7	197	34.0	90	15.5	97	16.7	159	27.5	46	7.9
65 years and over	1,058	436	41.2	422	39.9	183	17.3	154	14.5	349	33.0	133	12.5
65 to 74 years	615	264	42.9	253	41.1	111	18.0	99	16.2	206	33.5	79	12.8
75 years and over	443	172	38.8	169	38.2	72	16.3	54	12.2	143	32.3	54	12.1
Female													
Total	**20,617**	**14,193**	**68.8**	**12,927**	**62.7**	**4,423**	**21.5**	**7,820**	**37.9**	**11,403**	**55.3**	**3,648**	**17.7**
Under 18 years	6,360	5,449	85.7	4,826	75.9	1,520	23.9	3,217	50.6	4,451	70.0	1,333	21.0
18 to 24 years	2,911	1,718	59.0	1,631	56.0	530	18.2	927	31.8	1,466	50.4	477	16.4
25 to 34 years	3,017	2,256	74.8	2,050	68.0	607	20.1	1,317	43.6	1,861	61.7	550	18.2
35 to 44 years	2,484	1,808	72.8	1,566	63.0	541	21.8	932	37.5	1,372	55.2	376	15.2
45 to 54 years	1,877	1,136	60.5	1,065	56.8	474	25.3	604	32.2	875	46.6	304	16.2
55 to 59 years	823	442	53.7	425	51.6	169	20.5	227	27.6	327	39.7	119	14.5
60 to 64 years	747	330	44.1	325	43.5	167	22.4	163	21.8	264	35.3	114	15.2
65 years and over	2,398	1,056	44.0	1,039	43.3	415	17.3	433	18.0	787	32.8	375	15.6
65 to 74 years	1,105	528	47.8	517	46.7	229	20.7	247	22.4	409	37.0	193	17.5
75 years and over	1,293	528	40.8	522	40.4	186	14.4	185	14.3	378	29.2	182	14.0
Household relationship													
Total[a]	**36,997**	**25,022**	**67.6**	**22,681**	**61.3**	**7,552**	**20.4**	**13,390**	**36.2**	**20,009**	**54.1**	**5,959**	**16.1**
65 years and over	3,457	1,492	43.2	1,461	42.3	598	17.3	586	17.0	1,136	32.9	508	14.7
In families[b]	26,564	20,470	77.1	18,256	68.7	5,865	22.1	11,398	42.9	16,556	62.3	4,732	17.8
Householder	7,854	5,690	72.5	5,142	65.5	1,703	21.7	3,177	40.4	4,639	59.1	1,420	18.1

TABLE 2.12

Program participation status of household—persons below poverty level, 2004 [CONTINUED]

[Numbers in thousands. People who lived with someone (a nonrelative or a relative) who received aid. Not every person tallied here received the aid themselves].

	Total	In household that received means-tested assistance		In household that received means-tested assistance excluding school lunch		In household that received means-tested cash assistance		In household that received food stamps		In household in which one or more persons were covered by Medicaid		Lived in public or authorized housing	
		Number	Percent	Number	Percent	Number	Percent	Number	Percent	Number	Percent	Number	Percent
Under 65 years	7,062	5,360	75.9	4,833	68.4	1,563	22.1	3,038	43.0	4,366	61.8	1,348	19.1
65 years and over	792	330	41.7	309	39.0	139	17.6	138	17.4	273	34.4	72	9.1
Related children under 18 years[e]	12,460	10,826	86.9	9,604	77.1	3,018	24.2	6,389	51.3	8,821	70.8	2,689	21.6
Under 6 years	4,737	4,108	86.7	3,852	81.3	1,241	26.2	2,508	52.9	3,631	76.6	1,141	24.1
6 to 17 years	7,723	6,718	87.0	5,752	74.5	1,777	23.0	3,880	50.2	5,190	67.2	1,548	20.0
Own children 18 years and over[g]	1,775	1,239	69.8	1,142	64.4	442	24.9	640	36.0	1,009	56.9	267	15.0
In married-couple families[f]	11,824	7,879	66.6	6,631	56.1	1,439	12.2	3,328	28.1	5,957	50.4	787	6.7
Husbands[f]	3,222	1,852	57.5	1,588	49.3	390	12.1	789	24.5	1,405	43.6	205	6.4
Under 65 years	2,739	1,698	62.0	1,438	52.5	318	11.6	730	26.7	1,272	46.5	161	5.9
65 years and over	484	154	31.8	150	31.0	72	14.9	59	12.2	133	27.5	44	9.1
Wives[f]	3,222	1,852	57.5	1,588	49.3	390	12.1	789	24.5	1,405	43.6	205	6.4
Under 65 years	2,859	1,750	61.2	1,488	52.0	339	11.9	744	26.0	1,317	46.1	175	6.1
65 years and over	363	102	28.2	101	27.8	51	13.9	45	12.5	88	24.1	30	8.2
Related children under 18 years[e]	4,581	3,671	80.1	3,009	65.7	544	11.9	1,572	34.3	2,751	60.1	342	7.5
Under 6 years	1,751	1,416	80.9	1,269	72.5	214	12.2	651	37.2	1,194	68.2	166	9.5
6 to 17 years	2,831	2,254	79.6	1,740	61.5	330	11.6	921	32.5	1,557	55.0	176	6.2
Own children 18 years and over[g]	568	337	59.4	302	53.2	70	12.3	126	22.2	274	48.3	29	5.2
In families with male householder, no spouse present	1,917	1,356	70.8	1,139	59.5	332	17.3	541	28.2	1,032	53.9	209	10.9
Householder	658	452	68.6	391	59.3	116	17.6	182	27.6	354	53.8	70	10.6
Under 65 years	597	422	70.6	364	61.0	109	18.3	172	28.8	329	55.2	68	11.4
65 years and over	61	30	48.8	26	42.8	7	10.7	10	16.0	25	40.2	2	3.0
Related children under 18 years[e]	747	620	83.1	507	68.0	140	18.7	265	35.6	468	62.7	101	13.5
Under 6 years	309	244	78.8	214	69.3	58	18.6	115	37.3	202	65.4	51	16.6
6 to 17 years	437	377	86.2	293	67.1	82	18.8	150	34.4	266	60.8	50	11.4
Own children 18 years and over[g]	141	79	55.9	70	50.0	15	10.7	31	21.9	63	44.5	5	3.3
In families with female householder, no spouse present	12,823	11,235	87.6	10,485	81.8	4,095	31.9	7,529	58.7	9,566	74.6	3,735	29.1
Householder	3,973	3,387	85.2	3,162	79.6	1,197	30.1	2,205	55.5	2,880	72.5	1,146	28.8
Under 65 years	3,700	3,225	87.2	3,015	81.5	1,131	30.6	2,127	57.5	2,750	74.3	1,116	30.2
65 years and over	273	161	59.1	147	54.0	66	24.1	78	28.7	130	47.6	30	10.8
Related children under 18 years[e]	7,132	6,535	91.6	6,088	85.4	2,335	32.7	4,551	63.8	5,601	78.5	2,246	31.5
Under 6 years	2,677	2,448	91.4	2,369	88.5	969	36.2	1,742	65.0	2,234	83.4	924	34.5
6 to 17 years	4,455	4,087	91.8	3,719	83.5	1,366	30.7	2,810	63.1	3,367	75.6	1,322	29.7
Own children 18 years and over[g]	1,066	823	77.2	770	72.2	357	33.5	483	45.3	672	63.0	233	21.8
In unrelated subfamilies[c]	570	434	76.2	391	68.7	79	13.8	179	31.5	376	66.0	31	5.4
Under 18 years	314	246	78.3	221	70.4	47	14.9	107	34.2	213	67.8	16	5.1
Under 6 years	103	80	77.3	75	72.5	19	18.5	41	39.7	70	67.7	6	6.0
6 to 17 years	211	166	78.7	146	69.4	28	13.1	66	31.5	143	67.8	10	4.6
18 years and over	256	189	73.8	170	66.5	32	12.5	72	28.2	163	63.8	15	5.7

TABLE 2.12

Program participation status of household—persons below poverty level, 2004 [CONTINUED]

[Numbers in thousands. People who lived with someone (a nonrelative or a relative) who received aid. Not every person tallied here received the aid themselves].

	Total	In household that received means-tested assistance		In household that received means-tested assistance excluding school lunch		In household that received means-tested cash assistance		In household that received food stamps		In household in which one or more persons were covered by Medicaid		Lived in public or authorized housing	
		Number	Percent	Number	Percent	Number	Percent	Number	Percent	Number	Percent	Number	Percent
Unrelated individuals[d]	9,864	4,117	41.7	4,034	40.9	1,608	16.3	1,812	18.4	3,077	31.2	1,197	12.1
Male	4,284	1,754	40.9	1,708	39.9	675	15.8	763	17.8	1,333	31.1	444	10.4
Under 65 years	3,828	1,543	40.3	1,497	39.1	586	15.3	692	18.1	1,174	30.7	363	9.5
Living alone	1,497	597	39.9	597	39.9	285	19.0	318	21.3	445	29.7	242	16.2
65 years and over	456	211	46.3	211	46.3	89	19.6	70	15.4	160	35.0	81	17.8
Living alone	390	170	43.7	170	43.7	73	18.7	58	14.8	125	32.0	75	19.3
Female	5,580	2,363	42.3	2,326	41.7	933	16.7	1,050	18.8	1,743	31.2	752	13.5
Under 65 years	3,938	1,654	42.0	1,617	41.1	659	16.7	769	19.5	1,248	31.7	450	11.4
Living alone	1,727	826	47.8	826	47.8	394	22.8	446	25.8	586	33.9	376	21.8
65 years and over	1,642	709	43.2	709	43.2	274	16.7	280	17.1	495	30.2	302	18.4
Living alone	1,513	653	43.1	653	43.1	247	16.3	262	17.3	445	29.4	298	19.7

[a]Universe: All people except unrelated individuals under age 15 (such as foster children). Since the Current Population Survey (CPS) asks income questions not only to people age 15 and over, if a child under 15 is not part of a family by birth, marriage, or adoption, we do not know their income and cannot determine whether or not they are poor. Those people are excluded from the totals so as not to affect the percentages.

[b]People in families: People who are related to the householder by birth, marriage, or adoption. People who are related to each other but not to the householder are counted elsewhere (usually as unrelated subfamilies).

[c]People in unrelated subfamilies: People who are not related to the householder, but who are related to each other, either as a married couple or as a parent-child relationship with an unmarried child under 18.

[d]Unrelated individuals: People who are not in primary families (the householder's family) or unrelated subfamilies.

[e]People in families with related children. People living in a family where at least one member is a related child—a person under 18 who is related to the householder but is not the householder or spouse.

[f]In married-couple families the householder may be either the husband or wife.

[g]Own children: Sons and daughters, including stepchildren and adopted children, of the householder.

SOURCE: "Pov26: Program Participation Status of Household—Poverty Status of People: 2004, All Races—Below Poverty Level," in *Current Population Survey, 2005 Annual Social and Economic Supplement*, U.S. Census Bureau, 2005, http://pubdb3.census.gov/macro/032005/pov/new26_002_01.htm (accessed January 2, 2007)

FIGURE 2.7

FIGURE 2.8

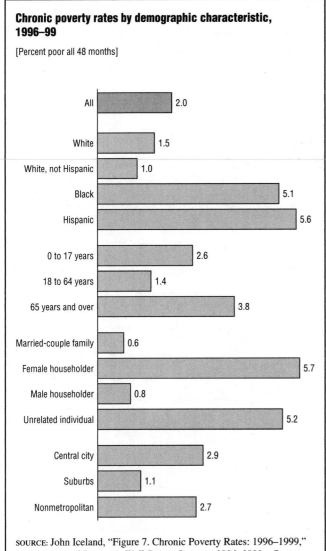

Chronic poverty rates by demographic characteristic, 1996–99

[Percent poor all 48 months]

All	2.0
White	1.5
White, not Hispanic	1.0
Black	5.1
Hispanic	5.6
0 to 17 years	2.6
18 to 64 years	1.4
65 years and over	3.8
Married-couple family	0.6
Female householder	5.7
Male householder	0.8
Unrelated individual	5.2
Central city	2.9
Suburbs	1.1
Nonmetropolitan	2.7

SOURCE: John Iceland, "Figure 7. Chronic Poverty Rates: 1996–1999," in *Dynamics of Economic Well-Being: Poverty, 1996–1999—Current Population Reports*, U.S. Census Bureau, July 2003, http://www.census.gov/prod/2003pubs/p70-91.pdf (accessed January 2, 2007)

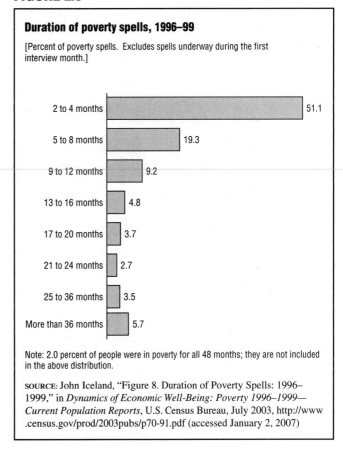

Duration of poverty spells, 1996–99

[Percent of poverty spells. Excludes spells underway during the first interview month.]

2 to 4 months	51.1
5 to 8 months	19.3
9 to 12 months	9.2
13 to 16 months	4.8
17 to 20 months	3.7
21 to 24 months	2.7
25 to 36 months	3.5
More than 36 months	5.7

Note: 2.0 percent of people were in poverty for all 48 months; they are not included in the above distribution.

SOURCE: John Iceland, "Figure 8. Duration of Poverty Spells: 1996–1999," in *Dynamics of Economic Well-Being: Poverty 1996–1999—Current Population Reports*, U.S. Census Bureau, July 2003, http://www.census.gov/prod/2003pubs/p70-91.pdf (accessed January 2, 2007)

FIGURE 2.9

FIGURE 2.10

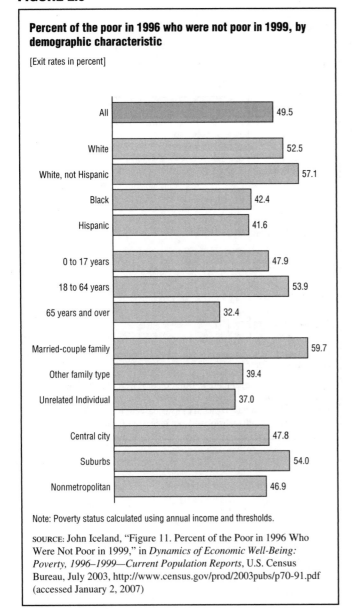

Percent of the poor in 1996 who were not poor in 1999, by demographic characteristic

[Exit rates in percent]

Note: Poverty status calculated using annual income and thresholds.

SOURCE: John Iceland, "Figure 11. Percent of the Poor in 1996 Who Were Not Poor in 1999," in *Dynamics of Economic Well-Being: Poverty, 1996–1999—Current Population Reports*, U.S. Census Bureau, July 2003, http://www.census.gov/prod/2003pubs/p70-91.pdf (accessed January 2, 2007)

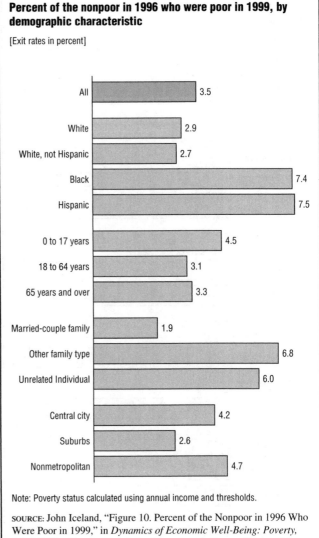

Percent of the nonpoor in 1996 who were poor in 1999, by demographic characteristic

[Exit rates in percent]

Note: Poverty status calculated using annual income and thresholds.

SOURCE: John Iceland, "Figure 10. Percent of the Nonpoor in 1996 Who Were Poor in 1999," in *Dynamics of Economic Well-Being: Poverty, 1996–1999—Current Population Reports*, U.S. Census Bureau, July 2003, http://www.census.gov/prod/2003pubs/p70-91.pdf (accessed January 2, 2007)

TABLE 2.13

Poverty status by age, sex, race, and Hispanic origin, 2004

[Numbers in thousands; people in the labor force for 27 weeks or more]

Age and sex	Total	White	Black or African American	Asian	Hispanic or Latino ethnicity	Below poverty level Total	White	Black or African American	Asian	Hispanic or Latino ethnicity	Rate[a] Total	White	Black or African American	Asian	Hispanic or Latino ethnicity
Total, 16 years and older	140,908	115,662	15,819	6,039	18,296	7,836	5,615	1,670	266	1,930	5.6	4.9	10.6	4.4	10.5
16 to 19 years	4,208	3,550	410	103	595	430	319	80	7	93	10.2	9.0	19.5	7.0	15.6
20 to 24 years	13,327	10,792	1,591	410	2,363	1,557	1,164	279	33	310	11.7	10.8	17.5	8.2	13.1
25 to 34 years	30,867	24,453	3,959	1,598	5,728	2,227	1,508	577	57	709	7.2	6.2	14.6	3.6	12.4
35 to 44 years	35,003	28,295	4,200	1,702	4,814	1,774	1,266	382	85	491	5.1	4.5	9.1	5.0	10.2
45 to 54 years	33,705	28,057	3,633	1,357	3,127	1,195	852	251	53	225	3.5	3.0	6.9	3.9	7.2
55 to 64 years	18,578	15,938	1,609	717	1,362	548	423	89	20	88	3.0	2.7	5.6	2.8	6.5
65 years and older	5,221	4,577	417	152	308	106	83	11	10	14	2.0	1.8	2.6	6.3	4.4
Men, 16 years and older	75,887	63,368	7,401	3,284	11,174	3,799	2,892	621	154	1,156	5.0	4.6	8.4	4.7	10.3
16 to 19 years	2,068	1,736	209	48	346	188	126	46	3	45	9.1	7.3	22.1	b	13.1
20 to 24 years	7,102	5,854	756	204	1,479	686	525	109	19	173	9.7	9.0	14.5	9.4	11.7
25 to 34 years	17,203	13,973	1,842	911	3,695	1,067	808	185	27	447	6.2	5.8	10.0	3.0	12.1
35 to 44 years	19,001	15,658	1,942	957	2,931	875	678	132	52	297	4.6	4.3	6.8	5.4	10.1
45 to 54 years	17,737	15,001	1,704	688	1,783	641	471	113	35	143	3.6	3.1	6.6	5.2	8.0
55 to 64 years	9,870	8,557	752	389	773	276	228	35	11	44	2.8	2.7	4.6	2.7	5.6
65 years and older	2,906	2,589	196	87	166	66	56	1	7	7	2.3	2.2	0.7	8.6	4.2
Women, 16 years and older	65,022	52,294	8,419	2,755	7,122	4,036	2,723	1,049	112	774	6.2	5.2	12.5	4.1	10.9
16 to 19 years	2,140	1,814	201	54	249	241	193	34	5	48	11.3	10.6	16.8	b	19.2
20 to 24 years	6,225	4,938	835	206	883	871	640	170	14	136	14.0	12.9	20.3	7.0	15.4
25 to 34 years	13,664	10,479	2,117	688	2,033	1,159	700	393	30	262	8.5	6.7	18.6	4.4	12.9
35 to 44 years	16,002	12,637	2,258	746	1,883	899	587	250	34	194	5.6	4.6	11.1	4.5	10.3
45 to 54 years	15,968	13,057	1,928	670	1,343	554	381	138	18	82	3.5	2.9	7.1	2.6	6.1
55 to 64 years	8,707	7,381	858	328	589	272	195	55	10	45	3.1	2.6	6.4	2.9	7.6
65 years and older	2,316	1,988	221	65	142	40	27	10	2	7	1.7	1.4	4.3	b	4.7

Note: Estimates for the above race groups (white, black or African American, and Asian) do not sum to totals because data are not presented for all races. In addition, people whose ethnicity is identified as Hispanic or Latino may be of any race and, therefore, are classified by ethnicity as well as by race.

[a]Number below the poverty level as a percent of the total in the labor force for 27 weeks or more.

[b]Data not shown where base is less than 80,000.

SOURCE: "Table 2. People in the Labor Force for 27 Weeks or More: Poverty Status by Age, Sex, Race, and Hispanic or Latino Ethnicity, 2004," in *A Profile of the Working Poor, 2004*, U.S. Department of Labor, Bureau of Labor Statistics, December 2006, http://www.bls.gov/cps/cpswp2004.pdf (accessed January 23, 2007)

TABLE 2.14

Poverty status by educational attainment, race, ethnicity, and sex, 2004

[Numbers in thousands]

Educational attainment, race, and Hispanic or Latino ethnicity	Total	Men	Women	Below poverty level Total	Men	Women	Rate[a] Total	Men	Women
Total, 16 years and older	**140,908**	**75,887**	**65,022**	**7,836**	**3,799**	**4,036**	**5.6**	**5.0**	**6.2**
Less than a high school diploma	16,013	10,032	5,981	2,427	1,341	1,087	15.2	13.4	18.2
Less than 1 year of high school	5,055	3,490	1,566	846	562	284	16.7	16.1	18.1
1–3 years of high school	9,226	5,463	3,763	1,368	672	696	14.8	12.3	18.5
4 years of high school, no diploma	1,732	1,079	653	214	106	107	12.3	9.8	16.4
High school graduates, no college[b]	42,922	24,129	18,792	2,792	1,382	1,410	6.5	5.7	7.5
Some college or associate degree	40,570	19,818	20,753	1,903	727	1,176	4.7	3.7	5.7
Some college, no degree	27,385	13,706	13,679	1,499	575	924	5.5	4.2	6.8
Associate degree	13,186	6,112	7,073	404	152	252	3.1	2.5	3.6
Bachelor's degree and higher[c]	41,404	21,908	19,495	714	350	364	1.7	1.6	1.9
White, 16 years and older	**115,662**	**63,368**	**52,294**	**5,615**	**2,892**	**2,723**	**4.9**	**4.6**	**5.2**
Less than a high school diploma	12,957	8,410	4,547	1,790	1,072	718	13.8	12.7	15.8
Less than 1 year of high school	4,374	3,095	1,279	728	497	231	16.6	16.1	18.0
1–3 years of high school	7,296	4,450	2,846	935	492	444	12.8	11.0	15.6
4 years of high school, no diploma	1,287	865	422	128	84	44	9.9	9.7	10.4
High school graduates, no college[b]	34,898	19,844	15,054	1,939	1,009	930	5.6	5.1	6.2
Some college or associate degree	33,356	16,621	16,736	1,362	559	804	4.1	3.4	4.8
Some college, no degree	22,312	11,419	10,893	1,062	447	616	4.8	3.9	5.7
Associate degree	11,044	5,202	5,842	300	112	188	2.7	2.2	3.2
Bachelor's degree and higher[c]	34,450	18,494	15,957	523	252	271	1.5	1.4	1.7
Black or African American, 16 years and older	**15,819**	**7,401**	**8,419**	**1,670**	**621**	**1,049**	**10.6**	**8.4**	**12.5**
Less than a high school diploma	2,022	1,054	968	490	185	305	24.3	17.6	31.5
Less than 1 year of high school	303	174	130	57	25	32	18.8	14.3	25.0
1–3 years of high school	1,406	724	681	359	141	218	25.5	19.5	32.0
4 years of high school, no diploma	313	156	157	74	19	55	23.7	12.3	35.1
High school graduates, no college[b]	5,867	3,052	2,815	697	286	411	11.9	9.4	14.6
Some college or associate degree	4,825	2,023	2,803	383	101	283	7.9	5.0	10.1
Some college, no degree	3,450	1,464	1,986	307	74	233	8.9	5.1	11.7
Associate degree	1,375	558	817	77	27	50	5.6	4.8	6.1
Bachelor's degree and higher[c]	3,105	1,272	1,833	99	49	50	3.2	3.8	2.7
Asian, 16 years and older	**6,039**	**3,284**	**2,755**	**266**	**154**	**112**	**4.4**	**4.7**	**4.1**
Less than a high school diploma	498	236	261	50	28	22	10.1	11.8	8.5
Less than 1 year of high school	224	114	110	25	17	8	10.9	14.5	7.3
1–3 years of high school	203	96	107	19	10	10	9.6	10.0	9.2
4 years of high school, no diploma	71	26	44	6	2	4	[d]	[d]	[d]
High school graduates, no college[b]	1,146	644	502	61	38	23	5.3	5.8	4.7
Some college or associate degree	1,235	611	625	76	41	35	6.1	6.7	5.6
Some college, no degree	820	415	404	64	33	30	7.8	8.0	7.5
Associate degree	416	195	220	12	7	5	2.9	3.8	2.1
Bachelor's degree and higher[c]	3,161	1,793	1,367	79	48	31	2.5	2.7	2.3
Hispanic or Latino ethnicity, 16 years and older	**18,296**	**11,174**	**7,122**	**1,930**	**1,156**	**774**	**10.5**	**10.3**	**10.9**
Less than a high school diploma	6,608	4,509	2,098	1,170	733	437	17.7	16.3	20.8
Less than 1 year of high school	3,530	2,508	1,022	660	458	202	18.7	18.3	19.8
1–3 years of high school	2,535	1,628	908	437	228	209	17.2	14.0	23.0
4 years of high school, no diploma	542	373	169	73	47	26	13.5	12.5	15.6
High school graduates, no college[b]	5,461	3,341	2,119	462	278	184	8.5	8.3	8.7
Some college or associate degree	4,043	2,110	1,933	231	114	118	5.7	5.4	6.1
Some college, no degree	2,968	1,573	1,395	176	91	85	5.9	5.8	6.1
Associate degree	1,075	537	538	55	23	32	5.1	4.2	6.0
Bachelor's degree and higher[3]	2,185	1,214	971	66	31	35	3.0	2.6	3.6

Note: Estimates for the above race groups (white, black or African American, and Asian) do not sum to totals because data are not presented for all races. In addition, people whose ethnicity is identified as Hispanic or Latino may be of any race and, therefore, are classified by ethnicity as well as by race.
[a]Number below the poverty level as a percent of the total in the labor force for 27 weeks or more.
[b]Includes people with a high school diploma or equivalent.
[c]Includes people with bachelor's, master's, professional, and doctoral degrees.
[d]Data not shown where base is less than 80,000.

SOURCE: "Table 3. People in the Labor Force for 27 Weeks or More: Poverty Status by Educational Attainment, Race, Hispanic or Latino Ethnicity, and Sex, 2004," in *A Profile of the Working Poor, 2004*, U.S. Department of Labor, Bureau of Labor Statistics, December 2006, http://www.bls.gov/cps/cpswp2004.pdf (accessed January 23, 2007)

TABLE 2.15

Poverty status of families, by selected characteristics, 2004

[Numbers in thousands]

Characteristic	Total families	At or above poverty level	Below poverty level	Rate*
Total primary families	**63,912**	**59,652**	**4,261**	**6.7**
With related children under 18 years	36,154	32,565	3,589	9.9
Without children	27,758	27,087	671	2.4
With one member in the labor force	27,307	23,696	3,611	13.2
With two or more members in the labor force	36,605	35,956	649	1.8
With two members	30,960	30,361	599	1.9
With three or more members	5,645	5,595	50	.9
Married-couple families	48,675	46,725	1,950	4.0
With related children under 18 years	26,288	24,742	1,546	5.9
Without children	22,387	21,983	404	1.8
With one member in the labor force	16,727	15,255	1,471	8.8
Husband	12,664	11,463	1,202	9.5
Wife	3,477	3,249	228	6.6
Relative	585	543	42	7.1
With two or more members in the labor force	31,949	31,470	479	1.5
With two members	27,241	26,793	448	1.6
With three or more members	4,708	4,677	31	.7
Families maintained by women	10,944	9,019	1,925	17.6
With related children under 18 years	7,548	5,793	1,755	23.3
Without children	3,396	3,226	170	5.0
With one member in the labor force	7,937	6,143	1,793	22.6
Householder	6,611	5,009	1,602	24.2
Relative	1,326	1,134	191	14.4
With two or more members in the labor force	3,007	2,875	132	4.4
Families maintained by men	4,293	3,908	385	9.0
With related children under 18 years	2,319	2,030	289	12.4
Without children	1,975	1,878	96	4.9
With one member in the labor force	2,644	2,298	347	13.1
Householder	2,217	1,932	285	12.9
Relative	427	366	61	14.3
With two or more members in the labor force	1,649	1,611	39	2.3

Note: Data relate to primary families with at least one member in the labor force for 27 weeks or more.
*Number below the poverty level as a percent of the total in the labor force for 27 weeks or more.

SOURCE: "Table 5. Primary Families: Poverty Status, Presence of Related Children, and Work Experience of Family Members in the Labor Force for 27 Weeks or More, 2004," in *A Profile of the Working Poor, 2004*, U.S. Department of Labor, Bureau of Labor Statistics, December 2006, http://www.bls.gov/cps/cpswp2004.pdf (accessed January 23, 2007)

TABLE 2.16

Poverty status and labor market problems of full-time wage and salary workers, 2004

[Numbers in thousands]

Poverty status and labor market problems	Total	At or above poverty level	Below poverty level	Rate[a]
Total, full-time wage and salary workers	109,297	105,520	3,777	3.5
No unemployment, involuntary part-time employment, or low earnings[b]	90,805	90,076	729	.8
Unemployment only	5,612	5,188	424	7.6
Involuntary part-time employment only	2,325	2,270	55	2.4
Low earnings only	7,244	5,620	1,623	22.4
Unemployment and involuntary part-time employment	998	924	74	7.4
Unemployment and low earnings	1,318	789	530	40.2
Involuntary part-time employment and low earnings	682	461	221	32.4
Unemployment, involuntary part-time employment, and low earnings	313	191	122	38.8
Unemployment (alone or with other problems)	8,242	7,093	1,149	13.9
Involuntary part-time employment (alone or with other problems)	4,318	3,847	472	10.9
Low earnings (alone or with other problems)	9,557	7,062	2,495	26.1

[a]Number below the poverty level as a percent of the total in the labor force for 27 weeks or more.
[b]The low-earnings threshold in 2004 was $278.03 per week.

SOURCE: "Table 8. People in the Labor Force for 27 Weeks or More: Poverty Status and Labor Market Problems of Full-Time Wage and Salary Workers, 2004," in *A Profile of the Working Poor, 2004*, U.S. Department of Labor, Bureau of Labor Statistics, December 2006, http://www.bls.gov/cps/cpswp2004.pdf (accessed January 23, 2007)

FIGURE 2.11

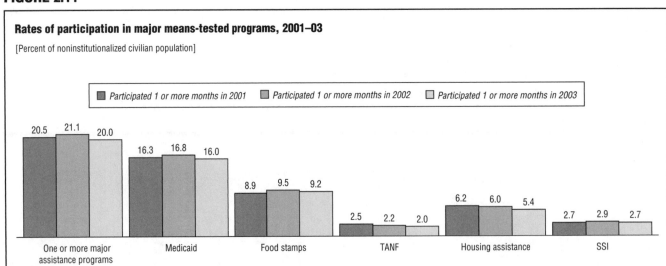

Rates of participation in major means-tested programs, 2001–03

[Percent of noninstitutionalized civilian population]

■ Participated 1 or more months in 2001　■ Participated 1 or more months in 2002　□ Participated 1 or more months in 2003

Notes: TANF is Temporary Assistance for Needy Families. SSI is Supplemental Security Income.

SOURCE: Tracy A. Loveless and Jan Tin, "Figure 4. Program Participation Rates for Major Means-Tested Programs: 2001, 2002, and 2003," in *Dynamics of Economic Well-Being: Participation in Government Programs, 2001 through 2003, Who Gets Assistance?—Current Population Reports*, U.S. Census Bureau, October 2006, http://www.census.gov/prod/2006pubs/p70-108.pdf (accessed January 2, 2007)

FIGURE 2.12

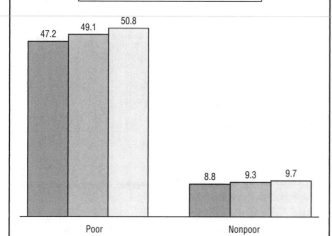

Average monthly rates of participation in major means-tested programs, by poverty status, 2001–03

[Percent of noninstitutionalized civilian population]

- ■ Average monthly participation rate for 2001
- ■ Average monthly participation rate for 2002
- □ Average monthly participation rate for 2003

SOURCE: Tracy A. Loveless and Jan Tin, "Figure 7. Average Monthly Participation Rates in Major Means-Tested Programs by Poverty Status: 2001, 2002, and 2003," in *Dynamics of Economic Well-Being: Participation in Government Programs, 2001 through 2003, Who Gets Assistance?—Current Population Reports*, U.S. Census Bureau, October 2006, http://www.census.gov/prod/2006pubs/p70-108.pdf (accessed January 2, 2007)

FIGURE 2.13

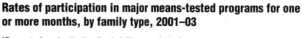

Rates of participation in major means-tested programs for one or more months, by family type, 2001–03

[Percent of noninstitutionalized civilian population]

- ■ Participated 1 or more months in 2001
- ■ Participated 1 or more months in 2002
- □ Participated 1 or more months in 2003

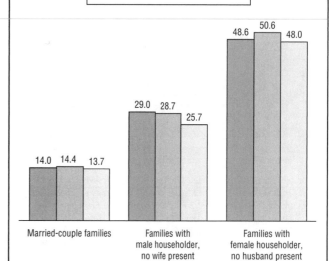

SOURCE: Tracy A. Loveless and Jan Tin, "Figure 14. Program Participation for 1 or More Months in Major Means-Tested Programs by Family Type: 2001, 2002, and 2003," in *Dynamics of Economic Well-Being: Participation in Government Programs, 2001 through 2003, Who Gets Assistance?—Current Population Reports*, U.S. Census Bureau, October 2006, http://www.census.gov/prod/2006pubs/ p70-108.pdf (accessed January 2, 2007)

FIGURE 2.14

FIGURE 2.15

Average monthly rates of participation in major means-tested programs, by educational level, 2001–03

[Percent of noninstitutionalized civilian population. People 18 years and older.]

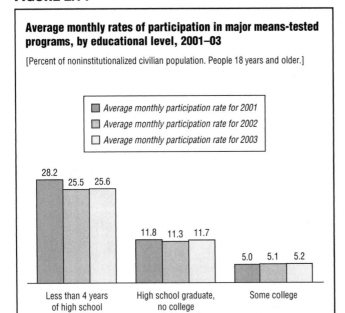

SOURCE: Tracy A. Loveless and Jan Tin, "Figure 17: Average Monthly Participation Rates in Major Means-Tested Programs by Educational Attainment: 2001, 2002, and 2003," in *Dynamics of Economic Well-Being: Participation in Government Programs, 2001 through 2003, Who Gets Assistance?—Current Population Reports*, U.S. Census Bureau, October 2006, http://www.census.gov/prod/2006pubs/p70-108 .pdf (accessed January 2, 2007)

Median spell length in major means-tested programs, by type of program, 2001–03

[In months]

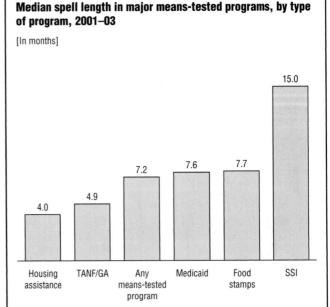

Notes: TANF is Temporary Assistance for Needy Families. GA is government assistance. SSI is Supplemental Security Income.

SOURCE: Tracy A. Loveless and Jan Tin, "Figure 20. Median Spell Length by Program: January 2001–December 2003," in *Dynamics of Economic Well-Being: Participation in Government Programs, 2001 through 2003, Who Gets Assistance?—Current Population Reports*, U.S. Census Bureau, October 2006, http://www.census.gov/prod/ 2006pubs/p70-108.pdf (accessed January 2, 2007)

TABLE 2.17

Median spell length in major means-tested programs, by type of program and demographic characteristics, 2001–03

[In months]

Characteristic	Any means-tested programs[a] Median	TANF/GA Median	Supplemental Security Income Median	Food stamps Median	Medicaid Median	Housing assistance[b] Median
All recipients[c]	7.2	4.9	15.0	7.7	7.6	4.0
Race and Hispanic origin[d]						
White	7.1	4.0	15.0	7.4	7.6	3.9
Not Hispanic	7.0	4.0	11.7	7.5	7.6	3.9
Black	7.5	6.5	11.8	8.6	7.9	7.5
Asian or Pacific Islander	3.9	11.4	(X)	7.1	7.0	3.7
Hispanic	7.2	4.0	22.3	7.0	7.7	3.9
Not Hispanic	7.2	5.4	11.9	7.8	7.6	4.0
Age[e]						
Under 18 years	7.9	6.3	11.3	8.8	9.7	7.0
18 to 64 years	5.4	4.0	15.0	7.1	7.4	3.9
65 years and older	4.0	(B)	15.7	19.8	4.9	7.9
Sex						
Men	7.0	5.7	15.2	7.2	7.7	3.9
Women	7.3	4.4	12.0	8.2	7.6	5.0
Educational attainment (people 18 and older)						
Less than high school graduate	7.4	4.3	19.7	10.2	7.7	7.2
High school graduate, no college	5.6	3.9	16.2	7.0	7.2	3.9
Some college	3.9	3.9	7.9	5.2	5.0	3.8
Disability status (people 15 to 64 years old)						
With a work disability	7.8	4.0	19.3	11.6	9.3	7.6
With no work disability	4.5	4.0	7.8	6.5	7.1	3.8
Residence						
Metropolitan	7.1	5.9	11.9	7.6	7.6	4.0
Central city	7.1	6.9	11.9	7.8	7.6	4.4
Noncentral city	7.2	5.6	13.4	7.3	7.6	3.9
Nonmetropolitan	7.4	3.8	19.0	7.9	7.9	3.9
Region						
Northeast	7.2	7.2	15.6	9.0	7.6	4.0
Midwest	7.3	5.3	11.7	7.7	7.8	7.3
South	7.2	3.8	12.9	8.0	7.6	3.9
West	7.0	5.1	11.5	6.1	7.6	3.9
Family status						
In families	7.2	4.9	11.5	7.6	7.7	4.0
In married-couple families	6.9	3.9	11.5	6.0	7.3	3.8
In families with a female householder, no husband present	7.7	5.8	11.3	8.8	9.9	7.6
In families with a male householder, no wife present	7.3	3.8	15.7	8.4	7.8	3.8
Unrelated individuals	5.2	4.6	(X)	9.5	7.6	3.9
Employment and labor force status (people 18 and older)						
Employed full-time[f]	3.8	3.7	3.9	3.9	3.9	3.7
Employed part-time	6.6	3.7	11.6	6.3	7.3	4.0
Unemployed	7.2	3.9	(B)	8.4	7.5	5.1
Not in labor force	7.2	4.7	19.0	11.4	7.5	7.3

TABLE 2.17

Median spell length in major means-tested programs, by type of program and demographic characteristics, 2001–03 [CONTINUED]

[In months]

Characteristic	Any means-tested programs[a] Median	TANF/GA Median	Supplemental Security Income Median	Food stamps Median	Medicaid Median	Housing assistance[b] Median
Family income-to-poverty ratio[g]						
Under 1.00	10.0	5.9	(X)	11.5	11.4	7.6
1.00 and over	6.0	3.9	11.3	5.8	7.3	3.8

(X) Not applicable. (B) The sample size is too small for analysis.

[a]Major means-tested programs include Temporary Assistance for Needy Families (TANF), General Assistance (GA), Supplemental Security Income (SSI), food stamps, Medicaid, and housing assistance.

[b]Median duration cannot be computed when more than half of the spells are continuing in the last month of data collection. (This situation is especially likely to occur for elderly recipients whose incomes from other sources are unlikely to rise over time.)

[c]Median duration for each program is derived only for those who begin participating in each program at the start of the survey, while those who are already in the program at the start of the survey are excluded from the analysis.

[d]Hispanics may be any race.

[e]Age, educational attainment, and other variables are measured at the time the spells begin, except that, for those who are already on programs at the start of the survey, these characteristics are measured at the first interview.

[f]Full-time and part-time employment reflects the average employment status.

[g]Family income-to-poverty threshold ratio reflects the monthly poverty status. A ratio of under 1.00 indicates that a person is in poverty, whereas a ratio of higher than or equal to 1.00 indicates that a person is not in poverty.

SOURCE: Tracy A. Loveless and Jan Tin, "Table A7. Median Duration of Participation in Major Means-Tested Programs by Program: 2001–2003 (in months)," in *Dynamics of Economic Well-Being: Participation in Government Programs, 2001 through 2003, Who Gets Assistance?—Current Population Reports* U.S. Census Bureau, October 2006, http://www.census.gov/prod/2006pubs/p70-108.pdf (accessed January 2, 2007)

CHAPTER 3
PUBLIC PROGRAMS TO FIGHT POVERTY

There are many methods which the federal government and the states use to combat poverty. There are a variety of programs that provide assistance to those in or at risk of poverty. These are often referred to as welfare. Some of these programs, like Temporary Aid for Needy Families (TANF), are designed to help people improve their situation so they will no longer be poor. The Supplemental Security Income (SSI) program provides assistance to people who have conditions that make it difficult to earn a living. A number of programs, including Food Stamps and Medicaid, are intended to help those in poverty meet their basic needs for food, shelter, and medical care (these programs are discussed in Chapter 7). Besides welfare programs, the government has established programs and policies like the minimum wage and unemployment compensation that are intended to help people avoid poverty in the first place.

The most far-reaching welfare law is the Personal Responsibility and Work Opportunity Reconciliation Act (PRWORA). First enacted in 1996 and renewed since, PRWORA replaced a welfare system based primarily on the Aid to Families with Dependent Children (AFDC) program with one centered on TANF. Critics of AFDC felt that the system produced welfare dependency rather than temporary assistance to help recipients move into a job and off welfare. TANF was specifically designed to limit the amount of time individuals could receive benefits, and to require that they work. The intention of the law was to reduce the number of people receiving welfare by bringing them into the workforce and out of poverty. PRWORA also changed some other welfare programs to place greater emphasis on these priorities.

According to the U.S. Department of Health and Human Services (HHS), in *Temporary Assistance for Needy Families Program (TANF): Sixth Annual Report to Congress* (November 2004, http://www.acf.hhs.gov//programs/ofa/annualreport6/chapter10/chap10.pdf), the welfare caseload fell from a monthly average of 4.5 million families during fiscal year (FY) 1996 to an average of 2.1 million families per month during FY 2002, a drop of 53%. This represented the largest welfare caseload decline in history. Observers agreed that some of the decline was the result of a strong economy in which unemployment was around 4%, an unprecedented low, rather than welfare reform. For example, a study conducted by the City University of New York and cited by the HHS in *Temporary Assistance for Needy Families Program (TANF): Fourth Annual Report to Congress* (April 2002, http://www.acf.hhs.gov/programs/ofa/opreweb/ar2001/indexar.htm) attributes 60% of the reductions in caseloads to welfare reform and 20% to the effects of a robust economy.

Critics of PRWORA question if the reduction in welfare caseloads are really a good thing. They are concerned that the system's time limits and its focus on moving people off of welfare and into work forces some individuals off of benefits even if they have a genuine need for them. For instance in states that are unable to provide jobs with a living wage the PRWORA system may merely move the poor population from welfare into low-wage work and deeper into poverty. In the fact sheet "TANF at 10" (August 17, 2006, http://www.cbpp.org/8-17-06tanf.htm), Sharon Parrott and Arloc Sherman note that the share of poor children who received TANF benefits dropped by half from 1995 to 2003, from 62% in 1995 to 31% in 2003. Parrott and Sherman state, "More than half—57%—of the caseload decline during the first decade of welfare reform reflects a decline in the extent to which TANF programs serve families that are poor enough to qualify, rather than to a reduction in the number of families who are poor enough to qualify for aid." As a result of these concerns, modifications to welfare legislation continue to be proposed.

PERSONAL RESPONSIBILITY AND WORK OPPORTUNITY RECONCILIATION ACT

Title I: Block Grants

Under the PRWORA each state receives a single block grant (a lump sum of money) for TANF programs. The amount of money available under TANF has remained steady at about $16 billion per year. However, Gene Falk points out in *Temporary Assistance for Needy Families (TANF) Block Grant: FY2007 Budget Proposals* (March 3, 2006, http://www.nationalaglawcenter.org/assets/crs/RS22385.pdf) that in constant dollars federal welfare spending has steadily decreased since 2001.

States have considerable control over how they implement the programs covered by the block grant, but the act requires that:

- Families on welfare for five cumulative years no longer receive further cash assistance. States can set shorter time limits and can exempt up to 20% of their caseload from the time limits.

- To count toward meeting the work requirement, a state must require individuals to participate in employment (public or private), on-the-job training, community service, work experience, vocational training (up to twelve months), or child care for other workers for at least twenty hours per week. State and local communities are responsible for the development of work, whether by creating community service jobs or by providing income subsidies or hiring incentives for potential employers.

- Unmarried parents under the age of eighteen must live with an adult or with adult supervision and must participate in educational or job training to receive benefits. In addition, the law encourages second-chance homes (discussed later in this chapter) to provide teen parents with the skills and support they need. The law also provides $50 million per year in new funding for state abstinence education activities, geared toward discouraging teen pregnancy through abstinence rather than through birth control.

None of the block grant funds can be used for adults who have been on welfare for over five years or who do not work after receiving benefits for two years. However, states are offered some flexibility in how to spend their TANF funds.

Title II: Supplemental Security Income

The PRWORA redefined the term *disability* for children who receive Supplemental Security Income (SSI). A child is considered disabled if he or she has a medically determinable physical or mental impairment that results in marked and severe functional limitations that can be expected to cause death or has lasted or can be expected to last at least twelve months. The PRWORA removed "maladaptive behavior" as a medical criterion from the listing of impairments used for evaluating mental disabilities in children.

Title III: Child Support

To be eligible for federal funds, each state must operate a Child Support Enforcement program that meets federal guidelines. The state must establish centralized registries of child support orders and centers for collection and disbursement of child support payments, and parents must sign their child support rights over to the state to be eligible for TANF benefits. The state must also establish enforcement methods, such as revoking the driver's and professional licenses of delinquent parents. The HHS's Administration for Children and Families notes in the fact sheet "Office of Child Support Enforcement" (October 2006, http://www.acf.hhs.gov/opa/fact_sheets/cse_factsheet.html) that in FY 2005 the program collected $23 billion at a cost of $5.4 billion. Federal funding for this program continues to increase; in FY 2005, $3.5 billion in federal funding was provided to states to help fund their programs; in FY 2006, $3.9 billion was provided.

To receive full benefits, a mother must cooperate with state efforts to establish paternity. She may be denied assistance if she refuses to disclose the father.

Title IV: Restricting Welfare and Public Benefits for Noncitizens

The PRWORA originally severely limited or banned benefits to most legal immigrants who entered the country on or after the date on which the bill became law. Ineligibility continued for a five-year period or until they attained citizenship. In addition, states had the option of withholding eligibility for Medicaid, TANF, and other social services from legal immigrants already residing in the United States. Refugees, including those who had come for political asylum or other sanctuary, veterans, and Cuban/Haitian immigrants were exempted from the five-year ban.

Illegal immigrants no longer had any entitlement to benefit programs, such as TANF or Medicaid. They could receive emergency medical care, short-term disaster relief, immunizations, and treatment for communicable diseases (in the interest of public health). They could also use community services such as soup kitchens and shelters, some housing programs, and school lunches/breakfasts if their children were eligible for free public education. States established programs to verify the legal residence of immigrants before paying benefits and may elect to deny Women, Infants, and Children (WIC) benefits and other child nutrition programs to illegal aliens.

The Balanced Budget Act of 1997 and the Noncitizen Technical Amendment Act of 1998 invested $11.5 billion to restore disability and health benefits to 380,000 legal immigrants who were in the United States before welfare reform became law on August 22, 1996. The Balanced Budget Act also extended the SSI and Medicaid eligibility period for refugees and people seeking asylum from five years after entry to seven years to give these residents more time to naturalize.

Title V: Child Protection

The PRWORA gave states the authority to use current federal funds to pay for foster care for children in child care institutions. It extended the enhanced federal match for statewide automated child welfare information systems through 1997 and appropriated $6 million per year (FY 1996 to FY 2002) for a national random sample study of abused and neglected children.

Title VI: Child Care

The law required that states maintain spending for child care for low-income families at the level of FY 1994 or FY 1995, whichever was greater, to be eligible for federally matched funds. Mandatory funding was set at $13.9 billion through June 30, 2004, with states receiving an estimated $1.2 billion per year before matching began. The remainder of the funds was available for state matching at the Medicaid rate. Total federal and state expenditures on child care totaled $3.2 billion in 2000, an increase of 60% over 1999 ($2 billion). The Congressional Budget Office (CBO), in *Cost Estimate* (January 27, 2006, http://www.cbo.gov/ftpdocs/70xx/doc7028/s1932 conf.pdf), states that the Deficit Reduction Act of 2005, which reauthorized the PRWORA, provides for increased annual federal funding for child care by $11.7 billion by 2010.

As under prior law, states must establish standards for prevention and control of infectious diseases, such as immunization programs, and for building codes and physical safety in child care institutions. Child care workers must also receive minimal training in health and safety. However, many low-income people rely on informal sources of child care, including relatives and friends.

Pamela Holcomb et al. indicate in *Child Care Subsidies and TANF: A Synthesis of Three Studies on Systems, Policies, and Parents* (2006, http://www.urban.org/Uploaded PDF/311302_synthesis.pdf) that despite increased federal funding for child care, the need outweighs the resources available under the law. As a result of more parents working while still on welfare or leaving welfare to work, the critical need for child care has become more pronounced. In *The Changing Role of Welfare in the Lives of Low-Income Families with Children* (August 2006, http://www.urban.org/ UploadedPDF/311357_occa73.pdf), Pamela Loprest and

Sheila Zedlewski report that only 21.4% of families who received TANF monies in 2002 received help paying for child care in that year. Even though the child care support system gives priority to families leaving welfare for work over other low-income families, only four out of ten families (40.8%) that had recently stopped receiving TANF monies received help paying for child care.

Title VII: Child Nutrition Programs

The PRWORA continued existing child nutrition programs, such as the school lunch and breakfast programs. Maximum reimbursement was reduced, however, for the Summer Food Service Program and for some institutional food programs. States were allowed to decide whether to include or exclude legal immigrants from these programs. According to the U.S. Department of Agriculture (USDA), in *FY 2007 Budget Summary and Annual Performance Plan* (2007, http://www.obpa.usda.gov/budsum/ 2007/fy07budsum.pdf), the budget for FY 2007 child nutrition programs was $13.8 billion, an increase of $439 million over the previous year.

Title VIII: Food Stamps and Commodities

The law reduced maximum benefits to the level of the Thrifty Food Plan, the index set by the USDA that reflects the amount of money needed to purchase food to meet minimal nutrition requirements. Benefits were indexed to the rate of inflation so that they increase as inflation rises.

The law also restructured the way certain expenses and earnings were counted in establishing eligibility for food stamps. Under the PRWORA, when recipients' benefits are calculated, their countable monthly income is reduced by several deductions, including a standard deduction, a deduction for excessively high shelter expenses, a dependent care deduction, and medical expenses for the elderly and disabled. These deductions raised food stamp allotments. In the fact sheet "Food Stamp Program" (January 4, 2007, http://www.fns.usda.gov/fsp/applicant_recipients/ fs_Res_Ben_Elig.htm), the USDA reports that through September 30, 2007, the maximum monthly allotment for a household of one was $155, for a household of two was $284, for a household of three was $408, and for a household of four was $518.

By law, all food stamp recipients who are eighteen to fifty years old and without children (known as able-bodied adults without dependents [ABAWD]) must work at least part time or be limited to three months of assistance in a thirty-six-month period. Recipients who were in a workfare program (a welfare program that usually requires recipients to perform public-service duties) for thirty days but lost their placement may qualify for an additional three months of food stamps. (This provision was revised to allow states to exempt 15% of ABAWD recipients from this restriction.)

PRWORA Reauthorization

Since 1996 many changes have been made to the PRWORA. The PRWORA was reauthorized through 2010 when President George W. Bush signed the Deficit Reduction Act of 2005 in February 2006. This bill did not increase funding for TANF programs and further restricted eligibility requirements. The Communications Workers of America noted critically in "TANF Reauthorization" (March 2, 2006, http://www.cwa-legislative.org/fact-sheets/page.jsp?itemID=27482970) that the basic TANF block grant did not increase with inflation but remained capped at $16 billion. Funding for child care was set at $2 billion for each year between 2006 and 2010. Child support enforcement funding was reduced. Drug testing became required for every TANF applicant and recipient. Finally, the bill allowed TANF funds to be used to promote the value of marriage through public advertising and high school and adult classes and mentoring programs.

ELIGIBILITY FOR TANF AND BENEFIT PAYMENTS

Under TANF, states decide how much to aid a needy family. No federal guidelines exist for determining eligibility, and no requirement mandates that states aid all needy families. Though TANF does not require states to have a need standard or a gross income limit, as the AFDC did, many states have based their TANF programs in part on their earlier practices.

The maximum benefit is the amount paid to a family with no countable income. (Federal law specifies what income counts toward figuring benefits and what income, such as child support, is to be disregarded by the state.) The maximum benefit is to be paid only to those families that comply with TANF's work requirements or other program requirements established by the state, such as parental and personal responsibility rules.

Although most states vary benefits according to family size, some eliminate or restrict benefit increases because of the birth of a new child to a recipient already receiving benefits, in effect penalizing poor families for having children. Instead, benefits depend on family size at the time of enrollment in sixteen states. Idaho pays a flat monthly grant that is the same regardless of family size. Wisconsin pays benefits based on work activity of the recipient and not on family size. Five states provide an increase in benefits to TANF families following the birth of an additional child.

Most states did not change their maximum benefits between July 1994 and January 2003, despite the major changes brought about by the PRWORA. When taking inflation into account, the value of benefits in most states has actually declined. (See Table 3.1.)

Most families receiving TANF benefits are also eligible for food stamps. A single benefit determination is made for both cash and food assistance. Though the eligibility and benefit amounts for TANF are determined by the states, food stamp eligibility and benefit amounts are determined by federal law and are consistent in all states.

Food stamp benefits, which are administered by the USDA, are not counted in determining the TANF cash benefit. However, TANF benefits are considered part of a family's countable income in determining food stamp benefits, which are reduced $0.30 for each dollar of countable income. Therefore, food stamp benefits are higher in states with lower TANF benefits and vice versa. As of January 1, 2003, combined monthly benefits for a family of three were lowest in Mississippi ($525), Puerto Rico ($532), Tennessee ($535), Texas ($546), and Arkansas ($549). (See Table 3.2.) Alaska ($1,157) and Hawaii ($1,012) had the highest combined benefit for a family of three. (Poverty guidelines are higher in these two states because of higher costs of living.) Other states that paid the most in benefits included Vermont ($902), California ($881 in region 1), and New York ($898 in Suffolk County).

Who Gets TANF Benefits?

In 2003 an average of 3.7 million people, or 1.3% of the population, received TANF benefits each month. (See Table 3.3.) Some groups in the population were more likely to receive these benefits than others. Children under eighteen years old were more likely than adults to receive TANF benefits—3.4%—compared with only 0.7% of adults aged eighteen to sixty-four years and 0.1% of adults aged sixty-five and older. Women were more likely than men to receive TANF benefits (1.5% and 1.1%, respectively), reflecting their role as the primary caretakers of children.

A higher proportion of African-Americans (3.7%) received TANF benefits each month in 2003 than any other racial or ethnic group. (See Table 3.3.) Among other groups, 2.7% of Hispanics, 1.5% of Asians and Pacific Islanders, and 0.5% of non-Hispanic whites received benefits, on average, each month.

Single female-headed families were by far the most likely family group to receive TANF benefits each month in 2003. More than one out of twenty of these families (5.6%) received TANF benefits each month, compared with 1.3% of single male-headed families and 0.5% of married-couple families. (See Table 3.3.)

Adults who had a high school education or less were much more likely than their better-educated peers to receive TANF in 2003, reflecting the difficulty of earning

TABLE 3.1

Maximum AFDC/TANF benefit[a] for a family of three (parent with two children), by state, selected years 1994–2003

State	July 1994	July 1996	July 1998	January 2000	January 2002	January 2003	Percent real change from July 1994 to January 2003[b]
Alabama	164	164	164	164	164	215	−7.0
Alaska	923	923	923	923	923	923	−18.3
Arizona	347	347	347	347	347	347	−18.3
Arkansas	204	204	204	204	204	204	−18.3
California	607	596	565	626	679	679	−8.6
Colorado	356	356	356	356	356	356	−18.3
Connecticut	680	636	636	636	636	636	−23.6
Delaware	338	338	338	338	338	338	−18.3
District of Columbia	420	415	379	379	379	379	−26.3
Florida	303	303	303	303	303	303	−18.3
Georgia	280	280	280	280	280	280	−18.3
Hawaii	712	712	570	570	570	570	−34.6
Idaho	317	317	276	293	293	309	−20.4
Illinois	377	377	377	377	377	396	−14.2
Indiana	288	288	288	288	288	288	−18.3
Iowa	426	426	426	426	426	426	−18.3
Kansas	429	429	429	429	429	429	−18.3
Kentucky	262	262	262	262	262	262	−18.3
Louisiana	190	190	190	190	240	240	3.2
Maine	418	418	439	461	485	485	−5.2
Maryland	373	373	388	417	472	473	3.69
Massachusetts	579	565	565	565	618	618	−12.8
Michigan–Washtenaw County	489	489	489	489	489	489	−18.3
Minnesota	532	532	532	532	532	532	−18.3
Mississippi	120	120	120	170	170	170	15.7
Missouri	292	292	292	292	292	292	−18.3
Montana	416	438	461	469	494	507	−0.5
Nebraska	364	364	364	364	364	364	−18.3
Nevada	348	348	348	348	348	348	−18.3
New Hampshire	550	550	550	575	600	625	−7.2
New Jersey	424	424	424	424	424	424	−18.3
New Mexico	389	389	439	439	439	389	−18.3
New York–New York City	577	577	577	577	577	577	−18.3
New York–Suffolk County	703	703	703	703	703	703	−18.3
North Carolina	272	272	272	272	272	272	−18.3
North Dakota	431	431	440	457	477	477	−9.6
Ohio	341	341	362	373	373	373	−10.7
Oklahoma	324	307	292	292	292	292	−26.4
Oregon	460	460	460	460	460	460	−18.3
Pennsylvania	421	421	421	421	421	421	−18.3
Rhode Island	554	554	554	554	554	554	−18.3
South Carolina	200	200	201	204	205	205	−16.3
South Dakota	430	430	430	430	469	483	−8.3
Tennessee	185	185	185	185	185	185	−18.3
Texas	188	188	188	201	201	201	−12.7
Utah	414	416	451	451	474	474	−6.5
Vermont	650	633	656	708	709	709	−10.9
Virginia	354	354	354	354	389	389	−10.3
Washington	546	546	546	546	546	546	−18.3
West Virginia	253	253	253	328	453	453	46.2
Wisconsin	517	517	673	673	673	673	6.3
Wisconsin–W2 Transitions	517	517	628	628	628	628	−0.8
Wyoming	360	360	340	340	340	340	−22.9

[a]This table presents maximum benefits generally available to families without income. Some states pay larger benefits to certain categories of recipients. For example, Hawaii and Massachusetts have a separate benefit schedule for persons whom they exempt from work. Also, some states supplement benefits for families with special needs.
[b]The inflation factor used to convert July 1994 dollars to January 2003 dollars was 1.2244 (representing the change in the Consumer Price Index for all urban consumers).
Notes: AFDC is Aid to Families with Dependent Children. TANF is Temporary Assistance for Needy Families.

SOURCE: "Table 7.10. Maximum AFDC/TANF Benefit for a Family of Three (Parent with Two Children), July 1994–January 2003," in *The Green Book*, U.S. House of Representatives, Committee on Ways and Means, 2004, http://waysandmeans.house.gov/media/pdf/greenbook2003/Section7.pdf (accessed January 11, 2007)

a living wage without some higher education. In that year 1.4% of adults who had not received a high school diploma received TANF assistance each month, compared with 0.5% of high school graduates and 0.2% of adults who had attended college. (See Table 3.3.)

Because TANF is designed to help those most in need, it is not surprising that most people who received TANF in 2003 were poor. In that year 6.1% of people below the poverty line received TANF assistance each month, compared with 0.5% of people who lived in

TABLE 3.2

Maximum combined TANF and food benefits for single-parent family from one to six persons, January 1, 2003

State	Family size					
	1	2	3	4	5	6
Alabama	$294	$429	$556	$676	$789	$926
Alaska	597	952	1,157	1,455	1,526	1,732
Arizona	322	488	649	797	939	1,106
Arkansas	220	409	549	678	797	945
California–region 1	414	679	881	1,071	1,241	1,436
California–region 2	402	660	859	1,044	1,210	1,402
Colorado	329	492	655	807	955	1,126
Connecticut	460	655	851	1,023	1,181	1,367
Delaware	319	485	642	790	929	1,094
District of Columbia	346	504	671	829	970	1,152
Florida	305	464	618	760	895	1,054
Georgia	287	460	602	736	861	1,000
Hawaii	503	762	1,012	1,244	1,460	1,711
Idaho	395	512	622	721	813	929
Illinois	335	500	683	809	953	1,113
Indiana	276	456	607	747	880	1,037
Iowa	307	548	704	851	980	1,140
Kansas	366	542	706	853	987	1,146
Kentucky	309	453	589	734	865	1,015
Louisiana	261	427	574	704	826	969
Maine	340	550	745	932	1,110	1,312
Maryland	326	557	737	905	1,060	1,223
Massachusetts	471	658	838	1,004	1,165	1,351
Michigan–Washtenaw County	392	576	748	920	1,079	1,288
Michigan–Wayne County	372	555	727	899	1,058	1,267
Minnesota	354	602	778	939	1,085	1,254
Mississippi	249	398	525	641	749	882
Missouri	274	460	610	744	868	1,015
Montana	388	578	761	932	1,097	1,286
Nebraska	334	501	661	809	951	1,117
Nevada	340	498	649	790	923	1,080
New Hampshire	521	685	843	986	1,120	1,293
New Jersey	292	521	703	846	983	1,144
New Mexico	340	513	678	833	980	1,152
New York–Suffolk County	491	699	898	1,082	1,261	1,440
North Carolina	305	461	596	713	823	957
North Dakota	376	560	740	906	1,066	1,250
Ohio	335	509	667	827	974	1,133
Oklahoma	305	453	610	757	892	1,051
Oregon	396	572	728	900	1,059	1,241
Pennsylvania	329	527	700	865	1,022	1,194
Puerto Rico	271	405	532	648	756	889
Rhode Island	408	610	794	949	1,096	1,269
South Carolina	260	410	549	678	800	945
South Dakota	426	598	744	878	1,005	1,158
Tennessee	234	395	535	663	781	926
Texas	223	418	546	673	784	929
Utah	371	562	738	893	1,039	1,200
Vermont	531	719	902	1,061	1,216	1,375
Virginia	348	522	678	820	973	1,124
Washington	423	604	788	954	1,115	1,302
West Virginia	423	576	723	863	989	1,142

TABLE 3.2

Maximum combined TANF and food benefits for single-parent family from one to six persons, January 1, 2003 [CONTINUED]

State	Family size					
	1	2	3	4	5	6
Wisconsin–community service	(*)	767	877	976	1,068	1,184
Wisconsin–W2 transitions	(*)	735	845	944	1,036	1,153

Notes:
Food stamp calculations assume that the family does not receive an excess shelter deduction. In many states with low TANF (Temporary Assistance for Needy Families) benefits, combined benefits shown reflect the maximum food stamp allotment for the family size, but in some states the excess shelter deduction would increase food stamps (by up to $110 monthly–more in Alaska and Hawaii). Calculations assume a single-parent family with no earned income.
*Wisconsin has no one-person families in its regular W-2 (TANF) program. Pregnant women without children are ineligible and "child-only" recipients have been moved into special programs of kinship care and SSI (Supplemental Security Income) caretaker supplements. The kinship care payment is $215 monthly per child; the SSI caretaker supplement program provides $250 monthly for the first eligible child and $150 for each additional child.

SOURCE: "Table 7-12. Maximum Combined TANF and Food Benefits for Single-Parent Family from One to Six Persons, January 1, 2003," in *The Green Book*, U.S. House of Representatives, Committee on Ways and Means, 2004, http://waysandmeans.house.gov/media/pdf/greenbook2003/Section7.pdf (accessed January 11, 2007).

receive TANF benefits is much lower than the lifetime limit. Between 2001 and 2003 TANF recipients received benefits for a median of 4.9 months. (See Table 2.17 in Chapter 2.) Children under eighteen years old tended to received TANF for a longer period; they received benefits for a median of 6.3 months, compared with a median of four months for adults aged eighteen to sixty-four.

Asians and Pacific Islanders had a much higher median duration of participation in TANF than did other racial and ethnic groups. Between 2001 and 2003 Asians and Pacific Islanders had a median duration of 11.4 months, compared with 6.5 months for African-Americans and four months for Hispanics and non-Hispanic whites. (See Table 2.17 in Chapter 2.)

People in families headed by a single female had a higher median duration of participation in TANF than did other family types. Between 2001 and 2003 these families had a median duration of 5.8 months, compared with 3.9 months for married-couple families and 3.8 months in families headed by a single male. (See Table 2.17 in Chapter 2.)

Teen Mothers

TANF contains provisions to encourage two-parent families and reduce out-of-wedlock births. Several provisions deal specifically with the reduction of births among teen mothers. According to Rebecca A. Maynard, in *Kids Having Kids: A Robin Hood Foundation Special Report on the Costs of Adolescent Childbearing* (1996, http://www.robinhood.org/approach/KHK.pdf), teen mothers tend to have less education and fewer job skills than older mothers.

families with incomes above the poverty line. (See Table 3.3.)

Most states have imposed a lifetime limit of five years for the receipt of TANF benefits for adults, although states are allowed to extend benefits for hardship cases or victims of domestic violence. Some states have set limits less than five years. Families in which there is no adult head of household are exempt from time limits. The actual median amount of time recipients

TABLE 3.3

Average monthly program participation rates for TANF or general assistance, by selected characteristics, 2001–03

Characteristic	Temporary Assistance for Needy Families(TANF)/General Assistance Participation rates (in percent)		
	2001	2002	2003
Total number of recipients[a]	3,935	3,584	3,667
As percent of the population	1.4	1.3	1.3
Race and Hispanic origin[b]			
White	0.9	0.8	0.8
Not Hispanic	0.6	0.5	0.5
Black	4.2	3.8	3.7
Asian or Pacific Islander	2.0	1.8	1.5
Hispanic	2.9	2.7	2.7
Not Hispanic	1.2	1.1	1.1
Age			
Under 18 years	3.7	3.3	3.4
18 to 64 years	0.7	0.7	0.7
65 years and older	0.1	0.1	0.1
Sex			
Men	1.2	1.1	1.1
Women	1.6	1.5	1.5
Educational attainment (people 18 and older)			
Less than high school graduate	1.7	1.6	1.4
High school graduate, no college	0.6	0.5	0.5
Some college	0.3	0.2	0.2
Disability status (people 15 to 64 years old)			
With a work disability	2.1	1.6	1.5
With no work disability	0.6	0.6	0.7
Residence			
Metropolitan	1.4	1.3	1.3
Central city	2.5	2.3	2.3
Noncentral city	0.8	0.7	0.8
Nonmetropolitan	1.3	1.2	1.1
Region			
Northeast	1.6	1.4	1.5
Midwest	1.2	1.1	1.1
South	1.0	0.9	0.9
West	2.1	2.0	1.9
Family status			
In families	1.6	1.5	1.5
In married-couple families	0.5	0.5	0.5
In families with a female householder, no husband present	6.5	5.8	5.6
In families with a male householder, no wife present	1.4	1.1	1.3
Unrelated individuals	0.4	0.3	0.3
Employment and labor force status (people 18 and older)			
Employed full-time[c]	0.1	0.1	0.1
Employed part-time	0.7	0.5	0.5
Unemployed	3.2	2.7	2.6
Not in labor force	1.2	1.2	1.1

TABLE 3.3

Average monthly program participation rates for TANF or general assistance, by selected characteristics, 2001–03 [CONTINUED]

Characteristic	Temporary Assistance for Needy Families(TANF)/General Assistance Participation rates (in percent)		
	2001	2002	2003
Marital status (people 18 and older)			
Married	0.3	0.3	0.3
Separated, divorced, or widowed	0.9	0.7	0.7
Never married	1.2	1.2	1.1
Family income-to-poverty ratio[d]			
Under 1.00	7.2	6.7	6.1
1.00 and over	0.4	0.4	0.5

[a]In thousands.
[b]Hispanics may be any race.
[c]Full-time and part-time employment reflect the monthly employment status.
[d]Family income-to-poverty threshold ratio reflects the monthly poverty status. A ratio of under 1.00 indicates that a person is in poverty, whereas a ratio of higher than or equal to 1.00 indicates that a person is not in poverty.

SOURCE: Tracy A. Loveless and Jan Tin, Table A-2. Average Monthly Program Participation Rates for Temporary Assistance for Needy Families or General Assistance by Selected Characteristics: 2001–03, in *Dynamics of Economic Well-Being: Participation in Government Programs, 2001 Through 2003: Who Gets Assistance?* Current Population Reports, U.S. Census Bureau, P70-108, October 2006, http://www.census.gov/prod/2006 pubs/p70-108.pdf (accessed January 2, 2007)

Teen mothers have a much higher participation rate in major means-tested government programs than do mothers in other age groups. The U.S. Bureau of the Census finds that in 2001 half (50%) of unmarried mothers aged fifteen to nineteen who had had a child in the last year received some form of government assistance, compared with 16% of all unmarried mothers who had had a child in the last year. (See Figure 3.1.) However,

older unmarried mothers were more likely than younger unmarried mothers to receive TANF in particular. In 2001, 68,000 of 670,000 unmarried mothers aged fifteen to twenty-four years who had had a child in the last year, or 10.1%, received TANF, but 54,000 of 365,000 unmarried mothers aged twenty-five to thirty-four years, or 14.8%, received TANF in that year. (See Table 3.4.)

The birth rate for unmarried teens is high, although it declined in the 1990s. (See Figure 3.2.) Between 1991 and 2003 the birth rate for fifteen- to seventeen-year-olds fell significantly, from a birth rate of 30.8 per one thousand unmarried girls in that age group to 20.3 per one thousand. Births to teenagers represent a concern to society because teen mothers tend to have less education and less ability to support and care for their children. In addition, Maynard indicates that babies born to teen mothers are:

- More likely to be born prematurely and to be of low birth weight

- At risk for health problems, lower cognitive skills, and behavioral problems

- Less likely to grow up in homes with their fathers, possibly causing emotional as well as financial problems

- At greater risk to be abused

To receive TANF benefits, states are required to submit plans detailing their efforts to reduce out-of-wedlock

FIGURE 3.1

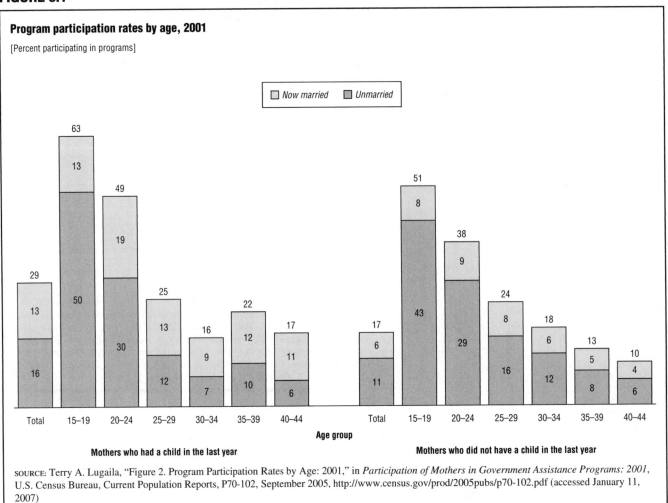

Program participation rates by age, 2001

[Percent participating in programs]

SOURCE: Terry A. Lugaila, "Figure 2. Program Participation Rates by Age: 2001," in *Participation of Mothers in Government Assistance Programs: 2001*, U.S. Census Bureau, Current Population Reports, P70-102, September 2005, http://www.census.gov/prod/2005pubs/p70-102.pdf (accessed January 11, 2007)

births, especially among teenagers. To be eligible for TANF benefits, unmarried minor parents are required to remain in high school or its equivalent as well as to live in an adult-supervised setting. One provision in the law allows for the creation of second-chance homes for teen parents and their children, a type of home that already existed in some states. These homes require that all residents either enroll in school or participate in a job-training program. They also provide parenting and life skills classes as well as counseling and support services.

A performance bonus that is separate from the TANF block grant rewards states for reductions in out-of-wedlock births combined with a decline in the abortion rate. Grant money is also available for states to implement abstinence-only education programs. In addition, the welfare-reform law directs the HHS to provide a strategy to prevent unmarried teen pregnancies and to ensure that 25% of the communities in the United States implement a teen pregnancy prevention program. The CBO reports in the *Cost Estimate* that the 2006 reauthorization of the PRWORA provided an additional $73 million per year for FY 2006 through FY 2015 to fund healthy marriage

initiatives—a variety of activities designed to promote the value of marriage to the general population and teach interpersonal skills to help ensure the stability of marital relationships.

THE WELFARE-TO-WORK CONCEPT

TANF recipients are expected to participate in work activities while receiving benefits. After twenty-four months of assistance, states must require recipients to work at least part time to continue to receive cash benefits. States are permitted to exempt certain groups from the work-activity requirements, including parents of young children (up to one year) and disabled adults. The TANF law defines the work activities that count when determining a state's work participation rate.

As part of their plans, states must require parents to work after two years of receiving benefits. In 2000 states were required to have 40% of all parents, and at least one adult in 90% of all two-parent families, engaged in a work activity for a minimum of twenty hours per week for single parents and thirty-five hours per week for at least one adult in two-parent families. This work require-

TABLE 3.4

Program participation status of mothers 15 to 44 years with a birth in the last year, by marital status and age, 1996 and 2001

[Numbers in thousands]

Marital status and age of mother	Total		Participants[b]									Nonparticipants[d]		1996[e]	
			Total												
	Number	Partici-pation rate[a]	Number	Percent	TANF	Food stamps	WIC	Medicaid	Housing assis-tance	Other[c]		Number	Percent	Number	Partici-pation rate[a]
Mothers who had a child in the last year	4,066	29.4	1,194	100.0	171	559	449	767	239	44		2,872	100.0	3,859	41.5
Now married[f]															
Total	**2,899**	**18.2**	**526**	**44.1**	**50**	**166**	**248**	**251**	**80**	**21**		**2,373**	**82.6**	**2,730**	**27.7**
15 to 24 years	493	41.7	206	17.2	24	56	100	110	19	12		287	10.0	586	55.4
25 to 34 years	1,840	12.9	237	19.9	21	83	111	102	52	3		1,603	55.8	1,634	21.7
35 to 44 years	567	14.8	84	7.0	5	27	37	39	9	6		483	16.8	510	15.2
Unmarried[g]															
Total	**1,167**	**57.2**	**667**	**55.9**	**121**	**394**	**201**	**516**	**159**	**23**		**499**	**17.4**	**1,129**	**74.7**
15 to 24 years	670	59.8	400	33.5	68	225	112	310	103	13		269	9.4	672	80.9
25 to 34 years	365	56.0	205	17.1	54	134	73	165	42	5		161	5.6	356	68.0
35 to 44 years	132	(B)	62	5.2	—	35	17	41	14	5		69	2.4	101	(B)
Mothers who did not have a child in the last year	31,174	17.1	5,334	100.0	577	2,941	449	3,484	1,834	154		25,841	00.0	31,633	21.7
Now married[f]															
Total	**20,675**	**8.4**	**1,747**	**32.8**	**110**	**808**	**201**	**1,011**	**414**	**42**		**18,929**	**73.3**	**21,760**	**11.5**
15 to 24 years	1,049	24.3	255	4.8	14	119	46	144	61	3		794	3.1	1,119	34.4
25 to 34 years	6,833	10.7	729	13.7	42	332	101	416	191	7		6,105	23.6	8,061	14.7
35 to 44 years	12,793	6.0	763	14.3	54	357	54	451	162	32		12,030	46.6	12,581	7.5
Unmarried[g]															
Total	**10,499**	**34.2**	**3,587**	**67.2**	**467**	**2,133**	**248**	**2,473**	**1,421**	**112**		**6,912**	**26.7**	**9,873**	**44.2**
15 to 24 years	1,758	48.6	854	16.0	134	422	131	626	324	25		904	3.5	1,592	63.5
25 to 34 years	3,724	37.9	1,411	26.4	212	919	92	982	551	33		2,314	9.0	3,609	50.1
35 to 44 years	5,017	26.4	1,322	24.8	121	792	25	865	546	55		3,695	14.3	4,672	33.1

— Represents or rounds to zero.
(B) Derived measure not shown when base is less than 200,000.
[a]Percent of mothers currently participating or covered by one or more programs.
[b]Currently participating in or covered by one or more programs.
[c]Includes general assistance and other welfare.
[d]Not currently participating in any program.
[e]Data for 1996 may vary due to analysis of additional assistance programs.
[f]Includes married spouse present, married spouse absent (excluding separated).
[g]Includes separated, divorced, widowed, and never married.
Notes: TANF is Temporary Assistance for Needy Families. WIC is Women, Infants and Children (public health program).

SOURCE: Terry A. Lugaila, "Table 2. Program Participation Status of Mothers 15 to 44 Years with a Birth in the Last Year by Marital Status and Age: 1996 and 2001," in *Participation of Mothers in Government Assistance Programs: 2001*, U.S. Census Bureau, Current Population Reports, P70-102, September 2005, http://www.census.gov/prod/2005pubs/p70-102.pdf (accessed January 11, 2007)

FIGURE 3.2

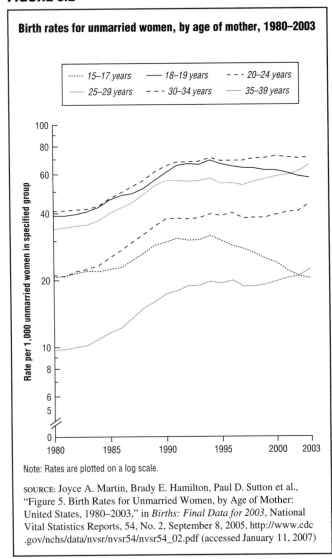

Birth rates for unmarried women, by age of mother, 1980–2003

Legend:
- 15–17 years
- 18–19 years
- 20–24 years
- 25–29 years
- 30–34 years
- 35–39 years

Rate per 1,000 unmarried women in specified group

Note: Rates are plotted on a log scale.

SOURCE: Joyce A. Martin, Brady E. Hamilton, Paul D. Sutton et al., "Figure 5. Birth Rates for Unmarried Women, by Age of Mother: United States, 1980–2003," in *Births: Final Data for 2003*, National Vital Statistics Reports, 54, No. 2, September 8, 2005, http://www.cdc.gov/nchs/data/nvsr/nvsr54/nvsr54_02.pdf (accessed January 11, 2007)

ment is becoming stricter. The 2006 reauthorization of PRWORA required 50% of all TANF recipients to work in 2006, increasing by 5% each year to 70% in 2010.

TANF recipients required to work must spend a minimum number of hours per week engaged in one of the following activities:

- An unsubsidized job (no government help)
- A subsidized private job
- A subsidized public job
- Work experience
- On-the-job training
- Job search and job readiness (a usual maximum of six weeks, total)
- Community service
- Vocational educational training (a twelve-month maximum)

- Job skills training
- Education related to employment
- High school or a general equivalency diploma completion
- Providing child care for a community service participant.

Additional provisions apply to young parents who are under the age of twenty and are either household heads or married and who lack a high school diploma. They will be considered "engaged in work" if they either maintain satisfactory attendance in high school (no hours specified) or participate in education directly related to work (twenty hours per week).

Education and Training

Reflecting a work-first philosophy, the 1996 welfare law limits the number of TANF recipients who may get work credit through participation in education and training. No more than 30% of TANF families who are counted as engaged in work may consist of people who are participating in vocational educational training. Vocational educational training is the only creditable work activity not explicitly confined to high school dropouts.

Finding and Creating Jobs for TANF Recipients

Job availability is one of the most difficult challenges facing states in moving recipients to work from welfare. While the national unemployment rate fell from a high of 7.5% in 1992 to 4% in 2000, it then began to rise again, hitting 6% in 2003. In 2006 it had fallen again to 4.6% ("Annual Average Unemployment Rate, Civilian Labor Force 16 Years and Over," U.S. Department of Labor, Bureau of Labor Statistics, February 6, 2007, http://www.bls.gov/cps/prev_yrs.htm). However, even in times of low national unemployment, unemployment in some areas of the country might be much higher, and the skill level of unemployed people may not match the skills required for available jobs. Welfare recipients often lack job skills and work experience. If suitable jobs cannot be found, states must create work-activity placements and may use TANF block grant funds to do so.

Welfare agencies have had to change their focus and train staff to function more as job developers and counselors than as caseworkers. They make an initial assessment of recipients' skills as required by TANF. They may then develop personal responsibility plans for recipients, identifying what is needed (for example, training, job-placement services, and support services) to move them into the workforce.

States have developed a variety of approaches to finding and creating job opportunities. Although most rely on existing unemployment offices, many states have tried other options to help recipients find work:

- Collaboration with the business community to develop strategies that provide recipients with the skills and training employers want

- Use of several types of subsidies for employers who hire welfare recipients directly (subsidizing wages, providing tax credits to employers, and subsidizing workers' compensation and unemployment compensation taxes)

- Targeting state jobs for welfare recipients

- Financial encouragement for entrepreneurship and self-employment

- Creation of community service positions, often within city departments, such as parks and libraries (recipients usually participate in this workfare as a condition of continuing to receive benefits rather than wages)

The results of these efforts to find welfare recipients work have been mixed. The Urban Institute reports that in fact, TANF agencies have built relationships with outside agencies in order to fulfill work program requirements, especially with nonprofit agencies; however, building partnerships with the for-profit business community occurred much less often. In addition, local TANF agencies rarely built partnerships with state agencies, but they did involve community-based nonprofit agencies, workforce development agencies, and occasionally other public agencies, like the public school system, in order to find jobs for welfare recipients. However, not all local TANF agencies made even these connections (Karin Martinson and Pamela A. Holcomb, "Reforming Welfare: Institutional Change and Challenges," The Urban Institute, July 2002, http://www.urban.org/url.cfm?ID=310535). In addition, at times of a slower economy, like in the early 2000s, fewer jobs existed for former welfare recipients (Pamela J. Loprest, "Fewer Welfare Leavers Employed in Weak Economy," The Urban Institute, August 2003, http://www.urban.org/url.cfm?ID=310837).

In *Building an Employment Focused Welfare System: Work First and Other Work-Oriented Strategies in Five States* (June 1998, http://www.urban.org/UploadedPDF/WORKFST.PDF), Pamela A. Holcomb et al. offer in-depth comparative analyses of how well states are adapting to work-oriented welfare systems. This study of five selected states shows that strategies to promote employment, supported by a strong economy, were effective in moving significant numbers of welfare recipients into jobs. Holcomb et al.'s report is based on site visits in early 1997 to Indiana, Massachusetts, Oregon, Virginia, and Wisconsin, states that have experienced large caseload declines. These five states had begun reorganizing their welfare systems to emphasize a work-first approach before Congress passed the 1996 welfare reform law.

According to Holcomb et al., typical practices in all five states included:

- Making the job search the first and major activity

- Restricting participation in education and training

- Imposing stricter participation and work requirements

- Enforcing heavy penalties for noncompliance

- Setting time limits on assistance

Nonetheless, despite the similarities, each state had its own unique plan for welfare reform. For instance, Virginia gave recipients the greatest opportunity to combine assistance with employment but also imposed harsh penalties for noncompliance. Both Virginia and Massachusetts required work sooner than the other states and depended heavily on community-service programs to engage recipients in some form of work. Of the states studied, Oregon had developed the most successful program for creating subsidized job opportunities for welfare recipients.

However, Holcomb et al. warn that a work-first approach alone cannot help all welfare recipients. It works best for individuals who are already fairly employable. It is less effective in helping those with significant barriers to employment or in helping recipients stay employed. After tracking a sample of recipients over a one-year period, Holcomb et al. find that, by the end of that year, 31% to 44% of the participants were still receiving cash assistance or were back on welfare, whether they had a job or not.

Norma B. Coe et al., in *Does Work Pay? A Summary of the Work Incentives under TANF* (December 1998, http://www.urban.org/UploadedPDF/anf28.pdf), look at the welfare-to-work program from the point of view of a benefit recipient. They find that the nation's social service system provides incentive for a single mother with two children to work, even at minimum wage. By supplementing her wage with tax credits, food stamps, and other available public assistance, a single mother can raise her family's income to 120% of the poverty level. However, because of decreasing public programs available to her if she earned more, that same mother would have little incentive to try to increase her earnings to $9 per hour.

States are now turning their attention to the needs of those with barriers to employment, including health problems, low educational and skill levels, difficulties speaking English, substance abuse, mental health problems, and victimization by domestic violence. These are people who require intensive supportive services to obtain employment and for whom a work-first approach is not appropriate.

In "Welfare Reform Mostly Worked" (July 24, 2005, http://www.urban.org/publications/900824.html), Olivia A. Golden, the assistant secretary for children and families in the HHS under President Bill Clinton, presents her thoughts concerning welfare reform. She believes the welfare-to-work model "mostly worked" in the sense that welfare caseloads have dropped and that most low-income parents are now working to support their families. However, even though welfare-to-work was successful, its success brought about additional problems. She states that "in less than a decade, welfare has faded as a means of support for impoverished families. Many of these families are working long hours despite low wages, shrinking health-insurance coverage and serious trade-offs between work and decent care for their children. Yet, neither our politics nor our policies have adjusted to our success at bringing more of these parents into the labor force."

In *Assessing the New Federalism, Eight Years Later* (2005, http://www.urban.org/UploadedPDF/311198_ANF_EightYearsLater.pdf), Golden identifies many successes of the welfare-to-work policies, including the increase in the percentage of welfare recipients who worked rising from 22% in 1997 to 33% in 1999, while declining as a result of a weaker economy in the early twenty-first century; the rise in work activity among those most likely to use welfare, namely single mothers with a high school education or less; the finding that employers were willing to hire welfare recipients; the fact that most families that left welfare had at least one working adult; and that about one-third of former welfare recipients who worked had health insurance benefits. However, there were also some problems, including that roughly 25% of those who left welfare were back on assistance two years later. In addition, many welfare recipients face multiple barriers to working that need to be addressed.

Support Services Necessary for Moving Recipients to Work

CHILD CARE. The offer of affordable child care is one critical element in encouraging low-income mothers to seek and keep jobs. In *Child Care Subsidies and TANF*, Holcomb et al. note that "child care is a key work support that can help those leaving cash assistance for work keep their jobs and avoid returning to welfare." According to Karen Schulman and Helen Blank, in *Child Care Assistance Policies 2005: States Fail to Make Up Lost Ground, Families Continue to Lack Critical Supports* (September 2005, http://www.nwlc.org/pdf/ChildCareSubsidyReport_September2005.pdf), child care for one child costs from $4,000 to $10,000 per year. In other words, child care for one child, at a minimum, would consume more than a third of the income of a family with one adult working full time and earning the minimum wage. As such, subsidies are essential.

The 1996 welfare reform law created a block grant to states for child care. The amount of the block grant was equivalent to what states received under the AFDC. However, states that maintain the amount that they spent for child care under the AFDC are eligible for additional matching funds. The block grant and the supplemental matching funds are referred to as the Child Care Development Fund (CCDF). In addition, states were given the option of transferring some of their TANF funds to the CCDF or spending them directly on child care services. The Urban Institute reports in the fact sheet "Government Work Supports and Low-Income Families: Facts and Figures" (July 2006, http://www.urban.org/UploadedPDF/900981_worksupports.pdf) that the amount allocated for child care through the CCDF and TANF tripled between 1996 and 2002, from $4 billion to $12 billion.

Because states may use TANF funds for child care, they have more flexibility than before to design child care programs, not only for welfare recipients but also for working-poor families who may need child care support to continue working and stay off welfare. States determine who is eligible for child care support, how much those parents will pay (often using a sliding fee scale), and the amount a state will reimburse providers of subsidized care. Children under the age of thirteen are eligible for child care subsidies; depending on the state, families with incomes from 111% to 287% of the federal poverty level in 2005 were eligible, although few states guaranteed payments to all eligible families. For example, the Urban Institute notes in "Government Work Supports and Low-Income Families" that in 2005 twenty states either had waiting lists or had stopped taking applications for child care subsidies.

The Administration for Children and Families reports in the "FFY 2005 CCDF Data Tables" (November 29, 2006, http://www.acf.hhs.gov/programs/ccb/data/ccdf_data/05acf800/list.htm) that in FY 2005 states provided child care subsidies to approximately 1.8 million low-income children in one million families. Approximately 73% of the children were cared for in child care centers or licensed family child care homes. The remaining 27% of children were cared for in more informal settings, including arrangements with friends and relatives. Despite the dramatic increase in the provision of child care to low-income families, many eligible families were still not receiving assistance. About one in five (19%) families served nationally were receiving TANF assistance.

TRANSPORTATION AND ACCESS TO JOBS. According to the U.S. Department of Transportation (DOT), in "Use of TANF, WtW, and Job Access Funds for Transportation" (1998, http://www.fta.dot.gov/printer_friendly/grants_financing_3715.html), transportation is another critical factor facing welfare recipients moving into a job. Recipients without a car must depend on public transportation. Yet two out of three new jobs are in suburban areas, often outside the range of public transportation, whereas three out of four welfare recipients live in rural areas or central cities. Even when jobs are accessible to public transportation, many day care centers and schools are not. Some jobs require weekend or night shift work, when public transportation schedules are limited. Even for those recipients with cars, the expense of gas and repairs can deplete earnings.

To promote employment, the vehicle asset limits under TANF are broader than under the AFDC. Even though each state has the flexibility to determine its own vehicle asset level, all states have chosen to increase the limit for the value of the primary automobile in the family beyond that set under the AFDC. Over half the states now have no limits on the value of one vehicle, while many other states have raised the vehicle asset limit.

The DOT notes that states use a variety of approaches to provide transportation for TANF recipients moving into the workforce, such as:

- Reimbursing work-related transportation expenses (automobile expenses or public transportation)

- Providing financial assistance in the form of loans or grants to purchase or lease an automobile

- Filling transit service gaps, such as new routes or extended hours

- Providing transit alternatives, such as vanpools or shuttle services

- Offering entrepreneurial opportunities for recipients to become transportation providers

- Transferring TANF funds to the Social Services Block Grant to develop the transportation infrastructure for the working poor in rural areas and inner cities

UNEMPLOYMENT COMPENSATION

To qualify for unemployment compensation benefits, an unemployed person usually must have worked recently for a particular employer for some period and for a certain amount of pay. Almost all wage and salary workers and most of the civilian labor force are covered by unemployment insurance. Most of those not covered were people who were self-employed, agricultural or domestic workers, certain alien farm workers, and railroad workers (who have their own unemployment program).

According to the *Unemployment Insurance Chartbook* (March 5, 2007, http://www.doleta.gov/unemploy/chartbook.cfm), the U.S. Department of Labor's Employment and Training Administration indicates that even though most wage and salary workers were covered in 2006 by the unemployment compensation insurance system, only 35% of unemployed workers received unemployment benefits.

Unemployment compensation varies widely by state. Figure 3.3 shows the percentages of unemployed receiving benefits in each state in 2003. The states with the highest rates of those receiving unemployment compen-

sation were Pennsylvania and Massachusetts; South Dakota and New Mexico had the lowest rates.

Even though the maximum a state may offer is thirty-nine weeks of coverage (except for special programs), all states provide up to twenty-six weeks of benefits, except Massachusetts and Washington, which offer thirty weeks. Benefits vary dramatically from state to state. In 2002 the average weekly benefits in Massachusetts ($357), New Jersey ($336), Rhode Island ($336), Minnesota ($321), and Colorado ($302) were significantly higher than those offered by Puerto Rico ($108), Alabama ($182), Mississippi ($186), Louisiana ($192), Alaska ($194), and Arizona ($195). (See Table 3.5.)

Unemployment insurance helps workers avoid poverty. In *Is the Unemployment Insurance System a Safety Net for Welfare Recipients Who Exit Welfare for Work?* (June 2001, http://wdr.doleta.gov/conference/pdf/rangarajan.pdf), Anu Rangarajan, Walter Corson, and Robert G. Wood find evidence that the unemployment insurance system was protecting low-wage workers following the enactment of welfare reform in 1996. After examining a group of former welfare recipients who exited welfare between July 1997 and June 1998, Rangarajan, Corson, and Wood find that between 50% and 60% of people leaving welfare for work were eligible for unemployment insurance, compared with 20% to 35% found in earlier studies. Nonetheless, almost 40% of those who left welfare for work were ineligible for benefits. Some of those who left the welfare rolls were ineligible for benefits because they quit their jobs. This study was conducted during a strong economic period, and more research is needed to determine whether unemployment insurance provides a safety net to low-wage workers and those leaving welfare during periods of slower economic growth and recessions.

The unemployment rate of African-American and Hispanic workers is higher than that of white and Asian workers. In 2005 the unemployment rate for white male workers aged sixteen years and over was 4.4% and for Asian male workers of the same age was 4%, compared with 10.5% for African-Americans and 5.4% for Hispanics. (See Table 3.6.) Single men and women have a higher unemployment rate than others. The unemployment rate for single women in 2005 was 8.3%, compared with 5.4% for widowed, divorced, or separated women and 3.3% for married women; the unemployment rate for single men in 2005 was 9.5%, compared with 5.6% of widowed, divorced, or separated men and 2.8% for married men.

FEDERAL MINIMUM WAGE

The federal minimum wage dates back to the passage of the Fair Labor Standards Act of 1938, which established basic national standards for minimum wages, overtime pay,

FIGURE 3.3

Unemployment compensation recipiency rates, by state, 2003

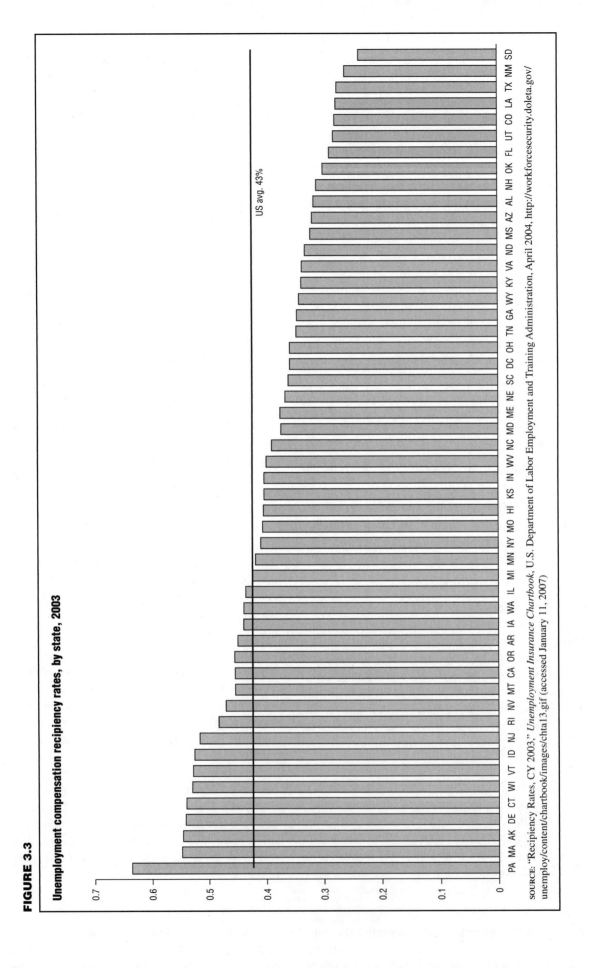

SOURCE: "Recipiency Rates, CY 2003," *Unemployment Insurance Chartbook*, U.S. Department of Labor Employment and Training Administration, April 2004, http://workforcesecurity.doleta.gov/unemploy/content/chartbook/images/chta13.gif (accessed January 11, 2007)

TABLE 3.5

Amount and duration of weekly benefits for total unemployment under regular state programs, by state, 2005

| State or area | Average weekly benefit for total unemployment | | Average weekly insured unemployment | Average actual duration (weeks) |
	Amount (dollars)[a]	Percent of average weekly wages[b]		
Total	**266.62**	**34.6**	**2,661,400**	**15.3**
Alabama	182.01	27.9	27,911	11.5
Alaska	193.91	25.8	12,443	14.3
Arizona	194.76	26.8	29,157	15.6
Arkansas	229.61	38.7	27,743	13.9
California	277.46	31.4	362,655	17.4
Colorado	301.77	38.2	25,197	13.9
Connecticut	295.42	29.0	39,624	16.7
Delaware	247.47	28.9	8,151	16.6
District of Columbia	266.67	22.7	4,529	19.5
Florida	226.35	32.3	88,748	15.2
Georgia	244.65	33.0	53,727	11.5
Hawaii	337.42	49.8	6,258	14.1
Idaho	235.25	40.3	13,131	12.7
Illinois	285.38	34.1	136,324	18.2
Indiana	278.07	41.1	54,078	13.0
Iowa	271.26	42.9	24,444	12.5
Kansas	278.47	43.2	20,002	15.3
Kentucky	259.56	40.2	30,330	13.5
Louisiana	192.29	30.2	65,746	12.5
Maine	240.24	38.9	10,683	14.8
Maryland	256.64	31.2	35,939	15.3
Massachusetts	356.64	37.2	82,111	17.9
Michigan	290.13	36.7	139,408	14.3
Minnesota	321.59	41.2	46,797	15.0
Mississippi	186.34	33.2	28,814	11.3
Missouri	205.79	30.1	50,455	15.4
Montana	220.58	40.5	7,436	14.9
Nebraska	225.65	36.6	11,917	13.7
Nevada	258.31	34.9	18,479	13.9
New Hampshire	252.12	32.5	6,550	11.8
New Jersey	336.04	35.5	113,897	18.1
New Mexico	217.70	35.8	11,792	17.5
New York	276.05	27.7	190,686	18.0
North Carolina	257.71	37.6	76,893	12.9
North Dakota	238.41	42.1	3,466	12.1
Ohio	260.99	36.7	100,554	15.2
Oklahoma	221.49	37.2	16,877	15.2
Oregon	261.26	37.5	45,526	15.2
Pennsylvania	291.89	38.6	167,857	16.6
Rhode Island	336.42	45.8	12,400	15.5
South Carolina	216.66	34.6	38,468	13.7
South Dakota	211.49	38.5	2,597	12.3
Tennessee	212.11	31.1	43,657	13.7
Texas	261.34	34.1	127,933	14.2
Utah	263.37	41.9	10,606	12.7
Vermont	267.14	41.1	6,222	13.6
Virginia	245.74	31.1	31,305	12.5
Washington	296.86	38.3	58,771	14.7
West Virginia	225.12	38.4	13,964	15.0
Wisconsin	252.82	37.2	72,716	13.3

TABLE 3.5

Amount and duration of weekly benefits for total unemployment under regular state programs, by state, 2005 [CONTINUED]

| State or area | Average weekly benefit for total unemployment | | Average weekly insured unemployment | Average actual duration (weeks) |
	Amount (dollars)[a]	Percent of average weekly wages[b]		
Wyoming	241.52	38.6	2,791	11.8
Outlying areas				
Puerto Rico	108.28	25.1	43,118	18.3
Virgin Islands	237.00	37.6	517	16.1

[a]Includes dependents' allowances for states that provide such benefits.
[b]Based on average total weekly wage in current year.

SOURCE: Adapted from "Table 9.A2. Summary Data on State Programs, by State or Other Area, 2005," in *Annual Statistical Supplement, 2006*, Social Security Administration, 2007, http://www.ssa.gov/policy/docs/statcomps/supplement/2006/9a.html#table9.a2 (accessed January 11, 2007)

and the employment of child workers. The provisions of the act have been extended to cover many other areas of employment since 1938.

The first minimum wage instituted in 1938 was $0.25 an hour. Over the years it gradually increased, reaching $4.25 in 1991. In July 1996 Congress passed legislation that raised the minimum wage to $5.15 in 1997 by means of two $0.45 increases. (See Table 3.7.) In 2007 the mini-mum wage was still $5.15, although twenty-nine states had minimum wage rates higher than the federal rate. Kansas had a minimum wage rate lower than the federal rate for the few jobs not covered by the federal minimum wage. It is worth noting that the minimum wage is a cash wage only and includes no health care or other fringe benefits that higher paid workers typically enjoy.

The minimum wage remained unchanged from 1981 to 1990. When inflation is taken into account, the minimum wage actually decreased in value by about $2. The increases in 1996 and 1997 still left the real value of the minimum wage well below the 1978 value. (See Figure 3.4.) A person working forty hours per week for fifty weeks per year at minimum wage ($5.15 per hour) would gross $206 per week, or $10,300 per year, well below the poverty level for a family of three ($16,600 in 2007). (See Table 1.1 in Chapter 1.) For adults, this means that day laborers (those without a permanent job who look for a job every day) and those employed in many service jobs for minimum wages will not be able to earn enough to escape from poverty.

In January 2007 the U.S. House of Representatives overwhelmingly passed a measure to increase the mini-mum wage from $5.15 per hour to $7.25 per hour, offering hope that the minimum wage would be increased for the first time in a decade. The Senate approved the measure in February but also called for tax breaks for small busi-nesses. As of spring 2007, the measure still required reconciliation between the House and the Senate.

Who Works for Minimum Wage?

After the recession of 1990–91 and the slow recovery in 1992, 4.2 million workers in 1993 earned the minimum wage or less. In 1996 nearly ten million workers were directly affected by the minimum-wage increase. Often,

TABLE 3.6

Unemployed persons by marital status, race, ethnicity, age, and sex, 2004–05

Marital status, race, Hispanic or Latino ethnicity, and age	Men				Women			
	Thousands of persons		Unemployment rates		Thousands of persons		Unemployment rates	
	2004	2005	2004	2005	2004	2005	2004	2005
Total, 16 years and over	**4,456**	**4,059**	**5.6**	**5.1**	**3,694**	**3,531**	**5.4**	**5.1**
Married, spouse present	1,466	1,287	3.1	2.8	1,244	1,168	3.5	3.3
Widowed, divorced, or separated	608	563	6.3	5.6	828	768	5.9	5.4
Single (never married)	2,381	2,209	10.5	9.5	1,621	1,595	8.7	8.3
White, 16 years and over	**3,282**	**2,931**	**5.0**	**4.4**	**2,565**	**2,419**	**4.7**	**4.4**
Married, spouse present	1,161	1,011	2.9	2.5	996	922	3.3	3.0
Widowed, divorced, or separated	466	415	5.9	5.0	600	548	5.5	4.9
Single (never married)	1,655	1,505	9.1	8.2	969	949	7.1	6.8
Black or African American, 16 years and over	**860**	**844**	**11.1**	**10.5**	**868**	**856**	**9.8**	**9.5**
Married, spouse present	200	177	5.6	5.1	149	144	5.3	5.2
Widowed, divorced, or separated	104	119	8.9	9.5	179	166	7.8	7.3
Single (never married)	556	548	18.2	16.9	540	546	14.4	13.9
Asian, 16 years and over	**153**	**141**	**4.5**	**4.0**	**124**	**118**	**4.3**	**3.9**
Married, spouse present	64	61	2.9	2.7	62	62	3.4	3.3
Widowed, divorced, or separated	14	11	5.8	3.6	24	23	6.3	5.5
Single (never married)	75	68	7.8	7.2	39	32	5.6	4.5
Hispanic or Latino ethnicity, 16 years and over	**755**	**647**	**6.5**	**5.4**	**587**	**544**	**7.6**	**6.9**
Married, spouse present	275	231	4.4	3.6	228	202	6.2	5.4
Widowed, divorced, or separated	85	69	5.8	4.5	130	103	7.9	6.2
Single (never married)	394	347	10.3	8.7	229	239	9.6	9.8
Total, 25 years and over	**2,980**	**2,617**	**4.4**	**3.8**	**2,531**	**2,453**	**4.4**	**4.2**
Married, spouse present	1,399	1,232	3.1	2.7	1,139	1,071	3.3	3.1
Widowed, divorced, or separated	584	538	6.2	5.5	781	730	5.7	5.3
Single (never married)	997	848	8.0	6.6	611	651	6.3	6.4
White, 25 years and over	**2,225**	**1,929**	**3.9**	**3.4**	**1,773**	**1,699**	**3.8**	**3.6**
Married, spouse present	1,108	966	2.8	2.5	911	845	3.1	2.9
Widowed, divorced, or separated	447	395	5.7	4.9	563	519	5.3	4.8
Single (never married)	670	567	7.0	5.7	299	335	4.6	4.9
Black or African American, 25 years and over	**545**	**507**	**8.4**	**7.6**	**589**	**568**	**7.9**	**7.5**
Married, spouse present	191	170	5.5	5.0	141	133	5.2	4.9
Widowed, divorced, or separated	101	113	8.8	9.2	172	160	7.7	7.2
Single (never married)	253	223	13.5	11.1	276	275	11.1	10.4
Asian, 25 years and over	**117**	**102**	**3.9**	**3.3**	**93**	**102**	**3.7**	**3.8**
Married, spouse present	63	61	2.9	2.7	55	60	3.1	3.3
Widowed, divorced, or separated	13	11	5.7	3.6	21	23	5.9	5.5
Single (never married)	41	30	6.6	5.0	17	19	4.2	4.5
Hispanic or Latino ethnicity, 16 years and over	**477**	**401**	**5.1**	**4.1**	**408**	**372**	**6.6**	**5.8**
Married, spouse present	253	214	4.2	3.5	202	174	5.9	5.0
Widowed, divorced, or separated	75	63	5.5	4.4	121	98	7.8	6.1
Single (never married)	149	124	7.4	5.7	84	99	6.8	7.7

Note: Estimates for the above race groups (white, black or African American, and Asian) do not sum to totals because data are not presented for all races. In addition, persons whose ethnicity is identified as Hispanic or Latino may be of any race and, therefore, are classified by ethnicity as well as by race. Beginning in January 2005, data reflect revised population controls used in the household survey.

SOURCE: "24. Unemployed Persons by Marital Status, Race, Hispanic or Latino Ethnicity, Age, and Sex," in Household Data Annual Averages, Bureau of Labor Statistics, 2006, http://www.bls.gov/cps/cpsaat24.pdf (accessed January 11, 2007)

employers use the minimum wage as a standard for low-paying jobs, perhaps paying $1 or $2 above minimum wage for a particular job.

Even though workers must receive at least the minimum wage for most jobs, there are some exceptions in which a person may be paid less than the minimum wage. Full-time students working on a part-time basis in the service and retail industries or at the student's academic institution, certain disabled people, and workers who are "customarily and regularly" tipped may receive less than the minimum wage.

According to the U. S. Department of Labor's Bureau of Labor Statistics, in *Characteristics of Minimum Wage Workers: 2004* (April 2005, http://www.bls.gov/cps/minwage 2004pdf.pdf), approximately 2 million American workers are paid at or below the minimum wage. Most of those who work for the minimum wage or below (74.6%) are employed in the service sector. About two-thirds (1.3 million

TABLE 3.7

Federal minimum wage rates under the Fair Labor Standards Act, selected years 1938–97

Effective date	1938 act[a]	1961 amendments[b]	1966 and subsequent amendments[c] Nonfarm	1966 and subsequent amendments[c] Farm
Oct. 24, 1938	$0.25			
Oct. 24, 1939	$0.30			
Oct. 24, 1945	$0.40			
Jan. 25, 1950	$0.75			
Mar. 1, 1956	$1.00			
Sept. 3, 1961	$1.15	$1.00		
Sept. 3, 1963	$1.25			
Sept. 3, 1964		$1.15		
Sept. 3, 1965		$1.25		
Feb. 1, 1967	$1.40	$1.40	$1.00	$1.00
Feb. 1, 1968	$1.60	$1.60	$1.15	$1.15
Feb. 1, 1969			$1.30	$1.30
Feb. 1, 1970			$1.45	
Feb. 1, 1971			$1.60	
May 1, 1974	$2.00	$2.00	$1.90	$1.60
Jan. 1, 1975	$2.10	$2.10	$2.00	$1.80
Jan. 1, 1976	$2.30	$2.30	$2.20	$2.00
Jan. 1, 1971			$2.30	$2.20
Jan. 1, 1978		$2.65 for all covered, nonexempt workers		
Jan. 1, 1979		$2.90 for all covered, nonexempt workers		
Jan. 1, 1980		$3.10 for all covered, nonexempt workers		
Jan. 1, 1981		$3.35 for all covered, nonexempt workers		
Apr. 1, 1990[d]		$3.80 for all covered, nonexempt workers		
Apr. 1, 1991		$4.25 for all covered, nonexempt workers		
Oct. 1, 1996[e]		$4.15 for all covered, nonexempt workers		
Sept. 1, 1997		$5.15 for all covered, nonexempt workers		

[a]The 1938 act was applicable generally to employees engaged in interstate commerce or in the production of goods for interstate commerce.

[b]The 1961 amendments extended coverage primarily to employees in large retail and service enterprises as well as to local transit, construction, and gasoline service station employees.

[c]The 1966 amendments extended coverage to state and local government employees of hospitals, nursing homes, and schools, and to laundries, dry cleaners, and large hotels, motels, restaurants, and farms. Subsequent amendments extended coverage to the remaining federal, state and local government employees who were not protected in 1966, to certain workers in retail and service trades previously exempted, and to certain domestic workers in private household employment.

[d]Grandfather clause: employees who do not meet the tests for individual coverage, and whose employers were covered by the Fair Labor Standards Act (FLSA), on March 31, 1990, and fail to meet the increased annual dollar volume (ADV) test for enterprise coverage, must continue to receive at least $3.35 an hour.

[e]A subminimum wage—$4.25 an hour—is established for employees under 20 years of age during their first 90 consecutive calendar days of employment with an employer.

SOURCE: "Federal Minimum Wage Rates under the Fair Labor Standards Act," U.S. Department for Labor, Employment Standards Administration, http://www.dol.gov/esa/minwage/chart.htm (accessed January 11, 2007)

---

out of two million, or 66.1%) of minimum-wage workers in 2004 were women, whereas 1.2 million of two million workers (61.9%) who earned minimum wage or less were part-time workers. (See Table 3.8.) White workers predominate among minimum-wage workers; 1.7 million of two million workers were white (83.9%), 250,000 were Hispanic (12.5%), 227,000 were African-American (11.3%), and 38,000 were Asian (1.9%).

SUPPLEMENTAL SECURITY INCOME

SSI is a means-tested income assistance program authorized by Title XVI of the Social Security Act. The SSI program replaced the combined federal-state pro-

grams of Old Age Assistance, Aid to the Blind, and Aid to the Permanently and Totally Disabled in fifty states and the District of Columbia. However, these programs still exist in the U.S. territories of Guam, Puerto Rico, and the Virgin Islands. Since the first payments in 1974, SSI has provided monthly cash payments to needy aged, blind, and disabled individuals who meet the eligibility requirements. States may supplement the basic federal SSI payment.

A number of requirements must be met to get financial benefits from SSI. First, a person must meet the program criteria for age, blindness, or disability. The aged, or elderly, are people sixty-five years old and older. To be considered legally blind, a person must have vision of 20/200 or less in the better eye with the use of corrective lenses, have tunnel vision of twenty degrees or less (can only see a small area straight ahead), or have met state qualifications for the earlier Aid to the Blind program.

A person is disabled if he or she cannot earn money at a job because of a physical or mental illness or injury that may cause his or her death, or if the condition lasts for twelve months or longer. Those who met earlier state Aid to the Permanently Disabled requirements may also qualify for assistance.

Children under the age of eighteen (or age twenty-two if a full-time student) and unmarried may qualify for SSI if they have a medically determinable physical or mental impairment that substantially reduces their ability to function independently as well as effectively engage in age-appropriate activities. This impairment must be expected to last for a continuous period of more than twelve months or to result in death.

Because SSI is a means-tested benefit, a person's income and property must be counted before he or she can receive benefits. In *The Green Book* (2003, http://waysandmeans.house.gov/media/pdf/greenbook2003/Section3.pdf), the Committee on Ways and Means of the U.S. House of Representatives indicates that in 2003 individuals and couples receiving Social Security benefits could not earn more than $572 and $849 per month, respectively. In addition, in 2003 a person could have no more than $2,000 worth of property, and a couple could have no more than $3,000 worth of property (mainly in savings accounts or stocks and bonds). Not included in countable resources are the person's home, as well as household goods and personal effects worth less than $2,000. The first $4,500 of the fair market value of a car is not counted. A car is not counted at all if a member of the household uses it to go to and from work or to medical treatments or if it has been adapted for a disabled person. Someone applying for SSI may have life insurance with a cash value of $1,500 or less and/or a burial policy up to the same value.

FIGURE 3.4

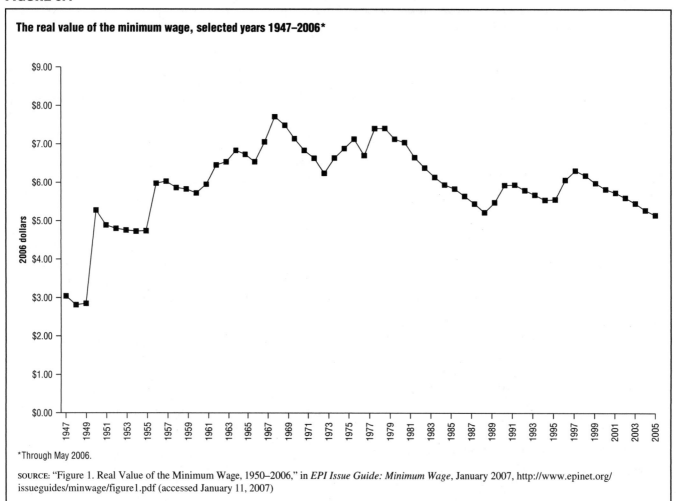

The real value of the minimum wage, selected years 1947–2006*

*Through May 2006.

SOURCE: "Figure 1. Real Value of the Minimum Wage, 1950–2006," in *EPI Issue Guide: Minimum Wage*, January 2007, http://www.epinet.org/issueguides/minwage/figure1.pdf (accessed January 11, 2007)

Recipients of SSI Benefits

The Social Security Administration's Office of Research, Evaluation, and Statistics reports in *Fast Facts and Figures about Social Security* (September 2006, http://www.ssa.gov/policy/docs/chartbooks/fast_facts/2006/fast_facts06.pdf) that 7.1 million people received SSI payments in December 2005. Of these, 82% were disabled, 17% were elderly, and 1% were blind. (See Figure 3.5.) Most of those receiving SSI were between the ages of eighteen and sixty-four (57%). Between 1974 and 2004 the number of elderly recipients declined, whereas the number of disabled recipients increased. Table 3.9 shows the annual amount of payments by source of payment and category from 1974 through 2004. About half—48.4%—of SSI recipients in 2004 were female; 51.6% were male. (See Table 3.10.)

TAX RELIEF FOR THE POOR

Both conservatives and liberals hailed the Tax Reform Act of 1986 as a major step toward relieving the tax burden of low-income families, one group of Americans whose wages and benefits have been eroding since 1979. The law enlarged and inflation-proofed the Earned Income Tax Credit (EITC), which provides a refundable tax credit that both offsets taxes and often operates as a wage supplement. Only those who work can qualify. The amount is determined, in part, by how much each qualified individual or family earned. It is also adjusted to the size of the family. To be eligible for the family EITC, workers must live with their children, who must be under nineteen years old or full-time students under twenty-four years old.

The maximum credit for 2005 was $2,662 for taxpayers with one child, $4,400 for taxpayers with more than one child, and $399 for people with no children. (See Figure 3.6.) Families received less if their income was low because they were also eligible for public assistance. A family of four received the maximum benefit if its earnings were slightly below the poverty line, but many families well above the poverty line received some credit. Single-parent families with one child were eligible for some credit up to an income of $31,030, whereas single-parent families with at least two children were eligible for some credit up to an income of $35,263. Benefits phased down gradually when income surpassed $15,000 and phased out entirely for single-parent families with two or more children that earned more than $35,000.

TABLE 3.8

Workers paid hourly rates at or below minimum wage, by selected characteristics, 2004

Characteristic	Number of workers (in thousands)				Percent distribution				Percent of workers paid hourly rates			
	Total paid hourly rates	At or below $5.15 per hour			Total paid hourly rates	At or below $5.15 per hour				At or below $5.15 per hour		
		Total	At $5.15	Below $5.15		Total	At $5.15	Below $5.15	Total	At $5.15	Below $5.15
Age and sex											
Total, 16 years and over	73,939	2,003	520	1,483	100.0	100.0	100.0	100.0	2.7	0.7	2.0
16 to 24 years	16,174	1,022	272	750	21.9	51.0	52.3	50.6	6.3	1.7	4.6
16 to 19 years	5,433	497	168	329	7.3	24.8	32.3	22.2	9.1	3.1	6.1
25 years and over	57,765	982	249	733	78.1	49.0	47.9	49.4	1.7	0.4	1.3
Men, 16 years and over	36,806	680	210	470	49.8	33.9	40.4	31.7	1.8	0.6	1.3
16 to 24 years	8,305	366	127	239	11.2	18.3	24.4	16.1	4.4	1.5	2.9
16 to 19 years	2,672	179	78	101	3.6	8.9	15.0	6.8	6.7	2.9	3.8
25 years and over	28,500	314	83	231	38.5	15.7	16.0	15.6	1.1	0.3	0.8
Women, 16 years and over	37,133	1,323	310	1,013	50.2	66.1	59.6	68.3	3.6	0.8	2.7
16 to 24 years	7,869	655	145	510	10.6	32.7	27.9	34.4	8.3	1.8	6.5
16 to 19 years	2,761	319	90	229	3.7	15.9	17.3	15.4	11.6	3.3	8.3
25 years and over	29,265	668	166	502	39.6	33.3	31.9	33.9	2.3	0.6	1.7
Race, sex and Hispanic or Latino ethnicity											
White[a]	59,877	1,681	395	1,286	81.0	83.9	76.0	86.7	2.8	0.7	2.1
Men	30,255	554	161	393	40.9	27.7	31.0	26.5	1.8	0.5	1.3
Women	29,621	1,126	234	892	40.1	56.2	45.0	60.1	3.8	0.8	3.0
Black or African American[a]	9,417	227	99	128	12.77	11.3	19.0	8.6	2.4	1.1	1.4
Men	4,243	89	40	49	5.7	4.4	7.7	3.3	2.1	0.9	1.2
Women	5,174	138	59	79	7.0	6.9	11.3	5.3	2.7	1.1	1.5
Asian[a]	2,672	38	8	30	3.6	1.9	1.5	2.0	1.4	0.3	1.1
Men	1,295	15	3	12	1.8	0.7	0.6	0.8	1.2	0.2	0.9
Women	1,378	23	5	18	1.9	1.1	1.0	1.2	1.7	0.4	1.3
Hispanic or Latino[a]	12,073	250	82	168	16.3	12.5	15.8	11.3	2.1	0.7	1.4
Men	7,183	98	32	66	9.7	4.9	6.2	4.5	1.4	0.4	0.9
Women	4,890	151	49	102	6.6	7.5	9.4	6.9	3.1	1.0	2.1
Full- and part-time status and sex											
Full-time workers[b]	55,739	760	177	583	75.4	37.9	34.0	39.3	1.4	0.3	1.0
Men	30,951	300	77	223	41.9	15.0	14.8	15.0	1.0	0.2	0.7
Women	24,788	460	100	360	33.5	23.0	19.2	24.3	1.9	0.4	1.5
Part-time workers[b]	18,046	1,240	343	897	24.4	61.9	66.0	60.5	6.9	1.9	5.0
Men	5,770	378	132	246	7.8	18.9	25.4	16.6	6.6	2.3	4.3
Women	12,276	861	210	651	16.6	43.0	40.4	43.9	7.0	1.7	5.3

Note: Data exclude all the self-employed, both unincorporated and incorporated.

[a]Detail for the race groups (white, black or African American, and Asian) will not sum to totals because data are not presented for all races. In addition, persons whose ethnicity is identified as Hispanic or Latino may be of any race and, therefore, are classified by ethnicity as well as race.

[b]The distinction between full- and part-time workers is based on hours usually worked. These data will not sum to totals because full- or part-time status on the principal job is not identifiable for a small number of multiple jobholders.

SOURCE: "Table 1. Employed Wage and Salary Workers Paid Hourly Rates with Earnings at or Below the Prevailing Federal Minimum Wage by Selected Characteristics, 2004 Annual Averages," in *Characteristics of Minimum Wage Workers: 2004*, U.S. Department of Labor, Bureau of Labor Statistics, April 2005, http://www.bls.gov/cps/minwage2004pdf.pdf (accessed January 11, 2007)

The largest EITC benefits go to families that no longer need welfare. The gradual phaseout and the availability of the EITC at above-poverty income levels help to stabilize a parent's employment by providing additional money to cover expenses associated with working, such as child care and transportation. Research finds that the EITC has been an effective work incentive and has significantly increased work participation among single mothers. The Urban Institute states in "Government Work Supports and Low-Income Families" that eight out of ten low-income working families are eligible to receive the tax credit and that the EITC is the support program with the highest participation rate.

Those who do not owe income tax, or who owe an amount smaller than the credit, receive a check directly from the Internal Revenue Service for the credit due them. Most recipients claim the credit when they file an income tax form. Robert Greenstein concludes in "The Earned Income Tax Credit: Boosting Employment, Aiding the Working Poor" (August 17, 2005, http://www.cbpp.org/7-19-05eic.htm) that the EITC lifted 4.4 million people, including 2.4 million children, out of poverty in 2003. Without the credit, the poverty rate among children would have been almost 25% higher.

Although the Tax Reform Act of 1986 has helped ease the burden of federal taxes, most of the poor still pay

FIGURE 3.5

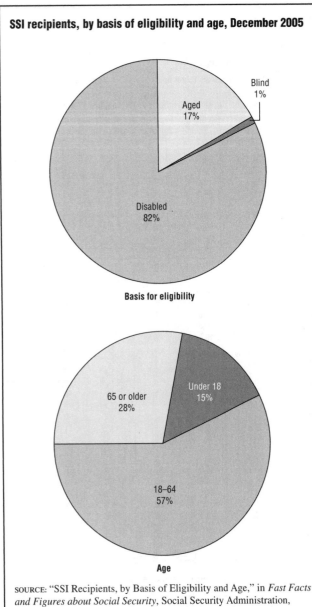

SSI recipients, by basis of eligibility and age, December 2005

Basis for eligibility

Age

SOURCE: "SSI Recipients, by Basis of Eligibility and Age," in *Fast Facts and Figures about Social Security*, Social Security Administration, Office of Policy, Office of Research, Evaluation, and Statistics, September 2006, http://www.ssa.gov/policy/docs/chartbooks/fast_facts/2006/fast_facts06.pdf (accessed January 11, 2007).

a substantial share of their income in state and local taxes. To relieve this tax burden and increase the number of single parents working, eighteen states have enacted a state EITC to supplement the federal credit. These state programs boost the income of families that move from welfare to work and prevent states from taxing poor families deeper into poverty.

OVERLAPPING SERVICES

Not surprisingly, poor households that receive one form of social welfare assistance are likely to qualify for and receive others. For example, during 2002, 37.6% of households receiving TANF also received housing assistance, 62.3% received free or reduced-price school meals, 80.8% received food stamps, and almost all (99.6%) were on Medicaid. (See Table 3.11.) Similarly, among households receiving SSI, 40.2% received food stamps, 17.7% received free or reduced-price school meals, 22.9% lived in public or subsidized rental housing, and 96.4% were on Medicaid. About 18.2% of those receiving Social Security and 17.8% of people receiving Medicare were also on Medicaid.

Among households receiving food stamps, 16.2% received TANF, 30.2% received SSI, 30.5% received Social Security, and 26% were on Medicare. (See Table 3.12.) (The figures do not add up to 100% because some people received more than one benefit.) About 10.8% of those receiving WIC also received TANF benefits.

Between 1984 and 2002 the percentage of AFDC/TANF and SSI households who received other benefits fluctuated, but, generally, the coverage for most nonveteran benefit programs increased initially but then declined following the passage of the PRWORA in 1996. The percentage of households receiving both AFDC/TANF and food stamps declined, from 87.2% in 1995 to 80.8% in 2002. (See Table 3.13.) The percentage receiving both SSI and food stamps also declined over this period, from 50% to 40.2%.

In "Government Work Supports and Low-Income Families," the Urban Institute points out how important the "package of supports" could be to working, low-income families. The package could include Medicaid, food stamps, child care subsidies, and the EITC. According to the Urban Institute, in 2002 a single parent with two children working full time and earning $10,000 (the minimum wage) could receive about $23,600 in work supports. However, most working families did not receive all the supports they could have; in fact, only 7% of families with incomes below the federal poverty level received all four supports in 2002.

TABLE 3.9

Total annual amount of SSI payments, by source of payment and eligibility category, selected years 1974–2004

[In thousands of dollars]

Year	Total	Federally administered	Federal SSI	State supplementation Total	State supplementation Federally administered	State supplementation State administered[a]
All recipients						
1974	5,245,719	5,096,813	3,833,161	1,412,558	1,263,652	148,906
1975	5,878,224	5,716,072	4,313,538	1,564,686	1,402,534	162,152
1980	7,940,734	7,714,640	5,866,354	2,074,380	1,848,286	226,094
1985	11,060,476	10,749,938	8,777,341	2,283,135	1,972,597	310,538
1990	16,598,680	16,132,959	12,893,805	3,704,875	3,239,154	465,721
1995	27,627,658	27,037,280	23,919,430	3,708,228	3,117,850	590,378
2000	31,564,439	30,671,699	27,290,248	4,274,191	3,381,451	892,740
2001	33,060,819	32,165,856	28,705,503	4,355,316	3,460,353	894,963
2002	34,566,844	33,718,999	29,898,765	4,668,079	3,820,234	847,845
2003	35,604,829	34,693,278	30,688,029	4,916,800	4,005,249	911,551
2004	36,961,099	36,065,358	31,886,509	5,074,590	4,178,849	895,741
Aged						
1974	2,503,407	2,414,034	1,782,742	720,665	631,292	89,373
1975	2,604,792	2,516,515	1,842,980	761,812	673,535	88,277
1980	2,734,270	2,617,023	1,860,194	874,076	756,829	117,247
1985	3,034,596	2,896,671	2,202,557	832,039	694,114	137,925
1990	3,736,104	3,559,388	2,521,382	1,214,722	1,038,006	176,716
1995	4,467,146	4,239,222	3,374,772	1,092,374	864,450	227,924
2000	4,811,048	4,537,914	3,595,384	1,225,603	942,530	283,073
2001	4,958,644	4,664,076	3,708,527	1,250,117	955,549	294,568
2002	5,085,554	4,802,792	3,751,491	1,334,063	1,051,301	282,762
2003	5,147,380	4,856,875	3,758,070	1,389,310	1,098,805	290,505
2004	5,173,378	4,894,070	3,773,901	1,399,477	1,133,324	266,153
Blind						
1974	130,195	125,791	91,308	38,887	34,483	4,404
1975	130,936	127,240	92,427	38,509	34,813	3,696
1980	190,075	185,827	131,506	58,569	54,321	4,248
1985	264,162	259,840	195,183	68,979	64,657	4,322
1990	334,120	328,949	238,415	95,705	90,534	5,171
1995	375,512	367,441	298,238	77,274	69,203	8,071
2000	394,484	385,832	312,144	82,324	73,688	8,636
2001	407,371	398,624	323,895	83,476	74,729	8,747
2002	426,409	416,454	335,405	91,004	81,049	9,955
2003	419,352	409,293	325,878	93,473	83,415	10,058
2004	421,817	412,414	327,446	94,371	85,364	9,007
Disabled						
1974	2,601,936	2,556,988	1,959,112	642,824	597,876	44,948
1975	3,142,476	3,072,317	2,378,131	764,345	694,186	70,159
1980	5,013,948	4,911,792	3,874,655	1,139,293	1,037,137	102,156
1985	7,754,588	7,593,427	6,379,601	1,374,987	1,213,826	161,161
1990	12,520,568	12,244,622	10,134,007	2,386,561	2,110,615	275,946
1995	22,778,547	22,430,612	20,246,415	2,532,132	2,184,197	347,935
2000	26,189,350	25,764,675	23,399,442	2,844,868	2,365,233	479,635
2001	27,611,303	27,125,707	24,695,630	2,915,673	2,430,077	485,596
2002	28,996,405	28,499,771[b]	25,811,887[b]	3,184,518	2,687,884	496,634
2003	29,966,210	29,429,428[b]	26,606,400[b]	3,359,810	2,823,028	536,782
2004	31,257,856	30,745,406	27,785,246	3,472,610	2,960,160	512,450

[a]Includes data not distributed by category.
[b]Revised data.
Note: SSI is Supplemental Security Income.

SOURCE: "Table 7.A4. Total Payments, by Eligibility Category and Source of Payment, Selected Years 1974–2004," in *Annual Statistical Supplement to the Social Security Bulletin, 2005*, Social Security Administration, Office of Policy, Office of Research, Evaluation, and Statistics, February 2006, http://www.ssa.gov/policy/docs/statcomps/supplement/2005/supplement05.pdf (accessed January 11, 2007)

TABLE 3.10

Number and percentage distribution of federally administered awards, by sex, age, and eligibility category, 2004

Sex and age	Total	Adults			Blind and disabled children[a]
		Aged	Blind	Disabled	
All persons					
Number	856,190	105,850	4,070	558,850	187,420
Percent	100.0	100.0	100.0	100.0	100.0
Percentage distribution by sex					
Male	51.6	37.6	55.8	49.6	65.1
Female	48.4	62.4	44.2	50.4	34.9
Percentage distribution by age					
Under 5	8.3	—	—	—	38.0
5–9	5.8	—	—	—	26.5
10–14	5.2	—	—	—	23.6
15–17	2.0	—	—	—	9.2
18–21	5.4	—	15.0	7.3	2.8
22–29	6.2	—	15.5	9.4	—
30–39	10.5	—	14.7	16.0	—
40–49	17.8	—	17.9	27.1	—
50–59	20.6	—	24.3	31.3	—
60–64	5.6	—	7.9	8.5	—
65–69	6.9	54.2	1.7	0.3	—
70–74	2.6	21.2	1.0	b	—
75–79	1.5	11.8	1.0	b	—
80 or older	1.6	12.9	1.0	b	—
Male					
Number	441,560	39,790	2,270	277,420	122,080
Percent	100.0	100.0	100.0	100.0	100.0
Under 5	9.8	—	—	—	35.6
5–9	8.1	—	—	—	29.2
10–14	6.7	—	—	—	24.4
15–17	2.3	—	—	—	8.4
18–21	5.9	—	15.0	8.3	2.4
22–29	6.5	—	15.9	10.2	—
30–39	9.9	—	16.3	15.6	—
40–49	16.9	—	15.9	26.8	—
50–59	19.5	—	25.6	30.8	—
60–64	5.1	—	8.8	8.0	—
65–69	5.3	56.6	1.8	0.3	—
70–74	2.1	22.8	0.9	b	—
75–79	1.0	11.4	b	b	—
80 or older	0.8	9.1	b	b	—
Female					
Number	414,630	66,060	1,800	281,430	65,340
Percent	100.0	100.0	100.0	100.0	100.0
Under 5	6.7	—	—	—	42.4
5–9	3.4	—	—	—	21.3
10–14	3.5	—	—	—	22.1
15–17	1.7	—	—	—	10.7
18–21	4.9	—	15.0	6.3	3.5
22–29	5.9	—	15.0	8.6	—
30–39	11.2	—	12.8	16.4	—
40–49	18.8	—	20.6	27.5	—
50–59	21.7	—	22.8	31.8	—
60–64	6.1	—	6.7	9.4	—
65–69	8.6	52.7	1.7	0.4	—
70–74	3.2	20.2	1.1	b	—
75–79	1.9	12.0	2.2	b	—
80 or older	2.4	15.1	2.2	b	—

Note: — not applicable.

[a]Includes students aged 18–21.

[b]Less than 0.05 percent.

SOURCE: "Table 7.E2. Percentage Distribution of Federally Administered Awards, by Sex, Age, and Eligibility Category, 2004," in *Annual Statistical Supplement to the Social Security Bulletin, 2005*, Social Security Administration, Office of Policy, Office of Research, Evaluation, and Statistics, February 2006, http://www.ssa.gov/policy/docs/statcomps/supplement/2005/supplement05.pdf (accessed January 11, 2007)

FIGURE 3.6

The Federal Earned Income Tax Credit, tax year 2005

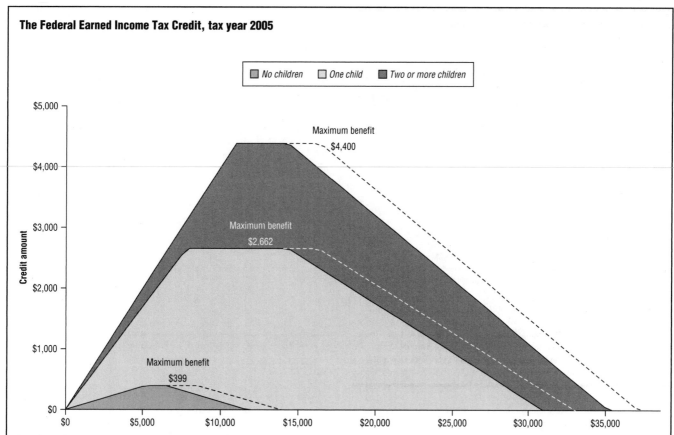

Note: Married couples with income in the phaseout range qualify for a higher credit than single parents—shown by dashed lines.

SOURCE: Ami Nagle and Nicholas Johnson, "Figure 2. The Federal Earned Income Tax Credit in Tax Year 2005," in *A Hand Up: How State Earned Income Tax Credits Help Working Families Escape Poverty in 2006*, Center on Budget and Policy Priorities, March 2006, http://www.cbpp.org/3-8-06sfp.pdf (accessed January 11, 2007)

TABLE 3.11

Percent of recipients in multiple federal assistance programs, 2002

Other assistance programs	Ways and Means assistance programs				
	TANF	SSI	Social Security	Unemployment compensation	Medicare
Food stamps	80.8	40.2	6.7	10.6	6.3
WIC	35.1	5.2	1.2	8.4	0.8
Medicaid	99.6	96.4	18.2	23.5	17.8
Free or reduced-price school meals	62.3	17.7	4.3	16.1	3.0
Public or subsidized rental housing	37.6	22.9	5.6	3.0	5.6
VA compensation or pensions	1.0	3.6	4.6	1.4	4.8
Number of recipients in households receiving benefits (in thousands)	1,393	5,207	31,358	3,209	28,452

Notes: Table shows number of recipient households for February–May 2002. Tables read that 80.8 percent of households with TANF (Temporary Assistance for Needy Families) recipients also received food stamp benefits. SSI is Supplemental Security Income. WIC is Women, Infants and Children. VA is Veteran Affairs.

SOURCE: "Table 15. Overview 1. Percent of Recipients in Programs within the Jurisdiction of the Committee on Ways and Means Receiving Assistance from Other Major Federal Programs, 2002," in *The Green Book*, U.S. House of Representatives, Committee on Ways and Means, 2004, http://waysandmeans.house.gov/media/pdf/greenbook2003/15OVERVIEW.pdf (accessed January 11, 2007)

TABLE 3.12

Recipients of federal assistance programs receiving aid from multiple programs, by percent and number, 2002

Ways and Means assistance programs	Other assistance programs					
	Food stamps	WIC	Free or reduced-price school meals	Public or subsidized rental housing	Medicaid	VA compensation or pensions
TANF	16.2	10.8	9.0	10.9	8.0	0.6
SSI	30.2	6.0	9.6	24.8	29.0	7.0
Social Security	30.5	8.1	13.9	36.9	32.9	54.4
Unemployment compensation	4.9	6.0	5.4	2.0	4.4	1.7
Medicare	26.0	5.1	9.0	33.5	29.2	52.3
Number of recipients in households receiving benefits (in thousands)	6,924	4,517	9,620	4,795	17,322	2,639

Note: Table shows number of recipient households for February–May 2002. Tables read that 16.2 percent of households with food stamp recipients also received TANF (Temporary Assistance for Needy Families). WIC is Women, Infants and Children. VA is Veteran Affairs. SSI is Supplemental Security Income.

SOURCE: "Table 15. Overview 2. Percent of Recipients in Other Major Federal Assistance Programs Receiving Assistance Under Programs within the Jurisdiction of the Committee on Ways and Means, 2002," in *The Green Book*, U.S. House of Representatives, Committee on Ways and Means, 2004, http://waysandmeans.house.gov/media/pdf/greenbook2003/15OVERVIEW.pdf (accessed January 11, 2007)

TABLE 3.13

Percent of households receiving TANF or SSI and also receiving assistance from other programs, selected years, 1984–2002

Assistance program	1984	1987	1990	1992	1993	1994	1995	1997–98	2002
AFDC/TANF:									
Food stamps	81.4	81.7	82.7	86.2	88.9	88.3	87.2	81.0	80.8
WIC	15.3	18.6	18.7	21.5	18.5	21.4	24.7	30.6	35.1
Free or reduced-price school meals	49.2	55.6	52.7	55.5	56.9	57.5	63.1	60.3	62.3
Public or subsidized rental housing	23.0	19.4	34.7	29.5	33.1	30.3	31.1	21.2	37.6
Medicaid	93.2	95.5	97.6	96.2	97.6	96.4	97.2	97.3	99.6
VA compensation or pensions	2.8	1.9	1.3	1.9	1.1	1.1	0.8	1.1	1.0
Number of households receiving benefits (in thousands)	3,585	3,527	3,434	4,057	4,831	4,906	4,652	3,008	1,391
SSI:									
Food stamps	46.5	39.7	41.3	46.2	48.0	50.1	50.0	43.7	40.2
WIC	2.5	2.5	3.0	4.3	3.7	5.4	5.6	5.5	5.2
Free or reduced-price school meals	12.7	11.9	15.3	18.2	21.3	23.8	25.2	18.4	17.7
Public or subsidized rental housing	21.6	20.0	21.4	23.8	23.9	24.9	24.1	23.4	22.9
Medicaid	100.0	99.6	99.7	99.8	99.5	100.0	100.0	95.0	96.4
VA compensation or pensions	4.7	7.7	5.7	4.0	4.5	3.9	3.6	2.8	3.6
Number of households receiving benefits (in thousands)	3,008	3,341	3,037	3,957	3,861	4,223	4,580	4,772	5,207

Note: Data on households interviewed between February and May 2002. AFDC/TANF is Aid to Families with Dependent Children/Temporary Assistance for Needy Families. WIC is Women, Infants and Children. VA is Veteran Affairs. SSI is Supplemental Security Income

SOURCE: "Table 15. Overview 3. Percent of Households Receiving TANF or SSI and Also Receiving Assistance from Other Programs, Selected Years, 1984–2002," in *The Green Book*, U.S. House of Representatives, Committee on Ways and Means, 2004, http://waysandmeans.house.gov/media/pdf/green book2003/15OVERVIEW.pdf (accessed January 11, 2007)

CHAPTER 4

CHARACTERISTICS OF THE HOMELESS

AUTHORITATIVE ESTIMATES OF HOMELESSNESS
The Facts Are Hard to Determine

Broad national assessments of homelessness were undertaken by several agencies and organizations during the 1980s and mid-1990s, including *A Report to the Secretary on the Homeless and Emergency Shelters* (1984) by the U.S. Department of Housing and Urban Development (HUD), Martha R. Burt and Barbara Cohen's *America's Homeless: Numbers, Characteristics, and Programs that Serve Them* (1989), and Martha R. Burt et al.'s *Homelessness: Programs and the People They Serve, Findings of the National Survey of Homeless Assistance Providers and Clients* (December 1999, http://www.urban.org/UploadedPDF/homelessness.pdf). In 2002 Burt and other researchers summarized the difficulty of addressing homelessness without a continuing census or other governmental program to track the homeless population in *Evaluation of Continuums of Care for Homeless People* (May 2002, http://www.huduser.org/publications/pdf/continuums_of_care.pdf). Burt et al. note:

> Basically, there are only three sources or original data on which to base estimates of incidence (the number of people homeless on a single day) for the nation as a whole—HUD's 1984 effort (HUD, 1984), the Urban Institute's 1987 study (Burt and Cohen, 1989), and the 1996 National Survey of Homeless Providers and Clients (Burt, Aron, and Lee, 2001). Any national estimates offered by anyone for any years other than 1984, 1987, and 1996 are projections or manipulations of one of these three data sources, and include assumptions of population change or growth that are not grounded in data. HUD's 1984 study was based on a survey of providers, who supplied their best guesses as to the size of the homeless population in their cities. Only the 1987 and 1996 studies are based on statistically reliable samples of homeless people using homeless assistance programs. Using these three data sources, the number of people homeless at any one time appears to have grown substantially from the mid-1980s until the mid-

1990s—from 250,000–350,000 in 1984 (HUD's "most reliable range") to 500,000–600,000 in 1987, to 640,000–840,000 in 1996. Best guesses or projections of the number of people homeless during the course of a year come from various different sources (Burt, Aron, and Lee, 2001; Culhane et al., 1994; Link et al., 1994, 1995) (there are no truly reliable national data). These estimates, using very different approaches, nevertheless converge on figures that between 2.5 and 3.5 million people (including children) experience at least one night of homelessness within a given year.

Even these data, considered by the government to be reliable, are based on small samples. The data in Burt et al.'s *Homelessness*, the most recent and most widely used study, were based on interviews with 6,307 homeless program representatives and 4,207 users of homeless programs in 1996. The total number of people homeless at some point in 1996 was derived by projection from this sample. Even though such methods of estimating are common in statistical analysis, they also show that current knowledge about homelessness is, at best, partial.

The National Alliance to End Homelessness collects more recent information that can be used to measure changes in homelessness over time. In 2005 it compiled data from 463 local Continuum of Care point-in-time counts from across the nation and published an estimate of the national homeless population in *Homelessness Counts* (January 10, 2007, http://www.endhomelessness.org/content/article/detail/1440). The alliance estimates that in January 2005, 744,313 people experienced homelessness. Of these, 56% were living in shelters or transitional housing and 44% were unsheltered. More than half (59%) were single adults and 41% were living in the 98,452 homeless families counted. Almost a quarter (23%) of homeless people were chronically homeless—in other words, they had been homeless for a long period or repeatedly. The alliance cautions that point-in-time estimates only tell how many people are homeless at a given time and that, in reality, many more people experience homeless at some point in a given year.

How Numbers Are Used

The ordinary citizen, hearing of the homeless, envisions people, including children, who live on the street permanently and sleep in cardboard boxes under bridges or in cars. There are, of course, people in this category, but they are the minority among the homeless. HUD labels such people the chronically homeless and estimates their number at around 150,000. According to the *Emergency and Transitional Shelter Population: 2000—Census 2000 Special Reports* (October 2001, http://www.census.gov/prod/2001pubs/censr01-2.pdf) by Annetta C. Smith and Denise I. Smith, this estimate is close to the number of people counted in the 2000 census as inhabiting emergency and transitional shelters (170,706 individuals). *Homelessness Counts* estimates that about 171,192 people were chronically homeless in January 2005. Most of the homeless are not chronically homeless but are temporarily without a residence. After some period of homelessness they find permanent shelter or move in with relatives; although people who have moved in with family as well as people who are doubled up are also counted as homeless by some programs and homeless advocates.

A more accurate definition of the homeless population is the group of people who are, on any day, without proper shelter. When agencies or the media cite numbers in the 600,000 to 800,000 range, they mean the size of the homeless population at any one point in time. Individuals are continuously joining this population while others are leaving it. If all people who are homeless at some point during a given year were counted, the number would reach between 2.5 million and 3.5 million individuals, as indicated by Burt et al. in *Evaluation of Continuums of Care for Homeless People.*

The manner in which the annual projections for 1996 were derived is shown in Table 4.1. The data for October, projected from counts of homeless services seekers, show that an estimated 36,900 individuals began spells of homelessness during the week surveyed, whereas the total number of people in the homeless population in any one week was estimated to be 444,000. The annual projection assumed that each week 36,900 became homeless and an equal number passed out of the homeless status. Multiplying 36,900 by the fifty-one weeks remaining in the year, and then adding that total to the average homeless population in a week, produced the 2.3 million count of people who were homeless at least once in 1996. This number does not mean that there were 2.3 million homeless during the entire span of 1996.

TABLE 4.1

Estimated number of people likely to be homeless at least once during the year, October 1996 and February 1996

	New homeless spells begun in last week	Average week estimate	Annual projection
	A	**B**	**C**
February 1996	52,000	842,000	3.5 million
October 1996	36,900	444,000	2.3 million

Note: The projection is developed by taking column A times 51 weeks and adding the result to column B. Column B represents the estimated constant population of homeless in any one week. The assumption is that a population of the size shown in column A is continuously passing into and also out of homeless status throughout the year. Data for February were based on the estimates of homeless program employees, data for October on interviews with the homeless.

SOURCE: "Number Likely to Be Homeless at Least Once in a Given Year," in *America's Homeless II: Populations and Services,* Urban Institute, February 2000, http://www.urban.org/UploadedPDF/900344_AmericasHomelessII.pdf (accessed January 11, 2007)

Counting Homeless Children

Sometimes stories in the media, such as Ralph da Costa Nunez and Laura M. Caruso's "Are Shelters the Answer to Family Homelessness" (*USA Today,* January 1, 2003), cite 600,000 homeless and one million homeless children. Such statements double count the homeless with two different sources of incompatible data. Under the McKinney-Vento Homeless Assistance Act of 1987, the U.S. Department of Education is required to file a report on homeless children served by the act. The Department of Education obtains the data from school districts; school districts use different methods of estimation. In its *Report to the President and Congress on the Implementation of the Education for Homeless Children and Youth Program under the McKinney-Vento Homeless Assistance Act* (2006, http://www.ed.gov/programs/homeless/rpt2006.doc), the Department of Education states that 602,568 children who experienced homelessness at some point during the year were enrolled during the 2003–04 school year. (See Table 4.2.) This number is almost certainly much lower than the number of children who actually experienced homelessness during that period, as the homeless status of children does not always come to the attention of school officials and many homeless children are not enrolled in school.

PROFILES OF THE HOMELESS

Gender and Race

Studies of homeless people and surveys of officials knowledgeable about homeless clients conducted since the 1990s show similar patterns of gender and racial data for the homeless, although the percentages vary from study to study.

TABLE 4.2

Homeless children and youth enrolled in grades K–12 during the 2003–04 school year

Grades	Number enrolled
K–5	338,982
6–8	153,500
9–12	110,086
Total all grades	**602,568**

SOURCE: "Table 1. Homeless Children and Youth Enrolled in School during the 2003–04 School Year," in *Report to the President and Congress on the Implementation of the Education for Homeless Children and Youth Program under the McKinney-Vento Homeless Assistance Act*, U.S. Department of Education, April 2006, http://www.ed.gov/programs/homeless/rpt2006.doc (accessed October 2, 2006)

Data collected for the 2006 U.S. Conference of Mayors survey show that in almost all cities surveyed, single males greatly outnumbered single females among the homeless. Single males represented a particularly high proportion of the homeless population in Nashville, Tennessee (74%), Miami, Florida (69%), and Salt Lake City, Utah (66.5%). (See Table 4.3.) The highest proportion of single females was in Santa Monica, California, where one-third (34%) of homeless people were single females. Detroit, Michigan, had a particularly high percentage of families among its homeless population (75%), followed by Des Moines, Iowa (61%), and Kansas City, Missouri (56%).

The racial composition of the homeless varied from city to city in the Conference of Mayors survey. (See Table 4.3.) Whites were the largest group in Charleston, South Carolina (52%), Denver, Colorado (37%), Des Moines (61%), Phoenix, Arizona (45%), Portland, Oregon (56%), and Salt Lake City (63%). In all other cities surveyed African-Americans were the largest group among the homeless. They were particularly overrepresented in Chicago, Illinois (80%), Philadelphia, Pennsylvania (77%), Norfolk, Virginia (75%), and Cleveland, Ohio (74%).

The Association of Gospel Rescue Missions (AGRM) regularly surveys the homeless population at more than one hundred missions serving inner cities. The AGRM surveys are based on large numbers of homeless served. In 2005, for example, 22,000 individuals were surveyed at rescue missions around the country. AGRM data show that men were 76% of the homeless in 2005. (See Table 1.11 in Chapter 1.) The racial/ethnic composition of the homeless population the AGRM served in 2005 was 45% white, 38% African-American, 10% Hispanic, 5% Native American, and 1% Asian.

In *Homelessness*, Burt et al. report that 68% of the homeless population was male and 32% was female. Forty-one percent of the homeless were white, 40% African-American, 11% Hispanic, 8% Native American, and 1% of other races. (See Table 1.12 in Chapter 1.)

TABLE 4.3

Composition of the homeless population, November 2005–October 2006

City	Families	Men	Women	Youth	African-American	White	Hispanic	Asian	Native American	Mentally ill	Substance abusers	Employed	Veterans	Single parent families	Family members who are children
Boston	37	52	11	0	44	31	20	5	0	21	39	44	7	90	56
Charleston	19	62	10	9	42	52	2	0	4	37	75	20	32	92	20
Charlotte	0	0	0	0	0	0	0	0	0	0	0	0	0	0	0
Chicago	26.2	57.4	16.4	0	80	10	9	0.3	1	6	23	11	6.9	92.9	66.8
Cleveland	12	56	32	0	74	21	4	0	1	22	56	0	20	99	65
Denver	54	29	13	4	31	37	22	2	8	28	41	15	6	38	31
Des Moines	61	18	18	3	24	61	10	1	2	21	9	32	19	45	37
Detroit	75	15	6.3	3.7	0	0	0	0	0	40	57	0	24	0	0
Kansas City	56	27	16	1	53.3	37.8	6.7	1.2	0.2	0	0	0	13	94	69
Los Angeles	29	56	23	2	48	25	20	0	0	36	49	0	18	15	20
Louisville metro	14	61	21	4	39	36	2	0.2	0.3	8	11	28	25	90	59.6
Miami	14	69	17	0	0	0	0	0	0	0	0	0	0	0	0
Nashville	11	74	15	0	54	43	3	0	0	18	43	4	15	92	60
Norfolk	20	60	20	0	75	23	1.6	0	0.4	0	0	0	0	94	62
Philadelphia	36	44.3	17.23	0	77	11.59	5.4	1.43	0.22	21.33	34.28	0	0	29	66
Phoenix	32	53	13	0.8	13	45	25	0	3	25	26	0	4	0	66
Portland	41	35	22	2	18	56	20	2	4	18	24	10	8	50	51
Salt Lake City	19.7	66.5	13.8	0	10	63	18	2	7	13	21	16	14	56	60
San Francisco	20	63	17	0	37	30	17	4	12	0	0	0	0	56	54
Santa Monica	7	58	34	1	34	51	13	1	1	34	41	11.3	7.6	60	83
Seattle	38	45	16	0	28	35	9	2	4	23	24	9	11	80	23
St. Paul	21	62	12	4	44	39	9	2	2	47	34	30	26	90	61
Trenton	0	0	0	0	0	0	0	0	0	100	40	55	26	88	83

SOURCE: "Composition of the Homeless Population," in *Hunger and Homelessness Survey: A Status Report on Hunger and Homelessness in America's Cities—A 23-City Survey*, U.S. Conference of Mayors and Sodexho, December 2006, http://usmayors.org/uscm/hungersurvey/2006/report06.pdf (accessed Januay 21, 2007)

These surveys exhibit similar patterns. More of the homeless were male than female, but these proportions have been gradually changing. Burt et al. report that while 40% of the homeless were African-American, only 11% of the total U.S. population was African-American. Thus, African-Americans were overrepresented among the ranks of the homeless. (See Table 1.12 in Chapter 1.) Hispanic representation among the homeless (11%) was near their share of total population (9%). Native Americans were homeless (8%) in greater proportion to their share of the total population (1%), and other ethnic groups were homeless (1%) in lower proportion to their share of the total population (3%).

Family Structure

According to Burt et al. in *Homelessness*, 62% of homeless men and 16% of homeless women were single—meaning they were homeless without a spouse or children. (See Table 1.12 in Chapter 1.) The 2006 Conference of Mayors survey finds that 30% of homeless people were in families with children, 51% were single men, 17% were single women, and 2% were unaccompanied youth. (See Table 4.4.) According to the survey, since 1994 the proportion of families among the homeless has generally declined. Data from the Conference of Mayors survey show city-by-city estimates of children as a percent of homeless family members. (See Table 4.3.) Values range from 20% of homeless family members in Los Angeles, California, and Charleston, to 83% in Trenton, New Jersey, and Santa Monica.

Homelessness Counts did not break down its count of the 2005 homeless population by gender, but by individuals (59%) and people in families (41%). The AGRM survey presents data about the family structure of homeless families. According to the survey, 14% of homeless families in 2005 were couples without children, 61% were women with children, 6% were men with children, and 19% were intact families—couples with children. (See Table 1.11 in Chapter 1.)

Age

Burt et al. find in *Homelessness* that 38% of the homeless were between thirty-five and forty-four years of age, 25% were between ages twenty-five and thirty-four, and 17% were between ages forty-five and fifty-four. The AGRM survey for 2005 shows that 20% of the homeless were between ages twenty-six and thirty-five, 29% were between ages thirty-six and forty-five, and 27% were between ages forty-six and sixty-five. (See Table 1.11 in Chapter 1.) The largest group in both surveys was the thirty-five to forty-five group—that is, adults in their middle years.

CHILDREN AND YOUTHS. Homeless children and youths have always received special attention from the public and welfare agencies. In the terminology of the

nineteenth century, children are considered "worthy" poor, because if they are homeless, it is because of events beyond their control.

Estimates provided by the Conference of Mayors give some indication of the proportion of children and runaway teens (unaccompanied youth) among the homeless population. In 2006, 30% of the homeless population in the twenty-three surveyed cities were in family groups and 24% were children. (See Table 4.4.)

The Conference of Mayors also surveyed the proportion of unaccompanied youth in the homeless population; in 2006 these teens not under adult supervision made up 2% of the homeless population in surveyed cities. (See Table 4.4.) The proportion of unaccompanied youth had steadily dropped from a high of 7% in 2000.

The Department of Education collects estimates of homeless children from selected school district records. The data exclude infants but include some children of pre-school age. The department's tallies show a total of 602,568 children and youth of school age (see Table 4.2), and another 19,343 children of preschool age that had been served during the year. Of these children, about half (50.3%) lived doubled up with relatives or friends; a quarter (25.3%) lived in shelters, 10% lived in hotels or motels, and 2.6% were unsheltered—in other words, sleeping outside, in vehicles, or in abandoned buildings. (See Figure 4.1.)

Even though the 2006 Department of Education report omits estimates of the total number of homeless children in the population, *Education for Homeless Children and Youth Program, Report to Congress, Fiscal Year 2000* (2001, http://www.ed.gov/programs/homeless/rpt2000.doc) includes this information. The department finds that of total children estimated by school districts to be homeless in 2000, only a portion were enrolled and even a smaller number attended school regularly. Among the estimated 343,340 homeless elementary students, 305,920 (89.1%) were enrolled and 271,906 (79.2%) attended regularly. However, Arun Venugopal, in "Advocates Say City Undercounts Homeless Kids" (September 14, 2006, http://www.wnyc.org/news/articles/64264), indicates that the Department of Education undercounts the number of homeless kids, which would place the number of homeless kids not enrolled in or attending school even higher. For example, in the *2005 Greater Los Angeles Homeless Count* (January 2006, http://www.lahsa.org/homelesscount2005/pdfs/LAHSA%20Report%20-%20Final%20Version6-4.pdf), a survey of homeless respondents in Los Angeles, the Los Angeles Homeless Services Authority finds that 31.8% of homeless families with school-age children stated their children were not attending school. Unfortunately, even when homeless children do attend school they have less than optimal conditions for educational achievement.

An example of the poor educational achievement of homeless youths is shown in the *Homeless Census and*

TABLE 4.4

Indicators of hunger and homelessness in large urban areas, 1991–2006

Indicator	1991	1992	1993	1994	1995	1996	1997	1998	1999	2000	2001	2002	2003	2004	2005	2006
Hunger																
Increase in demand for emergency food	26%	18%	13%	12%	9%	11%	16%	14%	18%	17%	23%	19%	17%	14%	12%	7%
Cities in which demand for food increased	93%	96%	83%	83%	72%	83%	86%	78%	85%	83%	93%	100%	88%	96%	76%	74%
Increase in demand by families for food assistance	26%	14%	13%	14%	10%	10%	13%	14%	15%	16%	19%	17%	18%	13%	7%	5%
Portion of those requesting food assistance who are families with children	68%	68%	67%	64%	63%	62%	58%	61%	58%	62%	54%	48%	59%	56%	54%	70%
Demand for emergency food unmet	17%	21%	16%	15%	18%	18%	19%	21%	21%	13%	14%	16%	14%	20%	18%	23%
Cities in which food assistance facilities must turn people away	79%	68%	68%	73%	59%	50%	71%	47%	54%	46%	33%	32%	56%	48%	43%	26%
Cities which expect demand for emergency food to increase next year	100%	89%	100%	81%	96%	96%	92%	96%	84%	71%	100%	100%	87%	88%	90%	72%
Homelessness																
Increase in demand for emergency shelter	13%	14%	10%	13%	11%	5%	3%	11%	12%	15%	13%	19%	13%	6%	6%	9%
Cities in which demand increased	89%	88%	81%	80%	63%	71%	59%	72%	69%	76%	81%	88%	80%	70%	71%	68%
Demand for emergency shelter unmet	15%	23%	25%	21%	19%	20%	27%	26%	25%	23%	37%	30%	30%	23%	14%	23%
Cities in which shelters must turn people away	74%	75%	77%	72%	82%	81%	88%	67%	73%	56%	44%	56%	84%	81%	79%	77%
Cities which expect demand for shelter to increase next year	100%	93%	88%	71%	100%	100%	100%	93%	92%	72%	100%	100%	88%	88%	93%	68%
Composition of homeless population																
Single men	50%	55%	43%	48%	46%	45%	47%	45%	43%	44%	40%	41%	41%	41%	43%	51%
Families with children	35%	32%	34%	39%	36%	38%	36%	38%	36%	36%	40%	41%	40%	40%	33%	30%
Single women	12%	11%	11%	11%	14%	14%	14%	14%	13%	13%	14%	13%	14%	14%	17%	17%
Unaccompanied youth	3%	2%	4%	3%	4%	3%	4%	3%	4%	7%	4%	5%	5%	5%	3%	2%
Children	24%	22%	30%	26%	25%	27%	25%	25%	NA	NA	NA	NA	NA	NA	NA	24%
Severely mentally ill	29%	28%	27%	26%	23%	24%	27%	24%	19%	22%	22%	23%	23%	23%	22%	16%
Substance abusers	40%	41%	48%	43%	46%	43%	43%	38%	31%	37%	34%	32%	30%	30%	30%	26%
Employed	18%	17%	18%	19%	20%	18%	17%	22%	21%	26%	20%	22%	17%	17%	15%	13%
Veterans	23%	18%	21%	23%	23%	19%	22%	22%	14%	15%	11%	10%	10%	10%	11%	9%

SOURCE: "Hunger and Homelessness in America's Cities: A Sixteen-Year Comparison," in *Hunger and Homelessness Survey: A Status Report on Hunger and Homelessness in America's Cities—A 23-City Survey*, U.S. Conference of Mayors and Sodexho, December 2006, http://usmayors.org/uscm/hungersurvey/2006/report06.pdf (accessed January 21, 2007)

FIGURE 4.1

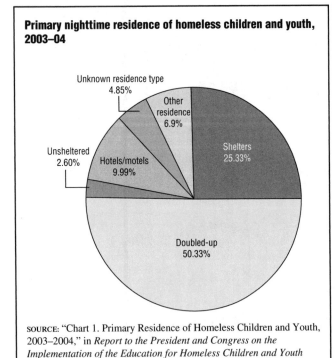

Primary nighttime residence of homeless children and youth, 2003–04

Unknown residence type 4.85%

Other residence 6.9%

Unsheltered 2.60%

Hotels/motels 9.99%

Shelters 25.33%

Doubled-up 50.33%

SOURCE: "Chart 1. Primary Residence of Homeless Children and Youth, 2003–2004," in *Report to the President and Congress on the Implementation of the Education for Homeless Children and Youth Program under the McKinney-Vento Homeless Assistance Act*, U.S. Department of Education, April 2006, http://www.ed.gov/programs/homeless/rpt2006.doc (accessed October 2, 2006)

Homeless Youth/Foster Teen Study (2002, http://www.appliedsurveyresearch.org/www/products/MC_Homeless02_report.pdf), a study of unaccompanied homeless youths conducted in Monterey County, California. According to the study's findings, 21% of sixteen-year-olds, 22% of seventeen-year-olds, 33% of eighteen-year-olds, 51% of nineteen-year-olds, 59% of twenty-year-olds, and 70% of twenty-one-year-olds were below grade level. Only 13% of the homeless youths in the study had a high school diploma or general equivalency diploma. The remaining 87% were performing below grade level.

The study shows that many homeless youth aged fourteen to twenty-one had been in the foster care system and had become homeless after emancipation (leaving foster care). Although this study is only a countywide survey, it confirms that children formerly in foster care are represented in higher numbers among the homeless than in the population at large. Ten percent of the unaccompanied homeless youths in the Monterey County study were at one time in the foster care system, whereas only 0.3% of the general population aged fourteen to twenty-one were ever in foster care.

Educational Achievement

The poor educational achievement of homeless youth puts them at an increased risk for homelessness in their adulthoods. After investigating the education of homeless people, Burt et al. find in *Homelessness* that 38% had less

than a high school diploma, 34% had completed high school, and 28% had some education beyond high school. (See Table 1.12 in Chapter 1.) The homeless were less educated than the population as a whole. In 1996, 18% of the U.S. adult population had less than a high school education, 34% had a high school diploma, and 48% had some education beyond high school.

Military Background

Burt et al. also report in *Homelessness* that in 1996, 23% of the homeless were veterans, whereas 13% of people in the general population were veterans. Citing U.S. Department of Veterans Affairs sources, the National Coalition for Homeless Veterans (NCHV) states in "Background and Statistics" (2005, http://www.nchv.org/background.cfm) that about two hundred thousand veterans are homeless on any given day, and up to four hundred thousand experience homelessness annually. Of homeless veterans, 96% are male and 4% are female. Almost half (47%) served during Vietnam; two-thirds (67%) served for three years or more and one-third (33%) were stationed in a war zone. Forty-five percent of homeless veterans have mental illness and half abuse drugs or alcohol.

In "Survey Confirms 'War on Terror' Veterans Are Seeking Homeless Assistance" (January 12, 2005, http://www.nchv.org/news_article.cfm?id=101)—a small survey of nineteen homeless veteran service providers to determine the effects of the wars in Iraq and Afghanistan on homeless veteran numbers—the NCHV finds that those nineteen service providers had served sixty-seven veterans from these wars. Linda Boone, the executive director of the NCHV, states that these veterans were likely to request assistance sooner and in greater numbers than did veterans of other foreign wars.

DURATION AND RECURRENCE OF HOMELESSNESS

Most homeless people will become homeless again. In *Homelessness*, Burt et al. note that 51% of all homeless people surveyed in that year had been homeless before. The AGRM finds in its 2005 survey that 66% of the homeless had been homeless before—26% had been homeless once before, 18% had been homeless twice before, and 22% had been homeless three or more times before. (See Table 1.11 in Chapter 1.)

Thirty-nine percent of the homeless studied by Burt et al. had been homeless less than six months, and 59% had been homeless for more than half a year. Fifty-nine percent of the homeless surveyed by the AGRM in 2005 had been homeless less than one year, and more than one-third had been homeless for more than a year.

These studies confirm that homelessness is usually a recurring experience and lasts for months at a time, suggesting that programs that help the homeless do not uniformly help clients solve the basic problems that can lead to life on the streets.

THE RURAL HOMELESS

Most studies on the homeless have been focused on urban areas, leaving the impression that this problem exists only on city sidewalks. Homelessness is more common in the cities, where the bulk of the population resides, but many areas of rural America also experience the phenomenon. According to *Rural Poverty at a Glance* (July 2004, http://www.ers.usda.gov/publications/rdrr100/rdrr100.pdf), the U.S. Department of Agriculture's Economic Research Service reports that rural communities have higher poverty rates than do urban areas. Rural communities have fewer official shelters and fewer public places (for example, heating grates, subways, or train stations), where the homeless can find temporary shelter. Therefore, they are more likely to live in a car or a camper, or with relatives in overcrowded or run-down housing. Finding the rural homeless is therefore more difficult for investigators of the problem.

The National Coalition for the Homeless (NCH) reports in the fact sheet "Rural Homelessness" (June 2006, http://www.nationalhomeless.org/publications/facts/Rural.pdf) that the rural homeless are more likely to be white, female, married, and currently working than are the urban homeless. They are also more likely to be homeless for the first time and generally experience homelessness for a shorter period than the urban homeless. Furthermore, the NCH notes that domestic violence is more likely to be a cause of homelessness in rural areas and that alcohol and substance abuse is less likely to be a cause.

Burt et al. determine in *Homelessness* that 21% of all homeless people in their study lived in suburban areas and 9% lived in rural communities. The rural homeless surveyed were more likely to be working, or to have worked recently, than the urban homeless—65% of the rural homeless had worked for pay in the last month. Homeless people living in rural areas were also more likely to be experiencing their first spell of homelessness (60%). In 55% of the cases the homeless period lasted three months or less.

Patricia A. Post, in *Hard to Reach: Rural Homelessness and Health Care* (January 2002, http://www.nhchc.org/Publications/RuralHomeless.pdf), argues that rural residents typically deal with a lack of permanent housing not by sleeping on the streets, like their urban counterparts, but by first moving in with a series of friends, second moving into abandoned shacks, cars, or campgrounds, and finally moving to cities in search of employment. They also differ from urban homeless people in many ways: They have less education, typically hold temporary jobs with no benefits, are less likely to receive government assistance or have health insurance, and are more likely to have been incar-

cerated for a period. According to the National Rural Network in *Why Rural Matters II: The Rural Impact of the Administration's FY07 Budget Proposal* (March 2006), budget cuts under President George W. Bush exacerbate the problems of the rural poor and homeless because disproportionate cuts to rural areas result in a significant disadvantage.

Several types of rural areas generate higher-than-average levels of homelessness, including regions that:

- Are primarily agricultural—residents often lose their livelihood because of reduced demand for farm labor or because of a shrinking service sector
- Depend on declining extractive industries, such as mining or timber
- Are experiencing economic growth—new or expanding industrial plants often attract more job seekers than can be absorbed
- Have persistent poverty, such as Appalachia and the rural South, where the young and able-bodied may have to relocate before they can find work

TRENDS IN HOMELESSNESS
Poverty Estimates

There is an undeniable connection between homelessness and poverty. People in poverty live from day to day with little or no safety net for times when unforeseen expenses arise. If a family's resources are small, expenditures on necessities such as food, shelter, or health care have to be carefully decided and sometimes sacrificed. Should one spend money on food, a visit to the doctor, buying necessary medicines, or paying the rent? In 2007 a full-time job paying minimum wage for forty hours per week provided an income of just $10,712 annually. (The federal poverty guideline for 2007 for one person was $9,800, and for two people it was $13,200; see Table 1.1 in Chapter 1.) Being poor often means that an illness, an accident, or a missed paycheck can be enough to cause homelessness.

Housing costs for such a family may be out of reach, costing from 50% to 75% of the family income. According to da Costa Nunez and Caruso, low-income and high-rent payments often result in substandard housing accommodation, doubled up living, or living on the street or in a public shelter. The necessity of basic sustenance and medical care usually leaves little money left to meet housing needs. People in poverty have further difficulties finding housing if they have previously defaulted on their rent or house payments, with the result of becoming homeless.

After large decreases in the poverty rate in the 1960s and 1970s, the poverty rate increased in the 1990s to a high of 15.1% in 1993. (See Table 1.2 in Chapter 1.)

Steady gains in decreasing the proportion of people living below the poverty threshold were made between 1994 and 2001. However, between 2002 and 2005 the poverty rate once again rose, to a high of 12.7% in 2004. It had decreased slightly to 12.6% in 2005. In that year thirty-seven million people lived below the poverty level.

Burt et al. indicate in *Evaluation of Continuums of Care for Homeless People* that whether using a low or high estimate of the number of homeless people in the nation, the number of homeless increased sharply between 1984 and 1987, at the same time that the poverty rate was decreasing. The number of homeless people continued to increase gradually until 1996, even as the poverty rate declined again in the 1990s.

No strong correlation between poverty and homelessness can be seen in these data; however, there is an obvious relationship between homelessness and poverty. There are no wealthy homeless people. Most likely, the lack of a correlation is due to the number of homeless being underestimated in the earlier years.

Numbers of Homeless People

Homeless counts have been based on surveys centered on facilities that provide services to the homeless (such as shelters and soup kitchens). These are permanent sites where some contact with the homeless is possible. The number of such facilities has increased substantially since the passage of the McKinney-Vento Homeless Assistance Act. The Urban Institute reports in *America's Homeless II: Populations and Services* (February 1, 2000, http://www.urban.org/Presentations/AmericasHomelessII/toc.htm) that shelter and housing for the homeless increased from an estimated 275,000 beds in 1988 to 607,000 beds in 1996; big city food service programs increased from 97,000 meals in 1987 to 380,100 meals in 1996. With an ever-larger base of support facilities, the ability of researchers to reach more and more precise estimates of populations served has improved.

Trend data on the growth or decline of homelessness, comparable in precision to data collected by the U.S. Bureau of the Census on poverty levels, are still not available. Other but more limited data support the relationship between poverty and homelessness. Data collected by Smith and Smith on the population in emergency and transitional shelters show a decline in that population from 178,638 in the 1990 census to a total of 170,706 in the 2000 census. (See Table 4.5.) During that period the economy exhibited strong growth.

Table 4.5 shows these data with regional breakdowns of the homeless population. In 2000, 30.7% of the sheltered population were found in the Northeast, a region with 19% of the total U.S. population. The West also had a disproportionate share of homeless people in shelters;

TABLE 4.5

Population in emergency and transitional shelters by region, 1990 and 2000

Area	Population in shelters				Total 2000 U.S. population Percent
	1990		2000		
	Number	Percent	Number	Percent	
United States	178,638	100.0	170,706	100.0	100.0
Region					
Northeast	60,077	33.6	52,369	30.7	19.0
Midwest	27,245	15.3	28,438	16.7	22.9
South	42,407	23.7	42,471	24.9	35.6
West	48,909	27.4	47,428	27.8	22.5

SOURCE: Adapted from Annetta C. Smith and Denise I. Smith, "Table 1. Population in Emergency and Transitional Shelters for the United States, Regions, States, and Puerto Rico: 1990 and 2000," in *Emergency and Transitional Shelter Population: 2000—Census 2000 Special Reports*, U.S. Census Bureau, October 2001, http://www.census.gov/prod/2001pubs/censr01-2.pdf (accessed January 11, 2007)

27.8% of the sheltered were found in the region, yet it had only 22.5% of the total population. The Midwest and the South had smaller shares of the sheltered than of their total populations, which might suggest that a greater proportion of people on the coasts were homeless than people in the middle of the country, or it may suggest that a greater proportion of homeless people on the coasts were sheltered.

Patrick Markee, in *Fall Update: Rising Family Homelessness in New York City* (September 28, 2006, http://www.coalitionforthehomeless.org/public_website/advocacy/Fall_Update_2006), notes a month-by-month pattern of increasing homelessness during 2006. The number of homeless families and the number of homeless children had both increased by 11% between January and September of that year. According to Markee, the number of new homeless families that entered a New York City shelter increased by 4.4% between fiscal year 2005 and fiscal year 2006. The number of people housed in shelters for the homeless in 2006 was at historically high levels.

Trends Profiled by Mayors

The Conference of Mayors reports that requests for emergency shelter increased in the cities surveyed in 2006 by an average of 9%, up from 6% the previous year. (See Table 4.4.) An average of 23% of the requests for emergency shelter by all homeless people went unmet in 2006, an increase from the previous year's low of 14%. More than three out of four (77%) cities had to turn people away from shelters at some point during the year. Officials in 68% of the cities surveyed expected that requests for emergency shelter by homeless individuals and families would increase in 2007.

TABLE 4.6

Past-year change in local city conditions and assessment of seriousness of problems, 2005

	Change in condition since last year			Current status of condition		
Code/condition	Improved	Worsened	No change	Major problem	Moderate problem	Minor/no problem
A. Violent crime	34%	13%	53%	7%	37%	56%
B. Unemployment	24%	28%	48%	18%	42%	40%
C. Impacts of unfunded mandates/preemption	3%	58%	39%	33%	47%	19%
D. City fiscal condition	32%	29%	37%	18%	45%	37%
E. Cable TV rates/broadband internet availability	24%	30%	47%	7%	34%	59%
F. Family stability	9%	16%	75%	8%	38%	54%
G. Race/ethnic relations	18%	8%	74%	5%	31%	64%
H. Vitality of neighborhoods	39%	10%	51%	7%	36%	57%
I. Police/community relations	45%	8%	47%	5%	25%	70%
J. Overall economic conditions	37%	26%	37%	19%	44%	37%
K. Poverty	7%	25%	68%	15%	41%	45%
L. Volunteerism/community services	42%	9%	49%	5%	21%	74%
M. Availability of quality affordable housing	26%	29%	45%	22%	42%	36%
N. Quality of public education	27%	19%	54%	18%	32%	50%
O. Homelessness	5%	22%	73%	8%	33%	59%
P. City relationships w/community groups	46%	7%	47%	2%	19%	79%
Q. Youth violence and crime	15%	20%	65%	9%	43%	48%
R. Regional/area-wide problem solving	43%	13%	44%	12%	40%	48%
S. Infrastructure	45%	22%	33%	18%	45%	37%
T. Traffic congestion	11%	55%	35%	29%	44%	27%
U. Local environmental quality	23%	11%	66%	6%	33%	61%
V. Federal relations with your city	21%	14%	65%	6%	33%	61%
W. State relations with your city	27%	25%	48%	14%	37%	49%
X. Public school relations with your city	34%	14%	52%	6%	26%	68%
Y. Drugs/alcohol abuse	7%	31%	62%	20%	50%	30%
Z. Vitality of downtown/main street	52%	14%	34%	17%	45%	38%
AA. Availability of child care	15%	9%	76%	5%	34%	61%
BB. Recreation	48%	8%	44%	5%	27%	68%
CC. Civility in public life	21%	21%	58%	6%	26%	68%
DD. Family-friendliness of city	41%	5%	54%	2%	18%	80%
EE. Overall sense of "community"	50%	7%	43%	4%	26%	70%
FF. Efficiency of municipal service delivery	48%	4%	48%	5%	23%	72%
GG. Public transportation/transit service	23%	14%	63%	12%	40%	48%
HH. Cost and availability of health services	9%	55%	36%	35%	43%	22%
II. Homeland security/emergency preparedness	46%	5%	49%	9%	37%	54%
JJ. Availability/quality of after-school programs	22%	10%	68%	9%	39%	52%
KK. Population changes/migration	17%	21%	62%	11%	36%	52%
LL. Economic health/vitality	35%	20%	45%	17%	38%	45%

SOURCE: Christiana Brennan, Elizabeth Wheel, and Christopher Hoene, "Specific Local Conditions," in *The State of America's Cities 2005: The Annual Opinion Survey of Municipal Elected Officials*, National League of Cities, 2005, http://www.nlc.org/content/Files/RMPSoACrpt05.pdf (accessed October 31, 2006)

National League of Cities

In 2005 the National League of Cities surveyed a random sample of the nation's municipal elected officials regarding issues and problems they faced in governing U.S. cities. When asked to indicate whether various conditions had improved or worsened in their cities in the previous year, 22% of the officials reported that homelessness had worsened in their cities, whereas only 5% said homelessness had improved. (See Table 4.6.) Eight percent believed homelessness was a major problem in their cities and 33% believed it was a moderate problem.

More than a quarter (29%) of city officials surveyed stated that the availability of quality affordable housing had decreased in the past year; slightly fewer (26%) believed the availability of housing had increased. More than one out of five (22%) thought the lack of affordable housing was a major problem in their cities, and another

42% believed it was a moderate problem. Officials also believed other conditions affecting homelessness had worsened; 28% believed unemployment had worsened, 26% believed overall economic conditions had worsened, and 25% believed poverty had worsened during the previous year. When officials were asked to list the top three most deteriorated conditions in their cities, homelessness was not in the top ten, as it had been in previous years, but "availability of quality affordable housing" ranked fifth at 18% percent. (See Table 4.7.)

EMPLOYMENT AND THE HOMELESS

It is extremely difficult for the homeless to escape their condition without a job. Yet it is equally difficult for the homeless to find and keep good jobs. In the fact sheet "Employment and Homelessness" (June 2006, http://www.nationalhomeless.org/publications/facts/Employment.

TABLE 4.7

Most deteriorated city conditions over past five years, 2005

Traffic congestion	34%
Impacts of unfunded mandates/preemption	29%
Cost and availability of health services	21%
City fiscal condition	20%
Availability of quality affordable housing	18%
Unemployment	15%
Drugs/alcohol abuse	14%
Overall economic conditions	13%
Infrastructure	13%
State relations with your city	12%

Note: Percent of city officials listing item as one of the three most deteriorated conditions in their community during the past five years.

SOURCE: Christiana Brennan, Elizabeth Wheel, and Christopher Hoene, "Table 2. Most Deteriorated Conditions," in *The State of America's Cities 2005: The Annual Opinion Survey of Municipal Elected Officials*, National League of Cities, 2005, http://www.nlc.org/content/Files/RMPSoACrpt05.pdf (accessed October 31, 2006)

pdf), the NCH lists the following barriers to employment for homeless people:

- Lack of education

- Lack of competitive work skills

- Lack of transportation

- Lack of day care

- Disabling conditions

In addition, the homeless, like other workers, are subject to the state of the labor market. The availability of jobs and the wages and benefits paid for the available jobs often determine whether or not people can remove themselves from homelessness.

Burt et al. indicate in *Homelessness* that 44% of homeless respondents reported working in the previous month. Two percent earned income as self-employed entrepreneurs—by peddling or selling belongings. Forty-two percent of the homeless respondents worked for, and were paid by, an employer. The 2006 Conference of Mayors report finds that 13% of the homeless in the survey cities were employed in full- or part-time jobs at the time of the survey.

The NCH states in "Employment and Homelessness" that advocates for the homeless are concerned that this dependency on wages, combined with the unfavorable labor market conditions, actually supports continued homelessness. Because most homeless people do not have more than a high school education and because a majority of the low paying jobs go to those with at least a high school education, advocates worry that the available job opportunities for homeless people provide an insufficient base for exiting homelessness.

It costs money to live. Even homeless people have needs that can only be met with money. From needing something as simple as a toothbrush or a meal, to money for a newspaper or a phone call to a job prospect, homeless people need money to begin to improve their lives. Out of the need to survive, homeless people have come up with a number of ways to earn money.

Day Labor

Regular work, characterized by a permanent and ongoing relationship between employer and employee, does not figure significantly in the lives and routines of most homeless, as it is usually unavailable or inaccessible. Homelessness makes getting and keeping regular work difficult because of the lack of a fixed address, communication, and, in many cases, the inability to get a good night's sleep, clean up, and dress appropriately. Studies find that the longer a person is homeless, the less likely he or she is to pursue wage labor and the more likely that person is to engage in some other form of work. For those who do participate in regular jobs, in most cases, the wages received are not sufficient to escape from living on the street.

Day labor—wage labor secured on a day-to-day basis, typically at lower wages and changing locations—is somewhat easier for the homeless to secure. Day labor may involve unloading trucks, cleaning up warehouses, cutting grass, or washing windows. Day labor often fits the abilities of the homeless because transportation may be provided to the work site, and appearance, work history, and references are less important than in regular employment. Equally attractive to a homeless person, day labor usually pays cash at quitting time, thus providing immediate pocket money. Day labor jobs are, however, by definition, without a future. They can provide for daily survival on the street but are not generally sufficient to get a person off the street. Consequently, many homeless turn to shadow work.

Shadow Work

Shadow work refers to methods of getting money that are outside the normal economy, some of them illegal. These methods include panhandling, scavenging, selling possessions, picking up cans and selling them, selling one's blood or plasma, theft, or peddling illegal goods, drugs, or services. A homeless person seldom engages in all these activities consistently but may turn to some of them as needed. Researchers estimate that 60% of homeless people engage in some shadow work. Shadow work is more common for homeless men than for homeless women. Theft is more common for younger homeless people.

In "Buddy, Can You Spare a Dime?: Homelessness, Panhandling, and the Public" (*Urban Affairs Review*,

January 2003), Barrett A. Lee and Chad R. Farrell note that a mixture of institutionalized assistance, wage labor, and shadow work is typical of those who live on the streets. Studies find that many homeless people are resourceful in surviving the rigors of street life and recommend that this resourcefulness be somehow channeled into training that can lead to jobs paying a living wage. However, the NCH reports in "Employment and Homelessness" that some observers suggest that homeless people who have adapted to street life may likely need transitional socialization programs as much as programs that teach them a marketable skill.

Institutionalized Assistance

According to David Snow et al., in "Material Survival Strategies on the Street: Homeless People as Bricoleurs, Homelessness in America" (Jim Baumohl, ed., *Homelessness in America*, 1996), institutionalized assistance refers to "established or routine monetary assistance patterned in accordance with tradition, legislation, or organizations." This would include institutionalized labor, such as that provided by soup kitchens, shelters, and rehabilitation programs that sometimes pay the homeless for work related to facility operation. The number of people employed by these agencies is a small percentage of the homeless population. In addition, the pay—room, board, and a small stipend—tends to tie the homeless to the organization rather than providing the means to get off the street.

Institutionalized assistance also includes income supplements provided by the government, family, and friends. According to Snow et al., even though a considerable number of the homeless may receive some financial help from family or friends, it is usually small. Women seem to receive more help from family and friends and to remain on the streets for shorter periods than men. Cash from family and friends seems to decline with the amount of time spent on the street and with age.

Street Newspapers: Bootstrap Initiatives

In the United States, as well as overseas, homeless people are writing, publishing, and selling their own newspapers. Many street newspaper publishers belong to the North American Street Newspaper Association (NASNA), which was organized in Chicago in 1996. The NASNA holds an annual conference, offers business advice and services, and supports street newspaper publishers in the same way that any professional organization supports its membership. It also lobbies the government on homeless issues. The NASNA (May 15, 2006, http://www.nasna.org/history.html) reports that more than forty cities in North America had street newspapers that provided opportunities for the homeless in 2006.

Generally, the street newspapers are loaned on credit to homeless vendors who then sell them for $1 or $2

each. At the end of the workday the vendor pays the publisher the agreed-on price and pockets the remainder as profit. For example, Boston's *Spare Change* newspaper publishes nine thousand copies every two weeks. Vendors purchase newspapers for $0.25 each and resell them for $1, pocketing $0.75 for each paper sold. Some street newspapers charge vendors nothing at all. California's *Street Spirit* and *Street Sheet* both make their papers free to vendors.

This cooperative arrangement among publishers, vendors, and consumers has many benefits:

- Creation of jobs
- Supports the work ethic
- Accommodates the mobility of homeless people
- Provides reliable employment despite crisis living conditions
- Informs the public about homelessness
- Erases stereotypes of the drunken, illiterate, "unworthy" homeless person
- Gives the writers and vendors a sense of accomplishment
- Provides immediate cash to people who desperately need it

Most of the homeless newspaper vendors have not been able to earn enough just from selling newspapers to move themselves from homelessness, but as the quality and availability of these publications grow, homeless people envision the street newspaper industry becoming a means of moving tens of thousands from homelessness.

EXITING HOMELESSNESS

Burt et al. note in *Homelessness* that homeless people say that the primary reason they cannot exit homelessness is insufficient income. Of those surveyed by Burt et al., 30% cited insufficient income and 24% cited lack of a job.

Burt et al. report that 81% of the "currently" homeless had incomes of less than $700 in the thirty days before the study; the average monthly income was $367. Most of the homeless in the study were receiving their income from Aid to Families with Dependent Children (now Temporary Assistance for Needy Families). Of the formerly homeless people surveyed, the median monthly income of $470 would amount to an annual income of $5,640, an amount well below the poverty level for a single person ($7,740 in 1996).

In the *2005 Greater Los Angeles Homeless Count*, the Los Angeles Homeless Services Authority reports that homeless people cited a variety of reasons having to do with money and income for not resecuring permanent housing. Over half (53%) said they could not afford monthly rent payments. Almost half (48%) said that they were unemployed or had no income and therefore could not secure permanent housing. One out of five (19%) said they had no money for moving expenses, and 16% said their bad credit would prevent them from getting permanent housing.

These findings clearly demonstrate the financial difficulty a homeless person encounters in trying to permanently exit homelessness or poverty. However, exiting homelessness—especially by the chronically homeless—

requires more than income. Persistent medical assistance, sometimes for an entire lifetime, has to be available for the mentally ill or for people with addiction and substance abuse problems. Furthermore, without programs such as job training, assistance with general education, help with socialization skills, and, in many instances, counseling, the maintenance of a degree of independent life for the long term can be difficult for the chronically homeless.

CHAPTER 5

THE HOUSING PROBLEM

At one time a home was defined as a place where a family resided, but as American society changed, so did the definition of home. A home is now considered a place where one or more people live, a private place to which they have legal right and where strangers may be excluded. It is the place where people keep their belongings and where they feel safe from the outside world. For housing to be considered a home, it should be permanent with an address. Furthermore, in the best of circumstances a home should not be substandard but should still be affordable. Many people would agree that a place to call home is a basic human right.

Those people who have no fixed address and no private space of their own are the homeless. The obvious solution to homelessness would be to find a home for everyone who needs one. There is enough housing available in the United States; as such, the problem lies in the affordability of that housing. Most of the housing in the United States costs far more than poor people can afford to rent or buy.

HIGH HOUSING COSTS AND HOMELESSNESS

According to Mary Cunningham and Sharon McDonald in *Promising Strategies to End Family Homelessness* (June 2006, http://www.hoopsforthehomeless.org/docs/hoopspaperfinal.pdf), research indicates that the primary cause of most homelessness is the inability to pay for housing, which is caused by some combination of low income and high housing costs. Even though many other factors may contribute to homelessness, such as a low level of educational achievement or mental illness, addressing these problems will seldom bring someone out of homelessness by itself. The underlying issue of not being able to afford housing will still need to be addressed.

Marybeth Shinn et al. conducted a study that shows no real difference exists between homeless people and the rest of society, other than housing affordability issues.

Shinn et al. conducted a five-year study of 564 homeless families and presented their results in "Predictors of Homelessness among Families in New York City: From Shelter Request to Housing Stability" (*American Journal of Public Health*, November 1998).

Shinn et al. find that when homeless families were provided with subsidies that allowed them to afford housing, 80% remained housed in their own residence for at least a year. This was true regardless of their social or personal attributes, such as their education level, race, or sex. This confirms the idea that while many homeless people face difficulties because of their personal backgrounds, these problems are not what drove most of them into homelessness. Furthermore, if given access to affordable housing, most will be able to take advantage of it.

The National Alliance to End Homelessness confirms that, in most ways, homeless people are no different from housed people. The alliance states in *Policy Book 2006* (August 17, 2006, http://www.endhomelessness.org/content/article/detail/586) that 80% of homeless people "have similar rates of mental illness, substance abuse disorders, physical ailments, and domestic violence experience. They have similar education levels and numbers of children." This group only needs affordable housing. The other 20% of homeless people can be characterized as chronically homeless, and they do differ substantially from the general population of poor people—they have higher rates of chronic disabilities, substance abuse disorders, physical disabilities, and human immunodeficiency virus/acquired immunodeficiency syndrome. These people need housing linked to other supportive services to help them move out of homelessness.

HOUSING THE POOR

When 30% or more of a meager income is spent on housing, hardship is the result. For that reason the federal government's official standard for low-income housing is

TABLE 5.1

Income and housing costs for owners and renters, 1975–2005

[In 2005 dollars]

Year	Monthly income		Home price	Mortgage rate	Before-tax mortgage payment	After-tax mortgage payment	Contract rent	Gross rent	Before-tax mortgage payment	After-tax mortgage payment	Contract rent	Gross rent
	Owner	Renter										
1975	4,417	2,618	130,524	8.9	938	817	613	657	21.2	18.5	23.4	25.1
1976	4,391	2,541	133,128	8.9	953	835	612	661	21.7	19.0	24.1	26.0
1977	4,406	2,557	138,273	8.8	985	917	611	666	22.4	20.8	23.9	26.0
1978	4,452	2,591	146,766	9.4	1,098	991	610	665	24.7	22.3	23.5	25.7
1979	4,459	2,535	147,931	10.6	1,227	1,092	589	645	27.5	24.5	23.2	25.4
1980	4,187	2,404	141,127	12.5	1,352	1,175	566	626	32.3	28.1	23.6	26.0
1981	4,067	2,372	135,294	14.4	1,480	1,267	560	623	36.4	31.2	23.6	26.3
1982	4,073	2,395	131,305	14.7	1,469	1,276	569	638	36.1	31.3	23.8	26.7
1983	4,164	2,389	131,099	12.3	1,237	1,081	585	659	29.7	25.9	24.5	27.6
1984	4,273	2,462	130,821	12.0	1,210	1,063	592	665	28.3	24.9	24.0	27.0
1985	4,387	2,498	132,592	11.2	1,152	1,015	608	679	26.3	23.1	24.4	27.2
1986	4,542	2,528	139,246	9.8	1,080	956	634	701	23.8	21.0	25.1	27.7
1987	4,571	2,503	143,790	9.0	1,037	950	637	698	22.7	20.8	25.4	27.9
1988	4,596	2,578	146,707	9.0	1,060	992	635	693	23.1	21.6	24.6	26.9
1989	4,657	2,665	148,731	9.8	1,156	1,073	629	686	24.8	23.0	23.6	25.8
1990	4,520	2,580	145,782	9.7	1,126	1,048	622	676	24.9	23.2	24.1	26.2
1991	4,452	2,473	142,549	9.1	1,039	973	618	672	23.3	21.9	25.0	27.2
1992	4,418	2,405	142,143	7.8	924	878	615	668	20.9	19.9	25.6	27.8
1993	4,382	2,380	140,964	6.9	838	806	611	664	19.1	18.4	25.7	27.9
1994	4,426	2,349	141,021	7.3	871	838	611	662	19.7	18.9	26.0	28.2
1995	4,467	2,410	141,626	7.7	908	870	608	658	20.3	19.5	25.3	27.3
1996	4,543	2,431	143,172	7.6	908	869	607	656	20.0	19.1	25.0	27.0
1997	4,646	2,486	145,545	7.5	918	878	610	660	19.8	18.9	24.6	26.5
1998	4,785	2,536	150,914	7.0	901	865	620	666	18.8	18.1	24.5	26.3
1999	4,890	2,626	155,338	7.1	943	900	626	669	19.3	18.4	23.8	25.5
2000	4,840	2,642	160,835	7.9	1,048	988	628	672	21.7	20.4	23.7	25.4
2001	4,742	2,620	168,791	6.9	1,005	954	637	687	21.2	20.1	24.3	26.2
2002	4,715	2,522	177,382	6.4	1,003	956	652	696	21.3	20.3	25.9	27.6
2003	4,740	2,438	185,077	5.7	964	944	656	704	20.3	19.9	26.9	28.9
2004	4,705	2,404	200,158	5.7	1,043	1,013	656	706	22.2	21.5	27.3	29.4
2005	4,672	2,430	219,000	5.9	1,164	1,119	654	709	24.9	23.9	26.9	29.2

Notes: All dollar amounts are expressed in 2005 constant dollars using the Bureau of Labor Statistics Consumer Price Index (CPI). Owner and renter incomes through 2004 are from Current Population Survey (CPS) published reports. Renters exclude those paying no cash rents. 2005 income is based on Moody's Economy.com estimate for all households, adjusted by the three-year average ratio of CPS owner and renter incomes to all household incomes. Home price is the 2005 median sales price of existing single-family homes determined by the National Association of Realtors, indexed by the Freddie Mac Conventional Mortgage Home Price Index. Mortgage rates are from the Federal Housing Finance Board Monthly Interest Rate Survey; 2005 value is the average of monthly rates. Mortgage payments assume a 30-year loan with 10% down. After-tax mortgage payment equals mortgage payment less tax savings of home ownership. Tax savings are based on the excess of housing (mortgage interest and real-estate taxes) plus non-housing deductions over the standard deduction. Non-housing deductions are set at 5% of income through 1986, 4.25% in 1987, and 3.5% from 1988 on. Contract rent equals median 2003 contract rent from the American Housing Survey, indexed by the CPI residential rent index with adjustments for depreciation in the stock before 1987. Gross rent is equal to contract rent plus fuel and utilities.

SOURCE: "Table A1. Income and Housing Costs, U.S. Totals: 1975–2005," in *The State of the Nation's Housing, 2006*, Joint Center for Housing Studies of Harvard University, 2006, http://www.jchs.harvard.edu/publications/markets/son2006/son2006.pdf (accessed January 11, 2007)

that rent and utilities should cost no more than 30% of the annual income of someone in poverty. "Low-income housing" is housing that is affordable to those in poverty based on that formula. In 2007 a family of two with an annual income of less than $13,200 was in poverty; a family of four was in poverty if their income was less than $20,000. (See Table 1.1 in Chapter 1.) Thus, in 2007 housing for a family of two at the poverty line should cost no more than one-third of $13,200 annually, or no more than $330 per month; for a family of four, housing should cost no more than one-third of $20,000 annually, or no more than $500 per month.

However, the price of rental units has been on the rise since 1975, at the same time that the real income of

renters has been declining. The Joint Center for Housing Studies (JCHS) of Harvard University reports that in 2005 dollars renters in 1975 had a median income of $2,618 per month and a median gross rent (including rent and utilities) of $657. (See Table 5.1.) By 2005 gross rent had risen while income had declined. In that year renters had a median income of $2,430 per month and a median gross rent of $709.

According to the U.S. Bureau of the Census, the median monthly gross rent for renter-occupied housing units was $728. (See Table 5.2.) As a result of such high rents, across the nation 45.7% of households in rental property spent 30% or more of their household income on rent. (See Table 5.3.) Renters in California faced partic-

TABLE 5.2

Median monthly housing costs for renter-occupied housing units, by state or territory, 2005

[Data are limited to the household population and exclude the population living in institutions, college dormitories, and other group quarters]

Rank	State	Median
1	Hawaii	$995
2	California	$973
3	New Jersey	$935
4	Massachusetts	$902
5	Maryland	$891
6	Nevada	$861
7	New Hampshire	$854
8	New York	$841
9	Connecticut	$839
10	Alaska	$832
10	District of Columbia	$832
12	Virginia	$812
13	Florida	$809
14	Delaware	$793
15	Rhode Island	$775
16	Colorado	$757
17	Washington	$741
18	Illinois	$734
	United States	$728
19	Arizona	$717
20	Georgia	$709
21	Minnesota	$692
22	Oregon	$689
23	Vermont	$683
24	Texas	$671
25	Utah	$665
26	Michigan	$655
27	Pennsylvania	$647
28	Wisconsin	$643
29	North Carolina	$635
30	Maine	$623
31	Indiana	$615
32	Ohio	$613
33	South Carolina	$611
34	Idaho	$594
35	Missouri	$593
36	Kansas	$588
37	New Mexico	$587
38	Tennessee	$583
39	Louisiana	$569
39	Nebraska	$569
41	Iowa	$559
42	Montana	$552
43	Arkansas	$549
44	Oklahoma	$547
45	Mississippi	$538
46	Wyoming	$537
47	Alabama	$535
48	Kentucky	$527
49	South Dakota	$500
50	West Virginia	$483
51	North Dakota	$479
	Puerto Rico	$380

Note: Data are based on a sample and are subject to sampling variability.

SOURCE: "R2514. Median Monthly Housing Costs for Renter-Occupied Housing," in *2005 American Community Survey*, U.S. Census Bureau, 2005, http://factfinder.census.gov/servlet/GRTTable?_bm=y&-eo_id=01000US&_box_head_nbr=R2514&-ds_name=ACS_2005_EST_G00_&-redoLog=false&-format=US-30&-mt_name=ACS_2005_EST_G00_R1704_US30&CONTEXT=grt (accessed January 11, 2007)

TABLE 5.3

Percent of renter-occupied units spending 30% or more of household income on rent and utilities, by state or territory, 2005

[Data are limited to the household population and exclude the population living in institutions, college dormitories, and other group quarters]

Rank	State	Percent
1	California	51.7
2	Florida	50.9
3	New York	48.3
4	Oregon	48.1
5	Michigan	47.6
5	New Jersey	47.6
7	Nevada	46.9
8	Colorado	46.5
9	Massachusetts	46.4
10	District of Columbia	46.3
11	Illinois	46.1
12	Washington	46.0
	United States	45.7
13	Vermont	45.7
14	Maryland	45.3
14	Rhode Island	45.3
14	Texas	45.3
17	Connecticut	44.8
17	Minnesota	44.8
19	Arizona	44.6
20	New Mexico	44.3
21	Georgia	44.2
22	Ohio	44.1
23	Hawaii	43.9
24	Indiana	43.4
24	Maine	43.4
26	Louisiana	42.9
26	Pennsylvania	42.9
28	New Hampshire	42.6
29	Delaware	42.5
30	North Carolina	42.3
31	Idaho	42.2
31	Virginia	42.2
33	South Carolina	41.9
34	Utah	41.6
34	Wisconsin	41.6
36	Missouri	41.4
37	Mississippi	41.3
37	Tennessee	41.3
39	Oklahoma	40.9
40	Montana	40.3
41	Kansas	40.2
42	Arkansas	40.0
42	Kentucky	40.0
44	Iowa	39.7
45	Alabama	38.8
46	Alaska	38.7
47	West Virginia	38.6
48	Nebraska	35.6
49	South Dakota	34.7
50	North Dakota	32.8
51	Wyoming	30.6
	Puerto Rico	33.0

Note: Data are based on a sample and are subject to sampling variability.

SOURCE: "R2515. Percent of Renter-Occupied Units Spending 30 Percent or More of Household Income on Rent and Utilities: 2005," in *2005 Community Survey*, U.S. Census Bureau, 2005, http://factfinder.census.gov/servlet/GRTTable?_bm=y&-geo_id=01000US&_box_head_nbr=R2515&-ds_name=ACS_2005_EST_G00_&_lang=en&-redoLog=false&-format=US-30&-mt_name=ACS_2005_EST_G00_R2514_US30&-CONTEXT=grt (accessed January 11, 2007)

ularly difficult circumstances. The median monthly rent there was the highest in the continental United States ($973) and more than half (51.7%) of renters spent 30% or more of their household income on housing.

Homeownership is also well beyond the reach of most low-income families. Walt Malony, in "Existing-Home Sales Holding at a Sustainable Pace" (September 25, 2006,

FIGURE 5.1

Rise in housing prices compared with income growth, selected years 1994–2005

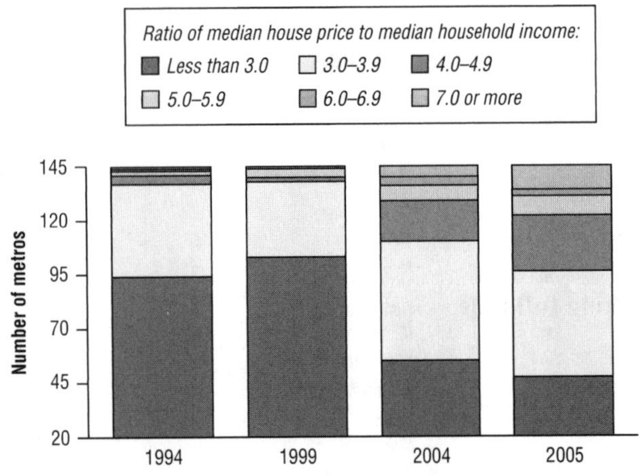

Ratio of median house price to median household income:
- ■ Less than 3.0
- □ 3.0–3.9
- ■ 4.0–4.9
- ☐ 5.0–5.9
- ▨ 6.0–6.9
- ▨ 7.0 or more

SOURCE: "Figure 10. Since 1999, House Prices Have Rocketed Past Incomes in Most Metros," in *The State of the Nation's Housing, 2006,* Joint Center for Housing Studies of Harvard University, 2006, http://www.jchs.harvard.edu/publications/markets/son2006/son2006.pdf (accessed Ocober 3, 2006)

TABLE 5.4

Top ten conditions selected by city officials as most important to address*, 2005

Traffic congestion	26%
City fiscal conditions	25%
Infrastructure	20%
Availability of quality affordable housing	18%
Overall economic conditions	18%
Impacts of unfunded mandates and preemption of local authority	17%
Vitality of downtown and main street	16%
Cost and availability of health services	15%
Economic health and vitality	15%
Unemployment	14%

*Percent of city officials listing item as one of the three most important conditions to address during the next two years.

SOURCE: Christiana Brennan, Elizabeth Wheel, and Christopher Hoene, "Table 1. Most Important Conditions to Address," in *The State of America's Cities 2005: The Annual Opinion Survey of Municipal Elected Officials,* National League of Cities, 2005, http://www.nlc.org/content/Files/RMPSoACrpt05.pdf (accessed October 3, 2006)

http://www.realtor.org/press_room/news_releases/2006/ehs_aug06_existing_home_sales_holding.html), reports that in August 2006 the median price for all housing types was $225,000, down 1.7% from August 2005, when the median price was $229,000. The JCHS notes that between 1994 and 2005 home ownership was becoming increasingly out of reach for all but those in the highest income brackets in most metropolitan areas. (See Figure 5.1.)

Not Enough Affordable Units Available

Researchers from every discipline agree that the number of housing units that are affordable to the poor is insufficient to meet needs. In *Changing Priorities: The Federal Budget and Housing Assistance, 1976–2005* (October 2004, http://es.nlihc.org/doc/cp04.pdf), Cushing N. Dolbeare, Irene Basloe Saraf, and Sheila Crowley quote a finding by a congressional commission that there were almost two million fewer units of housing affordable to low-income households than there were in 2004.

In December 2000 Congress established the bipartisan Millennial Housing Commission to examine the role of the federal government in meeting the nation's housing needs. In *Meeting Our Nation's Housing Challenges* (May 30, 2002, http://permanent.access.gpo.gov/lps19766/www.mhc.gov/mhcfinal.pdf), the commission states that "there is simply not enough affordable housing. The inadequacy of supply increases dramatically as one moves down the ladder of family earnings. The challenge is most acute for rental housing in high-cost areas, and the most egregious problem is for the very poor."

The limited availability of affordable housing is a problem across the nation. In *The State of America's Cities 2005: The Annual Opinion Survey of Municipal Elected Officials* (2005, http://www.nlc.org/ASSETS/5C8EBE817F604AE093F6072BD398F7E0/rmpsoacrpt05.pdf), an annual opinion survey of municipal elected officials, Christiana Brennan, Elizabeth Wheel, and Christopher Hoene find that 18% of city officials believed that increasing the availability of quality affordable housing should be a high priority for the federal government. (See Table 5.4.)

At Risk of Becoming Homeless

The severe shortage of affordable housing means that many low-income people and families constantly face the threat of homelessness, and the problem is not getting better. In *Affordable Housing Needs: A Report to Congress on the Significant Need for Housing* (2005, http://www.huduser.org/Publications/pdf/AffHsgNeedsRpt2003.pdf), the U.S. Department of Housing and Urban Development's (HUD) Office of Policy Development and Research notes that the number of low-income households paying more than 30% of their income in rent or living in substandard housing remained unchanged between 1995 and 2003. Approximately 5% of U.S. households experienced during that time "worst-case needs." The Office of Policy Development and Research defines families with "worst-case needs" as those who:

- Are renters

- Do not receive housing assistance from federal, state, or local government programs

- Have incomes below 50% of their local area median family income, as determined by HUD

- Pay more than one-half of their income for rent and utilities, or live in severely substandard housing

In other words, these are extremely impoverished people who do not own their housing and can barely afford to pay their housing costs or can only afford to stay in the worst housing. Of all housed people, they are the ones closest to being forced into homelessness. The Office of Policy Development and Research reports that in 2003, 11.4 million people in 5.2 million households had worst-case housing needs. Of these households, 29% were families with children, and 22% were elderly households. These households had an average income of $883 per month and an average gross monthly rent of $669, a rent burden of 76%. The Office of Policy Development and Research notes that four out of ten families with children that needed affordable housing actually had an adult wage earner who worked full time for low wages.

The Office of Policy Development and Research also finds that there was an adequate number of rental housing units to provide affordable housing to households with incomes above 40% of the area median income, but that there were far fewer adequate housing units available to the poorest households, especially in urban areas. In addition, some higher-income households occupied housing units that cost less than 30% of their income, restricting the units available to lower-income households. Some of the housing available was substandard as well. Furthermore, the housing stock affordable to low-income people is continually shrinking. The JCHS, in *The State of the Nation's Housing, 2006* (http://www.jchs.harvard .edu/publications/markets/son2006/son2006.pdf), states that the inventory of housing stock that is affordable to renter households with incomes of $16,000 or less had plunged by 1.2 million between 1993 and 2003.

For as long as worst-case needs have been reported by HUD, affordability rather than housing quality has been the main problem facing renters. A household that spends more than 50% of its income on housing is considered severely cost-burdened. In *State of the Nation's Housing: 2006*, the JCHS finds that the number of households with severe cost burdens—those that paid more than half their income for housing—increased by nearly two million between 2001 and 2004 to a record 15.8 million households. Almost half (46%) of households in the bottom income quartile were severely cost burdened in 2004.

Working Families Struggle to Keep Up

The National Low Income Housing Coalition (NLIHC), in *Out of Reach, 2006* (December 2006, http://www.nlihc .org/oor/oor2006/?CFID=8698180&CFTOKEN=35268835), analyzes the fair market rent (FMR)—HUD's estimate of what a household seeking modest rental housing must expect to pay for rent and utilities—for a two-bedroom rental unit in relation to the median hourly wage. In 2006 the hourly wage needed to pay the FMR for a two-

bedroom apartment spending no more than 30% of one's income on rent was $16.31. However, the median hourly wage in the United States was under $15, the average renter earned $13 per hour or less, and the federal minimum wage was $5.15 per hour. The NLIHC states that not only can minimum wage workers not find an affordable two-bedroom apartment but also "there is not a county in the country where a full-time minimum wage worker can afford even a one-bedroom apartment at the FMR." In most cities in the nation the housing wage was at least twice the federal minimum wage. In other words, to afford the FMR for a two-bedroom apartment, a household must have two or three minimum-wage workers working full time.

REASONS FOR THE LACK OF LOW-INCOME HOUSING

The major reasons for the lack of low-income housing are declining federal support; bureaucratic red tape, fraud, and waste; and a variety of local factors that affect new construction.

Declining Federal Support

The development and operation of low-income housing units depends in large part on government funding administered by HUD. Dolbeare, Saraf, and Crowley state that "the federal government's high water mark for housing assistance was the mid-1970s and funding has not come near that level in the years since. Nor will it in the next five years, absent a major policy and funding shift." Between 1976 and 2004 the housing assistance budget authority decreased 48%; in addition, in 1976 low-income housing units were being built, whereas in 2004 the budget mainly maintained existing units. In fact, because of public housing demolitions, the number of low-income housing units had declined overall by 2004.

Fraud, Waste, and Delays Hamper Rehabilitation

A major HUD goal is to increase the supply of affordable, decent, and safe rental housing, but it has not been particularly successful in this regard. In *Department of Housing and Urban Development: Status of Achieving Key Outcomes and Addressing Major Management Challenges* (July 2001, http://www.gao.gov/new.items/d01833.pdf), the U.S. General Accounting Office (GAO; now the Government Accountability Office), notes that HUD programs had been plagued by fraud, waste, and errors.

One of the federal housing production programs administered by HUD is the Urban Revitalization Demonstration Program, commonly known as HOPE VI. This program provides grants to local public housing authorities, who contract with private developers to rehabilitate public housing. The GAO notes in *Public Housing: HUD's Oversight of HOPE VI Sites Needs to Be More Consistent* (May 2003, http://www.gao.gov/new.items/

TABLE 5.5

Appropriations for public housing, fiscal years 2002–06

Millions of dollars

| | Fiscal year | | | | | |
	2002	2003	2004	2005	2006*	Total
Operating fund	$3,495	$3,577	$3,579	$2,438	$3,564	$16,653
Capital fund	2,843	2,712	2,696	2,579	2,439	13,269
Hope VI	574	570	149	143	99	1,535
Total	**$6,912**	**$6,859**	**$6,424**	**$5,160**	**$6,102**	**$31,457**

*Budget totals include the 1.0 percent across the board rescission to nondefense discretionary resources provided in fiscal year 2006 regular appropriations acts per P.L. No: 109-148.

SOURCE: David G. Wood, "Table 1. Appropriations for the Public Housing Program for Fiscal Years 2002–2006," in *Public Housing: Information on the Roles of HUD, Public Housing Agencies, Capital Markets, and Service Organizations*, U.S. Government Accountability Office, February 15, 2006, http://www.gao.gov/new.items/d06419t.pdf (accessed October 24, 2006)

d03555.pdf) that between fiscal year (FY) 1993 and FY 2001, HUD awarded about $4.5 billion in HOPE VI revitalization grants to 98 public housing authorities for 165 sites. In 2002 Congress charged the GAO with investigating and reporting on progress and HUD's oversight of the projects. The GAO reports that as of December 31, 2002, construction was complete on only 15 of the 165 sites. About one-quarter (27%) of the planned rehabilitation work had been done but nearly half (47%, or $2.1 billion) of the grant money had been spent, meaning that the projects were severely over budget. Work had been completed by the deadline on only three of the grants, and the construction deadlines had expired on forty-two grants. For FY 2004 the Bush administration proposed eliminating the HOPE VI program altogether; however, the program was funded at $149 million, down 73.8% from the $570 million funded in FY 2003. (See Table 5.5.) The program was cut even further in FY 2006, to $99 million.

Low Profit Margins Bring Neglect

HUD contracts with private owners limit profits and often limit the monies put back into the property for repairs. The existing housing available to renters at the lowest income levels often suffers from lack of upkeep. Neglected maintenance results in deterioration and sometimes removal from the housing inventory altogether.

According to *The State of the Nation's Housing, 2003* (2003, http://www.jchs.harvard.edu/publications/markets/son2003.pdf), the JCHS notes that about 705,000 tenants receiving government housing assistance in 2003 lived in substandard conditions. HUD data show that in 2003 an affordable unit existed for every household that earned 40% of the area medium income. However, as Figure 5.2 shows, housing units were only both affordable and available for households earning 60% of the

area medium income. Furthermore, a significant proportion of those housing units are substandard or inadequate. In fact, there is not enough affordable, available, and adequate housing available to house all low-income families.

Factors That Inhibit Construction

Construction of low-income units has been hampered by community resistance, by regulations that increase the cost of construction, and by limits on federal tax credits that make new construction unprofitable.

In his "Dissenting Statement to the Report of the Millennial Housing Commission" (May 31, 2002, http://www.heritage.org/Research/Welfare/WM102.cfm), Robert Rector complains, "It is a simple fact that those cities that have the greatest 'affordability' problem are those that have 'smart growth' or other regulatory policies that severely limit new housing growth. Policies such as restrictive zoning, antiquated building codes, and high impact fees for new construction reduce housing supply and greatly increase costs for everyone in a community."

These regulatory policies are put in place in part because, to many people, the prospect of low-income subsidized housing is synonymous with rising crime, falling property values, and overcrowded classrooms, and it is cause for protest. Resistance to the construction of low-income housing is said to be evidence of a "not in my backyard" (NIMBY) way of thinking. However, in *From NIMBY to Good Neighbors: Recent Studies Reinforce That Apartments Are Good for a Community* (May 1, 2006, http://www.nmhc.org/Content/ServeFile.cfm?FileID=5408), the National Multi Housing Council summarizes research showing that smart growth may depend on the development of more high-density housing, such as apartments. The council states, "The good news is that there is an ever-increasing body of research that indicates that apartments (including affordable apartments) are not a threat to local property values and are a net plus to communities."

However, developers complain that there is no profit to be made from building and operating low-income housing. To counteract this, the 1986 Low-Income Housing Tax Credit program gave the states $1.25 per capita in tax credits toward the private development of low-income housing. In "A New Era for Affordable Housing" (*National Real Estate Investor*, March 1, 2003), H. Lee Murphy reports on the National Council of State Housing Agencies' data indicating that construction hit a high in 1994, when 117,100 apartment units were built with the credits. Skyrocketing construction costs brought a decline in new construction, which reached a low of 66,900 units in 2000. In 2001 Congress raised the per capita allotment to $1.75 and provided that the formula would rise each year with inflation. The tax credits

FIGURE 5.2

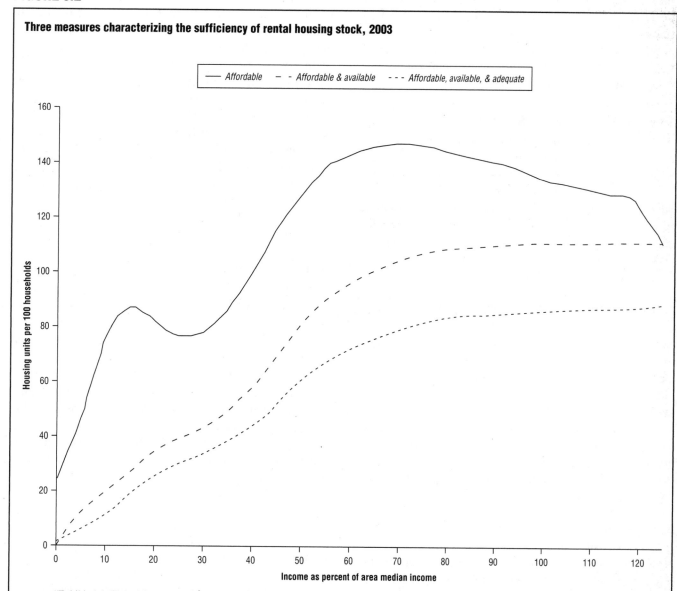

Three measures characterizing the sufficiency of rental housing stock, 2003

—— Affordable — - Affordable & available - - - Affordable, available, & adequate

y-axis: Housing units per 100 households

x-axis: Income as percent of area median income

SOURCE: "Exhibit 4-1. Three Measures Characterize the Sufficiency of the U.S. Rental Housing Stock, 2003," in *Affordable Housing Needs: A Report to Congress on the Significant Need for Housing*, U.S. Department of Housing and Urban Development, Office of Policy Development and Research, 2005, http://www.huduser.org/Publications/pdf/AffHsgNeedsRpt2003.pdf (accessed October 3, 2006)

financed the construction of 75,000 new units in 2001. Stan Luxenberg reports in "Affordable Housing Shortage" (*National Real Estate Investor*, September 1, 2006) that between 2002 and 2006 tax credits subsidized the construction of about 125,000 units per year. However, this rate of construction still did not keep pace with the number of affordable housing units that are demolished each year.

HABITAT FOR HUMANITY

One group dedicated to solving the housing problem one house at a time was the brainchild of Millard Fuller and Linda Fuller, who formed Habitat for Humanity International (HFHI) with a group of supporters in 1976. The purpose of this worldwide Christian service organization is to provide simple housing for the needy, built by volunteers assisted by the future homeowner. The homeowner assumes an interest-free, thirty-year mortgage, and materials are funded through donations and fund-raising activities. The idea is to give people assistance accompanied by responsibility.

By 2007 the HFHI had built more than two hundred thousand houses that sheltered one million people worldwide. According to the HFHI (2007, http://www.habitat .org/how/factsheet.aspx), homes in developing countries may cost as little as $800 to build, whereas the average house in the United States can cost nearly $60,000. Not all houses are new; the organization also restores older homes. Many volunteers travel to other countries to build homes. The HFHI (2007, http://www.habitat.org/how/ carter.aspx) notes that the most famous volunteers, the former president Jimmy Carter and his wife, Rosalynn, made their first work trip in 1984 to New York City, sparking widespread interest in the movement. An annual event since that time, the weeklong Jimmy Carter Work Project built fifty-four homes in Benton Harbor and Detroit, Michigan, in June 2005.

WHERE THE HOMELESS LIVE

When faced with high rents and low housing availability, many poor people become homeless. What happens to them? Where do they live? Research shows that after becoming homeless, many people move around, staying in one place for a while, then moving on to another place. Many homeless people take advantage of homeless shelters at some point. Such shelters may be funded by the federal government, by religious organizations, or by other private homeless advocates.

Emergency Housing: Shelters and Transitional Housing

Typically, a homeless shelter provides dormitory-style sleeping accommodations and bathing facilities, with varying services for laundry, telephone calls, and other needs. Residents are often limited in the length of their stays and must leave the shelter during the day under most circumstances. By contrast, transitional housing is intended to bridge the gap between the shelter or street and permanent housing, with appropriate services to move the homeless into independent living. It may be a room in a hotel or motel, or it may be a subsidized apartment.

Counting the Homeless in Shelters

The Census Bureau conducted a point-in-time count of the homeless population living in shelters for the 2000 census, and the results were published by Annetta C. Smith and Denise I. Smith in *Emergency and Transitional Shelter Population: 2000—Census 2000 Special Reports* (October 2001, http://www.census.gov/prod/2001pubs/censr01-2.pdf). Smith and Smith report a decline in the number of people living in homeless shelters—from 178,638 people in 1990 to 170,706 people in 2000. Based on their own experience, advocates for the homeless deny that there could have been a decline in the numbers. They criticize the Census Bureau's count as flawed, arguing that the survey excluded shelters with fewer than one hundred beds and could not provide a full picture of homelessness because it was conducted over only three nights. Smith and Smith caution that the Census Bureau's count is not "representative of the entire population that could be defined as living in emergency and transitional shelters."

Other evidence suggests that the homeless population housed in shelters is not only increasing, but would increase more dramatically if more shelter beds became available. The Conference of Mayors reports in the *Hun-ger and Homelessness Survey* that in 2006 the overall number of emergency shelter beds increased by an estimated 8%. At the same time the number of requests for emergency shelter beds increased over the previous year in the twenty-three major cities surveyed. Requests by homeless families with children increased by an average of 5%; requests by single homeless individuals increased by an average of 9%. Of all the cities surveyed, 68% reported an increase in requests for shelter by homeless individuals, and 59% reported an increase in requests by homeless families. Many of the cities had to turn homeless people and families away. On average, 23% of shelter requests by homeless people overall went unmet, and 29% of the shelter requests by homeless families went unmet that year.

Homeless Children and Youth

In 2002, researchers attempted to count the number of homeless people in Monterey County, California, focusing on what was called "the fastest growing segment of the homeless population," homeless youth (*Homeless Census and Homeless Youth/Foster Teen Study*, County of Monterey, California, 2002). Based on an actual count and interviews with 2,681 homeless individuals, the researchers estimated that between 8,686 and 11,214 people were homeless in Monterey County at some time during 2002. The majority of those interviewed (65%) were found on the street, 14% were in transitional housing, and 6% were in emergency shelters.

Of the individuals counted, more than one-fifth (21%) were between the ages of fourteen and eighteen. The youths were asked to describe their current living situation. The majority (61%) reported staying temporarily with family or friends. More than one-fifth (22%) reported they were living outdoors, 6.1% were living in a shelter, and 11.5% were living in an automobile/van. This particular segment of the homeless tended to shy away from shelters, especially if they were underage and feared interference from the authorities.

Counts by the public school system give some idea of both the numbers of homeless children and where they live. In accordance with the provisions of the Education for Homeless Children and Youth program, Title VII-B of the McKinney-Vento Homeless Assistance Act (42 USC 11431 et seq.), states that receive funds under the act must submit a report to the U.S. Department of Education regarding the estimated number of homeless children in the state. According to the most recent count (*Report to Congress Fiscal Year 2000*, Washington, DC, 2000), in 2000 there were an estimated 866,899 homeless children in forty-six reporting states. More than one-third (35%) of these children lived in shelters; 35% stayed doubled up with others, presumably family or friends; 25% lived in motels and the like. Most distressing for those concerned about the health and well-being of children was that 38,732 children lived unsheltered. By far the greatest number of unsheltered children (17,640) lived in California.

Illegal Occupancy

Poor neighborhoods are often full of abandoned buildings. Even the best-intentioned landlords cannot afford to maintain their properties in these areas. Many have let their buildings deteriorate or have simply walked away, leaving the fate of the building and its residents in the hands of the government. Despite overcrowding and unsafe conditions, many homeless people move into these dilapidated buildings illegally, glad for what shelter they can find. Municipal governments, overwhelmed by long waiting lists for public housing, by a lack of funds and personnel, and by an inadequate supply of emergency shelter beds, are often unable or unwilling to strictly enforce housing laws, allowing the homeless to become squatters rather than forcing them into the streets. Some deliberately turn a blind eye to the problem, knowing they have no better solution for the homeless.

The result is a multitude of housing units with deplorable living conditions—tenants bedding down in illegal boiler basements, sharing beds with children or in-laws, or sharing bathrooms with strangers. The buildings may have leaks and rot, rusted fire escapes, and rat and roach infestations. Given the alternative, many homeless people feel lucky to be sheltered at all.

RISK OF SQUATTING. However, squatting can leave the homeless vulnerable to legal remedies or public criticism. The most dramatic case in recent years took place in December 1999 in Worcester, Massachusetts. Tom Kirchofer reports in "Homeless Couple Charged in Firefighter Deaths" (December 8, 1999, http://www.firehouse.com/worcester/charged.html) that a homeless couple had taken up residence in an abandoned building in the city. One of them allegedly knocked over a candle during an argument and the building caught fire. The Worcester fire department was called, and six firefighters were killed while fighting the fire. The homeless man and woman were each charged with involuntary manslaughter. The public outcry against the homeless couple, and against homeless people in general, reached national proportions. Frustration ran rampant in the ranks of homeless advocates. Most believed the Worcester couple was guilty of nothing more than trying to stay alive. Nicole Witherbee, the policy coordinator for the Massachusetts Coalition for the Homeless, voiced her frustration: "We make laws all the time, they can't panhandle, they can't loiter, we don't have enough shelter beds, so when they go into abandoned buildings it's trespassing. So where is it they're supposed to be?"—underscoring the lack of options and resources homeless people deal with daily.

CHAPTER 6
DEALING WITH THE PROBLEM OF HOMELESSNESS

FEDERAL GOVERNMENT AID FOR THE HOMELESS

What should the role of the government be in combating homelessness? Some people believe it is the duty of the government to take care of all citizens in times of need. Others point out that government help has often been misdirected or inadequate; in some instances, it has even added to the problem. Some people assert that people in trouble should solve their problems themselves. Federal programs for the homeless reflect a consensus that limited government help is important and necessary, but that homeless people also need to help themselves.

Since 1860 the federal government has been actively involved with the housing industry, specifically the low-income housing industry. In 1860 the government conducted the first partial census of housing—by counting slave dwellings. Twenty years later the U.S. census focused on the living quarters of the rest of the population, conducting a full housing census. Since then the federal government has played an increasingly larger role in combating housing problems in the United States:

- 1937—The U.S. Housing Act of 1937 established the Public Housing Administration (which was later merged into the Federal Housing Administration [FHA] and the U.S. Department of Housing and Urban Development [HUD]) to create low-rent housing programs across the country through the establishment of local public housing agencies.

- 1949—The Housing Act of 1949 set the goals of "a decent home and a suitable environment" for every family and authorized an 810,000-unit public housing program over the next six years. Title I of the act created the Urban Renewal program; and Title V created the basic rural housing program under the FHA, which put the federal government directly into the mortgage business.

- 1965—Congress established HUD. Its goal was to create a new rent supplement program for low-income households in private housing.

- The Housing and Community Development Act of 1974 created a new leased-housing program that included a certificate (voucher) program, expanding housing choices for low-income tenants. The voucher program soon became known as Section 8, after the section of the act that established it.

MCKINNEY-VENTO HOMELESS ASSISTANCE ACT

Widespread public outcry over the plight of the homeless in the early 1980s prompted Congress to pass the Stewart B. McKinney Homeless Assistance Act of 1987. Congress renamed the act the McKinney-Vento Homeless Assistance Act in 2000 to honor Representative Bruce Vento's service to the homeless. The range and reach of the act has broadened over the years. Most of the money authorized by the act went, initially, toward the funding of homeless shelters. The program also funded a Supportive Housing program, a Shelter Plus Care program, and the Single Room Occupancy program besides the Emergency Shelter Grant program. Amendments to the act later enabled funding and other services to support permanent housing and other programs to help the homeless. HUD administers most McKinney-Vento funds.

In 2007 programs administered under the McKinney-Vento Homeless Assistance Act fell into three distinct categories. A cluster of activities known as the Continuum of Care programs provided competitive grants intended to help communities and organizations provide comprehensive services to the homeless. A noncompetitive formula grant program, the Emergency Shelter Grants Program, provided funds for emergency shelters to states, large cities, urban counties, and U.S. territories. The Title V program freed properties for use to house the homeless.

Continuum of Care

In *Homeless Assistance Programs* (July 18, 2006, http://www.hud.gov/offices/cpd/homeless/programs/index.cfm), HUD notes that the concept behind Continuum of Care programs is as follows: "A continuum of care system is designed to address the critical problem of homelessness through a coordinated community-based process of identifying needs and building a system to address those needs. The approach is predicated on the understanding that homelessness is not caused merely by a lack of shelter, but involves a variety of underlying, unmet needs—physical, economic, and social."

Nonprofit groups and local government entities applying for funds under these programs are expected to survey and assess local needs and to write a comprehensive plan for combating homelessness and meeting needs. Grant recipients are required to assess their clients' progress and make changes in the program in response to ongoing evaluation. Three major programs and some additional demonstration and rural efforts have developed over the years.

SUPPORTIVE HOUSING PROGRAM. The aim of the Supportive Housing Program (SHP) is to provide housing and services that will enable homeless clients to achieve economic independence and control over their lives. The SHP provides up to $400,000 in matching funds for construction of new buildings for housing homeless people; it also provides funding for the acquisition or refurbishing of existing buildings. The program underwrites 75% of the operating cost, including administration, and up to 80% of the cost of support programs. These programs must help clients achieve independence by providing skills training, child care, education, transportation assistance, counseling, and job referrals. Elements of the program include transitional housing for twenty-four months, permanent housing for the disabled, supportive services without housing, havens for the hard-to-reach and the mentally ill, and other innovative programs to solve problems of homelessness.

SHELTER PLUS CARE. The Shelter Plus Care Program helps agencies that specifically target the hardest-to-serve homeless: those with mental and physical disabilities living on the street or in shelters, including drug addicts and acquired immunodeficiency syndrome (AIDS) sufferers. The program provides for rental assistance funded by HUD and other sources. Housing in this program can be in the form of group homes or individual units with supportive services. Grant funds must be matched with local dollars. Subsidies for projects are available for ten years; assistance to sponsors and tenants is available for five years. A range of supportive services for tenants must be funded through other sources. Rental assistance includes four types of contracts:

1. Tenant-Based Rental Assistance—Direct contract with a low-income tenant

2. Project-Based Rental Assistance—Building owner contracts

3. Sponsor-Based Rental Assistance—Contracts with nonprofit organizations

4. Single-Room Occupancy-Based Rental Assistance— Single-room occupancy contracts provided by public housing authorities (PHAs)

SINGLE-ROOM OCCUPANCY. Single-room occupancy housing is housing in a dormitory-style building where each person has his or her own private room but shares kitchens, bathrooms, and lounges. Single-room occupancy housing is generally the cheapest type of housing available. Funding is intended to encourage the establishment and operation of such housing. Subsidy payments fund a project for a period of ten years in the form of rental assistance in amounts equal to the rent, including utilities, minus the portion of rent payable by the tenants.

OTHER PROGRAM COMPONENTS. Other programs folded under the Continuum of Care designation by HUD include demonstration programs for safe havens for the homeless and innovative homeless programs as well as rural homeless housing programs.

Emergency Shelter Grants

The Emergency Shelter Grants program provides homeless persons with basic shelter and essential supportive services. It can assist with the operational costs of the shelter facility, and for the administration of the grant. ESG also provides short-term homeless prevention assistance to persons at imminent risk of losing their own housing due to eviction, foreclosure, or utility shutoffs.

—HUD, *Emergency Shelter Grants (ESG) Program* (February 16, 2007, http://www.hud.gov/offices/cpd/homeless/programs/esg/)

The Emergency Shelter Grant program is HUD's formula grant program administered as a part of its community planning and development grant program. Recipients of funding are states, large cities, urban counties, and U.S. territories that have filed consolidated community development plans with HUD. The program is called a formula program because the amounts allocated are based in part on population and poverty levels within the planning entities that participate. Grant funds flow from governmental entities to organizations that actually operate shelters and provide services to homeless people or people at risk of becoming homeless. Money may be used to help individuals avoid homelessness by providing them with emergency funds. All grantees except for state governments must match grant funds dollar for dollar.

TABLE 6.1

Requirements of four U.S. Department of Housing and Urban Development (HUD) McKinney-Vento programs

Program requirement	Emergency shelter grants	Supportive housing program	Shelter plus care	Single-room occupancy
Type of grants	Formula grant	Competitive grant	Competitive grant	Competitive grant
Eligible applicants	States Metropolitan cities Urban counties Territories	States Local governments Other governmental agencies Private nonprofit organizations Community mental health centers that are public nonprofit organizations	States Local governments Public housing authorities	Public housing authorities Private nonprofit organizations
Eligible program services	Emergency shelter Essential social services	Transitional housing Permanent housing for people with disabilities Supportive services only Safe havens Innovative supportive housing	Tenant based rental assistance Sponsor based rental assistance Project based rental assistance Single-room occupancy based rental assistance	Single-room occupancy housing
Eligible activities	Renovation/conversion Major rehabilitation Supportive service Operating costs Homelessness prevention activities	Acquisition Rehabilitation New construction Leasing Operating and administrative costs Supportive services only	Rental assistance	Rental assistance
Eligible population	Homeless individuals and families People at risk of becoming homeless	Homeless individuals and families for transitional housing and supportive services Disabled homeless individuals for permanent housing Hard-to-reach mentally ill homeless individuals for safe havens	Disabled homeless individuals and their families	Homeless individuals
Initial term of assistance	1 year	Up to 3 years	5 or 10 years	10 years
Matching funds	States: no match for first $100,000 and dollar-for-dollar match for rest of funds. Local governments: dollar-for-dollar match for all funds.	Dollar-for-dollar match for acquisition, rehabilitation, and new construction grants. Operating costs must be shared by 25 percent in the first 2 years and 50 percent in the third year. A 25-percent match for supportive service grants No match for grants used for leasing or administrative costs.	Dollar-for-dollar match of the federal shelter grant to pay for supportive services	No match required

SOURCE: Stanley Czerwinsky, "Table 3. Requirements of Four HUD McKinney-Vento Programs," in *Homelessness: Improving Program Coordination and Client Access to Programs*, U.S. General Accounting Office, March 2002, http://www.gao.gov/new.items/d02485t.pdf (accessed January 11, 2007)

Title V

HUD maintains information about and publishes listings of federal properties categorized as unutilized, underutilized, in excess, or in surplus. States, local governments, and nonprofit organizations can apply to use such properties to house the homeless. Title V does not provide funding; it provides properties to agencies for housing use. Groups may apply for funding under the Continuum of Care program to modify, refurbish, or adapt such structures for residential uses.

Consolidations, New Initiatives, and Reorganizations

HUD's programs, particularly those under Continuum of Care, have overlapping objectives yet operate under separate rules and requirements. (See Table 6.1.) The U.S. General Accounting Office (GAO; now the Government Accountability Office) studied the McKinney programs in 1999 and concluded in *Homelessness: Coordination and Evaluation of Programs Are Essential* (February 1999, http://www.gao.gov/archive/1999/rc99049.pdf) that the number of programs and the differences between them

create barriers to their efficient use. According to Stanley J. Czerwinski, in *Homelessness: Improving Program Coordination and Client Access to Programs* (March 6, 2002, http://www.gao.gov/new.items/d02485t.pdf), even though "HUD has taken actions that have improved the coordination of homeless assistance programs within communities and have helped reduce some of the administrative burdens that separate programs cause," consolidating the McKinney-Vento programs could harm homeless people if a system was not first devised to hold mainstream programs accountable for serving the homeless.

HUD's program administrators evidently reached much the same conclusions as the GAO. In its fiscal year (FY) 2004 budget request to Congress and again in its FY 2005 budget summary, HUD proposed consolidating its three major programs under Continuum of Care, along with the demonstration and rural assistance programs, into a single Homeless Assistance Grants program. The GAO believed that this consolidation would facilitate comprehensive delivery of services while reducing administrative expenses, both at HUD and on the part of grant recipients. In *Annual Performance Plan, Fiscal Year 2007* (August 2006, http://www.hud.gov/offices/cfo/reports/pdfs/app2007.pdf), HUD proposes "consolidating HUD homeless programs into a single, more streamlined program." In FY 2007 HUD's proposed budget for programs to help the homeless was a record $1.5 billion, a $209 million increase over FY 2006.

In 2004 HUD proposed that Congress fund a new program called the Samaritan Initiative. The new program targeted an estimated 150,000 individuals HUD considers chronically homeless. The FY 2007 HUD budget proposed setting aside up to $200 million for programs to help end chronic homelessness.

The National Coalition for the Education of Homeless Children and Youth reports in "HEARTH Act Introduced: Amends HUD Definition of Homeless, Improves Support for All Homeless Populations" (February 6, 2007) that in February 2007 the Homeless Emergency Assistance and Rapid Transition to Housing Act was introduced in the House of Representatives to reauthorize the McKinney-Vento Homeless Assistance Programs. This act would more closely align the HUD definition of homelessness with the definition of other government agencies, expand resources for supportive services, including shelters, emphasize the prevention of homelessness, and provide for greater decision-making power and flexibility at the local level.

Education for Homeless Children and Youth

In response to reports that over 50% of homeless children were not attending school regularly, Congress enacted the McKinney-Vento Homeless Assistance Act's Education for Homeless Children and Youth program in 1987. The program ensures that homeless children and youth have equal access to the same free, appropriate education, including preschool education, provided to other children. Education for Homeless Children and Youth also provides funding for state and local school districts to implement the law. States are required to report estimated numbers of homeless children and the problems encountered in serving them.

The McKinney-Vento Homeless Education Act was scheduled to be considered for reauthorization in 2007 as part of the reauthorization of the No Child Left Behind Act. The last reauthorization of the act in 2001 included the following new guidelines.

- Homeless children cannot be segregated.

- Transportation has to be provided to and from schools of origin if requested (a school of origin is the school the student attended when permanently housed, or the school in which the student was last enrolled).

- In case of a placement dispute, immediate enrollment is required pending the outcome.

- Local education agencies must put the "best interest of the child" first in determining the feasibility of keeping children in their school of origin.

- Local education agencies must designate a local liaison for homeless children and youth.

- States have to subgrant 50% to 75% of their allotments under Education for Homeless Children and Youth competitively to local education agencies.

At the time the McKinney-Vento Homeless Assistance Act was passed, only an estimated 57% of homeless children were enrolled in school. By 2000 the percentage had increased to 88%. In the 2003–04 school season more homeless children were enrolled in elementary school than in middle school or high school. (See Table 4.2 in Chapter 4.) Even though the data appear inconclusive because elementary school children may be more likely to be homeless, thus accounting for their greater numbers, the data seem to suggest that older homeless children may be less likely to be enrolled in school than elementary school-age children.

However, in implementing the legislation, school districts found that barriers arose in areas such as residency, guardian requirements, incomplete or missing documentation (including immunization records and birth certificates), and transportation. Consequently, some school districts established separate schools for homeless children. As of 2002 there were an estimated forty separate schools for the homeless nationwide, according to Kristen Kreisher in "Educating Homeless Children" (*Children's Voice*, September–October 2002), and even though separate schools were outlawed with the 2001 reauthorization of the act, those schools that already existed were allowed to remain.

Transportation became an issue for school districts providing education to homeless students. Nicole Brode reports in "New York's School Choice Leaves More Homeless Children with Hour-Plus Commutes" (*Knight-Ridder/Tribune Business News*, February 10, 2003) that Homes for the Homeless found that over a third of the 226 students in one New York shelter in 2003 faced commutes of over an hour because their parents had opted to keep their children in the same schools they had attended before they became homeless, a right guaranteed by the new law. The Maricopa County School Foundation reports in "Pappas Kids" (2007, http://www.pappaskids.org/faq.html) that in 2007 the Thomas J. Pappas schools for the homeless in Phoenix and Tempe, Arizona, reported that sixteen buses traveled one thousand miles each day to transport children to and from school.

FEDERALLY SUBSIDIZED HOUSING

The national effort to provide housing for those in need is far more massive than would be indicated by the expenditure

TABLE 6.2

Department of Housing and Urban Development (HUD) budget authority for homeless and public housing programs, 2005–07

[Dollars in millions]

Discretionary programs	2005 Enacted	2006 Enacted	2007 Estimate
Public and Indian housing			
Housing certificate fund	2,710	(2,050)	(2,000)
Tenant-based rental assistance	10,600	15,808	15,920
Public housing capital fund	2,579	2,439	2,178
Revitalization of severely distressed public housing projects	$143	$99	($99)
Public housing operating fund	2,438	3,564	3,564
Native American housing block grants	622	624	626
Homeless assistance grants	1,241	1,327	1,536
Faith-based prisoner re-entry initiative	—	—	[25]
Transfer to working capital fund	[2]	[1]	[2]
Technical assistance and management information systems	[11]	[12]	[10]
Shelter plus care (renewals)	[214]	[255]	[285]
Samaritan homeless program	—	—	[200]
Rescission	(11)	—	—
Total, homeless	**[1,230]**	**[1,327]**	**[1,536]**

Note: Totals may differ from President's budget due to rounding.

SOURCE: Adapted from "Appendix B. Budget Authority by Program," in *Fiscal Year 2007 Budget Summary*, U.S. Department of Housing and Urban Development, February 2006, http://www.hud.gov/offices/cfo/reports/2007/cjs/part1/bdgtauthority.pdf (accessed October 24, 2006)

of about $1.5 billion on assistance to the homeless. HUD's expenditures on public and Native American housing were projected to be $20.2 billion in FY 2007. (See Table 6.2.) If these funds are added to projected expenditures on homeless programs, total spending on subsidized housing in FY 2007 would be $22.8 billion. Of this total, 6.6% is allocated directly to helping the homeless and 93.4% to various forms of housing assistance for the poor, which has the effect of helping people to avoid homelessness. To help people stay housed, the government has housing programs that help low-income people.

In 2002 over 5.1 million families, or 4.6% of U.S. households, lived in subsidized housing. (See Table 6.3.) Of those in subsidized housing, 2.6 million households had income below the officially defined poverty level; these poor households represented 2.3% of all households and just over half of all subsidized households (51%).

The U.S. Bureau of the Census provides estimates of families living in poverty and of poverty-stricken households (a sector that includes family as well as nonfamily groups and singles). Bernadette D. Proctor and Joseph Dalaker report in *Poverty in the United States: 2002* (September 2003, http://www.census.gov/prod/2003pubs/p60-222.pdf) that 7.2 million families, or 9.6% of all families, lived in poverty in 2002. According to *Income, Poverty, and Health Insurance Coverage in the Untied States: 2005—Current Population Reports* (August 2006, http://www.census.gov/prod/2006pubs/p60-231.pdf) by Carmen DeNavas-Walt, Bernadette D. Proctor, and Cheryl Hill Lee, the number of families living in poverty increased to 7.7 million families, or 9.9% of all families, in 2005. According to the Census

Bureau in *Statistical Abstract of the United States: 2004–2005* (2004, http://www.census.gov/prod/2004pubs/04statab/socinsur.pdf), in 2002 more than 5.1 million households lived in subsidized housing. In the 1990–2002 period, those in subsidized housing peaked in 2002. Total households living in subsidized housing increased by 15.3% during that time.

Most government housing programs are targeted to poor or low-income households. For this reason subsidized housing is means-tested, meaning that the income of those receiving help must be below a certain threshold. The qualifying income level—much like the definition of poverty—changes over time. Beneficiaries of housing assistance never receive cash outright. The benefits are therefore labeled "means-tested noncash benefits."

HUD has operated many different kinds of housing programs, but these can be classified under three headings: public housing owned by the government, tenant-based programs that provide people vouchers to subsidize rent, and project-based programs that underwrite the costs of private owners who, in turn, pledge to house low-income people.

Public housing and voucher programs account for roughly equal proportions of subsidized units. Project-based programs, also known as private subsidized projects, account for the most units, but these private subsidies take many forms, some quite complicated. A look at the major programs follows.

Public Housing

HUD's FY 2006 budget appropriations for public housing were $6.1 million, significantly lower than the

TABLE 6.3

Households receiving means-tested noncash benefits, selected years 1980–2002

[In thousands (82,368 represents 82,368,000), except percent. Households as of March of following year.]

| | | | | | 2002 | | | |
| | | | | | Below poverty level | | | Above poverty level |
Type of benefit received	1980	1990	1995	2000	Total	Number	Percent of total	
Total households	82,368	94,312	99,627	106,418	111,278	13,505	100	97,773
Receiving at least one noncash benefit	14,266	16,098	21,148	20,131	22,478	7,806	58	14,672
Not receiving cash public assistance	7,860	8,819	13,335	14,465	16,890	5,003	37	11,887
Receiving cash public assistance*	6,407	7,279	7,813	5,667	5,588	2,803	21	2,785
Total households receiving—								
Food stamps	6,769	7,163	8,388	5,563	6,245	3,834	28	2,411
School lunch	5,532	6,252	8,607	7,185	7,930	3,092	23	4,838
Public housing	2,777	4,339	4,846	4,689	5,125	2,593	19	2,532
Medicaid	8,287	10,321	14,111	14,328	16,765	6,182	46	10,583

*Households receiving money from Aid to Families with Dependent Children Program (beginning 2000, Temporary Assistance for Needy Families Program), Supplemental Security Income program or other public assistance programs.

Note: Data covers civilian noninstitutional population, including persons in the armed forces living off post or with their families on post. A means-tested benefit program requires that the household's income and/or assets fall below specified guidelines in order to qualify for benefits. There are general trends toward underestimation of noncash beneficiaries. Households are classified according to poverty status of family or nonfamily householder.

SOURCE: "No. 529. Households Receiving Means-Tested Noncash Benefits, 1980 to 2002," in *The 2007 Statistical Abstract: The National Data Book*, U.S. Census Bureau, http://www.census.gov/compendia/statab/social_insurance_human_services/government_transfer_payments_social_assistance/ (accessed January 11, 2007)

Public Housing Program budget in FY 2002 but almost $1 billion higher than in the previous year. (See Table 5.5 in Chapter 5.) David G. Wood notes in *Public Housing: Information on the Roles of HUD, Public Housing Agencies, Capital Markets, and Service Organizations* (February 15, 2006, http://www.gao.gov/new.items/d06419t.pdf) that HUD anticipated funding 1.2 million public housing units in FY 2006, unchanged from the previous year. However, the number of public housing units has been decreasing over a number of years, in part because of an initiative to remove, modernize, and refurbish many poorly constructed and dilapidated public housing units. Over three thousand public housing authorities manage the 1.2 million units. In FY 2006, $2.4 billion was allocated to the Capital Fund to finance major repairs and modernization of units, and $3.6 billion was allocated for operating costs. An additional $99 million was appropriated for the HOPE VI grant program to help housing agencies replace and revitalize the most severely distressed public housing and implement community service and supportive service improvements in those projects.

HUD provides a data server on public housing residents called the *Resident Characteristics Report* (http://www.hud.gov/offices/pih/systems/pic/50058/rcr/index.cfm). As of January 31, 2007:

- The average annual income was $12,030. Only 9% of the public housing population earned more than per $25,000 year.

- Among residents, 33% had wage income, 22% had Temporary Assistance for Needy Families income, 55% had Social Security income, and 19% had other income (the same person could have income from more than one source). Three percent had no income from any source.

- The average rental payment per unit was $278 per month.

- More than a third (37%) of families were headed by a single woman with children, 18% were headed by elderly, not disabled people, and 12% were headed by a senior citizen with a disability. A number of other, overlapping, categories were shown as well, but notably missing was a category for male-headed families with children.

- Over half (51%) of heads of households were white, 46% were black, and 2% were Asian. Over one in five heads of household (22%) were of Hispanic origin.

- Nearly half (47%) of households consisted of just one person, 20% of two, 15% of three, 10% of four, 5% of five, 2% of six, and 1% of seven people. No households had more than seven people.

- The 968,678 units reporting data had 2,109,428 household members, with an average household size of 2.2 people.

- Of units occupied, 7% had no bedroom, 34% had one, 30% had two, 23% had three, 5% had four, and 1% had five or more bedrooms.

- Many residents had lived much of their lives in public housing. Thirteen percent of the population had been in public housing for more than twenty years, 17% for ten to twenty years, 20% for five to ten years, 22% for two to five years, 12% for a year or two, and 17% had moved during the past year.

Management of public housing is handled by housing agencies (sometimes called authorities) established by local governments to administer HUD housing programs. The Housing Act of 1937 required that PHAs submit annual plans to HUD but also declared it to be the policy of the United States "to vest in public housing agencies that perform well, the maximum amount of responsibility and flexibility in program administration, with appropriate accountability to public housing residents, localities, and the general public."

PHAs thus operate under plans approved by HUD and under HUD supervision, but they are expected to operate with some independence accountable to their residents, local (or state) governments, and the public. Not all PHAs have "performed well," and HUD has been accused of lax supervision. PHAs and public housing generally reflect the distressed economic conditions of the population living in government-owned housing. Many PHAs have been charged with neglecting maintenance, with tolerating unsafe living conditions for tenants, and with fraudulent or careless financial practices.

Troubled housing refers to low-income projects that are badly deteriorated, are located in unsafe neighborhoods, or are in danger of being lost to market-rate housing conversion or foreclosure. In an effort to improve its accountability for the conditions of low-income housing, HUD began to implement a new Public Housing Assessment System (PHAS) in January 2000. The PHAS is used to measure the performance of PHAs. Four primary components of the assessment system are designed to ensure, through physical inspection, that PHAs meet the minimum standard of being decent, safe, sanitary, and in good repair; to oversee the finances of public housing authorities; to evaluate the effectiveness of the management of PHAs; and to receive feedback from PHA residents on housing conditions.

In *Public Housing: New Assessment System Holds Potential for Evaluating Performance* (March 2002, http://www.gao.gov/new.items/d02282.pdf), the GAO examines the implementation of the PHAS and its progress. The GAO finds that HUD had also formed the Public and Indian Housing Information Center, a database that collected additional information not addressed by the PHAS, such as compliance and funding. In 2002, of the existing 3,167 authorities investigated, 532 PHAs were "troubled" overall or in one area (16.8%), 827 were high performers (26.1%), and 1,808 were standard performers (57.1%). However, in that year HUD was only looking at one of its four criteria—the effectiveness of management—when determining if a PHA was troubled. The other three criteria were not being considered at that time but plans called for them to be incorporated into future evaluations.

The GAO confirms in "Major Management Challenges at the Department of Housing and Urban Development" (February 23, 2005, http://www.gao.gov/pas/2005/hud.htm) that HUD continued to have major problems. According to the GAO, HUD had made some progress in addressing management problems. However, because "some of HUD's corrective actions are still in the early stages of implementation and additional steps are needed to resolve ongoing problems," its rental housing assistance programs remain "high risk." Wood states that in many cases HUD's enforcement actions against "troubled" PHAs—such as technical assistance and training or sanctions such as withholding of funding—resulted in some improvements.

HOPE VI. As a result of the 1992 recommendations of the National Commission on Severely Distressed Public Housing, Congress authorized $300 million for an urban revitalization demonstration program in the FY 1993 Appropriations Act. James Bovard reports in "HUD's Biggest Farce?" (*Free Market*, November 2000) that the program came to be named HOPE VI. (The acronym stands for Housing Opportunities for People Everywhere.) Up to that point HUD had put in place four previous HOPE initiatives; no HOPE V was ever launched.

In *HOPE VI Program Authority and Funding History* (August 2003, http://www.hud.gov/offices/pih/programs/ph/hope6/about/fundinghistory.pdf), HUD indicates that the aim of HOPE VI was to eliminate or upgrade the eighty-six thousand deteriorated units identified by the 1992 commission. Between FY 1993 and FY 2002 HUD reported revitalization grants totaling $5 billion and expended $335.6 million on demolitions. Since 2002 funding for HOPE VI has dramatically declined, from $574 million in FY 2002 to just $99 million in FY 2006. (See Table 5.5 in Chapter 5.) Funding was down in part because the Bush administration proposed the elimination of the program altogether.

The 1992 findings of the National Commission on Severely Distressed Public Housing and the launch of an initiative such as HOPE VI (aimed at demolishing public housing) illustrates the sometimes troubled history of public housing. HOPE VI itself has been severely criticized by advocacy groups. The report *False HOPE: A Critical Assessment of the HOPE VI Public Housing Redevelopment Program* (June 2002, http://www.nhlp.org/html/pubhsg/FalseHOPE.pdf), which was prepared by the National Housing Law Project, the Poverty and Race Research Action Council, Sherwood Research Associates, and Everywhere and Now Public Housing Residents Organizing Nationally Together, finds that HOPE VI:

1. Appeared headed toward eliminating twice the number of units found to have been "severely distressed" by the commission

2. Eliminated rather than increased units available to the lowest income population

3. Made it difficult for residents to participate in program decisions

4. Failed to improve the "living environment" of those in HOPE VI sites

5. Failed to provide data on project outcomes

According to Will Fischer, in "Public Housing Squeezed between Higher Utility Costs and Stagnant Funding: Low-Income Families Will Bear Brunt of Shortfalls" (October 11, 2006, http://www.cbpp.org/10-11-06hous.htm), data on the number of public housing units available to house low-income people support the general charge that the number of units has declined from 1,273,500 in 1999 to 1,162,808 in 2005, a drop of 110,692 units. If people who inhabit units slated for demolition are not able to find accommodation under HUD Section 8 voucher programs, they are at greater risk of becoming homeless. The low-income housing crisis is made even more serious by regulations that allow PHAs to rent to people with incomes as high as 80% of the local median income. (An income of $47,700 is 80% of the national median income for a family of four.) Fischer indicates that renting to higher-income families increases the ability of these housing authorities to meet operating costs (and estimates that the FY 2007 Operating Fund is $1 billion short of what is needed to fully fund PHAs' operating budgets) but makes it much more difficult for lower-income families to find affordable and adequate housing.

Vouchers

Voucher programs pay a portion of the rent for qualifying families. Only low-income families are eligible, specifically those with incomes lower than half of an area's median income. Under some circumstances families with up to 80% of the local median income may also qualify; such cases may involve, for instance, families displaced by public housing demolition. The family pays 30% of its income in rent, with the remaining cost of their rent covered by the voucher. Vouchers are issued by the Public Housing Agency, which executes assistance contracts with the landlord, who must also qualify.

Two major voucher programs are available: tenant-based and project-based. In tenant-based programs, the voucher "follows" the tenant when the tenant moves to another qualifying unit. In project-based programs, the voucher is "attached" to a subsidized housing project. Families are directed to participating projects after they qualify. Tenants cannot automatically transfer their voucher in a project-based dwelling to another—but they may qualify for tenant-based vouchers after they move.

Besides these two basic programs, HUD also has five other voucher programs. Conversion vouchers are used to help tenants relocate when public housing is demolished. Family unification vouchers are used to help families stay together. Vouchers for people with disabilities and welfare-to-work vouchers assist the elderly or nonelderly disabled and families transitioning from welfare to work.

The homeownership voucher program, begun in 2002, provides vouchers to participants in the tenant-voucher programs who meet income and eligibility requirements to help them buy their first homes (under the law anyone who has not owned a home in the last three years is considered to be buying his or her first home). Participants must be employed and have an income of at least minimum wage. HUD reports in *Annual Performance Plan, Fiscal Year 2007* that the program assisted two thousand low-income families from 2002 through 2005; beginning in 2007 the program planned to assist two thousand families each year in buying their first homes.

In all these programs the housing supplied is privately owned and operated and rents paid are at or below fair market rent (FMR). HUD determines the FMR in every locality of the nation by an annual survey of new rental contracts signed in the past fifteen months. The FMR is set as the fortieth percentile of rents paid, meaning that 40% paid a lower rent and 60% paid a higher rent. HUD has chosen the fortieth percentile to increase housing choices while keeping budgets at reasonable levels. Table 6.4 presents FMRs used by HUD in a sample of cities around the country in 2006–07. Rents in certain cities are calculated at the fiftieth percentile under new HUD rules that went into effect in 2001 for thirty-nine markets, which resulted in a raise in the FMR in these localities.

Of the cities shown in Table 6.4, the highest FMR for a two-bedroom unit for 2006–07 was in San Francisco, California ($1,551 per month). The lowest FMR was in Bismarck, North Dakota ($536 per month).

Project-based Section 8 housing has declined dramatically because funding for new construction stopped in 1983 with some minor exceptions (including construction/rehabilitation aimed at supporting homeless programs). Support of housing in such units continues, but the housing stock is going out of use through demolitions and conversions. Thus, in 2005 the vast majority of Section 8 housing vouchers were tenant-based. Although tenant-voucher residents have a fractionally higher average

TABLE 6.4

Fair market rental rates for selected metropolitan areas, 2007

Area definition	Fair market rental rate				
	0 bedroom	1 bedroom	2 bedroom	3 bedroom	4 bedroom
Bismarck, ND	$412	$431	$536	$776	$798
San Juan–Guaynabo, PR	$419	$455	$506	$570	$792
Gulfport–Biloxi, MS	$517	$548	$640	$834	$857
Lexington–Fayette, KY	$437	$525	$647	$870	$897
Memphis, TN-MS-AR	$548	$596	$662	$882	$910
Cincinnati–Middletown, OH-KY-IN	$436	$516	$668	$894	$929
Charlotte–Gastonia–Concord, NC-SC	$588	$637	$707	$891	$1,036
Kansas City, MO-KS	$518	$622	$714	$966	$1,016
Salt Lake City, UT	$545	$592	$714	$1,005	$1,170
Albuquerque, NM	$502	$591	$746	$1,086	$1,303
Atlanta–Sandy Springs–Marietta, GA	$647	$700	$779	$948	$1,035
Dallas, TX HMFA.	$591	$658	$798	$1,059	$1,283
Orlando, FL	$655	$712	$814	$1,019	$1,200
Seattle–Bellevue, WA	$623	$710	$854	$1,207	$1,474
Minneapolis–St. Paul–Bloomington, MN-WI	$600	$707	$858	$1,123	$1,262
Las Vegas–Paradise, NV	$643	$754	$891	$1,237	$1,503
Philadelphia–Camden–Wilmington, PA-NJ-DE-MD	$676	$773	$923	$1,105	$1,314
Ann Arbor, MI	$685	$768	$934	$1,175	$1,210
Chicago–Naperville–Joliet, IL	$727	$832	$935	$1,143	$1,291
Flagstaff, AZ	$699	$831	$939	$1,208	$1,523
Baltimore–Towson, MD	$694	$784	$941	$1,208	$1,492
Anchorage, AK	$660	$751	$942	$1,356	$1,652
New Orleans–Metairie–Kenner, LA	$755	$836	$978	$1,256	$1,298
Portland, ME	$638	$757	$981	$1,236	$1,324
New York–Monmouth–Ocean, NY-NJ	$988	$1,069	$1,189	$1,462	$1,645
Los Angeles–Long Beach, CA	$843	$1,016	$1,269	$1,704	$2,051
Honolulu, HI	$888	$1,058	$1,279	$1,865	$2,196
Washington–Arlington–Alexandria, DC-VA-MD	$995	$1,134	$1,286	$1,659	$2,171
Boston–Cambridge–Quincy, MA-NH	$1,097	$1,164	$1,366	$1,634	$1,795
San Francisco, CA	$1,008	$1,239	$1,551	$2,071	$2,188

SOURCE: Adapted from "SCHEDULE B: FY 2007 Final Fair Market Rents for Existing Housing," U.S. Department of Housing and Urban Development, 2006, http://www.huduser.org/datasets/fmr/fmr2007f/FY2007F_SCHEDULEB_rev2.pdf (accessed October 23, 2006)

household income than public housing residents, they also have a larger family size. Therefore, two-thirds of voucher users (66%) and a little more than half (56%) of public housing residents have an extremely low income for their family size. (See Table 6.5.) The shift of the subsidized population from public housing toward voucher housing represents not an improvement so much as a change in policy, whereby the provision of housing in the future appears to be headed for privatization. Barbara Sard contends in "Housing Vouchers Should Be a Major Component of Future Housing Policy for the Lowest Income Families" (*Cityscape: A Journal of Policy Development and Research*, 2001) that tenant-based voucher programs give low-income people choices in housing and avoid problems of concentrating all poor people in housing projects.

Other Housing Assistance Programs

HUD maintains programs to help fund housing for specific groups, including people living with AIDS, elderly people, Native Americans and Native Hawaiians, and people with disabilities. The Prisoner Reentry Initiative, created in 2005, helps former prisoners find housing and job training and other services.

TABLE 6.5

Selected characteristics of subsidized housing populations, 2005

	Public housing	Tenant vouchers
Average income	$10,725	$11,080
Percent with income of:		
$0	5	4
$1–5,000	16	13
$5,001–10,000	41	39
$10,001–15,000	18	20
$15,001–20,000	9	12
$20,001–25,000	5	6
Above $25,000	7	6
Percent below 30% of median income	56	66
Average monthly payment	$243	$253
Race		
White	50	52
Black	46	44
American Indian/Alaska Native	1	1
Asian	2	3
Ethnicity		
Hispanic	21	17
Not-Hispanic	79	83
Average household size	2.2	2.6
Percent with 4 or more people	18	25
Percent with 2 bedrooms	30	37

SOURCE: Adapted from *Resident Characteristics Report*, U.S. Department of Housing and Urban Development, March 2005

TABLE 6.6

Funding for selected rural housing programs, selected fiscal years 1987–2007

[Dollars in millions]

Rural housing program	Total dollars spent, fiscal year 1987	Total dollars spent, fiscal year 1997	Total dollars requested, fiscal year 2007	Type of assistance
Single-family housing direct loans (sec. 502)	1,144.2	706.4	1,237.5	Loans subsidized as low as 1% interest
Single-family housing guaranteed loans (sec. 502)	NA	2,000.0	3,564.2	No money down, no monthly mortgage insurance loans
Single-family home repair grants and loans (sec. 504)	18.4	48.5	66.2	Grants for elderly and loans subsidized as low as 1% interest
Single-family housing mutual self-help grants (sec. 523)	7.6	26.2	37.6	Grants to nonprofit and public entities to provide technical assistance
Multifamily direct rural rental housing loans (sec. 515)	554.9	152.5	0	Loans to developers subsidized as low as 1% interest
Multifamily housing guaranteed loans (sec. 538)	NA	51.8	198.0	Guaranteed loans for developing moderate-income apartments
Multifamily housing farm labor grants and loans (secs. 516/514)	17.8	23.4	55.5	Grants and loans subsidized at 1% interest
Multifamily housing preservation grants (sec. 533)	19.1	7.6	9.9	Grants to nonprofit organizations, local governments, and Native American tribes, usually leveraged with outside funding
Multifamily housing rental assistance (sec. 521)	275.3	520.2	486.3	Rental assistance to about one-half the residents in RHS rental and farm labor units

SOURCE: Adapted from Bruce E. Foote, "Table 1a. Funding for Selected Rural Housing Programs, FY1980–FY2007," and "Table 1b. Funding for Selected Rural Housing Programs, FY1980–FY2007," in *USDA Rural Housing Programs: An Overview*, Library of Congress, Congressional Research Service, May 11, 2006, http://www.nationalaglawcenter.org/assets/crs/RL33421.pdf (accessed October 24, 2006)

In *Annual Performance Plan, Fiscal Year 2007*, HUD notes that the FY 2007 budget requested $40 million for the Self-Help Homeownership Opportunity Program, which would help approximately fifteen hundred families in that year. Other HUD programs aim to increase privately owned low-income housing stock. The FHA provides mortgage insurance for multifamily projects, and the Low-Income Housing Tax Credit program, which is available to developers who provide a portion of their projects at low rents, added an estimated 117,000 low-income units in 1994, down to only 70,000 units in 2005, according to the Danter Company, in "Statistical Overview of the LIHTC Program, 1987 to 2005" (July 11, 2006, http://www.danter.com/taxcredit/stats.htm). Funding under HUD's Community Development Block Grant program also has money for low-income housing.

HUD maintains demographic and income data only on participants in the major programs. For that reason information on the characteristics of participants in many other HUD subsidy programs aimed at low-income people is unavailable. The programs cited earlier do not include mortgage insurance and other FHA programs aimed to assist the more affluent general population to own a home.

RURAL HOUSING PROGRAMS. A variety of rural housing programs are administered by the Rural Housing Service (RHS), a division of the U.S. Department of Agriculture. (Table 6.6 lists program data for 1987, 1997, and 2007.)

These programs make federal money available for housing in rural areas, which are considered places with populations of fifty thousand people or less. Eligibility for rural housing programs is similar to that of subsidized urban programs. The requirements vary from region to region, and applicants must meet minimum and maximum income guidelines. The subsidies come in the form of grants or low-interest loans to repair substandard housing, subsidized mortgages for low-income home ownership, and grants to cover down payment and purchasing costs of low-income homes.

Table 6.6 shows the various programs that were available under RHS funding in millions of dollars. In 2007, $5.6 billion was appropriated for rural housing programs; of that, over $4.8 billion subsidized single-family home loans (sections 502 and 504) and $486 million provided rental assistance to families (section 521).

Much of the rural low-income housing where renters, migrant workers, and a high population of minorities live is substandard. There are four major areas affected by housing inadequacies: the Mississippi Delta, Native American trust lands, the colonias (poor neighborhoods) bordering Mexico, and Appalachia.

Unfortunately, like HUD, the RHS has been plagued by accusations of mismanagement. In 2003 William B. Shear finds in *Rural Housing Services: Opportunities to Improve Management* (June 19, 2003, http://www.gao.gov/new .items/d03911t.pdf) that the RHS could be improved by reducing costs and by centralizing administration. In May

2004 the GAO reports in *Rural Housing Service: Agency Has Overestimated Its Rental Assistance Budget Needs over the Life of the Program* (http://www.gao.gov/new.items/d04752.pdf) that the RHS has consistently overestimated its budget needs. In 2006 the GAO states in "Rural Housing Service: Overview of Program Issues" (March 10, 2005, http://www.gao.gov/highlights/d05382thigh.pdf) that "several issues prevent the agency from making the best use of resources," including: the policy of "grandfathering" communities, which inhibits an accurate determination of metropolitan versus rural areas; the consistent overestimation of the RHS's rental assistance budget needs and insufficient monitoring of the use of the agency's funds; and inaccurate data collection methods.

PROJECTS FOR ASSISTANCE IN TRANSITION FROM HOMELESSNESS. Projects for Assistance in Transition from Homelessness (PATH) is a federally funded program administered by the federal Center for Mental Health Services through grants to state mental health agencies. These state agencies provide PATH-funded services to homeless people with mental illness primarily through local or regional mental health service providers. PATH funds can be used for outreach, screening, diagnostic treatment, habilation, rehabilitation, community mental health services, case management, supportive and supervisory services in residential settings, and other housing-related services.

NOT KEEPING UP WITH DEMAND

HUD's programs are not able to provide assistance to everyone who qualifies and wants help, and those who are in the programs do not necessarily get all of the assistance they need. Testifying before the House Subcommittee on Housing and Community Opportunity on April 23, 2002, Telissa Dowling (http://commdocs.house.gov/committees/bank/hba79319.000/hba79319_1.HTM) of the New Jersey Department of Community Affairs Resident Advisory Board said that in 2002 about 1.5 million families took advantage of the Section 8 vouchers (also called Housing Choice vouchers). However, the rents permitted under the voucher program have not kept pace with actual rents in many markets. In his testimony before the same subcommittee, Roy Ziegler of the National Leased Housing Association reported that many Section 8 vouchers go unused because there are not enough rental units available to which the vouchers can be applied.

Funding is also a problem. The Joint Center for Housing Studies (JCHS) reports in *The State of the Nation's Housing, 2005* (2005, http://www.jchs.harvard.edu/publications/markets/son2005/son2005.pdf) that for the first time the federal government did not fund all housing vouchers in use in 2005. As shown in Table 6.7, the amount of subsidized housing and Section 8 housing vouchers declined

TABLE 6.7

Subsidized units available under public housing and voucher programs, 1998, 2003, and 2005

	1998	2003	2005
Public housing	1,300,493	1,241,466	1,220,937
Section 8 tenant vouchers	1,391,526	2,077,336	1,803,013
Section 8 project-based vouchers/certificates	1,001,939	817,274	9,833

SOURCE: Created by Melissa Doak for Information Plus from "Basic Counts," in *A Picture of Subsidized Households in 1998*, U.S. Department of Housing and Urban Development, August 28, 1998, http://www.huduser.org/datasets/assthsg/statedata98/ (accessed January 27, 2007), and *Resident Characteristics Report*, U.S. Department of Housing and Urban Development, March 2005

across all categories between 2003 and 2005. As a result of the decline in funding for Section 8 housing vouchers coupled with the rising costs of housing, waiting lists to get this housing assistance are long and sometimes closed altogether to new applicants.

Low-income people hoping for housing assistance from the federal government face formidable obstacles. According to the U.S. Department of Housing and Urban Development (HUD), in *Waiting in Vain: An Update on America's Housing Crisis* (1999), in 1998 a family spent an average of thirty-three months on a waiting list for HUD-assisted housing operated by the largest public housing authorities. The U.S. Conference of Mayors reports in the *Hunger and Homelessness Survey: A Status Report on Hunger and Homelessness in America's Cities, a 23-City Survey* (December 2006, http://www.usmayors.org/uscm/hungersurvey/2006/report06.pdf) that requests for government housing assistance were up in 86% of the surveyed cities in 2006. Section 8 waiting lists were long and often closed in surveyed cities. In January 2006, for example, 5,543 were on the Housing Choice Voucher waiting list in Boston; after the city reopened its waiting list for two weeks, 10,645 families were on the list. Seattle estimated it would take about seven or eight years to get through all the families on its Section 8 waiting list. New York City was not processing applications for Section 8 housing in January 2007 because of the shortfall in federal funding. Seventeen of twenty-three mayors surveyed believed high housing costs were a primary cause of homelessness in their cities.

RESTRICTIVE ORDINANCES

According to Tom Wetzel, in "What Is Gentrification?" (2004), the process of renewal and rebuilding that accompanies an influx of middle-class or affluent people into deteriorating areas is called gentrification. It typically displaces earlier—and usually poorer—residents, and often destroys ethnic communities. Even though gentrification has positive aspects—reduced crime, new investment in the community, and increased economic activity—these benefits are generally enjoyed by the newcomers while the existing residents are marginalized. When a neighborhood is gentrified, the visible homeless come to be seen as a blight on the quality of life of the new residents. The homeless can drive away tourists and frustrate the proprietors of area businesses, leading to efforts to remove the homeless from the community. The widening gap between the haves and the have-nots in American society is evident in the plight of homeless people. As more and more privately owned, federally subsidized apartment buildings and former "skid rows" were gentrified during the economic boom of the 1990s, more of the poorest people were forced into homelessness.

Recent years have seen an increase in the enactment of laws and ordinances intended to regulate the activities of homeless people. Moreover, in some areas homeless children even found themselves placed outside the regular public school system and segregated in special schools for the homeless. Advocates for the homeless contend that such practices deny the homeless their most basic human, legal, and political rights.

Some local ordinances prevent the homeless from sleeping on the streets or in parks, although there may not be enough shelter beds to accommodate every homeless person every night. The homeless may be turned out of shelters to fend for themselves during the day, yet local ordinances prevent them from loitering in public places or resting in bus stations, libraries, or public buildings. Begging or picking up cans for recycling may help the homeless to support themselves, yet often there are restrictions against panhandling (begging) or limits on the number of cans they can redeem. To see the homeless bathe or use the toilet in public makes people uncomfortable; consequently, laws are passed to prohibit such activities.

Are the homeless targeted by these laws and consequently denied their civil rights? Do such ordinances criminalize homelessness by singling out the minority (the unhoused) but not the majority (the housed)? For example, drinking alcoholic beverages in public is illegal, but the police may selectively enforce the law against street people while ignoring other drinkers, such as tourists. Ordinances disallowing life-sustaining activities performed by homeless individuals may be said to exclude the homeless from equal protection under the law.

Most measures regulating the behavior of the homeless are enacted at the community level. Sometimes the most restrictive of these laws have been challenged in federal court on the grounds that they violate the rights of the homeless people they seek to regulate. For example, a federal court may be asked to determine whether begging

or panhandling is considered protected conduct under the First Amendment (freedom of speech).

Criminalizing Homelessness

Homeless people live in and move about public spaces, and many Americans believe society has a right to control or regulate what homeless people can do in these shared spaces. A city or town may introduce local ordinances or policies designed to restrict homeless people's activities, remove their belongings, or destroy their nontraditional living places. In many cities municipal use of criminal sanctions to protect public spaces has come into conflict with efforts by civil rights and homeless advocates to prevent the criminalization of the necessary activities of the homeless population.

There have been other approaches. Several cities have proposed or created community courts specifically to handle "public nuisance" crimes. Other cities have implemented plans to privatize public property as a way of restricting the access of homeless people to certain areas.

Other localities pass ordinances that target homeless people in the hopes of driving them from the community. According to the National Coalition for the Homeless (NCH), in *A Dream Denied: The Criminalization of Homelessness in U.S. Cities* (January 2006, http://www.nationalhomeless.org/publications/crimreport/report.pdf), of 224 cities surveyed in 2006, 28% prohibited camping in some places and 16% prohibited it citywide; 27% prohibited sitting or lying in some public places; 39% prohibited loitering in some places and 16% prohibited it citywide; 43% prohibited begging in some places, 45% prohibited "aggressive" panhandling, and 21% had citywide prohibitions.

Violating Human Rights

In *A Dream Denied*, the NCH states that, as successful lawsuits have shown, "many of the practices and policies that punish the public performance of life-sustaining activities by homeless persons violate the constitutional rights of homeless persons." The NCH notes that nearly all the communities surveyed lacked sufficient shelter space to accommodate the homeless and suggests that the effort and money spent on bringing the homeless into the courthouse might better be directed toward addressing the nation's lack of affordable housing.

Antihomeless laws existed in some of the cities surveyed by the NCH. Prohibited or restricted behaviors fell under the categories of sanitation, begging, sleeping/camping, sitting/lying, loitering/loafing, and vagrancy.

The NCH names Sarasota, Florida; Lawrence, Kansas; Little Rock, Arkansas; Atlanta, Georgia; and Las Vegas, Nevada, as the five "meanest cities" based on the number of antihomeless laws passed or pending, the enforcement and severity of their laws, the local support for the "meanest" designation, and the "general political climate" with regard to the homeless, among other criteria. Two examples of the practices of these cities follow.

Sarasota tried a third time to criminalize homelessness after two previous antilodging laws were overturned as unconstitutional by Florida courts. The latest law explicitly targeted homeless people—to be arrested under the law, a person must have "no other place to live."

Even though Las Vegas lacks an adequate number of shelter beds, police regularly sweep homeless encampments and repeat misdemeanor offenders face extended jail time. The city considered making parks private to enable owners to kick out unwanted people. Mayor Oscar Goodman said, "I don't want them here. They're not going to be there. I'm not going to let it happen. They think I'm mean now; wait until the homeless try to go over there."

Rationale for Restrictive Ordinances

Local officials often restrict homeless people's use of public space to protect public health and safety—either of the general public, the homeless themselves, or both. Dangers to the public have included tripping over people and objects on sidewalks, intimidation of passersby caused by aggressive begging, and the spreading of diseases. Many people believe the presence of the homeless is unsightly and their removal improves the appearance of public spaces. Other laws are based on the need to prevent crime. New York's campaign is based on the broken windows theory of the criminologists James Q. Wilson and George Kelling (*Atlantic Monthly*, March 1982). They argue that allowing indications of disorder, such as a broken window or street people, to remain unaddressed shows a loss of public order and control, as well as apathy in a neighborhood, which breeds more serious criminal activity. Therefore, keeping a city neat and orderly should help to prevent crime.

All these are legitimate concerns to some degree. The problem, critics say, is that rather than trying to eliminate or reduce homelessness by helping the homeless find housing and jobs, most local laws try to change the behavior of the homeless by punishing them. They target the homeless with legal action, ignoring the fact that many would gladly stop living in the streets and panhandling if they had any feasible alternatives. Even though these laws may be effective in the sense that the shanties are gone and homeless people are not allowed to bed down in subway tunnels or doorways, the fact remains that homelessness has not been eradicated. Homeless people have simply been forced to move to a different part of town, have hidden themselves, or have been imprisoned, and all because they are doing something that they would gladly stop if they could. Furthermore, many of these laws have been challenged in court as violating the legal rights of the homeless people they target.

An Argument against Criminalization as Public Policy

In "Downward Spiral: Homelessness and Its Criminalization" (*Yale Law and Policy Review*, 1996), Maria Foscarinis, the founder of the National Law Center on Homelessness and Poverty, states that criminalization of the homeless is poor public policy for several reasons:

- It may be constitutionally unsound, especially in cities that are unable to offer adequate resources to their homeless residents.

- It leads to legal challenges, which may take years to resolve, regardless of outcome.

- Legal battles are costly and will deplete already scarce municipal resources that could be used on solutions to homelessness.

- Criminalization responses do not reflect public sentiment, but the will of a vocal, politically influential minority.

- Criminalization fosters divisiveness, pitting "us" (the housed) against "them" (the homeless).

- Like emergency relief, criminalization addresses the visible symptom of homelessness—the presence of homeless people in the public space—and neglects the true causes of homelessness.

- There is the fact that, in the long term, criminalization does not and cannot work. Like all humans, homeless people must eat, sleep, and occupy space. If they are prohibited from occupying one area, they must go somewhere else.

As an alternative to criminalization, Foscarinis suggests the following:

- Police advocacy programs, in which sweeps are replaced by outreach units—officers assigned to go out, with service providers, to homeless people to refer them to necessary services. Unless criminal activity is involved, the police remain in the background to provide security, and the presence of service providers prevents police from being too heavy-handed or harassing.

- Standing committees composed of homeless people, advocates, a police captain, and a representative of the city government to respond to complaints about the camping of homeless residents. The committee outreach team attempts to make alternative arrangements for the homeless. The police act only if criminal activity is involved, or if homeless people refuse alternative arrangements.

- Day-labor centers—buildings where homeless people can meet with employers to get jobs.

- One-stop access centers, which offer medical services, mental health services, social services, and job training at one location.

The NCH agrees with these suggestions. In *A Dream Denied*, it argues that criminalization does nothing to address the problem and that local government, police officials, and business groups should work with advocates and providers for the homeless to come up with solutions that prevent and end homelessness. For example, more resources should be made available for affordable housing projects and homeless shelters and other services. The NCH states that business groups can put resources toward solutions to end homelessness rather than toward lobbying for criminalization methods. The NCH contends that "as criminalization measures move people away from services, make it more difficult for people to move out of homelessness, and cost more due to incarceration and law enforcement costs than more constructive approaches, cities would be wise to seek constructive alternatives to criminalization. When cities work with homeless persons and advocates toward solutions to homelessness, instead of punishing those who are homeless or poor, everyone can benefit."

Alternative Strategies

Alternatives to criminalizing homeless behavior can be implemented with help from community leadership and homeless advocates, who have intimate knowledge from close contact with homelessness. In *A Dream Denied*, the NCH details the innovative programs that some cities have put in place to better deal with the problem of homelessness.

A key element of most successful programs is the partnering of governmental and police organizations with advocacy organizations. For example, in Broward County, Florida, the Taskforce for Ending Homelessness partnered with the Fort Lauderdale police department to create an outreach team that includes not only police officers but also a civilian advocate who was formerly homeless. After five years of operation the team had had over twenty-three thousand contacts with homeless individuals and had prevented an estimated twenty-four hundred arrests each year. In Columbus, Cleveland, and Cincinnati, Ohio, teams of trained workers visit homeless encampments at nontraditional hours to assist homeless people. Key to the success of the program is that they do not put many restrictions on the assistance they offer. In Washington, D.C., the downtown business community created a community day center for homeless people to provide services when shelters are closed. The center serves up to 260 people per day, providing them with laundry services and showers, as well as a morning meal.

CONSTITUTIONAL RIGHTS OF THE HOMELESS

The U.S. Constitution and its amendments, especially the Bill of Rights, guarantee certain freedoms and rights to all U.S. citizens, including the homeless. As more and more cities move to deal with homelessness by aggressively enforcing public place restrictions, the restrictions are increasingly being challenged in court as unconstitutional. Sometimes a city ordinance has been declared unconstitutional; at other times the courts have found that there were special circumstances that allowed the ordinance to stand.

There are many ways in which ordinances affecting the homeless can violate their rights. Many court challenges claim that the law in question is unconstitutionally broad or vague. Others claim that a particular law denies the homeless equal protection under the law or violates their right to due process, as guaranteed by the Fifth and Fourteenth Amendments. There are also cases based on a person's right to travel, and others that claim restrictions on the homeless constitute cruel and unusual punishment, which is prohibited by the Eighth Amendment. Many cities have ordinances against panhandling, but charitable organizations freely solicit in public places. As a result, according to those challenging the ordinances, the right to free expression under the First Amendment is unfairly made available to organizations but denied to the homeless.

The appearance of poverty should not deny an individual's right to be free from unreasonable search and seizure, as guaranteed by the Fourth Amendment. Often, homeless people's property has been confiscated or destroyed (such as camping gear or personal possessions) without warning because they were found on public property. Unfortunately, the state of homelessness is such that even the most personal living activities have to be performed in public. Denying these activities necessary for survival may infringe on an individual's rights under the Eighth Amendment.

The Fourteenth Amendment's right to equal protection under the law may be at issue when the homeless are cited for sleeping in the park, but others lying on the grass sunning themselves or taking a nap during a picnic, for instance, are not.

Testing the Constitutionality of Laws in Court

Some court cases test the law through civil suits, and others challenge the law by appealing convictions in criminal cases. Many advocates for the homeless, or the homeless themselves, challenge laws that they believe infringed on the rights of homeless people. The NCH argues that antipanhandling laws infringe on the First Amendment's right of free speech; that anticamping laws penalize people when no shelter space is available and violate the Eighth Amendment's right to be free from cruel and unusual punishment; that antiloitering laws are often unconstitutionally vague and violate the Due Process Clause of the Fourteenth Amendment; and that sweeps targeted toward cleaning public areas violate the Fourth Amendment's right to be free from unreasonable searches and seizures.

NO BED, NO ARREST. The concept of "no bed, no arrest" first arose out of a 1988 class action suit filed by the Miami Chapter of the American Civil Liberties Union on behalf of about six thousand homeless people living in the city of Miami. The city had a practice of sweeping the homeless from the areas where the Orange Bowl Parade and other related activities were held. The complaint alleged that the city had "a custom, practice and policy of arresting, harassing and otherwise interfering with homeless people for engaging in basic activities of daily life—including sleeping and eating—in the public places where they are forced to live. Plaintiffs further claim that the City has arrested thousands of homeless people for such life-sustaining conduct under various City of Miami ordinances and Florida Statutes. In addition, plaintiffs assert that the city routinely seizes and destroys their property and has failed to follow its own inventory procedures regarding the seized personal property of homeless arrestees and homeless persons in general."

In *Pottinger v. City of Miami* (76 F.3d 1154, 1992), the U.S. District Court for the Southern District of Florida ruled that the city's practices were cruel and unusual, in violation of the Eighth Amendment's ban against punishment based on status. (Only the homeless were being arrested.) Furthermore, the court found the police practices of taking or destroying the property of the homeless to be in violation of the Fourth and Fifth Amendments' rights of freedom from unreasonable seizure and confiscation of property.

The city appealed the district court's judgment. Ultimately, a settlement was reached in which the city of Miami agreed that a homeless person observed committing a "life-sustaining conduct" misdemeanor may be warned to stop, but if there is no available shelter, no warning is to be given. If there is an available shelter, the homeless person is to be told of its availability. If the homeless person accepts assistance, no arrest is to take place.

LOITERING OR WANDERING. In the year 2000, homeless street dwellers and shelter residents of the Skid Row area (the plaintiffs) sought a temporary restraining order (TRO) against the Los Angeles Police Department (the defendant), claiming that their rights guaranteed by the First and Fourth Amendments were being violated. The plaintiffs alleged that they were being stopped without cause and their identification demanded on threat of arrest, that they were being ordered to "move along" although they were not in anyone's way, that their belongings were being confiscated, and that they were being ticketed for loitering. In *Justin v. City of Los Angeles* (No. CV-00-12352 LGB, 2000 U.S. Dist. LEXIS 17881 [C.D. Cal. Dec. 5, 2000]), Judge Lourdes Baird denied a TRO that would have prevented the defendant from asking the plaintiffs to "move along." The TRO was granted with reference to the following actions when in the Skid Row area:

- Detention without reasonable suspicion
- Demand of identification on threat of arrest
- Searches without probable cause
- Removal from sidewalks unless free passage of pedestrians was obstructed
- Confiscation of personal property that was not abandoned
- Citation of those who may "annoy or molest" if interference was reasonable and free passage of pedestrians was not impeded

LIVING IN AN ENCAMPMENT. In 1996 advocates for the homeless sought an injunction against a Tucson, Arizona, resolution barring homeless encampments from city-owned property on Eighth Amendment and Equal Protection grounds. The court, in *Davidson v. City of Tucson* (924 F. Supp. 989), held that the plaintiffs did not have standing to raise a cruel and unusual punishment claim, as they had not been convicted of a crime and no one had been arrested under the ordinance. The Equal Protection claim failed because the court did not consider homeless people a suspect class and the right to travel did not include the right to ignore trespass laws or remain on property without regard to ownership.

LOITERING IN A TRAIN STATION. In 1995 plaintiffs challenged Amtrak's policy of arresting or ejecting people who appeared to be homeless or loitering in Penn Station in New York City, even though the individuals were not apparently committing crimes. The district court, in *Streetwatch v. National R.R. Passenger Corp.* (875 F. Supp. 1055), determined that Amtrak's rules of conduct were unacceptably vague and that their enforcement impinged on the plaintiffs' rights to freedom of movement and due process.

PANHANDLING. One of the notable court cases addressing panhandling involved Jennifer Loper, who moved from her parents' suburban New York home to beg on the streets of New York City. From time to time she and her friend William Kaye were ordered by police to move on, in accordance with the city ordinance, which stated: "A person is guilty of loitering when he: '(1) Loiters, remains or wanders about in a public place for the purpose of begging.'" In 1992 Loper and Kaye sued the city, claiming that their free speech rights had been violated and that the ordinance was unconstitutional. A district court declared the ordinance unconstitutional on First Amendment grounds. On appeal, the police department argued that begging has no expressive element that is protected by the First Amendment. In *Loper v. New York City Police Department* (999 F.2d 699 [2d Cir. 1993]), the U.S. Court of Appeals, Second Circuit, declared the city's ban on begging invalid, noting that the regulations applied to sidewalks, which have historically been acknowledged to be a public forum. The court agreed that the ban deprived beggars of all means to express their message. Even if a panhandler does not speak, "the presence of an unkempt and disheveled person holding out his or her hand or a cup to receive a donation itself conveys a message of need for support and assistance."

ZONING THE HOMELESS OUT OF DOWNTOWN. In 1998 Alan Mason, a homeless man, sought an injunction, damages, and relief against the city of Tucson and the city police for zoning homeless people. The suit alleged that homeless people were arrested without cause, were charged with misdemeanors, and were then released only if they agreed to stay away from the area where they had been arrested. Mason himself had been restricted from certain downtown areas, such as federal, state, and local courts (including the court in which his case was tried); voter registration facilities; a soup kitchen; places of worship; and many social and transportation agencies.

The plaintiff argued that such restrictions violated his constitutional right to travel, deprived him of liberty without due process in violation of the Fifth Amendment, and implicated the Equal Protection clause of the Fourteenth Amendment. In July 1998 the district court, in *Mason v. Tucson* (D. Arizona, 1998), granted a temporary injunction against enforcing the law, saying the zone restrictions were overbroad. The case was subsequently settled out of court.

CHAPTER 7
HEALTH AND HUNGER

HEALTH OF POOR PEOPLE
Connection between Poor Health and Poverty

The National Center for Health Statistics of the U.S. Department of Health and Human Services (HHS) points out in *Health, United States, 2006* (2006, http://www.cdc.gov/nchs/data/hus/hus06.pdf) that poverty causes poor health because of its connection with a nutritionally poor diet, substandard housing, exposure to the elements and environmental hazards, unhealthy lifestyle, and decreased access to and use of health care services. Jane Knitzer, the director of the National Center for Children in Poverty, testified before the House Committee on Ways and Means on January 27, 2007, that economic hardship in childhood is linked to poor health and that poor health adversely impacts educational attainment and future productivity, leading to a cycle of poverty (http://www.nccp.org/pub_wmt07.html).

Poor people are more likely to suffer from chronic conditions that limit their activities. According to *Health, United States, 2006*, in 2004, 11.9% of the population had such conditions. However, almost a quarter of people living below the poverty line (23%) suffered from chronic health complaints, compared with 16.3% of those whose household incomes were 100% to 199% of the poverty level and 9.2% of those whose incomes were 200% or more of the poverty level. In addition, 14.2% of adults with incomes below the poverty line had difficulty seeing even with corrective lenses, compared with 12% of people with incomes 100% to 199% of the poverty line and 7.4% of those with incomes 200% of the poverty line or higher.

Health, United States, 2006 also reports that poor respondents were much more likely to rate their health as only fair or poor, compared with their more affluent peers. In 2004 more than one in five people (21.3%) with incomes below the poverty level rated their health as fair or poor, compared with 14.4% of people with incomes 100% to 199% of the poverty level and only 6.3% of people with higher incomes.

Poor people also have more mental health problems. Only 1.7% of people with incomes 200% of the poverty level or higher reported they suffered from serious psychological distress in 2004. However, 5.4% of people with incomes 100% to 199% of the poverty line and 8.8% of people with incomes below the poverty level reported such psychological distress.

Access to Care

Health, United States, 2006 also reports that poor people have limited access to medical care. In 2004, 11.5% of those living below the poverty level reported not receiving care because of cost, and 13.5% reported delaying receiving health care because of cost in the previous year. In contrast, of those with incomes 100% to 199% of the poverty level, 10% reported not receiving care and 12.8% reported a delay in receiving care, whereas among those with incomes 200% of the poverty level or more, 3.3% reported not receiving care and 5.5% reported a delay in receiving care in the previous year. In addition, 14.2% of people with incomes below the poverty level did not get prescription drugs because of the cost, compared with 12.8% of people with incomes 100% to 199% of the poverty level and only 4.5% of those with higher incomes. The percentage of people unable to get prescription drugs because of their costs has risen markedly in all socioeconomic groups since 1997.

A higher percentage of poor and low-income children in 2003–04 had not visited the doctor in the previous twelve months than children in higher income families; this was particularly true among Hispanic children. According to *Health, United States, 2006*, over one in five Hispanic children living in households with incomes below the poverty level (21.8%) or with incomes 100% to 199% of the poverty level (20.9%) had not visited a doctor in the previous year, whereas 14.9% of Hispanic children living in households with incomes 200% or

FIGURE 7.1

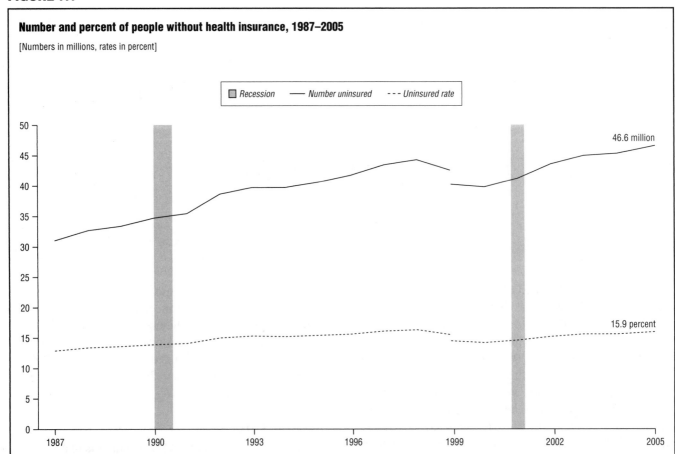

Number and percent of people without health insurance, 1987–2005

[Numbers in millions, rates in percent]

Notes: Respondents were not asked detailed health insurance questions before the 1988 Current Population Survey (CPS). These estimates also reflect the results of follow-up verification questions that were asked of people who responded "no" to all questions about specific types of health insurance coverage in order to verify whether they were actually uninsured. This change increased the number and percentage of people covered by health insurance, bringing the CPS more in line with estimates from other national surveys. The data points are placed at the midpoints of the respective years.

SOURCE: Carmen DeNavas-Walt, Bernadette D. Proctor, and Cheryl Hill Lee, "Figure 7. Number Uninsured and Uninsured Rate: 1987 to 2005," in *Income, Poverty, and Health Insurance Coverage in the United States: 2005—Current Population Reports*, U.S. Census Bureau, P60-231, August 2006, http://www.census.gov/prod/2006pubs/p60-231.pdf (accessed December 1, 2006)

more of the poverty level had not visited a doctor in the past year. Among white, non-Hispanic children, 12.3% of those living below the poverty level, 12.4% of those living at 100% to 199% of the poverty level, and 8.3% of those living at 200% or more of the poverty level had not seen a doctor in the previous year. Among African-American children, 12.9% of those living below the poverty level, 13.4% of those living at 100% to 199% of the poverty level, and 10.2% of those living at 200% or more of the poverty level had failed to see a doctor within the past year.

HEALTH INSURANCE

The scope of health issues regarding the impoverished and homeless in the United States is related in part to the number of uninsured Americans. Figure 7.1 shows that in 2005 the number of uninsured people was higher than it had been in decades. At that time 46.6 million people were uninsured. Figure 7.2 shows the average number of people from 2003 to 2005 who were without health insurance coverage by state. Texas (24.6%) had the highest percentage of uninsured people, whereas Minnesota (8.7%) had the lowest. Comparisons of two-year averages (2003–04 and 2004–05) show that the percentage of people without health insurance rose in eight states (California, Utah, Arizona, Florida, Georgia, South Carolina, Delaware, and Vermont) and dropped in only three (Idaho, Iowa, and New York). (See Figure 7.3.)

Children in poverty were much more likely than children in general to be uninsured in 2005 (19% and 11.2%, respectively). (See Figure 7.4.) However, this rate varied greatly by race. Hispanic children (21.9%) were far more likely to be uninsured than African-American children (12.5%), Asian children (12.2%), or white, non-Hispanic children (7.2%).

People without insurance are less likely to seek medical care. In "Out of Pocket Medical Spending

FIGURE 7.2

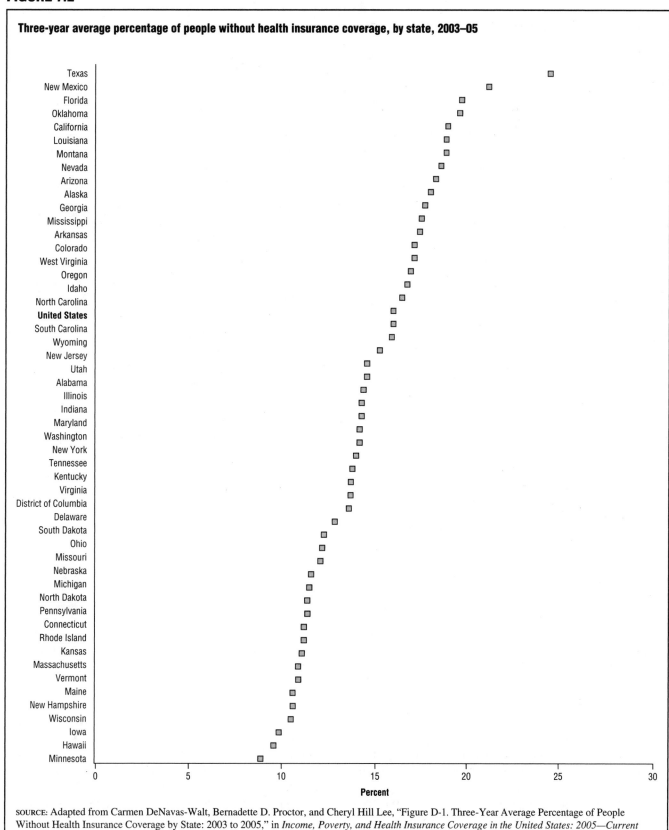

Three-year average percentage of people without health insurance coverage, by state, 2003–05

SOURCE: Adapted from Carmen DeNavas-Walt, Bernadette D. Proctor, and Cheryl Hill Lee, "Figure D-1. Three-Year Average Percentage of People Without Health Insurance Coverage by State: 2003 to 2005," in *Income, Poverty, and Health Insurance Coverage in the United States: 2005—Current Population Reports*, U.S. Census Bureau, P60-231, August 2006, http://www.census.gov/prod/2006pubs/p60-231.pdf (accessed December 1, 2006)

for Care of Chronic Conditions" (*Health Affairs*, November–December 2001), Stephen W. Hwang et al. note that "among chronically ill persons the uninsured had the highest out-of-pocket spending and were five times less likely to see a medical provider in a given year."

FIGURE 7.3

Differences in uninsured rates by state, 2003–04 to 2004–05

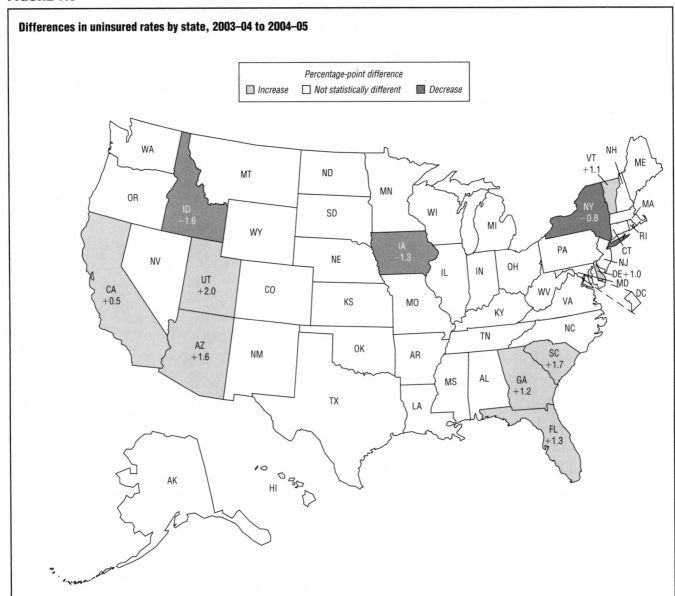

Note: The 2004 data have been revised to reflect a correction to the weights in the 2005 Annual Social and Economic Supplement (Census Bureau). The estimates also reflect improvements to the algorithm that assigns coverage to dependents.

SOURCE: Carmen DeNavas-Walt, Bernadette D. Proctor, and Cheryl Hill Lee, "Figure 9. Differences in 2-Year-Average Uninsured Rates by State: 2004–2005 less 2003–2004," in *Income, Poverty, and Health Insurance Coverage in the United States: 2005—Current Population Reports*, U.S. Census Bureau, P60-231, August 2006, http://www.census.gov/prod/2006pubs/p60-231.pdf (accessed December 1, 2006)

At the same time that overall money spent on health care in the United States is growing rapidly, government spending to help the uninsured has remained stagnant or declined. The Kaiser Commission notes in "Covering the Uninsured: Growing Need, Strained Resources" (January 2007, http://www.kff.org/uninsured/upload/7429-02.pdf) that between 2001 and 2004 health care expenses rose by nearly 14%, whereas federal spending on safety net programs—a network of hospitals, clinics, and health centers that are largely supported by government resources— increased from $19.8 billion in 2001 to $22.8 billion in 2004, an increase of 15.4%. However, because the number of uninsured grew by nearly five million people over that

period, federal spending per uninsured person actually declined, from $546 per person to $498 per person in constant 2004 dollars. The Kaiser Commission concludes, "As critical to the care of the uninsured as safety net providers are, they are unable to meet all the needs of the uninsured, particularly if resources continue to decrease as the number of uninsured increases."

Medicaid

Medicaid, which is authorized under Title XIX of the Social Security Act, is a federal-state program that provides medical insurance for low-income people who are aged, blind, disabled, or members of families with dependent

FIGURE 7.4

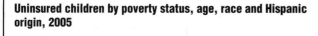

Uninsured children by poverty status, age, race and Hispanic origin, 2005

[By percent]

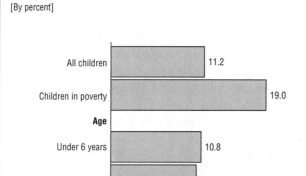

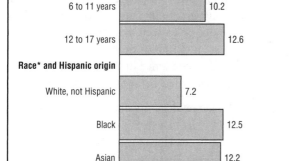

*Federal surveys now give respondents the option of reporting more than one race. Therefore, two basic ways of defining a race group are possible. A group such as Asian may be defined as those who reported Asian and no other race (the race-alone or single-race concept) or as those who reported Asian regardless of whether they also reported another race (the race-alone-or-in-combination concept). This figure shows data using the first approach (race alone). The use of the single-race population does not imply that it is the preferred method of presenting or analyzing data. The Census Bureau uses a variety of approaches. Information on people who reported more than one race, such as white and American Indian and Alaska Native or Asian and black or African American, is available from Census 2000 through American Fact Finder. About 2.6 percent of people reported more than one race in Census 2000.

SOURCE: Carmen DeNavas-Walt, Bernadette D. Proctor, and Cheryl Hill Lee, "Figure 8. Uninsured Children by Poverty Status, Age, and Race and Hispanic Origin: 2005," in *Income, Poverty, and Health Insurance Coverage in the United States: 2005—Current Population Reports*, U.S. Census Bureau, P60-231, August 2006, http://www.census.gov/prod/2006pubs/p60-231.pdf (accessed December 1, 2006)

TABLE 7.1

Number of Medicaid recipients, amount of payments, and average payment, by state, fiscal year 2002

State	Number of recipients	Total payments (millions of dollars)	Average payment (dollars)
United States*	49,754,619	213,491	4,291
Alabama	765,328	3,204	4,187
Alaska	109,641	686	6,264
Arizona	878,362	2,881	3,281
Arkansas	579,278	2,015	3,479
California	9,301,001	23,636	2,541
Colorado	425,878	2,166	5,086
Connecticut	479,051	3,245	6,774
Delaware	167,162	651	3,897
District of Columbia	193,494	1,027	5,308
Florida	2,676,235	9,827	3,672
Georgia	1,637,329	4,796	2,929
Hawaii	199,966	695	3,477
Idaho	176,499	791	4,487
Illinois	1,731,398	9,121	5,268
Indiana	849,427	3,725	4,386
Iowa	352,635	1,855	5,263
Kansas	289,349	1,501	5,188
Kentucky	808,294	3,459	4,280
Louisiana	898,824	3,234	3,599
Maine	275,826	1,716	6,223
Maryland	692,539	3,662	5,288
Massachusetts	1,065,636	6,387	5,994
Michigan	1,449,915	5,918	4,082
Minnesota	620,652	4,439	7,153
Mississippi	712,457	2,499	3,508
Missouri	1,036,150	4,071	3,929
Montana	103,617	532	5,143
Nebraska	255,771	1,255	4,907
Nevada	202,306	723	3,579
New Hampshire	104,138	745	7,161
New Jersey	954,491	5,497	5,759
New Mexico	798,665	1,796	2,250
New York	3,920,718	31,488	8,031
North Carolina	1,355,269	6,041	4,457
North Dakota	70,132	422	6,028
Ohio	1,656,124	9,186	5,547
Oklahoma	631,498	2,238	3,544
Oregon	621,462	2,136	3,438
Pennsylvania	1,627,261	8,523	5,238
Rhode Island	199,014	1,251	6,288
South Carolina	809,136	3,382	4,181
South Dakota	117,631	503	4,284
Tennessee	1,732,381	4,747	2,740
Texas	2,952,569	11,121	3,767
Utah	274,707	1,215	4,425
Vermont	153,731	607	3,950
Virginia	665,203	3,017	4,537
Washington	1,039,070	4,373	4,209
West Virginia	362,030	1,577	4,358
Wisconsin	716,298	3,605	5,034
Wyoming	59,071	280	4,748

*Excludes recipients in Puerto Rico and the Virgin Islands. Data are not available.

SOURCE: "Table 8.H1—Number of Recipients, Total Payments, and Average Payment, by State, Fiscal Year 2002," in *Annual Statistical Supplement to the Social Security Bulletin, 2005*, Social Security Administration, February 2006, http://www.ssa.gov/policy/docs/statcomps/supplement/2005/supplement05.pdf (accessed January 11, 2007)

children and for certain other pregnant women and children. Within federal guidelines, each state designs and administers its own program. For this reason there may be considerable differences from state to state as to who is covered, what type of coverage is provided, and how much is paid for medical services. States receive federal matching payments based on their Medicaid expenditures and the state's per capita income. The federal match ranges from 50% to 80% of Medicaid expenditures. Table 7.1 shows the number of recipients, the amount of payments, and the average payment per recipient for each state or territory in fiscal year (FY) 2002.

Although Medicaid eligibility had been linked to receipt of, or eligibility to receive, benefits under Aid to Families with Dependent Children or Supplemental Security Income, legislation gradually extended coverage in the 1980s and 1990s. Beginning in 1986 benefits were extended to low-income children and pregnant women not on welfare. States must cover children less than six years of age and pregnant women with family incomes below 133% of the federal poverty level. Pregnant women are only covered for medical services related to their pregnancies, whereas children receive full Medicaid coverage. The states may cover infants under one year old and pregnant women with incomes more than 133%, but not more than 185%, of the poverty level. As of January 1, 1991, Medicaid also began to cover aged and disabled people receiving Medicare whose incomes were below 100% of the poverty level.

States may deny Medicaid benefits to adults who lose Temporary Assistance for Needy Families (TANF) benefits because they refuse to work. However, the law exempts poor pregnant women and children from this provision, requiring their continued Medicaid eligibility. In addition, the welfare law requires state plans to ensure Medicaid for children receiving foster care or adoption assistance.

Carmen DeNavas-Walt, Bernadette D. Proctor, and Cheryl Hill Lee report in *Income, Poverty, and Health Insurance Coverage in the United States: 2005—Current Population Reports* (August 2006, http://www.census.gov/prod/2006pubs/p60-231.pdf) that 8.3 million children, or 11.2%, are uninsured. In an effort to reach these uninsured children, many states are simplifying the Medicaid application process. In addition, the 1996 welfare law gives states the option to use Medicaid to provide health care coverage to low-income working parents. About half (47%) of poor adults without children, 42% of poor parents, and 22% of poor children were uninsured in 2005. (See Figure 7.5.) Although the income of these households is below the federal poverty line, working poor parents have been ineligible for publicly funded health insurance. In addition, low-wage jobs often do not offer affordable employer-sponsored coverage. The number of uninsured working poor parents is likely to grow as welfare recipients move into the workforce, as required under the welfare reform law, unless states expand Medicaid to cover this group.

Medicaid accounted for 13% of all health coverage in 2005. (See Figure 7.6.) Medicaid is the single largest source of health insurance coverage for all children from families earning below 200% of the poverty line. African-American and Hispanic children were far more likely to have Medicaid coverage than were white or Asian and Pacific Islander children. DeNavas-Walt, Proctor, and Hill Lee note that in 2005, 44.9% of African-American children and 39.3% of Hispanic children were covered by Medicaid, compared with 18% of non-Hispanic white children and 15.9% of Asian children.

Of the 49.7 million people enrolled in Medicaid in 2002 (the latest year for which detailed statistics are available), the majority were dependent children under twenty-one years of age (24.6 million) and adults in families with

dependent children (13.2 million). (See Table 7.2.) The remainder of Medicaid recipients were disabled (8 million) or elderly (4.7 million). The number receiving Medicaid coverage had more than doubled since the mid-1970s, when approximately 22 million people were enrolled.

The rapid growth in spending for Medicaid has contributed to the concern over the rising cost of health care. Not accounting for inflation, spending skyrocketed from $6.3 billion in 1972 to $37.5 billion in 1985 to $213.5 billion in 2002. (See Table 7.2.) Of the $213.5 billion spent on Medicaid payments in 2002, most went for the disabled ($91.9 billion, or 43%) and the elderly ($51.7 billion, or 24.2%). In addition, considerable amounts were spent on dependent children under age twenty-one ($31.2 billion, or 14.6%) and adults in families with dependent children ($23.5 billion, or 11%). On average, in 2002 the Medicaid program spent $10,870 on every elderly recipient, $1,271 on each dependent child under twenty-one, and $11,408 on each disabled person in the program.

Medicare and Medicaid payments to physicians were cut after the year 2000. In "Bush Seeks Big Medicare and Medicaid Saving, but Faces Hard Fight" (*New York Times*, February 2, 2007), Robert Pear reports that more deep cuts in physician reimbursement in January 2007 were followed by the announcement that the Bush administration planned to ask Congress in February 2007 to cut more than $70 billion from Medicare and Medicaid over the following five years, as well as institute cuts in federal funding of Children's Health Insurance Programs. As a result of these cuts, some medical providers turned Medicaid and Medicare patients away. In "New AMA Survey Shows Medicare Cuts Will Harm Seniors' Access to Physician Care" (March 16, 2006, http://www.ama-assn.org/ama/pub/category/16117.html), the American Medical Association finds that 45% of physicians said they would either decrease or stop seeing new Medicare patients because of the pending 2007 cuts. As a result, access to health care for many low-income people has been compromised.

State Child Health Insurance Program

The Balanced Budget Act of 1997 set aside $24 billion over five years to fund the State Children's Health Insurance Program (SCHIP) in an effort to reach children who were uninsured. This was the nation's largest children's health care investment since the creation of Medicaid in 1965. SCHIP requires states to use the funding to cover uninsured children whose families earn too much for Medicaid but too little to afford private coverage. States may use this money to expand their Medicaid programs, design new child health insurance programs, or create a combination of both.

States must enroll all children who meet Medicaid eligibility rules in the Medicaid program rather than in the new SCHIP plan. They are not allowed to use SCHIP

FIGURE 7.5

Health insurance coverage of low-income adults and children, 2005

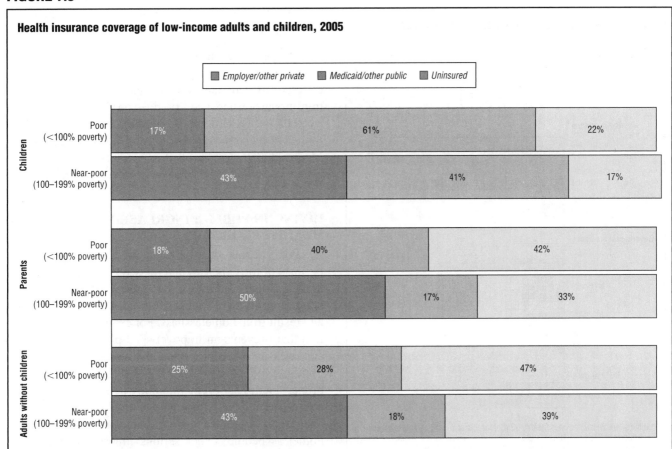

Note: Medicaid also includes State Children's Health Insurance Program (SCHIP) and other state programs, Medicare and military-related coverage. The federal poverty level was $19,971 for a family of four in 2005. Data may not total 100% due to rounding.

SOURCE: "Figure 22. Health Insurance Coverage of Low-Income Adults and Children, 2005," in *The Uninsured: A Primer: Key Facts about Americans without Health Insurance*, Kaiser Family Foundation, October 2006, http://www.kff.org/uninsured/upload/7451-021.pdf (accessed November 21, 2006). This information was reprinted with permission from the Henry J. Kaiser Family Foundation. The Kaiser Family Foundation, based in Menlo Park, California, is a nonprofit, private operating foundation focusing on the major health care issues facing the nation and is not associated with Kaiser Permanente of Kaiser Industries.

to replace existing health coverage. In addition, states must decide on what kind of cost-sharing, if any, to require of low-income families without keeping them from accessing the program. The only federal requirement is that cost-sharing cannot exceed 5% of family income. In *SCHIP Program Enrollment: June 2005 Update* (December 2006, http://www.kff.org/medicaid/upload/7607.pdf), Vernon K. Smith, David Rousseau, and Caryn Marks note that over four million children were enrolled in the SCHIP plan in 2005. As noted earlier, however, the Bush administration proposed in 2007 to cut funding for the program.

Health Care for the Homeless

In 1987 Congress passed the Stewart B. McKinney Homeless Assistance Act to provide services to the homeless, including job training, emergency shelter, education, and health care. Title VI of the act funds Health Care for the Homeless (HCH) programs. The HCH has become the national umbrella under which most

homeless health care initiatives operate. According to the HHS (March 7, 2006, http://bphc.hrsa.gov/hchirc/about/face_homelessness.htm), in 2004 about six hundred thousand people were served by HCH programs. In 2000 the government appropriated $88 million for HCH programs; by 2005 the appropriations had been increased to $145 million.

Nonprofit private organizations and public entities, including state and local government agencies, may apply for grants from the program. The grants may be used to continue to provide services for up to one year to individuals who have obtained permanent housing if services were provided to them when they were homeless.

The goal of the HCH programs is to improve the health of homeless individuals and families by improving access to primary health care and substance abuse services. The HCH provides outreach, counseling to clients explaining available services, case management, and linkages to services such as mental health treatment,

FIGURE 7.6

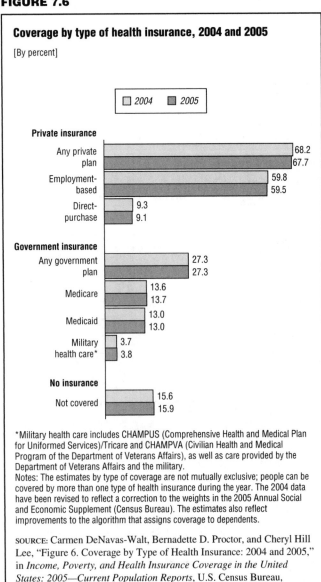

Coverage by type of health insurance, 2004 and 2005

[By percent]

☐ 2004   ■ 2005

Private insurance

Any private plan: 68.2 / 67.7
Employment-based: 59.8 / 59.5
Direct-purchase: 9.3 / 9.1

Government insurance

Any government plan: 27.3 / 27.3
Medicare: 13.6 / 13.7
Medicaid: 13.0 / 13.0
Military health care*: 3.7 / 3.8

No insurance

Not covered: 15.6 / 15.9

*Military health care includes CHAMPUS (Comprehensive Health and Medical Plan for Uniformed Services)/Tricare and CHAMPVA (Civilian Health and Medical Program of the Department of Veterans Affairs), as well as care provided by the Department of Veterans Affairs and the military.
Notes: The estimates by type of coverage are not mutually exclusive; people can be covered by more than one type of health insurance during the year. The 2004 data have been revised to reflect a correction to the weights in the 2005 Annual Social and Economic Supplement (Census Bureau). The estimates also reflect improvements to the algorithm that assigns coverage to dependents.

SOURCE: Carmen DeNavas-Walt, Bernadette D. Proctor, and Cheryl Hill Lee, "Figure 6. Coverage by Type of Health Insurance: 2004 and 2005," in *Income, Poverty, and Health Insurance Coverage in the United States: 2005—Current Population Reports*, U.S. Census Bureau, P60-231, August 2006, http://www.census.gov/prod/2006pubs/p60-231.pdf (accessed December 1, 2006)

housing, benefits, and other critical supports. Access to around-the-clock emergency services is available, as well as help in establishing eligibility for assistance and obtaining services under entitlement programs.

The HHS reports that of the six hundred thousand homeless people the HCH served in 2004, most of the clients (58%) were male. Almost two-thirds (63%) of homeless clients were members of minority groups: African-Americans made up 37%; Hispanics, 22%; Asians and Pacific Islanders, 2%; and Native Americans and Alaskan Natives, 2%.

The HHS indicates that clients between the ages of twenty and forty-four represented the largest portion of people served by the HCH programs in 2004 (51%), followed by individuals between the ages of forty-five

and sixty-four (30%), and children up to age nineteen (15%). Homeless people over age sixty-five made up 2% of clients served.

Of clients seen in HCH centers, the HHS notes that 40% lived in shelters at some point during treatment, 19% lived doubled up with family or acquaintances, 11% lived in transitional housing, and 11% lived on the street. The majority (71%) of HCH users had no medical care coverage. Of those who had some type of insurance, 23% were enrolled in Medicaid, 3% were enrolled in Medicare, 2% had private insurance, and 2% had some other type of insurance.

LIVING IN PUBLIC: INCREASED HEALTH PROBLEMS

Poor people can be catapulted into homelessness because of the expenses and missed work caused by poor health. Homelessness itself causes a person's health to deteriorate further. Thus, health problems can both cause and result from homelessness. For example, a health problem that prevents an impoverished person from working can result in a loss of income that leads to homelessness. For those living on the streets, lack of adequate shelter and proper facilities for maintaining personal hygiene can exacerbate illness. Alcoholism, mental illnesses, diabetes, and depression become visible and more pronounced in homeless people. Other serious illnesses (for example, tuberculosis [TB]) are almost exclusively associated with the unhealthy living conditions brought on by poverty. In general, experts agree that homeless people suffer from more types of illnesses, for longer periods of time, and with more harmful consequences than housed people. In addition, according to "Homelessness and Health" (2006, http://www.nhchc.org/Advocacy/PolicyPapers/Homeless Health2006.pdf), a policy statement by the National Health Care for the Homeless Council (NHCHC), health care delivery is complicated by a patient's homeless status, making management of chronic diseases such as diabetes, human immunodeficiency virus/acquired immunodeficiency syndrome (HIV/AIDS), and hypertension more difficult. Most Americans suffer illness and disease at some time in their lives, but for people experiencing homelessness and poverty, illness more often leads to serious health concerns or premature death.

There is a growing belief in the health care field that homelessness must be considered in epidemic terms—that massive increases in homelessness may result in a hastened spread of illness and disease, overwhelming the health care system. John Lozier, in *The Health Care of Homeless Persons* (2004, http://www.bhchp.org/BHCHP%20manual/pages/chapters.html), writes that "primary care clinics for indigent people generally operate beyond their capacity, are not well-located to serve people staying in shelters, and are not prepared to deal with the complex conditions often presented by homeless people." He conveys the sense of

TABLE 7.2

Number of total Medicaid recipients, total vendor payments, and average amounts, by type of eligibility category, 1972–2002

Year	Total	Aged 65 or older	Blind	Permanent and total disability	Dependent children under age 21	Adults in families with dependent children	Other
				Number of recipients (thousands)			
1972	17,606	3,318	108	1,625	7,841	3,137	1,576
1975	22,007	3,615	109	2,355	9,598	4,529	1,800
1980	21,605	3,440	92	2,819	9,333	4,877	1,499
1985	21,814	3,061	80	2,937	9,757	5,518	1,214
1986	22,515	3,140	82	3,100	10,029	5,647	1,362
1987	23,109	3,224	85	3,296	10,168	5,599	1,418
1988	22,907	3,159	86	3,401	10,037	5,503	1,343
1989	23,511	3,132	95	3,496	10,318	5,717	1,175
1990	25,255	3,202	83	3,635	11,220	6,010	1,105
1991	28,280	3,359	85	3,983	13,415	6,778	658
1992	30,926	3,742	84	4,378	15,104	6,954	664
1993	33,432	3,863	84	4,932	16,285	7,505	763
1994	35,053	4,035	87	5,372	17,194	7,586	779
1995	36,282	4,119	92	5,767	17,164	7,604	1,537
1996	36,118	4,285	95	6,126	16,739	7,127	1,746
1997	34,872	3,955	—	6,129	15,791	6,803	2,195
1998	40,649	3,964	—	6,638	18,964	7,908	3,176
1999*	40,300	4,241	—	7,303	20,119	8,552	846
2000*	42,886	4,289	—	7,479	21,086	10,543	862
2001*	46,163	4,420	—	7,703	22,533	11,639	869
2002*	49,754	4,759	—	8,055	24,583	13,245	903
				Total payments (millions of dollars)			
1972	6,300	1,925	45	1,354	1,139	962	875
1975	12,242	4,358	93	3,052	2,186	2,062	492
1980	23,311	8,739	124	7,497	3,123	3,231	596
1985	37,508	14,096	249	13,203	4,414	4,746	798
1986	41,005	15,097	277	14,635	5,135	4,880	980
1987	45,050	16,037	309	16,507	5,508	5,592	1,078
1988	48,710	17,135	344	18,250	5,848	5,883	1,198
1989	54,500	18,558	409	20,476	6,892	6,897	1,268
1990	64,859	21,508	434	23,969	9,100	8,590	1,257
1991	77,048	25,453	475	27,798	11,690	10,439	1,193
1992	90,814	29,078	530	33,326	14,491	12,185	1,204
1993	101,709	31,554	589	38,065	16,504	13,605	1,391
1994	108,270	33,618	644	41,654	17,302	13,585	1,467
1995	120,141	36,527	848	48,570	17,976	13,511	2,708
1996	121,685	36,947	869	51,196	17,544	12,275	2,853
1997	124,430	37,721	—	54,130	17,544	12,307	2,727
1998	142,318	40,602	—	60,375	22,806	14,833	3,702
1999*	147,372	40,470	—	63,028	20,765	15,141	7,966
2000*	168,442	44,560	—	72,772	23,490	17,671	9,948
2001*	186,913	48,431	—	80,493	26,770	20,096	11,121
2002*	213,491	51,732	—	91,889	31,247	23,459	15,162
				Average payment (dollars)			
1972	358	580	417	833	145	307	555
1975	556	1,205	850	1,296	228	455	273
1980	1,079	2,540	1,358	2,659	335	663	398
1985	1,719	4,605	3,104	4,496	452	860	658
1986	1,821	4,808	3,401	4,721	512	864	719
1987	1,949	4,975	3,644	5,008	542	999	761
1988	2,126	5,425	4,005	5,366	583	1,069	891
1989	2,318	5,926	4,317	5,858	668	1,206	1,079
1990	2,568	6,717	5,212	6,595	811	1,429	1,138
1991	2,725	7,577	5,572	6,979	871	1,540	1,813
1992	2,936	7,770	6,298	7,612	959	1,752	1,813
1993	3,042	8,168	7,036	7,717	1,013	1,813	1,824
1994	3,089	8,331	7,412	7,755	1,006	1,791	1,884
1995	3,311	8,868	9,256	8,422	1,047	1,777	1,762
1996	3,369	8,622	9,143	8,357	1,048	1,722	1,635

many public health officials that the health care system is facing a crisis because of homelessness when he states, "The public health system, which made great strides in the 20th century by eliminating unhealthy living conditions, seems ill-equipped to contend with the teeming shelters that are a throwback to the 19th century."

The rates of both chronic and acute health problems are disproportionately high among the homeless population. Except for obesity, strokes, and cancer, homeless people are far more likely than the housed to suffer from every category of chronic health problems. Conditions that require regular, uninterrupted treatment, such as

TABLE 7.2

Number of total Medicaid recipients, total vendor payments, and average amounts, by type of eligibility category, 1972–2002 [CONTINUED]

Year	Total	Aged 65 or older	Blind	Permanent and total disability	Dependent children under age 21	Adults in families with dependent children	Other
			Average payment (dollars)				
1997	3,568	9,538	—	8,832	1,111	1,809	3,597
1998	3,501	10,242	—	9,095	1,203	1,876	1,166
1999*	3,657	9,541	—	8,630	1,032	1,770	9,407
2000*	3,928	10,388	—	9,729	1,114	1,676	11,536
2001*	4,049	10,957	—	10,449	1,188	1,727	12,792
2002*	4,291	10,870	—	11,408	1,271	1,771	16,777

Notes: Fiscal year 1977 began in October 1976 and was the first year of the new federal fiscal cycle. Before 1977, the fiscal year began in July. Beginning in 1997, "disability" data includes blindness. "Children" includes foster care children, and "other" are "unknowns." In 1999 and 2000, "other" includes foster care children and "unknowns." In 2001 and 2002, "other" includes foster care children and "unknowns."
— not applicable.
*Excludes recipients in Puerto Rico and the Virgin Islands. Data are not available.

SOURCE: "Table 8.E2—Unduplicated Number of Recipients, Total Vendor Payments, and Average Payment, by Type of Eligibility Category, Selected Fiscal Years, 1972–2002," in *Annual Statistical Supplement to the Social Security Bulletin, 2005*, Social Security Administration, February 2006, http://www.ssa.gov/policy/docs/statcomps/supplement/2005/supplement05.pdf (accessed January 11, 2007)

TB, HIV/AIDS, diabetes, hypertension, malnutrition, severe dental problems, addictive disorders, and mental disorders, are extremely difficult to treat or control among those without adequate housing.

Street living comes with a set of health conditions that living in a home does not. Homeless people fall prey to parasites, frostbite, leg ulcers, and infections. They are also at greater risk of physical and psychological trauma resulting from muggings, beatings, and rape. With no safe place to store belongings, proper storage or administration of medications becomes difficult. In addition, some homeless people with mental disorders may use drugs or alcohol to self-medicate, and those with addictive disorders are more susceptible to HIV and other communicable diseases.

Homeless people may also lack the ability to access some of the basic rituals of self-care: bed rest, good nutrition, and good personal hygiene. For example, the luxury of taking it easy for a day or two is almost impossible for homeless people; they must often keep walking or remain standing all day to avoid criminal charges.

Unwell homeless people also remain untreated longer than their sheltered counterparts because obtaining food and shelter takes priority over health care. As a result, relatively minor illnesses go untreated until they develop into major emergencies, requiring expensive acute care treatment and long-term recovery.

At least one study suggests that the health of homeless people may be getting worse. In "A Comparison of the Health and Mental Health Status of Homeless Mothers in Worcester, Mass: 1993 and 2003" (*American Journal of Public Health*, August 2006), Linda F. Weinreb et al. report that between 1993 and 2003 homeless women and their families exhibited more acute and chronic mental health problems, especially major depression and post-traumatic stress disorder, their overall health declined, and their physical functioning became more limited. Their social functioning also became more impaired because of all of those factors. In addition, homeless women and their families were poorer in 2003 than in 1993 when inflation was taken into account. Weinreb et al. speculate that cuts in welfare spending and the decrease in the availability of affordable housing might be responsible for this trend.

Mortality Rates

James J. O'Connell, a physician with the Boston Health Care for the Homeless program, concludes in "Death on the Streets" (*Harvard Medical Alumni Bulletin*, Winter 1997) that even though the causes of the higher morbidity and mortality rates among Boston's homeless people are complex, there are elements of the homeless life that encourage early death. Some of these are exposure to extremes of weather and temperature; crowded shelter living, which increases the spread of communicable diseases such as TB and pneumonia; violence; the high frequency of medical and psychiatric illnesses; substance abuse; and inadequate nutrition. Stephen W. Hwang et al., in "Health Care Utilization among Homeless Adults Prior to Death" (*Journal of Health Care for the Poor and Underserved*, February 2001), find that of 558 deaths among the homeless population in Boston in 2001, within one year before death 27% of homeless people had no outpatient visits, emergency department visits, or hospitalizations. Hwang et al. conclude that even homeless people at high risk of death are underutilizing health care services.

In *King County 2003: Homeless Death Review* (November 2004, http://www.metrokc.gov/health/hchn/hchn-death-review.pdf), a 2003 study of homeless deaths in King County, Washington, the Health Care for the Homeless Network identifies seventy-seven people who had died while homeless in the county that year. Major causes of death included acute intoxication (26%), cardiovascular disease (17%), and homicide (9%). Most of the homeless deaths involved several illnesses before death; on average, those who died had had three health conditions before death.

In "The Risk of Death among Homeless Women: A Cohort Study and Review of the Literature" (*Canadian Medical Association Journal*, April 13, 2004), a study of deaths among homeless women in Toronto, Angela M. Cheung and Stephen W. Hwang find that homeless women aged eighteen to forty-four were ten times more likely to die than women in the general population of Toronto. Another key finding of the study is that the risk of death among young homeless women was nearly the same as the risk of death among homeless men of the same age.

James J. O'Connell, in *Premature Mortality in Homeless Populations: A Review of the Literature* (December 2005, http://www.nhchc.org/PrematureMortalityFinal.pdf), reviews the literature concerning the connection between homelessness and mortality. He finds that "a remarkable consistency ... transcends borders, cultures and oceans: homeless persons are 3–4 times more likely to die than the general population." In addition, he notes that the average age of death of homeless people in the studies reviewed was between forty-two and fifty-two years, despite a life expectancy of around eighty years in the United States. These premature deaths were highly associated with the coexistence of acute and chronic medical conditions with either mental illness or substance abuse.

Access to Care

Martha R. Burt et al. analyze in *Homelessness: Programs and the People They Serve, Findings of the National Survey of Homeless Assistance Providers and Clients* (December 1999, http://www.urban.org/UploadedPDF/homelessness.pdf) the results of the 1996 National Survey of Homeless Assistance Providers and Clients, the only survey of its kind (studies of the homeless tend to focus on local populations). The analysis shows that in the year preceding the survey, 25% of the clients studied had needed medical attention but were not able to see a doctor or a nurse. The study also reveals that newly housed people were even less likely to receive medical help when needed.

Burt et al. attribute the higher rate of health problems among newly housed people to several factors, including:

1. The loss of convenient health care in centers or shelters

2. The habit of enduring untreated ailments

3. A lack of health care benefits (common among people below the poverty level)

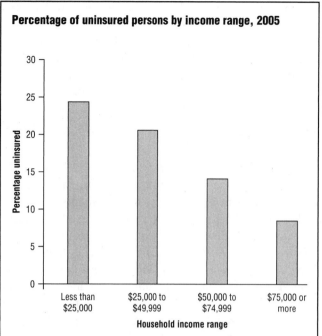

FIGURE 7.7

Percentage of uninsured persons by income range, 2005

SOURCE: Adapted from Carmen DeNavas-Walt, Bernadette D. Proctor, and Robert J. Mills, "Table 8. People With or Without Health Insurance Coverage by Selected Characteristics: 2004 and 2005," in *Income, Poverty, and Health Insurance Coverage in the United States: 2005— Current Population Reports*, U.S. Census Bureau, August 2006, http://www.census.gov/prod/2006pubs/p60-231.pdf (accessed December 1, 2006)

Figure 7.7 shows that the lower the income range of a household, the greater possibility the household would be uninsured in 2005. Among households with an annual income of less than $25,000 in 2005, almost a quarter (24.4%) were uninsured. Moreover, health insurance is becoming harder to obtain. Between 2004 and 2005 the percentage of uninsured people rose in every income bracket.

Lillian Gelberg et al. report in "The Behavioral Model for Vulnerable Populations: Application to Medical Care Use and Outcomes for Homeless People" (*Health Services Research*, February 2000) the results of a study on the prevalence of certain disease conditions among homeless adults, which revealed that 37% suffered from functional vision impairment, 36% from skin/leg/foot problems, and 31% tested positive for TB. Gelberg et al. indicate that homeless people who had a community clinic or private physician as a regular source of care exhibited better health outcomes. Gelberg et al. also suggest that clinical treatment of the homeless be accompanied by efforts to help them find permanent housing.

To fully understand why health care may not be readily available to the homeless population, one must look at the U.S health care system in general. In "U.S. Health-Care System Faces Cost and Insurance Crises: Rising

Costs, Growing Numbers of Uninsured and Quality Gaps Trouble World's Most Expensive Health-Care System" (*Lancet*, August 2, 2003), Michael McCarthy describes a system "lurching towards crisis." Health care costs continue to rise, as do the numbers of people who do not have insurance. DeNavas-Walt, Proctor, and Hill Lee note that between 2004 and 2005, even though the number of Americans living below the poverty line decreased by about ninety thousand, the number of uninsured Americans grew by 1.3 million.

McCarthy notes that even though most hospitals by law must provide care for the indigent, in reality an uninsured patient is less likely to receive any care at all and, if hospitalized, is less likely to receive a high quality of care than an insured patient. He cites *Care without Coverage: Too Little, Too Late* (2002), a study by the U.S. National Academy of Sciences Institute of Medicine. The study found that "uninsured patients who are hospitalized for a range of conditions are more likely to die in the hospital, to receive fewer services when admitted, and to experience substandard care and resultant injury than are insured patients."

AILMENTS OF HOMELESS PEOPLE

In the *Hartford Homeless Health Survey* (March 22, 2000, http://www.hchp.org/pdf/homeless.pdf), a survey of the homeless in Hartford, Connecticut, Eileen B. O'Keefe, Rose Maljanian, and Katherine M. McCormack counted 1,365 homeless people on the evening of December 13, 1999. The vast majority (87%) of survey respondents reported a prior diagnosis of at least one of seventeen chronic conditions. The most prevalent of these chronic conditions were drug and alcohol abuse, depression and other mental illnesses, hypertension, chronic bronchitis and emphysema, HIV/AIDS, asthma, and arthritis. Comparing the responses from the homeless survey against the rates for the general Hartford population revealed that homeless people suffered almost twice the rate of depression (41%) as the general population (23%) and three times the rate of chronic bronchitis and emphysema (22.7%). Even though these chronic diseases exist throughout the general population, difficulty in providing treatment to the homeless makes them worse, as do hunger and malnutrition.

Gillian Silver and Rea Pañares summarize in *The Health of Homeless Women: Information for State Mental and Child Health Programs* (2000, http://www.jhsph.edu/WCHPC/Publications/homeless.PDF) one study's findings regarding the health problems faced by homeless women, who made up about one-third (32%) of the homeless population. This group was prone to the same physical ailments reported by the general homeless population in Hartford but also reported high rates of gastrointestinal problems, neurological disorders, chronic obstructive pulmonary disease, and peripheral vascular disease. (See Table 7.3.)

Physical Disorders and Diseases

A description of a few chronic problems suffered by homeless people follows.

TUBERCULOSIS. Several kinds of acute, nonspecific respiratory diseases are common among homeless people. These diseases are easily spread through group living in overcrowded shelters without adequate nutrition. TB, a disease at one time almost eliminated from the general American population, has become a major health problem among the homeless. This disease is associated with exposure, poor diet, alcoholism, HIV, intravenous drug use, and other illnesses that lower the body's resistance to infection. TB is spread by long personal contact, making it a potential hazard not only to shelter residents but also to the general public.

The Centers for Disease Control and Prevention (CDC) notes in *Reported Tuberculosis in the United States, 2005* (September 2006, http://www.cdc.gov/tb/surv/surv2005/PDF/TBSurvFULLReport.pdf) that from 1953 to 1984 the United States experienced a decrease of 73.6% in the number of reported TB cases (from 84,304 cases to 22,255 cases). However, in 1984 the number of TB cases began to rise, reaching 25,701 cases in 1990. Rising homelessness and poverty account, in part, for the resurgence of TB. Poor ventilating systems in shelters and impoverished homes, as well as the inability to quarantine poor or transient victims, contribute to the rise. In 2005 the CDC found that 6.1% of those infected with TB were homeless, a much higher rate of infection than among the general population. (See Table 7.4.) State-by-state breakdowns showing high rates of infection among the homeless populations of some states give one indication of the contagious nature of the disease. In 2005, for example, Montana reported that 20% of those testing positive for TB were homeless, whereas Arkansas, Delaware, Maine, New Hampshire, North Dakota, and Vermont had no cases of TB among their homeless populations.

Clinical data from the federally funded HCH programs find prevalence rates for TB to be one hundred to three hundred times higher among the homeless than among the overall population. Maryam B. Haddad et al. report in "Tuberculosis and Homelessness in the United States, 1994–2003" (*Journal of the American Medical Association*, 2005) that many of the risk factors for tuberculosis in the United States overlap with the risk factors associated with homelessness, including having a history of incarceration or substance abuse. An additional contributing factor was the emergence of drug-resistant strains of TB. Experts report that to control the spread of TB, the homeless population must receive frequent

TABLE 7.3

Health problems faced by homeless women

Health issue	Key findings
Chronic disease	• The most common chronic physical conditions (excluding substance abuse) are hypertension, gastrointestinal problems, neurological disorders, arthritis and other musculoskeletal disorders, chronic obstructive pulmonary disease, and peripheral vascular disease.
Infectious disease	• The most common infectious diseases reported were chest infection, cold, cough, and bronchitis; reporting was the same for those formerly homeless, currently homeless, and other service users. • Homeless patients with tuberculosis (TB) were more likely to present with a more progressed form than nonhomeless. • Widespread screening for TB in shelters may miss most homeless persons because many do not live in the shelter, and instead present in emergency departments.
STDs/HIV/AIDS	• A mobile women's health unit in Chicago reported that of 104 female homeless clients, 30 percent had abnormal Pap smears—14 percent with atypia and 10 percent with inflammation; the incidence of chlamydia was 3 percent, gonorrhea 6 percent, and trichomoniasis 26 percent. • HIV infection was found to be 2.35 times more prevalent in homeless, drug-abusing women than homeless, drug-abusing men.
Stress	• Homeless mothers reported higher levels of stress, depression, and avoidant and anti-cognitive coping strategies than low-income, housed mothers.
Nutrition	• Currently and formerly homeless clients are more likely to report not getting enough to eat (28 and 25 percent respectively) than among all U.S. households (4 percent) and among poor households (12 percent). • Contrary to their opinions, homeless women and their dependents were consuming less than 50 percent of the 1989 recommended daily allowance for iron, magnesium, zinc, folic acid, and calcium. • Subjects of all ages consumed higher than desirable quantities of fats. • The health risk factors of iron deficiency anemia, obesity, and hypercholesterolemia were prevalent.
Smoking	• More than half of both homeless mothers and low-income housed mothers were current smokers, compared with 22.6 percent of female adults 18 years and over.
Violence	• Poor women are at higher risk for violence than women overall; poverty increases stress and lowers the ability to cope with the environment and live safely. • In a study of 436 sheltered homeless and poor housed women: 84 percent of these women had been severely assaulted at some point in their lives; 63 percent had been severely assaulted by parental caretakers while growing up; 40 percent had been sexually molested at least once before reaching adulthood; 60 percent had experienced severe physical attacks by a male intimate partner, and 33 percent had been assaulted by their current or most recent partner. • A study of 53 women homeless for at least three months in the past year demonstrated that this group is at a very high risk of battery and rape, with 91 percent exposed to battery and 56 percent exposed to rape.
Substance abuse	• Homeless women comprise a subpopulation at high risk for substance abuse; rates of substance use disorder range from 16 percent to 67 percent. There exists an imbalance between treatment need and treatment access. • Some homeless people with mental disorders may use drugs or alcohol to self-medicate.
Mental health/depression	• A case-control study of 100 homeless women with schizophrenia and 100 nonhomeless women with schizophrenia found that homeless women had higher rates of a concurrent diagnosis of alcohol abuse, drug abuse, antisocial personality disorder, and also had less adequate family support. • Many homeless women with serious mental illness are not receiving care; this is due to lack of perception of a mental health problem and lack of services designed to meet the needs of homeless women.

SOURCE: Gillian Silver and Rea Panares, "Table 2. Summary of Study Findings Related to Health Problems Faced by Homeless Women," in *The Health of Homeless Women: Information for State Mental and Child Health Programs*, Women's and Children's Health Policy Center, Johns Hopkins Bloomberg School for Public Health, 2000, http://www.jhsph.edu/WCHPC/Publications/homeless.PDF (accessed January 11, 2007)

screenings for TB, and the infected must get long-term care and rest. Few if any among the homeless can get such care.

A campaign for increased public awareness, particularly among members of the medical community, was launched in 1990 to identify and screen those at the greatest risk for TB. Some researchers, such as Po-Marn Kong et al. in "Skin-Test Screening and Tuberculosis Transmission among the Homeless" (*Emerging Infectious Diseases*, November 2002), tested pilot programs to better identify and treat homeless people infected with TB. Other studies, such as J. P. Tulsky et al. in "Can the Poor Adhere? Incentives for Adherence to TB Prevention in Homeless Adults" (*International Journal of Tuberculosis and Lung Disease*, January 2004), investigated how best to help homeless adults adhere to treatment for latent TB infection. In *Reported Tuberculosis in the United States*, the CDC notes that the number of reported TB cases in the United States declined to 14,097 in 2005, a 2.9% decrease from the year before.

SKIN AND BLOOD VESSEL DISORDERS. Frequent exposure to severe weather, insect bites, and other infestations make skin lesions fairly common among the homeless. Being forced to sit or stand for extended periods results in many homeless people being plagued with edema (swelling of the feet and legs), varicose veins, and skin ulcerations. This population is more prone to conditions that can lead to chronic phlebitis (inflammation of the veins). A homeless person with circulatory problems who sleeps sitting up in a doorway or a bus station can develop open lacerations that may become infected or maggot-infested if left untreated.

Regular baths and showers are luxuries to most homeless people, so many suffer from various forms of dermatitis (inflammation of the skin), often because of infestations of lice or scabies (a contagious skin disease caused by a parasitic mite that burrows under the skin to deposit eggs, causing intense itching). The lack of bathing increases the opportunity for infection to develop in cuts and other lacerations.

TABLE 7.4

Tuberculosis cases by homeless status[a], 2005

Reporting area	Total cases	Cases with information on homeless status		Cases reported as being homeless	
		No.	%	No.	%
United States	**13,234**	**13,126**	**99.2**	**795**	**6.1**
Alabama	201	201	100.0	11	5.5
Alaska	52	52	100.0	3	5.8
Arizona	244	227	93.0	21	9.3
Arkansas	105	103	98.1	0	0.0
California	2,753	2,721	98.8	179	6.6
Colorado	84	83	98.8	6	7.2
Connecticut	93	93	100.0	5	5.4
Delaware	25	25	100.0	0	0.0
District of Columbia	55	55	100.0	5	9.1
Florida	1,037	1,031	99.4	83	8.1
Georgia	463	463	100.0	41	8.9
Hawaii	109	109	100.0	1	0.9
Idaho	21	18	85.7	3	16.7
Illinois	550	543	98.7	23	4.2
Indiana	137	137	100.0	5	3.6
Iowa	51	51	100.0	3	5.9
Kansas	57	57	100.0	5	8.8
Kentucky	118	118	100.0	9	7.6
Louisiana	241	236	97.9	15	6.4
Maine	16	16	100.0	0	0.0
Maryland	266	266	100.0	13	4.9
Massachusetts	252	250	99.2	10	4.0
Michigan	238	237	99.6	6	2.5
Minnesota	179	179	100.0	4	2.2
Mississippi	100	100	100.0	11	11.0
Missouri	105	105	100.0	6	5.7
Montana	10	10	100.0	2	20.0
Nebraska	35	35	100.0	2	5.7
Nevada	107	107	100.0	8	7.5
New Hampshire	4	4	100.0	0	0.0
New Jersey	461	461	100.0	14	3.0
New Mexico	39	39	100.0	5	12.8
New York State[b]	287	286	99.7	8	2.8
New York City	943	919	97.5	52	5.7
North Carolina	309	309	100.0	20	6.5
North Dakota	6	5	83.3	0	0.0
Ohio	241	240	99.6	15	6.3
Oklahoma	125	125	100.0	12	9.6
Oregon	99	99	100.0	8	8.1
Pennsylvania	312	311	99.7	5	1.6
Rhode Island	44	44	100.0	2	4.5
South Carolina	235	235	100.0	16	6.8
South Dakota	16	16	100.0	1	6.3
Tennessee	277	277	100.0	32	11.6
Texas	1,424	1,423	99.9	70	4.9
Utah	25	25	100.0	1	4.0
Vermont	7	7	100.0	0	0.0
Virginia	330	330	100.0	8	2.4
Washington	247	246	99.6	40	16.3
West Virginia	27	27	100.0	1	3.7
Wisconsin	72	70	97.2	5	7.1
Wyoming	0	0	—	—	—
American Samoa[c]	5	5	100.0	0	0.0
Fed. States of Micronesia[c]	63	63	100.0	0	0.0
Guam[c]	53	53	100.0	0	0.0

HIV/AIDS. The CDC reports in *HIV/AIDS Surveillance Report, 2005* (2006, http://www.cdc.gov/hiv/topics/ surveillance/resources/reports/2005report/pdf/2005Surveilla nceReport.pdf) that in 2005, 35,537 new cases of HIV infection and 17,011 deaths of people with AIDS were reported. Since the beginning of the epidemic, 249,950 HIV cases that had not progressed to full-blown AIDS had been reported. In addition, at the end of 2005, 437,982 people were living with AIDS. The number of HIV/AIDS cases decreased each year between 2001 and 2004, but then increased in 2005; the number of AIDS cases actually increased each year between 2002 and 2005.

According to the news release "FDA Approves New Rapid HIV Test Kit" (November 7, 2002, http://www.fda .gov/bbs/topics/NEWS/2002/NEW00852.html), in November 2002 the U.S. Food and Drug Administration approved a rapid test for HIV infection that can provide results in

TABLE 7.4

Tuberculosis cases by homeless status[a], 2005 [CONTINUED]

Reporting area	Total cases	Cases with information on homeless status		Cases reported as being homeless	
		No.	%	No.	%
Marshall Islands[c]	60	57	95.0	0	0.0
N. Mariana Islands[c]	55	55	100.0	0	0.0
Puerto Rico[c]	108	108	100.0	2	1.9
Republic of Palau[c]	9	9	100.0	0	0.0
U.S. Virgin Islands[c]	—	—	—	—	—

[a]Homeless within past 12 months of tuberculosis diagnosis. Percentage based on 52 reporting areas (50 states, New York City, and the District of Columbia). Counts and percentages shown only for reporting areas with information reported for ≥75% of cases.
[b]Excludes New York City.
[c]Not included in U.S. totals.
Note: — indicate data not available.

SOURCE: "Table 30. Tuberculosis Cases and Percentages by Homeless Status, Age > or = 15: Reporting Areas, 2005," in *Reported Tuberculosis in the United States, 2005*, U.S. Department of Health and Human Services, Centers for Disease Control and Prevention, September 2006, http://www.cdc.gov/nchstp/tb/surv/surv2005/PDF/table30.pdf (accessed January 11, 2007)

twenty minutes. The HHS secretary Tommy G. Thompson explained the significance of the test: "Each year, 8,000 HIV-infected people who come to public clinics for HIV testing do not return a week later to receive their test results. With this new test, in less than a half an hour they can learn preliminary information about their HIV status, allowing them to get the care they need to slow the progression of their disease and to take precautionary measures to help prevent the spread of this deadly virus."

The CDC estimates that up to one-fourth of people infected with HIV are not aware of their condition. The CDC is working with health officials to make the rapid test widely available, particularly in places where likely victims reside, such as homeless shelters, drug treatment centers, and jails.

According to "Study: Disparity between Rich and Poor Mortality" (*AIDS Alert*, August 1, 2003), poor AIDS patients in San Francisco die sooner from AIDS. Within five years of diagnosis, fewer than 70% of people living in the city's poorest neighborhoods were still alive, compared with more than 85% of people who lived in the richest neighborhoods. Poor people with HIV usually have a number of co-occurring disorders, such as drug dependence, mental illness, and unstable housing arrangements. The lack of affordable and appropriate housing can be an acute crisis for these individuals, who need a safe shelter that provides protection and comfort, as well as a base from which to receive services, care, and support.

The National Alliance to End Homelessness points out in "Homelessness and HIV/AIDS" (August 10, 2006, http://www.endhomelessness.org/content/general/detail/1073) that HIV/AIDS is more prevalent in homeless populations. As many as 3.4% of homeless people are HIV positive, a rate that is three times higher than that of the general population. The high costs of medical care may even put individuals

with HIV/AIDS at a greater risk of homelessness. Furthermore, the homeless life poses a grave threat to the health of those with HIV/AIDS, whose immune systems are compromised by the disease. Shelter conditions expose people to dangerous infections, while exposure to the elements and malnutrition exacerbate chronic illness. In addition, homeless people have difficulty obtaining and using common HIV/AIDS medications.

Mental Health and Substance Abuse

Before the 1960s people with chronic mental illness were often committed involuntarily to state psychiatric hospitals. The development of medications that could control the symptoms of mental illness coincided with a growing belief that involuntary hospitalization was warranted only when a mentally ill person posed a threat to him- or herself or to others. Gradually, large numbers of mentally ill people were discharged from hospitals and other treatment facilities. Because the community-based treatment centers that were supposed to take the place of state hospitals were often either inadequate or nonexistent, many of these people ended up living on the streets.

In "Prevalence and Risk Factors for Homelessness and Utilization of Mental Health Services among 10,340 Patients with Serious Mental Illness in a Large Public Mental Health System" (*American Journal of Psychiatry*, February 2005), David P. Folsom et al. find that 15% of patients treated for serious mental illness were homeless at some point during a one-year period. Twenty percent of patients with schizophrenia, 17% of patients with bipolar disorder, and 9% of patients with depression were homeless. Folsom et al. find that mentally ill people are at a much higher risk of homelessness than the general population. They emphasize that homelessness among the mentally ill was associated with two other factors: substance use disorders and a lack of Medicaid insurance. Folsom et al. state, "Although it would be naïve to assume that treatment for substance abuse disorders and provision of Medicaid insurance could solve the problem of homelessness among persons with serious mental illness, further research is warranted to test the effect of interventions designed to treat patients with dual diagnoses and to assist homeless persons with serious mental illness in obtaining and maintaining entitlement benefits."

Many mentally ill homeless people do not realize how ill they are and how dependent they are on regular treatment. Others no longer believe the system can or will help them. This seems to have been borne out by Olga Acosta and Paul A. Toro's "Let's Ask the Homeless People Themselves: A Needs Assessment Based on a Probability Sample of Adults" (*American Journal of Community Psychology*, 2000), a 1999 survey of 301 homeless adults in Buffalo, New York. When Acosta and Toro asked homeless people what their greatest needs were, respondents listed affordable housing, safety, education, transportation, medical/dental treatment, and job training/placement. Formal mental health and substance abuse services were rated as unimportant by comparison, easy to obtain, and not satisfactory to people who had used them.

Table 7.3 shows the results of a study of one hundred homeless women with schizophrenia and one hundred nonhomeless women with schizophrenia. The study, which is summarized by Silver and Pañares, finds that homeless schizophrenic women had higher rates of co-occurring disorders, including alcohol and/or drug abuse and antisocial personality disorder.

Silver and Pañares note that families with children make up about 40% of the total homeless population, and the vast majority (about 90%) are female-headed. They report on a study of 436 sheltered homeless and low-income housed mothers. The study found that 84% of all these women had a history of having been severely assaulted at some point in their lives. Research shows that mothers with a history of abuse are more likely to have children with mental health problems.

PREVALENCE AND TREATMENT. There is some debate over the rate of mental disorders among homeless populations, but there is general agreement that it is greater among the homeless than the general population. The U.S. Conference of Mayors reports in *Hunger and Homelessness Survey: A Status Report on Hunger and Homelessness in America's Cities, a 23-City Survey* (December 2006, http://www.usmayors.org/uscm/hungersurvey/2006/report06.pdf) that an average of 16% of the homeless in the twenty-three surveyed cities were mentally ill and 26% were substance abusers in 2006. The National Resource and Training Center on Homelessness and Mental Illness indicates in "Get the Facts: Why Are So Many People with Serious Mental Illnesses Homeless?" (2007, http://www.nrchmi.samhsa.gov/facts/facts_question_3.asp) that a disproportionate percentage of the homeless population suffers from serious mental illnesses of the most "personally disruptive" kind, "including severe, chronic depression; bipolar disorder; schizophrenia; schizoaffective disorders; and severe personality disorders." An estimated 20% to 25% of the homeless population is afflicted, compared with only 4% of the general population.

Mentally ill homeless people present special problems for health care workers. They may not be as cooperative and motivated as other patients. Because of their limited resources, they may have difficulty getting transportation to treatment centers. They frequently forget to show up for appointments or take medications. They are often unkempt. The addition of drug abuse can make them unruly or unresponsive. Among people with severe mental disorders, those at greatest risk of homelessness are both the most severely ill and the most difficult to help.

The National Alliance on Mental Illness states in "Dual Diagnosis and Integrated Treatment of Mental Illness and Substance Abuse Disorder" (2003, http://www.nami.org/Template.cfm?Section=By_Illness&Template=/TaggedPage/TaggedPageDisplay.cfm&TPLID=54&ContentID=23049) that mental illness and substance abuse frequently occur together; clinicians call this dual diagnosis. Experts explain that in the absence of appropriate treatment, people with mental illness often resort to self-medication—that is, using alcohol or drugs to silence the voices or calm the fears that torment them. Approximately 50% of individuals with severe mental disorders also abuse drugs or alcohol. Homeless people with dual diagnoses are frequently excluded from mental health programs because of treatment problems created by their substance abuse and are excluded from substance abuse programs because of problems in treating their mental illness. Experts explain that the lack of an integrated system of care plays a major role in these people's recurrent homelessness and stress that transitional or assisted housing initiatives for homeless substance abusers must realistically address the issue of abstinence and design measures for handling relapses that do not place people back on the streets.

HEALTH OF HOMELESS CHILDREN

Evangeline R. Danseco and E. Wayne Holden, in "Are There Different Types of Homeless Families? A Typology of Homeless Families Based on Cluster Analysis" (*Family Relations*, 1998), seek to identify different types of homeless families and to examine children from these families. They studied 180 families, with a total of 348 children, participating in a comprehensive health care program for children of homeless families. The results show that homeless children consistently exhibited greater behavior problems and showed a trend of poorer cognitive, academic, and adaptive behaviors than children in the general population.

In "Homeless Children: What Every Health Care Provider Should Know" (2006, http://www.nhchc.org/Children/), Catherine Karr notes that homeless children experience a variety of behavioral and/or health disorders, including depression, developmental delay, asthma, respiratory infections, and gastrointestinal problems. Homeless children may also lack preventive care, such as immunizations, which leaves them vulnerable to preventable diseases. Failure to treat certain childhood conditions early (for example, ear infections) can lead to a lifetime of health problems. They also frequently suffer from malnutrition.

HEALTH OF HOMELESS VETERANS

According to Robert E. Klein and Donald D. Stockford, in *Data on the Socioeconomic Status of Veterans and on VA Program Usage* (May 2001, http://www1.va.gov/vetdata/docs/sesprogramnet5-31-01.ppt), in 1990 veterans were present in shelters at a rate of 149 per 100,000, compared with 126 per 100,000 of other males. The National Coalition for Homeless Veterans, citing U.S. Department of Veterans Affairs (VA) sources, states in "Background and Statistics" (2005, http://www.nchv.org/background.cfm) that of all homeless veterans, 4% are female, 45% suffer from mental illness, and half abuse drugs or alcohol. An estimated 200,000 veterans are homeless on any single night, and over the course of a year, nearly 400,000 experience homelessness at least one night. Almost half (47%) of homeless veterans served in Vietnam, two-thirds (67%) served in the military for three years or more, and a third (33%) were stationed in a war zone.

The VA operates many outreach programs designed specifically to help homeless veterans in areas of health, housing, and employment. Programs include outreach to homeless veterans who would not otherwise seek assistance; clinical assessment and referral for medical, psychiatric, or substance abuse treatment; supportive living programs; employment assistance; and transitional housing assistance.

VICTIMS OF VIOLENCE
Violence toward Homeless Women

Angela Browne and Shari Bassuk, in "Intimate Violence in the Lives of Homeless and Poor Housed Women: Prevalence and Patterns in an Ethnically Diverse Sample" (*American Journal of Orthopsychiatry*, April 1999), find that lifetime prevalence rates of physical and sexual assault among homeless women are particularly high. After surveying both homeless and poor, housed women, Browne and Bassuk find that although violence by intimate male partners is high in both groups, homeless women experience violence at a somewhat higher rate (63.3%) than poor, housed women (58%).

Homeless women (41%) are also more likely than poor, housed women (33%) to report a male partner threatening suicide. More than one-third (36%) of homeless women said their partner had threatened to kill them, compared with 31% of poor, housed women. Almost 27% of homeless women and 19.5% of poor, housed women needed or received medical treatment because of physical violence. Table 7.3 summarizes other studies related to violence and homeless women.

Hate Crimes

The National Coalition for the Homeless (NCH), in *Hate, Violence, and Death on Main Street, USA: A Report on Hate Crimes and Violence against People Experiencing Homelessness, 2006* (February 2007, http://www.nationalhomeless.org/getinvolved/projects/hatecrimes/2006report.pdf), reports "an alarming, nationwide sustained increase in reports of homeless men, women and even children being killed, beaten, and harassed." The NCH identifies 189 deaths and 425 nonlethal attacks on homeless people between 1999 and 2006—142 attacks in 2006 alone. The crimes occurred in 200 cities in 44 states and in Puerto Rico.

The NCH recommends the following actions to address the problem of violence against homeless individuals:

- "A public statement by the U.S. Department of Justice acknowledging that hate crimes and/or violence against people experiencing homelessness is a serious national trend"

- Justice Department guidelines "for local police on how to investigate and work with people experiencing homelessness" and recommendations for improvements to state law that would "better protect against violence directed against people experiencing homelessness, including tougher penalties"

- "Inclusion of housing status in the pending state and federal hate crimes legislation"

- "Awareness training at police academies and departments nationwide for trainees and police officers on how to deal effectively and humanely with people experiencing homelessness in their communities"

- "A U.S. Government Accountability Office...study into the nature and scope of hate crimes and/or violent acts and crimes that occur against people experiencing homelessness"

Homeless advocates have demanded that crimes against homeless people be defined as hate crimes, which may result in harsher penalties in federal courts. However, determining how many of these crimes occur is difficult. Some factors that affect the accuracy of the count are:

- The bodies of the victims are not always discovered.

- Bodies may be badly decomposed when found, preventing accurate identification of the cause of death.

- Local authorities may rule causes of death other than violence.

- Survivors do not always report crimes, and murdered victims cannot tell their own stories.

HUNGER
Extent of the Problem

During the 1980s a number of studies found that some Americans, especially children, were suffering from hunger. Many observers did not believe these reports or thought they had been exaggerated. In 1984 a Task Force on Food Assistance appointed by President Ronald Reagan found that it could not find evidence on the extent of hunger because there was no agreed-on way to measure hunger.

In response, the Food Research and Action Center (FRAC) in Washington, D.C., an advocacy group for the poor, launched the Community Childhood Hunger Identification Project (CCHIP) to determine the extent of hunger in the United States. The first FRAC survey conducted interviews in 2,335 households with incomes at or below 185% of poverty and with at least one child under twelve years of age. The results of this survey, as reported by Cheryl A. Wehler et al. in *Community Childhood Hunger Identification Project: A Survey of Childhood Hunger in the United States* (1991), indicated that 32% of U.S. households with incomes at or below 185% of the poverty level experienced hunger. At least one child out of every eight under twelve years of age suffered from hunger. Another 40% of low-income children were at risk for hunger.

Between 1992 and 1994 FRAC sponsored a second round of CCHIP surveys in nine states and the District of Columbia (5,282 low-income families with at least one child aged twelve or under). For the purposes of its report, FRAC defined hunger as food insufficiency—skipping meals, eating less, or running out of food—that occurred because of limited household resources. The results were reported by Cheryl A. Wehler et al. in *Community Childhood Hunger Identification Project: A Survey of Childhood Hunger in the United States* (1995). Based on the findings of the second CCHIP surveys, FRAC concluded that about four million children aged twelve and under experienced hunger in some part of one or more months during the previous year. Another 9.6 million children were at risk of becoming hungry.

The 1995 CCHIP survey studied one child in each household (the child with the most recent birthday) and found that, in comparison with nonhungry children, hungry children were:

- More than three times as likely to suffer from unwanted weight loss

- More than four times as likely to suffer from fatigue

- Almost three times as likely to suffer from irritability

- More than three times as likely to have frequent headaches

- Almost one and a half times as likely to have frequent ear infections

- Four times as likely to suffer from concentration problems

- Almost twice as likely to have frequent colds

Based on the findings from the 1991 and 1995 CCHIP surveys, FRAC concluded that although federal food programs are targeted to households most in need, a common barrier to program participation is a lack of information, particularly about eligibility guidelines. FRAC contended that if federal, state, and local governments made a greater effort to ensure that possible recipients were aware of their eligibility for food programs, such as Women, Infants, and Children (WIC) and the School Breakfast Program, there would be a large drop in hunger in the United States.

In 1997 the Urban Institute conducted the National Survey of American Families (NSAF; 2006, http://www.urban.org/center/anf/snapshots.cfm). Nearly half of low-income families (those with family incomes up to 200% of the federal poverty line) who were interviewed in 1997 reported that the food they purchased ran out before they got money to buy more or they worried they would run out of food. More children than adults lived in families that worried about or had trouble affording food—54% of low-income children experienced the problem. The NSAF was repeated in 1999 (2006, http://www.urban.org/publications/900841.html), and families reported fewer problems affording food than in 1997. Four in ten low-income families were either concerned about or had difficulty affording food, down from nearly 50% in 1997. However, approximately half of all low-income children still lived in families with difficulties affording food or concern about lack of food. A third NSAF was conducted in 2002, and results were released in 2004. According to Sandi Nelson, in "Trends in Parents' Economic Hardship" (*Snapshots of America's Families*, March 2004), the 2002 report showed that 51.3% of low-income parents faced food hardship, 59.3% of single parents experienced food hardship, and the gains between 1997 and 1999 had been all but erased.

Since 1995 the Food and Nutrition Service (FNS) of the U.S. Department of Agriculture (USDA) and the U.S. Bureau of the Census have conducted annual surveys of food security, low food security (or food insecurity), and very low food insecurity (previously called hunger). (Food-secure households are those that have access at all times to enough food for an active, healthy life. Low food security households are uncertain of having, or unable to acquire, enough food to meet basic needs at all times during the year.) According to Mark Nord, Margaret Andrews, and Steven Carlson, in *Household Food Security in the United States, 2005* (November 2006, http://www.ers.usda.gov/Publications/ERR29/ERR29.pdf), the survey is based on an eighteen-item scale:

1. Worried food would run out before (I/we) got money to buy more

2. Food bought did not last and (I/we) did not have money to get more

3. Could not afford to eat balanced meals

4. Adult(s) cut size of meals or skipped meals

5. Respondent ate less than felt he or she should

6. Adult(s) cut size or skipped meals in three or more months

7. Respondent hungry but did not eat because could not afford food

8. Respondent lost weight

9. Adult(s) did not eat for whole day

10. Adult(s) did not eat for whole day in three or more months

11. Relied on few kinds of low-cost food to feed child(ren)

12. Could not feed child(ren) balanced meals

13. Child(ren) were not eating enough

14. Cut size of child(ren)'s meals

15. Child(ren) were hungry

16. Child(ren) skipped meals

17. Child(ren) skipped meals in three or more months

18. Child(ren) did not eat for whole day

Figure 7.8 shows that the low food security rose steadily from 1999 to 2004, but dropped in 2005 to 1995 levels. The prevalence rate of very low food security also dropped in 2005. (Households with very low food security often worry that their food will run out, report that their food does run out before they have money to get more, cannot afford to eat balanced meals, often have adults who skip meals because there is not enough money for food, and report that they eat less than they should because of lack of money.) In 2005, 11% of households reported low food security at some time during the year, and 3.9% reported being very low food security. (See Figure 7.9.)

Unsurprisingly, poor and low-income households were more likely to experience very low food security during the year than were households with higher incomes. In 2005, 13.5% of households below the poverty line reported very low food security. (See Figure 7.10.) In comparison, 10.6% of households with an income-to-poverty ratio under 1.85 experienced very low food security, and only 1.7% of households with higher incomes experienced very low food security.

About 15.6% of all households with children experienced low food security in 2005; 0.7% experienced very low food security among the children. (See Table 7.5.) The poorest families experienced low food security most often; only 57.8% of households with an income-to-poverty ratio under 1.00 were food secure, compared with 59.4% of families with income-to-poverty ratios under 1.30, 65.8% of families with income-to-poverty ratios under 1.85, and 93% of families with income-to-poverty ratios of 1.85 and over. Families headed by married couples are much less likely to experience low food security than families headed by single females; only 9.9% of married-couple households compared with 30.8% of female-headed households reported low food security in 2005. Low food security was also more prevalent among African-American and Hispanic families, 27.4% and 21.6%, respectively, of whom experienced low food security, than among non-Hispanic whites, 11.8% of whom experienced low food security.

Emergency Food Assistance

America's Second Harvest (A2H; 2007, http://www.hungerinamerica.org/) is the nation's largest charitable hunger-relief organization, serving over twenty-five million people per year. In 2005 a study based on 52,878 interviews with clients and 31,342 questionnaires from A2H agencies was conducted, and findings were reported in *Hunger Study, 2006* (2007, http://www.hungerinamerica.org/key_findings/). The study finds the following characteristics of recipients of emergency food assistance:

- More than a third (36.4%) of the members of households served by the A2H National Network were children; and 8% were children age zero to five years.

- About a third (36%) of all emergency client households had at least one member working.

- More than two-thirds (68%) of the households had incomes below the poverty level.

- More than one in ten (12%) clients were homeless.

- About a third (35%) of client households also received Food Stamp Program benefits; 51% of families with young children participated in the WIC program, and 62% of households with school-age children participated in school lunch programs.

FIGURE 7.8

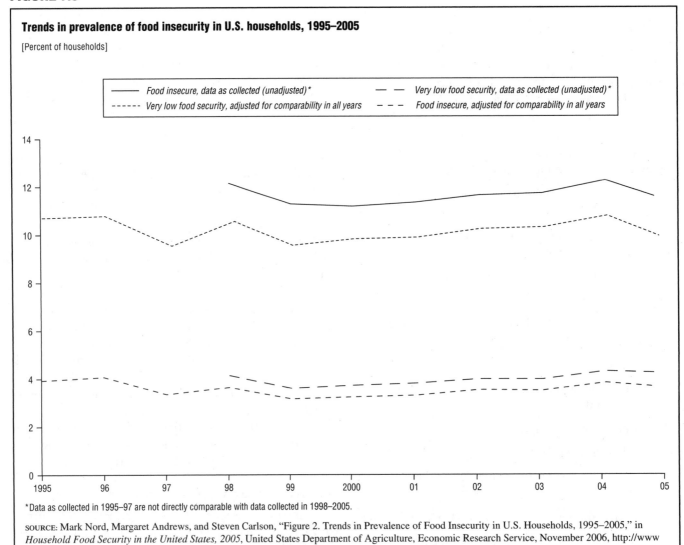

Trends in prevalence of food insecurity in U.S. households, 1995–2005

[Percent of households]

——— Food insecure, data as collected (unadjusted)*   — — Very low food security, data as collected (unadjusted)*

- - - - - Very low food security, adjusted for comparability in all years   – – – Food insecure, adjusted for comparability in all years

*Data as collected in 1995–97 are not directly comparable with data collected in 1998–2005.

SOURCE: Mark Nord, Margaret Andrews, and Steven Carlson, "Figure 2. Trends in Prevalence of Food Insecurity in U.S. Households, 1995–2005," in *Household Food Security in the United States, 2005*, United States Department of Agriculture, Economic Research Service, November 2006, http://www.ers.usda.gov/Publications/ERR29/ERR29.pdf (accessed January 21, 2007)

- About 40% of recipients at all program sites were non-Hispanic whites, 38% were African-American, 17% were Hispanic, and the rest were from other racial groups.

- Twenty-nine percent reported that at least one household member was in poor health.

- A significant proportion of clients had to choose between food and other necessities; 42% reported having to choose between paying for food and paying for utilities; 35% had to choose between paying for food and paying their rent or mortgage; and 32% had to choose between paying for food and paying for medical care.

Malnutrition among the Homeless

Homeless people face a daily challenge to fulfill their basic need for food. They often go hungry. This is borne out by Burt et al. in *Homelessness*. Clients of homeless assistance programs are found to have higher levels of food problems than poor people in general; 28% reported

not getting enough to eat sometimes or often, compared with 12% of poor American adults. More than one-third of the homeless clients had been hungry in the past thirty days but did not eat because they had no money for food (39%), and 40% reported going at least one whole day without eating. Undernourishment and vitamin deficiency can cause or aggravate other physical conditions.

Meg Wilson finds in "Health-Promoting Behaviors of Sheltered Homeless Women" (*Family and Community Health*, January–March 2005) that despite being homeless, many homeless women practiced "health-promoting behaviors." However, because of their homelessness, they had difficulty getting adequate nutrition.

The diet of homeless people, even those who live in shelters or cheap motels, is generally not balanced or of good quality. Homeless people often rely on ready-cooked meals, fast-food restaurants, garbage cans, and the sometimes infrequent meal schedules of free food sources, such

FIGURE 7.9

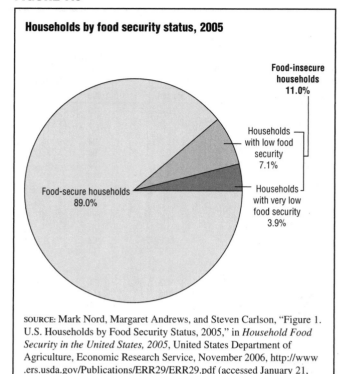

Households by food security status, 2005

Food-insecure households 11.0%

Food-secure households 89.0%

Households with low food security 7.1%

Households with very low food security 3.9%

SOURCE: Mark Nord, Margaret Andrews, and Steven Carlson, "Figure 1. U.S. Households by Food Security Status, 2005," in *Household Food Security in the United States, 2005*, United States Department of Agriculture, Economic Research Service, November 2006, http://www.ers.usda.gov/Publications/ERR29/ERR29.pdf (accessed January 21, 2007)

FIGURE 7.10

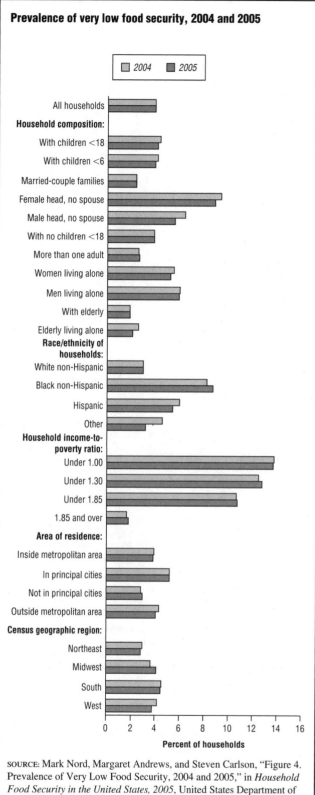

Prevalence of very low food security, 2004 and 2005

SOURCE: Mark Nord, Margaret Andrews, and Steven Carlson, "Figure 4. Prevalence of Very Low Food Security, 2004 and 2005," in *Household Food Security in the United States, 2005*, United States Department of Agriculture, Economic Research Service, November 2006, http://www.ers.usda.gov/Publications/ERR29/ERR29.pdf (accessed January 21, 2007)

as shelters, soup kitchens, and drop-in centers. However, many soup kitchens serve only one meal per day, and many shelters that serve meals—and not all them do—serve only two meals per day.

The Conference of Mayors reports that 74% of the twenty-three cities it surveyed in 2006 reported an increase in requests for emergency food assistance over the course of the year by an average of 7%. Nearly half (48%) of those requesting food assistance were children or their parents—and 18% of these requests went unmet. Even though 53% of the survey cities reported that they were able to provide an adequate quantity of food, almost two-thirds of the cities (63%) had to reduce the number of bags of food provided or the number of times people could receive food. Officials cited unemployment or underemployment, high housing, utility and transportation costs, medical or health costs, poverty, and lack of education as causes of hunger in their cities.

GOVERNMENT PROGRAMS TO COMBAT HUNGER

Food Stamps

The Food Stamp Program, which is administered by the USDA, is the United States' largest food assistance program. Food stamps are designed to help low-income families purchase a nutritionally adequate, low-cost diet. Generally, food stamps may only be used to buy food to be prepared at home. They may not be used for alcohol,

TABLE 7.5

Prevalence of food security and food insecurity in households with children, by selected household characteristics, 2005

Category	Total[a] 1,000	Food-secure households 1,000	Percent	Food-insecure households[b] 1,000	Percent	Households with very low food security among children 1,000	Percent
All households with children	39,601	33,404	84.4	6,197	15.6	270	0.7
Household composition:							
With children < 6	17,615	14,671	83.3	2,944	16.7	94	.5
Married-couple families	26,776	24,130	90.1	2,646	9.9	98	.4
Female head, no spouse	9,659	6,681	69.2	2,978	30.8	153	1.6
Male head, no spouse	2,536	2,082	82.1	454	17.9	19	.7
Other household with child[c]	630	511	81.1	119	18.9	0	0.0
Race/ethnicity of households:							
White non-Hispanic	24,962	22,020	88.2	2,942	11.8	111	.4
Black non-Hispanic	5,499	3,995	72.6	1,504	27.4	84	1.5
Hispanic[d]	6,722	5,267	78.4	1,455	21.6	63	.9
Other	2,417	2,121	87.8	296	12.2	11	.5
Household income-to-poverty ratio:							
Under 1.00	5,619	3,246	57.8	2,373	42.2	138	2.5
Under 1.30	7,424	4,408	59.4	3,016	40.6	158	2.1
Under 1.85	11,753	7,733	65.8	4,020	34.2	182	1.5
1.85 and over	21,522	20,008	93.0	1,514	7.0	62	.3
Income unknown	6,326	5,663	89.5	663	10.5	26	.4
Area of residence:[e]							
Inside metropolitan area	33,286	28,140	84.5	5,146	15.5	243	.7
In principal cities[f]	10,453	8,401	80.4	2,052	19.6	114	1.1
Not in principal cities	17,348	15,243	87.9	2,105	12.1	89	.5
Outside metropolitan area	6,315	5,264	83.4	1,051	16.6	27	.4
Census geographic region:							
Northeast	7,074	6,148	86.9	926	13.1	54	.8
Midwest	9,006	7,604	84.4	1,402	15.6	54	.6
South	14,318	11,949	83.5	2, 369	16.5	86	.6
West	9,203	7,701	83.7	1,502	16.3	77	.8
Individuals in households with children:							
All individuals in households with children	158,515	133,972	84.5	24,543	15.5	1,141	.7
Adults in households with children	84,911	72,770	85.7	12,141	14.3	536	.6
Children	73,604	61,201	83.1	12,403	16.9	606	.8

[a]Totals exclude households whose food security status is unknown because they did not give a valid response to any of the questions in the food security scale. In 2005, these represented 129,000 households with children (0. 3 percent.)
[b]Food-insecure households are those with low or very low food security among adults or children.
[c]Households with children in complex living arrangements, e.g., children of other relatives or unrelated roommate or boarder.
[d]Hispanics may be of any race.
[e]Metropolitan area residence is based on 2003 Office of Management and Budget delineation. Prevalence rates by area of residence are comparable with those for 2004 but are not precisely comparable with those of earlier years.
[f]Households within incorporated areas of the largest cities in each metropolitan area. Residence inside or outside of principal cities is not identified for about 17 percent of households in metropolitan statistical areas.

SOURCE: Mark Nord, Margaret Andrews, and Steven Carlson, "Prevalence of Food Security and Food Insecurity in Households with Children by Selected Household Characteristics, 2005," in *Household Food Security in the United States, 2005*, United States Department of Agriculture, Economic Research Service, November 2006, http://www.ers.usda.gov/Publications/ERR29/ERR29.pdf (accessed January 21, 2007).

tobacco, or hot foods intended to be consumed immediately, such as restaurant or delicatessen food.

The typical U.S. household spends about a third of its monthly income on food purchases. The Food Stamp program uses this fact in determining the amount of benefits to provide to a family. It calculates 30% of the family's earnings, and if that amount is insufficient to pay for an adequate diet then it supplies enough benefits to make up the difference. In many cases the "food stamps" benefit are actually provided electronically using a card similar to a bank debit card.

The cash value of these benefits is based on the size of the household and how much the family earns. The FNS notes in *Food Stamps Make America Stronger* (September 2006, http://www.fns.usda.gov/fsp/outreach/Translations/English/313Brochure-06.pdf) that households without an elderly or disabled member generally must have a monthly total (gross) cash income at or below 130% of the poverty level and may not have liquid assets (cash, savings, or other assets that can be easily sold) of more than $2,000. (If the household has a member aged sixty or older, the asset limit is $3,000.) The net monthly income limit (gross income minus any approved deductions for child care, some housing costs,

TABLE 7.6

Income chart for eligibility to receive food stamps, 2006–07

People in household	Gross monthly income*	Net monthly income*
1	$1,062	$ 817
2	1,430	1,100
3	1,799	1,384
4	2,167	1,667
5	2,535	1,950
6	2,904	2,234
7	3,272	2,517
8	3,640	2,800

*Larger households can have more income. Amounts are higher in Alaska and Hawaii. People who receive Supplemental Security Income in California are not eligible.

SOURCE: Income table in *Food Stamps Make America Stronger*, U.S. Department of Agriculture, Food and Nutrition Service, September 2006, http://www.fns.usda.gov/fsp/outreach/Translations/English/313Brochure-06 .pdf (accessed January 20, 2007)

TABLE 7.7

Food stamp program participation and costs, 1969–2006

Fiscal year	Average participation	Average benefit per person[a]	Total benefits	All other costs[b]	Total costs
	(Thousands)	(Dollars)	Millions of dollars		
1969	2,878	6.63	228.8	21.7	250.5
1970	4,340	10.55	549.7	27.2	576.9
1971	9,368	13.55	1,522.7	53.2	1,575.9
1972	11,109	13.48	1,797.3	69.4	1,866.7
1973	12,166	14.60	2,131.4	76.0	2,207.4
1974	12,862	17.61	2,718.3	119.2	2,837.5
1975	17,064	21.40	4,385.5	233.2	4,618.7
1976	18,549	23.93	5,326.5	359.0	5,685.5
1977	17,077	24.71	5,067.0	394.0	5,461.0
1978	16,001	26.77	5,139.2	380.5	5,519.7
1979	17,653	30.59	6,480.2	459.6	6,939.8
1980	21,082	34.47	8,720.9	485.6	9,206.5
1981	22,430	39.49	10,629.9	595.4	11,225.2
1982[c]	21,717	39.17	10,208.3	628.4	10,836.7
1983	21,625	42.98	11,152.3	694.8	11,847.1
1984	20,854	42.74	10,696.1	882.6	11,578.8
1985	19,899	44.99	10,743.6	959.6	11,703.2
1986	19,429	45.49	10,605.2	1,033.2	11,638.4
1987	19,113	45.78	10,500.3	1,103.9	11,604.2
1988	18,645	49.83	11,149.1	1,167.7	12,316.8
1989	18,806	51.85	11,702.4	1,231.8	12,934.2
1990	20,049	58.96	14,185.9	1,304.5	15,490.4
1991	22,625	63.87	17,339.4	1,431.5	18,770.9
1992	25,407	68.57	20,905.7	1,556.7	22,462.3
1993	26,987	67.95	22,006.0	1,646.9	23,653.0
1994	27,474	69.00	22,748.6	1,745.1	24,493.7
1995	26,619	71.27	22,764.1	1,855.5	24,619.5
1996	25,543	73.21	22,440.1	1,890.9	24,331.0
1997	22,858	71.27	19,548.9	1,936.5	21,485.4
1998	19,791	71.12	16,890.5	1,997.7	18,888.2
1999	18,183	72.27	15,769.4	1,941.0	17,710.8
2000	17,194	72.62	14,983.3	2,070.7	17,054.0
2001	17,318	74.81	15,547.4	2,242.1	17,789.5
2002	19,096	79.67	18,256.2	2,381.0	20,637.2
2003	21,259	83.90	21,404.3	2,410.0	23,814.3
2004	23,858	85.99	24,618.9	2,480.0	27,098.9
2005	25,674	92.72	28,565.7	2,562.4	31,128.1
2006	26,736	94.06	30,176.3	2,640.5	32,816.8

Notes: Fiscal year (FY) 2006 data are preliminary; all data are subject to revision.
[a]Represents average monthly benefits per person.
[b]Includes the federal share of state administrative expenses and employment and training programs. Also includes other federal costs (e.g., printing and processing of stamps; anti-fraud funding; program evaluation).
[c]Puerto Rico initiated food stamp operations during FY 1975 and participated through June of FY 1982. A separate nutrition assistance grant was begun in July 1982.

SOURCE: "Food Stamp Program Participaton and Costs," U.S. Department of Agriculture, Food and Nutrition Service, December 2006, http://www.fns .usda.gov/pd/fssummar.htm (accessed January 20, 2007)

and other expenses) must be 100% or less of the poverty level, or $1,667 per month for a family of four between 2006 and 2007. (See Table 7.6.)

With some exceptions, food stamps are automatically available to Supplemental Security Income and TANF recipients. Food stamp benefits are higher in states with lower TANF benefits because those benefits are considered a part of a family's countable income. To receive food stamps, certain household members must register for work, accept suitable job offers, or fulfill work or training requirements (such as looking or training for a job).

Even though the federal government sets guidelines and provides funding, the Food Stamp Program is actually carried out by the states. State agencies certify eligibility as well as calculate and issue benefit allotments. Most often, the welfare agency and staff that administer the TANF and Medicaid programs also run the Food Stamp Program. The regular Food Stamp Program operates in all fifty states, the District of Columbia, Guam, and the Virgin Islands. (Puerto Rico is covered under a separate nutrition-assistance program.)

Except for some small differences in Alaska, Hawaii, and the territories, the program is run the same way throughout the United States. The states pay 50% of the administrative costs, the federal government pays 100% of food stamp benefits and the other 50% of the operating costs. In 2001 the federal government paid $15.5 billion in food stamp benefits, but by 2006 it paid $30.2 billion in food stamp benefits, or an estimated average monthly benefit of $94.06 per recipient (based on preliminary data). (See Table 7.7.)

Food stamp participation decreased significantly after the Personal Responsibility and Work Opportunity Reconciliation Act of 1996, from a high of 27.5 million program participants in 1994 to a low of 17.2 million in 2000. (See Table 7.7.) However, after 2001 the economy began to worsen; as a result, participation rates crept up to near 1994 levels by 2006.

The Food Stamp Program is the nation's largest source of food assistance, helping about 6% of all Americans. The FNS reports in "Characteristics of Food Stamp Households, Fiscal Year 2005—Summary" (September 2006, http://www.fns .usda.gov/oane/MENU/Published/FSP/FILES/ Participation/ 2005CharacteristicsSummary.pdf) that in 2005, 50% of participants were children and 8% were aged sixty or older. Only four out of ten food stamp recipients lived in a household with earnings as the primary source of income, but most

TABLE 7.8

Maximum food stamp allotments, 2006–07

People in household	Maximum monthly allotment*
1	$155
2	284
3	408
4	518
5	615
6	738
7	816
8	932

*Larger households get higher amounts. Amounts are higher in Alaska and Hawaii. People who receive Supplemental Security Income in California are not eligible.

SOURCE: Maximum benefits table in *Food Stamps Make America Stronger*, U.S. Department of Agriculture, Food and Nutrition Service, September 2006, http://www.fns.usda.gov/fsp/outreach/Translations/English/313Brochure-06.pdf (accessed January 20, 2007)

food stamp households did not receive cash welfare benefits. Most food stamp households were poor; only 12% of food stamp households had incomes above the poverty level and 40% had incomes at or below half the poverty line.

Average monthly benefits per person rose from $34.47 in 1980 to a preliminary estimate of just over $94 in 2006, not accounting for inflation. (See Table 7.7.) Table 7.8 shows the maximum monthly food stamp allotments for 2006 to 2007 for households of varying sizes within the continental United States. During this period the maximum monthly benefit for a four-person household was $518.

National School Lunch and School Breakfast Programs

The National School Lunch Program (NSLP) and the School Breakfast Program (SBP) provide federal cash and commodity support to participating public and private schools and to nonprofit residential institutions that serve meals to children. Both programs have a three-level reimbursement system. Children from households with incomes at or below 130% of the poverty line receive free meals. Children from households with incomes between 130% and 185% of the poverty level receive meals at a reduced price (no more than $0.40). Table 7.9 shows the income eligibility guidelines, based on the poverty guidelines, effective from 2006 to 2007. The levels are higher for Alaska and Hawaii than in the forty-eight contiguous states, the District of Columbia, Guam, and other U.S. territories. Children in TANF families are automatically eligible to receive free breakfasts and lunches. Almost 90% of federal funding for the NSLP is used to subsidize free and reduced-price lunches for low-income children.

The NSLP was created in 1946 under the National School Lunch Act. In the school year 1996–97 the USDA

changed certain policies so that school meals would meet the recommendations of the Dietary Guidelines for America, the federal standards for what constitutes a healthy diet. About thirty million children, or 59.3% of all children served lunch, received free or reduced-price lunches in 2006. (See Table 7.10.) According to the Physicians Committee for Responsible Medicine, in "National School Lunch Program Background" (2006, http://www.healthyschoollunches.org/background/index.html), over 99,800 public and nonprofit private elementary and secondary schools and residential child care institutions participate in the program.

The SBP, which was created under the Child Nutrition Act of 1966, serves far fewer students than does the NSLP. The SBP also differs from the NSLP in that most schools offering the program are in low-income areas, and the children who participate in the program are mainly from low- and moderate-income families. In 2006 about 9.8 million students, or about 81.2% of all children served breakfast, participated. (See Table 7.11.)

Special Supplemental Food Program for Women, Infants, and Children

The Special Supplemental Food Program for Women, Infants, and Children (WIC) program provides food assistance as well as nutrition counseling and health services to low-income pregnant women, to women who have just given birth and their babies, and to low-income children up to five years old. Participants in the program must have incomes at or below 185% of poverty (all but five states use this cutoff level) and must be nutritionally at risk.

Under the Child Nutrition Act of 1966 nutritional risk includes abnormal nutritional conditions, medical conditions related to nutrition, health-impairing dietary deficiencies, or conditions that might predispose a person to these conditions. Pregnant women may receive benefits throughout their pregnancies and for up to six months after childbirth (up to one year for nursing mothers).

Those receiving WIC benefits get supplemental food each month in the form of actual food items or, more commonly, vouchers (coupons) for the purchase of specific items at the store. Permitted foods contain high amounts of protein, iron, calcium, vitamin A, and vitamin C. Items that may be purchased include milk, cheese, eggs, infant formula, cereals, and fruit or vegetable juices. Mothers participating in WIC are encouraged to breast-feed their infants if possible, but state WIC agencies will provide formula for mothers who choose to use it.

The USDA estimates that the national average monthly cost of a WIC food package in 2006 was $37.15 per participant, including food and administrative costs. (See Table 7.12.) In FY 2006 estimated federal costs for the WIC program were $5.1 billion, and the program served

TABLE 7.9

Income eligibility guidelines for free or reduced-price meals, 2006–07

Household size	Federal poverty guidelines — Annual	Reduced price meals—185% — Annual	Monthly	Twice per month	Every two weeks	Weekly	Free meals—130% — Annual	Monthly	Twice per month	Every two weeks	Weekly
48 contiguous states, District of Columbia, Guam and territories											
1	9,800	18,130	1,511	756	698	349	12,740	1,062	531	490	245
2	13,200	24,420	2,035	1,018	940	470	17,160	1,430	715	660	330
3	16,600	30,710	2,560	1,280	1,182	591	21,580	1,799	900	830	415
4	20,000	37,000	3,084	1,542	1,424	712	26,000	2,167	1,084	1,000	500
5	23,400	43,290	3,608	1,804	1,665	833	30,420	2,535	1,268	1,170	585
6	26,800	49,580	4,132	2,066	1,907	954	34,840	2,904	1,452	1,340	670
7	30,200	55,870	4,656	2,328	2,149	1,075	39,260	3,272	1,636	1,510	755
8	33,600	62,160	5,180	2,590	2,391	1,196	43,680	3,640	1,820	1,680	840
For each add'l family member, add	3,400	6,290	525	263	242	121	4,420	369	185	170	85
Alaska											
1	12,250	22,663	1,889	945	872	436	15,925	1,328	664	613	307
2	16,500	30,525	2,544	1,272	1,175	588	21,450	1,788	894	825	413
3	20,750	38,388	3,199	1,600	1,477	739	26,975	2,248	1,124	1,038	519
4	25,000	46,250	3,855	1,928	1,779	890	32,500	2,709	1,355	1,250	625
5	29,250	54,113	4,510	2,255	2,082	1,041	38,025	3,169	1,585	1,463	732
6	33,500	61,975	5,165	2,583	2,384	1,192	43,550	3,630	1,815	1,675	838
7	37,750	69,838	5,820	2,910	2,687	1,344	49,075	4,090	2,045	1,888	944
8	42,000	77,700	6,475	3,238	2,989	1,495	54,600	4,550	2,275	2,100	1,050
For each add'l family member, add	4,250	7,863	656	328	303	152	5,525	461	231	213	107
Hawaii											
1	11,270	20,850	1,738	869	802	401	14,651	1,221	611	564	282
2	15,180	28,083	2,341	1,171	1,081	541	19,734	1,645	823	759	380
3	19,090	35,317	2,944	1,472	1,359	680	24,817	2,069	1,035	955	478
4	23,000	42,550	3,546	1,773	1,637	819	29,900	2,492	1,246	1,150	575
5	26,910	49,784	4,149	2,075	1,915	958	34,983	2,916	1,458	1,346	673
6	30,820	57,017	4,752	2,376	2,193	1,097	40,066	3,339	1,670	1,541	771
7	34,730	64,251	5,355	2,678	2,472	1,236	45,149	3,763	1,882	1,737	869
8	38,640	71,484	5,957	2,979	2,750	1,375	50,232	4,186	2,093	1,932	966
For each add'l family member, add	3,910	7,234	603	302	279	140	5,083	424	212	196	98

SOURCE: "Income Eligibility Guidelines," in "Child Nutrition Programs–Income Eligibility Guidelines," *Federal Register*, vol. 71, March 15, 2006, http://www.fns.usda.gov/cnd/Governance/notices/iegs/IEG06-07.pdf (accessed January 20, 2007)

TABLE 7.10

National school lunch program participation and lunches served, 1969–2006

Fiscal year	Average participation				Total lunches served	Percent free/RP of total
	Free	Reduced price (RP)	Full price	Total		
	Millions					%
1969	2.9	*	16.5	19.4	3,368.2	15.1
1970	4.6	*	17.8	22.4	3,565.1	20.7
1971	5.8	0.5	17.8	24.1	3,848.3	26.1
1972	7.3	0.5	16.6	24.4	3,972.1	32.4
1973	8.1	0.5	16.1	24.7	4,008.8	35.0
1974	8.6	0.5	15.5	24.6	3,981.6	37.1
1975	9.4	0.6	14.9	24.9	4,063.0	40.3
1976	10.2	0.8	14.6	25.6	4,147.9	43.1
1977	10.5	1.3	14.5	26.2	4,250.0	44.8
1978	10.3	1.5	14.9	26.7	4,294.1	44.4
1979	10.0	1.7	15.3	27.0	4,357.4	43.6
1980	10.0	1.9	14.7	26.6	4,387.0	45.1
1981	10.6	1.9	13.3	25.8	4,210.6	48.6
1982	9.8	1.6	11.5	22.9	3,755.0	50.2
1983	10.3	1.5	11.2	23.0	3,803.3	51.7
1984	10.3	1.5	11.5	23.4	3,826.2	51.0
1985	9.9	1.6	12.1	23.6	3,890.1	49.1
1986	10.0	1.6	12.2	23.7	3,942.5	49.1
1987	10.0	1.6	12.4	23.9	3,939.9	48.6
1988	9.8	1.6	12.8	24.2	4,032.9	47.4
1989	9.7	1.6	12.9	24.2	4,004.9	47.2
1990	9.8	1.7	12.6	24.1	4,009.0	48.3
1991	10.3	1.8	12.2	24.2	4,050.7	50.4
1992	11.2	1.7	11.7	24.6	4,101.3	53.1
1993	11.7	1.7	11.4	24.9	4,137.7	54.8
1994	12.2	1.8	11.3	25.3	4,201.6	55.9
1995	12.4	1.9	11.4	25.7	4,253.3	56.4
1996	12.6	2.0	11.3	25.9	4,313.2	56.9
1997	12.9	2.1	11.3	26.3	4,409.0	57.6
1998	13.0	2.2	11.4	26.6	4,425.0	57.8
1999	13.0	2.4	11.6	27.0	4,513.6	57.6
2000	13.0	2.5	11.9	27.3	4,575.2	57.1
2001	12.9	2.6	12.0	27.5	4,585.2	56.8
2002	13.3	2.6	12.0	28.0	4,716.7	57.6
2003	13.7	2.7	11.9	28.4	4,763.0	58.5
2004	14.1	2.8	12.0	29.0	4,842.3	59.1
2005	14.6	2.9	12.2	29.6	4,976.1	59.4
2006	14.7	2.9	12.4	30.0	5,016.1	59.3

Notes: Fiscal year 2006 data are preliminary; all data are subject to revision.
Participation data are 9 month averages (summer months are excluded).
*Included with free meals.

SOURCE: "National School Lunch Program: Participation and Lunches Served," U.S. Department of Agriculture, Food and Nutrition Service, December 2006, http://www.fns.usda.gov/pd/slsummar.htm (accessed January 20, 2007)

approximately 8.1 million women, infants, and children. WIC works in conjunction with the Farmers' Market Nutrition Program, which was established in 1992, to provide WIC recipients with increased access, in the form of vouchers, to fresh fruits and vegetables.

WIC is not an entitlement program. That is, the number of participants is limited by the amount of funds available rather than by eligibility. In *WIC Participant and Program Characteristics, 2004* (March 2006, http://www.fns.usda.gov/oane/MENU/Published/WIC/FILES/pc2004.pdf), the FNS notes that of the approximately 8.6 million participants in 2004 (the most recent year for which detailed data are available), half (49.8%) were children and 25.7% were infants. In that year 24.5% of WIC participants were women; 11% were pregnant, 6%

were breastfeeding, and 7.5% were postpartum. Only about 7.9 million enrollees picked up their vouchers.

The FNS finds that 67% of WIC participants have household incomes at or below the poverty line, compared with 13% of the general population. In 2004, 9.4% of WIC recipients were also receiving TANF, 19.8% were also receiving food stamps, and 61.6% were also receiving Medicaid.

The FNS also notes that the ethnic composition of WIC recipients has been changing since 1992 as the percentage of Hispanic enrollees has risen and the percentage of non-Hispanic white and African-American enrollees has declined. In 2004, 39.2% of all WIC participants were Hispanic, 34.8% were non-Hispanic white, and 20% were African-American.

TABLE 7.11

National school breakfast program participation and meals served, 1969–2006

| Fiscal years | Total participation[a] | | | | Meals served | Free/red. price of total meals |
| | Free | Red. price | Paid | Total | | |
	Millions					Percent
1969	—	—	—	0.22	39.7	71.0
1970	—	—	—	0.45	71.8	71.5
1971	0.60	b	0.20	0.80	125.5	76.3
1972	0.81	b	0.23	1.04	169.3	78.5
1973	0.99	b	0.20	1.19	194.1	83.4
1974	1.14	b	0.24	1.37	226.7	82.8
1975	1.45	0.04	0.33	1.82	294.7	82.1
1976	1.76	0.06	0.37	2.20	353.6	84.2
1977	2.02	0.11	0.36	2.49	434.3	85.7
1978	2.23	0.16	0.42	2.80	478.8	85.3
1979	2.56	0.21	0.54	3.32	565.6	84.1
1980	2.79	0.25	0.56	3.60	619.9	85.2
1981	3.05	0.25	0.51	3.81	644.2	86.9
1982	2.80	0.16	0.36	3.32	567.4	89.3
1983	2.87	0.15	0.34	3.36	580.7	90.3
1984	2.91	0.15	0.37	3.43	589.2	89.7
1985	2.88	0.16	0.40	3.44	594.9	88.6
1986	2.93	0.16	0.41	3.50	610.6	88.7
1987	3.01	0.17	0.43	3.61	621.5	88.4
1988	3.03	0.18	0.47	3.68	642.5	87.5
1989	3.11	0.19	0.51	3.81	658.4	86.8
1990	3.30	0.22	0.55	4.07	707.5	86.7
1991	3.61	0.25	0.58	4.44	771.9	87.3
1992	4.05	0.26	0.61	4.92	852.4	88.0
1993	4.41	0.28	0.66	5.36	923.6	87.9
1994	4.76	0.32	0.75	5.83	1,001.5	87.4
1995	5.10	0.37	0.85	6.32	1,078.9	86.8
1996	5.27	0.41	0.90	6.58	1,125.7	86.5
1997	5.52	0.45	0.95	6.92	1,191.2	86.5
1998	5.64	0.50	1.01	7.14	1,220.9	86.1
1999	5.72	0.56	1.09	7.37	1,267.6	85.4
2000	5.73	0.61	1.21	7.55	1,303.4	84.2
2001	5.80	0.67	1.32	7.79	1,334.5	83.2
2002	6.03	0.70	1.41	8.15	1,404.7	82.9
2003	6.22	0.74	1.47	8.43	1,447.9	82.8
2004	6.52	0.80	1.58	8.90	1,524.8	82.4
2005	6.81	0.86	1.70	9.37	1,603.8	82.1
2006	6.99	0.92	1.85	9.77	1,660.0	81.2

Fiscal year 2006 data are preliminary; all data are subject to revision.
[a]Nine month average: October–May plus September.
[b]Included with free participation.

SOURCE: "School Breakfast Program Participation and Meals Served," U.S. Department of Agriculture, Food and Nutrition Service, December 2006, http://www.fns.usda.gov/pd/sbsummar.htm (accessed January 20, 2007)

TABLE 7.12

Special Supplemental Food Program for Women, Infants, and Children (WIC) program participation and costs, 1974–2006

| Fiscal year | Total participation[a] | Program costs | | | Average monthly food cost per person |
| | | Food | NSA | Total[b] | |
	(thousands)	(millions of dollars)			(dollars)
1974	88	8.2	2.2	10.4	15.68
1975	344	76.7	12.6	89.3	18.58
1976	520	122.3	20.3	142.6	19.60
1977	848	211.7	44.2	255.9	20.80
1978	1,181	311.5	68.1	379.6	21.99
1979	1,483	428.6	96.8	525.4	24.09
1980	1,914	584.1	140.5	727.7	25.43
1981	2,119	708.0	160.6	871.6	27.84
1982	2,189	757.6	190.5	948.8	28.83
1983	2,537	901.8	221.3	1,126.0	29.62
1984	3,045	1,117.3	268.8	1,388.1	30.58
1985	3,138	1,193.2	294.4	1,489.3	31.69
1986	3,312	1,264.4	316.4	1,582.9	31.82
1987	3,429	1,344.7	333.1	1,679.6	32.68
1988	3,593	1,434.8	360.6	1,797.5	33.28
1989	4,119	1,489.4	416.5	1,910.9	30.14
1990	4,517	1,636.8	478.7	2,122.4	30.20
1991	4,893	1,751.9	544.0	2,301.0	29.84
1992	5,403	1,960.5	632.7	2,600.6	30.24
1993	5,921	2,115.1	705.6	2,828.6	29.77
1994	6,477	2,325.2	834.4	3,169.3	29.92
1995	6,894	2,511.6	904.6	3,436.2	30.36
1996	7,186	2,689.9	985.1	3,695.4	31.20
1997	7,407	2,815.5	1,008.2	3,843.8	31.68
1998	7,367	2,808.1	1,061.4	3,890.4	31.76
1999	7,311	2,851.6	1,063.9	3,938.1	32.50
2000	7,192	2,853.1	1,102.6	3,982.1	33.06
2001	7,306	3,007.9	1,110.6	4,147.8	34.31
2002	7,491	3,129.7	1,182.3	4,339.8	34.82
2003	7,631	3,230.3	1,260.0	4,524.5	35.28
2004	7,904	3,561.9	1,273.3	4,888.0	37.55
2005	8,023	3,602.6	1,336.0	4,993.0	37.42
2006	8,087	3,605.6	1,431.9	5,091.0	37.15

[a]Participation data are annual averages (6 months in fiscal year 1974; 12 months all subsequent years).
[b]In addition to food and NSA costs, total expenditures includes funds for program evaluation, Farmers' Market Nutrition Program (fiscal year 1989 onward), special projects and infrastructure. Farmers' Market costs for fiscal year 2006 are not yet available.
NSA=Nutrition services and administrative costs. Nutrition services includes nutrition education, preventative and coordination services (such as health care), and promotion of breastfeeding and immunization.
Fiscal year 2006 data are preliminary; all data are subject to revision.

SOURCE: "WIC Program Participation and Costs," U.S. Department of Agriculture, Food and Nutrition Service, December 2006, http://www.fns.usda.gov/pd/wisummary.htm (accessed January 20, 2007)

IMPORTANT NAMES AND ADDRESSES

Administration for Children and Families
U.S. Department of Health and Human Services
370 L'Enfant Promenade SW
Washington, DC 20201
URL: http://www.acf.hhs.gov/

American Public Human Services Association
810 First St. NE, Ste. 500
Washington, DC 20002
(202) 682-0100
FAX: (202) 289-6555
URL: http://www.aphsa.org/

America's Second Harvest
35 E. Wacker Dr., Ste. 2000
Chicago, IL 60601
(312) 263-2303
1-800-771-2303
URL: http://www.secondharvest.org/

Association of Gospel Rescue Missions
1045 Swift St.
Kansas City, MO 64116-4127
1-800-624-5156
FAX: (816) 471-3718
URL: http://www.agrm.org/

Center for Law and Social Policy
1015 Fifteenth St. NW, Ste. 400
Washington, DC 20005
(202) 906-8000
FAX: (202) 842-2885
URL: http://www.clasp.org/

Center for the Study of Social Policy
1575 Eye St. NW, Ste. 500
Washington, DC 20005
(202) 371-1565
FAX: (202) 371-1472
URL: http://www.cssp.org/

Centers for Disease Control and Prevention
1600 Clifton Rd.
Atlanta, GA 30333
(404) 639-3534
1-800-311-3435
URL: http://www.cdc.gov/

Child Welfare League of America
440 First St. NW, Third Floor
Washington, DC 20001-2085
(202) 638-2952
FAX: (202) 638-4004
URL: http://www.cwla.org/

Children's Defense Fund
25 E St. NW
Washington, DC 20001
(202) 628-8787
E-mail: cdfinfo@childrensdefense.org
URL: http://www.childrensdefense.org/

Fannie Mae Foundation
3900 Wisconsin Ave. NW
Washington, DC 20016
(202) 752-7000
URL: http://www.fanniemaefoundation.org/

Food and Nutrition Service
3101 Park Center Dr.
Alexandria, VA 22302
URL: http://www.fns.usda.gov/fns/default.htm

Food Research and Action Center
1875 Connecticut Ave. NW, Ste. 540
Washington, DC 20009
(202) 986-2200
FAX: (202) 986-2525
E-mail: webmaster@frac.org
URL: http://www.frac.org/

Habitat for Humanity International
121 Habitat St.
Americus, GA 31709-3498
(229) 924-6935 x2551 or x2552
E-mail: publicinfo@habitat.org
URL: http://www.habitat.org/

Health Care for the Homeless Information Resource Center
Bureau of Primary Health Care
U.S. Department of Health and Human Services
Parklawn Bldg.
5600 Fishers Lane
Rockville, MD 20857
URL: http://bphc.hrsa.gov/hchirc/

Homes for the Homeless
36 Cooper Square, Sixth Floor
New York, NY 10003
(212) 529-5252
FAX: (212) 529-7698
E-mail: info@homesforthehomeless.com
URL: http://www.homesforthehomeless.com/

Housing Assistance Council
1025 Vermont Ave. NW, Ste. 606
Washington, DC 20005
(202) 842-8600
FAX: (202) 347-3441
E-mail: hac@ruralhome.org
URL: http://www.ruralhome.org/

Institute for Research on Poverty
University of Wisconsin—Madison
1180 Observatory Dr.
3412 Social Science Bldg.
Madison, WI 53706-1393
(608) 262-6358
FAX: (608) 265-3119
E-mail: djohnson@ssc.wisc.edu
URL: http://www.irp.wisc.edu/

Interagency Council on Homelessness
U.S. Interagency Council on Homelessness, Federal Center SW
409 Third St. SW, Ste. 310
Washington, DC 20024
(202) 708-4663
FAX: (202) 708-1216
URL: http://www.ich.gov/

Joint Center for Housing Studies
Harvard University
1033 Massachusetts Ave., Fifth Floor
Cambridge, MA 02138
(617) 495-7908
FAX: (617) 496-9957
URL: http://www.jchs.harvard.edu/index.htm

Kaiser Family Foundation
2400 Sand Hill Rd.
Menlo Park, CA 94025
(650) 854-9400
FAX: (650) 854-4800
URL: http://www.kff.org/

National Alliance of HUD Tenants
42 Seaverns Ave.
Boston, MA 02130
(617) 267-9564
FAX: (617) 522-4857
E-mail: naht@saveourhomes.org
URL: http://www.saveourhomes.org/

National Alliance on Mental Illness
Colonial Place Three
2107 Wilson Blvd., Ste. 300
Arlington, VA 22201-3042
(703) 524-7600
1-800-950-6264
FAX: (703) 524-9094
URL: http://www.nami.org/

National Association for the Education of Homeless Children and Youth
PO Box 26274
Minneapolis, MN 55426
(763) 545-0064
FAX: (763) 545-9499
E-mail: info@naehcy.org
URL: http://www.naehcy.org/

National Center for Children in Poverty
215 W. 125th St., Third Floor
New York, NY 10027
(646) 284-9600
FAX: (646) 284-9623
URL: http://www.nccp.org/

National Center for Homeless Education
915 Northridge St., Second Floor
Greensboro, NC 27403
1-800-755-3277
FAX: (336) 315-7457
E-mail: homeless@serve.org
URL: http://www.serve.org/nche

National Coalition for Homeless Veterans
333 1/2 Pennsylvania Ave. SE
Washington, DC 20003-1148
(202) 546-1969
1-800-VET-HELP
FAX: (202) 546-2063
E-mail: nchv@nchv.org
URL: http://www.nchv.org/

National Coalition for the Homeless
2201 P St. NW
Washington, DC 20037
(202) 462-4822
FAX: (202) 462-4823
E-mail: info@nationalhomeless.org
URL: http://www.nationalhomeless.org/

National Health Care for the Homeless Council
PO Box 60427
Nashville, TN 37206-0427
(615) 226-2292
FAX: (615) 226-1656
URL: http://www.nhchc.org/

National Housing Conference
1801 K St. NW, Ste. M-100
Washington, DC 20006-1301
(202) 466-2121
FAX: (202) 466-2122
URL: http://www.nhc.org/

National Housing Law Project
614 Grand Ave., Ste. 320
Oakland, CA 94610
(510) 251-9400
FAX: (510) 451-2300
E-mail: nhlp@nhlp.org
URL: http://www.nhlp.org/

National Law Center for Children and Families
225 N. Fairfax St.
Alexandria, VA 22314
(703) 548-5522
FAX: (703) 548-5544
URL: http://www.nationallawcenter.org/home/

National Law Center on Homelessness and Poverty
1411 K St. NW, Ste. 1400
Washington, DC 20005
(202) 638-2535
FAX: (202) 628-2737
URL: http://www.nlchp.org/

National League of Cities
1301 Pennsylvania Ave. NW, Ste. 550
Washington, DC 20004
(202) 626-3000
FAX: (202) 626-3043
E-mail: info@nlc.org
URL: http://www.nlc.org/

National Low Income Housing Coalition
727 Fifteenth St. NW, Sixth Floor
Washington, DC 20005

(202) 662-1530
FAX: (202) 393-1973
URL: http://www.nlihc.org/

National Resource and Training Center on Homelessness and Mental Illness
7500 Old Georgetown Rd., Ste. 900
Bethesda, MD 20814
1-800-444-7415
FAX: (301) 656-4012
E-mail: nrtc@cdmgroup.com
URL: http://www.nrchmi.samhsa.gov/

National Rural Housing Coalition
1250 Eye St. NW, Ste. 902
Washington, DC 20005
(202) 393-5229
FAX: (202) 393-3034
E-mail: nrhc@nrhcweb.org
URL: http://www.nrhcweb.org/

National Women's Law Center
11 Dupont Circle NW, Ste. 800
Washington, DC 20036
(202) 588-5180
FAX: (202) 588-5185
E-mail: info@nwlc.org
URL: http://nwlc.org/

Rural Policy Research Institute
University of Missouri
214 Middlebush Hall
Columbia, MO 65211-6200
(573) 882-0316
FAX: (573) 884-5310
E-mail: office@rupri.org
URL: http://www.rupri.org/

Social Security Administration
Office of Public Inquiries
Windsor Park Bldg.
6401 Security Blvd.
Baltimore, MD 21235
1-800-772-1213
URL: http://www.ssa.gov/

Urban Institute
2100 M St. NW
Washington, DC 20037
(202) 833-7200
URL: http://www.urban.org/

U.S. Conference of Mayors
1620 Eye St. NW
Washington, DC 20006
(202) 293-7330
FAX: (202) 293-2352
E-mail: info@usmayors.org
URL: http://www.usmayors.org/uscm/

U.S. Department of Housing and Urban Development
451 Seventh St. SW
Washington, DC 20410
(202) 708-1112
URL: http://www.hud.gov/

RESOURCES

The federal government remains the premier source of facts on many issues, including poverty, employment, welfare, and housing. Some particularly excellent sources of information from the U.S. Bureau of the Census are *Emergency and Transitional Shelter Population: 2000—Census 2000 Special Reports* (October 2001), *Income, Poverty, and Health Insurance Coverage in the United States: 2005—Current Population Reports* (August 2006), *Statistical Abstract of the United States: 2006* (2006), *America's Families and Living Arrangements: 2003* (November 2004), *Custodial Mothers and Fathers and Their Child Support: 2003* (July 2006), and *Children's Living Arrangements and Characteristics: March 2002* (June 2003).

The monthly *Employment and Earnings* of the U.S. Bureau of Labor Statistics (BLS) provides data on wages and work patterns, while the annual *A Profile of the Working Poor, 2003* (March 2005) details labor information about low-income workers. Many of the BLS data are published in the *Monthly Labor Review*. Other material used in preparing this book comes from the BLS's *Characteristics of Minimum Wage Workers: 2005* (May 2006) and *Household Data Annual Averages* (2006).

Other publications of the federal government used in this book include *Affordable Housing Needs: A Report to Congress on the Significant Need for Housing* (2005) and *Report to the President and Congress on the Implementation of the Education for Homeless Children and Youth Program under the McKinney-Vento Homeless Assistance Act* (2006). The U.S. Social Security Administration publishes the quarterly *Social Security Bulletin* and the *Annual Statistical Supplement to the Social Security Bulletin*, which provide a statistical overview of major welfare programs. The Administration for Children and Families of the U.S. Department of Health and Human Services publishes the *TANF Annual Report to Congress*, which describes the Temporary Assistance for Needy Families program. The National Center for Health Statistics, which

issues periodic reports on vital statistics such as birth rates and marital status as well as health status, is a part of the Centers for Disease Control and Prevention.

The Food and Nutrition Service of the U.S. Department of Agriculture provides detailed tables about the National School Lunch Program, the School Breakfast Program, the Food Stamp Program and its participants, and the Women, Infants, and Children program, as well as data from *Household Food Security in the United States, 2005* (November 2006) and *Food Stamps Make America Stronger* (September 2006).

The U.S. Government Accountability Office (GAO) investigates topics as requested by Congress. GAO publications used in this book include *Public Housing: Information on the Roles of HUD, Public Housing Agencies, Capital Markets, and Service Organizations* (February 2006) and *Homelessness: Improving Program Coordination and Client Access to Programs* (March 2002).

The periodically published *Green Book—Background Material and Data on Programs within the Jurisdiction of the Committee on Ways and Means* by the U.S. House of Representatives provides the most complete information on the U.S. welfare system in a single source. The annual *State Expenditure Report* of the National Association of State Budget Officers shows how the states and territories spend their welfare funds.

Many different organizations study the homeless and poor. Notable among them for many large studies on homelessness is the Urban Institute. This organization's ongoing studies of the homeless are among the largest and most comprehensive in the United States. Its publications were a major source of information for this volume, especially *The 1996 National Survey of Homeless Assistance Providers and Clients: A Comparison of Faith-Based and Secular Non-profit Programs* (March 2002) and *America's Homeless II: Populations and Services* (February 2000). Reports and data issued as part of the Urban Institute's Assessing the New Federalism project were also valuable resources, including "Trends in Parents' Economic Hardship" (March 2004), "Decade of Welfare Reform: Facts and Figures—Assessing the New Federalism" (June 2006), "Government Work Supports and Low-Income Families: Facts and Figures" (July 2006), and *The Changing Role of Welfare in the Lives of Low-Income Families with Children* (August 2006). America's Second Harvest, a charitable hunger-relief organization, prepared *Hunger Study, 2006* (2007).

Three other excellent sources of information on the national homeless population are the National League of Cities, the U.S. Conference of Mayors, and the Association of Gospel Rescue Missions. *The State of America's Cities 2005: The Annual Opinion Survey* (2005) by the National League of Cities contains valuable data on the scope of urban homelessness and how cities and regions try to deal with it. The Conference of Mayors' *Hunger and Homelessness Survey: A Status Report on Hunger and Homelessness in America's Cities, a 23-City Survey* (2006) and the Association of Gospel Rescue Missions' *Statistics and Studies: 2005 Snapshot Survey of the Homeless* (2005) also provide a great deal of information on the homeless population.

The many organizations that advocate for the homeless and their issues are also crucial sources for this book. The National Coalition for the Homeless is certainly one of the most important of these organizations. Its publication *A Dream Denied: The Criminalization of Homelessness in U.S. Cities* (January 2006) is particularly recommended. The Joint Center for Housing Studies of Harvard University, Health Care for the Homeless, the National Coalition for Homeless Veterans, the Millennial Housing Commission, the National Multi Housing Council, and the National Law Center on Homelessness and Poverty all provide extensive coverage of important aspects of the housing and homelessness issues.

Other nonprofit organizations whose materials were used in researching this book include the Finance Project, whose Welfare Information Network provides links to major organizations, reports, federal and state government agencies, and other sources of data; the Kaiser Family Foundation, an advocacy group that studies health and health insurance issues; and the Center on Law and Social Policy, a research and advocacy group that examines issues relating to low-income families.

INDEX

median household income, 12*t*

poverty and, 1, 4, 6–12

poverty estimates based on alternative measures of income, 13*t*

poverty rates by education, 45

poverty status/labor market problems of full-time wage and salary workers, 68*t*

program participation status of household, all income levels, 57*t*–59*t*

program participation status of household, persons below poverty level, 60*t*–62*t*

renter-occupied units spending 30% or more of household income on rent and utilities, 113 (*t*5.3)

shares of household income, 17*t*–18*t*

SSI qualifications, 89

TANF benefit eligibility and, 76

voucher programs and, 128

Income gap, 11–12

Income, Poverty, and Health Insurance Coverage in the United States: 2005—Current Population Reports (DeNavas-Walt, Proctor, and Lee)

on families in poverty, 125

on income of women, 12

as information resource, 167

on Medicaid, 142

Income-to-poverty ratios

description of, 2

poor, percent of U.S. population, 35

poverty thresholds, people with income below, 36*t*

Indiana, 83

Inflation, 87

Institutionalized assistance, 109

Insurance. *See* Health insurance

Internal Revenue Service (IRS), 91

"Intimate Violence in the Lives of Homeless and Poor Housed Women: Prevalence and Patterns in an Ethnically Diverse Sample" (Browne and Bassuk), 153

Is the Unemployment Insurance System a Safety Net for Welfare Recipients Who Exit Welfare for Work? (Rangarajan, Corson, and Wood), 85

J

Jail, 29

Jobs. *See* Work

Johnson, Lyndon B., 1

Joint Center for Housing Studies (JCHS)

on housing costs, 112, 114

on housing vouchers, 131

on lack of affordable housing, 115, 116

Jones, Arthur F., Jr., 12

Justin v. City of Los Angeles, 135

K

Kaiser Commission, 140

Kansas, minimum wage in, 87

Karr, Katherine, 153

Kaye, William, 135

Kelling, George, 133

Kids Having Kids: A Robin Hood Foundation Special Report on the Costs of Adolescent Childbearing (Maynard), 78–79

King County 2003: Homeless Death Review (Health Care for the Homeless Network), 146–147

Klein, Robert E., 153

Knitzer, Jane, 137

Koball, Heather, 45

Kong, Po-Marn, 149

Kreisher, Kristen, 124

L

Labor market, 52, 108

Las Vegas, Nevada, 132, 133

Laws, homeless, 131–134

Lee, Barrett A., 108–109

Lee, Cheryl Hill

on health insurance, 148

on income inequality, 12

on Medicaid, 142

on number of families in poverty, 125

Legislation and international treaties

Balanced Budget Act of 1997, 75, 142

Child Nutrition Act of 1966, 160

Deficit Reduction Act of 2005, 75, 76

Fair Labor Standards Act, 85, 87, 89*t*

Homeless Emergency Assistance and Rapid Transition to Housing Act, 124

Housing Act of 1937, 127

Housing Act of 1949, 121

Housing and Community Development Act of 1974, 121

McKinney-Vento Homeless Assistance Act, 13, 18, 30, 100, 106, 118, 121–124

National School Lunch Act, 160

Noncitizen Technical Amendment Act of 1998, 75

Personal Responsibility and Work Opportunity Reconciliation Act, 73, 74–76, 159

Social Security Act, 89

Stewart B. McKinney Homeless Assistance Act of 1987, 13, 143

Tax Reform Act of 1986, 11, 90–92

U.S. Housing Act of 1937, 121

"Let's Ask the Homeless People Themselves: A Needs Assessment Based on a Probability Sample of Adults" (Acosta and Toro), 152

Liabilities, 11

Loitering, 132, 135

Loper, Jennifer, 135–136

Loper v. New York City Police Department, 135–136

Loprest, Pamela, 75, 83

Los Angeles, California, 29, 135

Los Angeles Homeless Services Authority, 109–110

Loveless, Tracy A., 52

Low-income housing

lack of, reasons for, 115–117

price of, 112–114

public housing appropriations, 116*t*

rental housing stock, sufficiency of, 117*f*

standard for, 111–112

subsidized housing, 124–131

Low-Income Housing Tax Credit program, 116–117, 130

Low-income people. *See* Poor people

Lozier, John, 144–145

Luxenberg, Stan, 117

M

"Major Management Challenges at the Department of Housing and Urban Development" (U.S. Government Accountability Office), 127

Male-headed households, 37–38

Males. *See* Gender

Maljanian, Rose, 148

Malnutrition, 156–157

See also Hunger

Malony, Walt, 113–114

Marital status

child poverty and, 35

marital status of population 15 years old and over, by gender, 47*f*

poverty by family status, 37–38, 44

program participation status of mothers 15 to 44 years with a birth in the last year, by marital status and age, 81*t*

unemployed persons by marital status, race, ethnicity, age, and sex, 88*t*

See also Family status

Markee, Patricia, 106

Marks, Carolyn, 143

Martinson, Karin, 83

Mason, Alan, 136

Mason v. Tucson, 136

Massachusetts

jobs for welfare recipients, 83

squatting incident in, 119

"Material Survival Strategies on the Street: Homeless People as Bricoleurs, Homelessness in America" (Snow et al.), 109

Maynard, Rebecca A., 78–79

McCarthy, Michael, 148

McCormack, Katherine M., 148

McDonald, Sharon, 111

McKernan, Signe-Mary, 11

McKinney-Vento Homeless Assistance Act

Continuum of Care programs, 122

count of homeless children, 118

Transitional shelters
    number of homeless in, 100, 106, 118
    population in emergency/transitional
        shelters by region, 106*t*
    population in emergency/transitional
        shelters by state, 29*t*
    service of special populations, 31
Transportation
    of homeless students, 124
    to jobs, 84–85
Treaties. *See* Legislation and international
    treaties
"Trends in Parents' Economic Hardship"
    (Nelson), 154
Troubled housing, 127
Tuberculosis
    among homeless people, 144, 148–149
    tuberculosis cases by homeless status,
        150*t*–151*t*
"Tuberculosis and Homelessness in the
    United States, 1994–2003" (Haddad
    et al.), 148
Tucson, Arizona
    constitutional rights of homeless, 135
    zoning homeless out of downtown, 136
Tucson, Mason v., 136
Tulsky, J. P., 149
2005 Greater Los Angeles Homeless Count
    (Los Angeles Homeless Services
    Authority), 109–110

U
Unaccompanied youth, 102, 104
Unemployment
    amount/duration of weekly benefits, by
        state, 87*t*
    compensation, qualification for, 85
    compensation, recipiency rates, by state,
        86*f*
    problems of working poor, 52
    trends in, 82
    unemployed persons by marital status,
        race, ethnicity, age, and sex, 88*t*
    welfare caseload reduction and, 73
Unemployment Insurance Chartbook
    (U.S. Department of Labor's
    Employment and Training
    Administration), 85
Uninsured people. *See* Health insurance
Unmarried women
    birth rates for unmarried women, by age
        of mother, 82*f*
    program participation rates by age, 80*f*
    program participation status of mothers
        15 to 44 years with a birth in last year,
        81*t*
    teen mothers, 78–80
Urban areas
    city conditions, most deteriorated over
        past five years, 108*t*
    city conditions, past-year change in,
        seriousness of problems, 107*t*

hunger/homelessness indicators in large
    urban areas, 103*t*
poverty in, 36
Urban Institute
    on child care funds, 84
    estimates of homelessness, 99
    homeless population count by, 26,
        27*t*, 28
    on homeless services, 30, 31
    on homeless shelter, housing, 106
    on hunger, 154
    information resources, 167–168
    on overlapping services, 92
    on tax relief, 91
    on welfare assistance, 45
    on welfare reform, 83
Urban Revitalization Demonstration
    Program. *See* HOPE VI program
U.S. Bureau of Labor Statistics (BLS)
    on consumer expenditures, 2, 4
    information resources from, 167
    on minimum wage workers, 88–89
U.S. Bureau of the Census
    child support, 44
    duration of program spells, 52–53
    homeless population count, 26–28
    housing costs, 112–113
    hunger surveys, 154–155
    income definition and, 6–11
    income inequality, 11–12
    income-to-poverty ratios, 2
    information resources from, 167
    number of homeless in shelters, 118
    poor, characteristics of, 35
    poverty, length of time in, 49–50
    poverty by race, 44–45
    subsidized housing, 125
    teen mothers, 79
    welfare assistance, 45–46, 48–49
U.S. census, 26–28
U.S. Conference of Mayors
    causes of homelessness, 18
    emergency food assistance, 157
    family structure of homeless, 102
    homeless people and employment, 108
    homelessness estimates, 101
    homelessness trends profiled by, 106
    housing assistance, 131
    information resources from, 168
    mental health of homeless, 152
    number of homeless in shelters, 118
U.S. Constitution, 134–136
U.S. Department of Agriculture (USDA)
    on child nutrition programs, 75
    Food Stamp Program, 157–160
    National School Lunch Program, 160
    poverty level and, 1
    Special Supplemental Food Program
        for Women, Infants, and Children,
        160, 162

U.S. Department of Agriculture's Economic
    Research Service, 105
U.S. Department of Education
    count of homeless children, 102, 118–119
    report on homeless children, 100, 101
        (*t*4.2)
U.S. Department of Health and Human
    Services (HHS)
    Health Care for the Homeless, 143–144
    poverty guidelines, 1, 2*t*
    on welfare caseload reduction, 73
U.S. Department of Housing and Urban
    Development (HUD)
    budget authority for homeless and public
        housing programs, 125*t*
    establishment of, 121
    estimates of homelessness, 99
    on homeless services, 30
    HUD McKinney-Vento programs,
        requirements of four, 123*t*
    on lack of affordable housing, 114–117
    McKinney-Vento Homeless Assistance
        Act, 121–124
    programs not meeting demand, 131
    subsidized housing, 124–131
U.S. Department of Justice, 153
U.S. Department of Labor, 1
U.S. Department of Labor's Employment
    and Training Administration, 85
U.S. Department of Transportation (DOT),
    84–85
U.S. Department of Veteran Affairs, 153
U.S. Food and Drug Administration (FDA),
    150–151
U.S. Government Accountability Office
    (GAO)
    on HUD homeless assistance programs,
        123
    information resources from, 167
    on lack of affordable housing, 115–116
    on public housing, 127
    on rural housing program, 131
U.S. House of Representatives, 167
U.S. Housing Act of 1937, 121
U.S. National Academy of Sciences
    Institute of Medicine, 148
USDA. *See* U.S. Department of Agriculture
"Use of TANF, WtW, and Job Access
    Funds for Transportation" (U.S.
    Department of Transportation), 84–85

V
Vehicle asset limit, 85
Vento, Bruce, 121
Venugopal, Arun, 102
Veterans
    health problems of homeless veterans, 153
    number of homeless veterans, 104
Violence, against homeless people, 153–154
Virginia, jobs for welfare recipients, 83